Charles McKew Parr, Richard F. Burton

The Gold-Mines of Midian and the Ruined Midianite Cities

A Fortnight's Tour in North-Western Arabia

Charles McKew Parr, Richard F. Burton

The Gold-Mines of Midian and the Ruined Midianite Cities
A Fortnight's Tour in North-Western Arabia

ISBN/EAN: 9783744762021

Printed in Europe, USA, Canada, Australia, Japan

Cover: Foto ©Andreas Hilbeck / pixelio.de

More available books at **www.hansebooks.com**

THE GOLD-MINES OF MIDIAN

AND

THE RUINED MIDIANITE CITIES.

THE GOLD-MINES OF MIDIAN

AND

THE RUINED MIDIANITE CITIES.

A FORTNIGHT'S TOUR
IN NORTH-WESTERN ARABIA.

BY

RICHARD F. BURTON,

MEMBRE DE L'INSTITUT ÉGYPTIEN.

LONDON:
C. KEGAN PAUL & CO., 1, PATERNOSTER SQUARE.
1878.

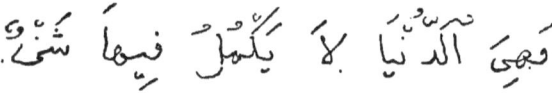

"We have the authority of Niebuhr, that the precious metals are not found or known to exist in Arabia, which has no mines either of gold or silver."—Crichton's *History of Arabia*, ii. 403.

"Namentlich sind es die Arabir, welche den grössten Theil des in Alterthum vorhandenen Goldes unter die menschen geschleudert haben."—Sprenger, *Alte Geographie*, etc., p. 299.

"Peregrinatio notitiam dabit gentium, novas tibi montium formas ostendit, inusitata spatia camporum et irriguas perennibus aquis valles, et alicujus fluminis sub observatione naturam."—*L. Annæi Senecæ*, Epist. civ.

TO

HIS HIGHNESS

ISMAIL I.,

KHEDIV OF EGYPT,

A RULER WHOSE LOVE OF PROGRESS

AND WHOSE PRINCELY HOSPITALITY

HAVE MADE THE NILE-VALLEY, ONCE MORE,

THE RESORT OF SCIENCE

AND

THE DELIGHT OF TRAVELLERS,

These Pages

ARE RESPECTFULLY AND GRATEFULLY INSCRIBED.

TO THE READER.

THE present publication should be considered a sequel and a continuation of my "Pilgrimage to El-Medinah and Meccah," from which the adventure forming its subject may be said to date. I have, therefore, dwelt at some length upon the mighty changes, the growths, and the developments of the last quarter century, which has produced the "Greater Egypt" of the present day : contenting myself, however, with contrasting the actual Alexandria, Cairo, and Suez with my descriptions of the same places in 1853–54.

The tale of the Mining-Cities of Midian reads, they say, like a leaf from the "Arabian Nights." Yet it is sober truth. My object has been to avoid, as much as possible, all play of fancy and the exaggerations of an explorer's enthusiasm. It is hardly necessary to state that my assertions are borne out by the Report of the Mineralogists officially appointed by H.M. the Viceroy of Egypt : and the labours of H.E. Gastinel-Bey and of M. George Marie have been carefully consulted before sending this volume to print.

How little is known of the country may be learned from the words of my friend Professor Aloys Sprenger,* the most scientific topographer of Arabia : " Es (die Station in oder bei Aynûnâ) ist reich an Palmen, trieb einst Feldbau, und es gibt Stellen, wo man (*in Rinnen ?*) Gold fand." The mineral wealth of the land is equally ignored by the *savant* Herr Albrecht Zehme,† the most modern geographical and historical "Sketcher" of the Peninsula. Finally, the heart of Ancient Midian was traversed by Dr. Edward Rüppell in 1826,‡ and by Dr. George Aug. Wallin in 1847 ;§ not to mention such names as Burckhardt, Wellsted, ‖ and Lieutenant (I.N.) Carless, who also surveyed the coast under Captain Moresby (I.N.), and my old

---

* Page 22, *Die alte Geographie Arabiens*. Bern. Huber, 1875.

† *Arabien und die Araber seit hundert Jahren.* Halle, 1875.

‡ *Reisen in Nubien Kerdofan*, etc. 1 vol. Wilmans, Frankfurt, A.M. 1829.

§ "Notes taken during a Journey through part of Northern Arabia :" *Journal R.G.S.*, vol. xx. of 1850.

‖ Lieutenant J. R., "Travels in Arabia." 2 vols. London : Murray, 1838.

and lamented friend Dr. Beke, whose last writings are quoted in a note to chap. xii. Yet, apparently, none of them ever fanned a pound of sand, broke a stone, or noticed an atom of metal.

It is not easy to explain how a naturalist like Rüppell could overlook the structure of the rocks, and pass through the old Ophir without suspecting the existence of the masses of metal around and below him. But at that time he was a fresh arrival, and the completely novel aspects of oriental scenery and life possibly bewildered him. Those who remember their sensations during their first month in India will understand what I mean. As regards the Ruined Cities, he was evidently not allowed to visit them by his escort, the Huwaytát—in those days a somewhat turbulent and dangerous tribe, fond of domineering over strange visitors. With respect to the gold in quartz and porphyry, Sprenger suggests, with much probability, that Rüppell, like the men of his day, some twenty years before the discoveries in California and Australia awoke the attention of the world, never dreamt of such treasures and paid no attention to the geological features which denote the presence of the precious metal. The other travellers seem to have been wholly innocent of natural history.

Gold has been connected with our earliest ideas of the Arabian peninsula, since William, the biographer of Thomas Becket, said, "Araby sends us gold." All have read in youth of the *plenas Arabum domos*, and *Icci beatis nunc Arabum invides gazis*. We, the members of the Khedivial Expedition, feel not a little proud of our new work in an old land; and we may rejoice in having added a name to the long list of mines and places given by the exhaustive Professor Sprenger.

The Reconnaissance, to call it by its true title, was hurriedly organized, while the advancing hot season left us little time for making collections. The choicest samples of metals were submitted, after return, to H.H. the Khediv; and the rest of the samples were sent for analysis to the Laboratory in the Cairene Citadel. My bottle full of reptiles and insects was forwarded to Dr. Smith of the British Museum; the land-shells of Wady Aynúnah to Mr. J. Gwyn Jeffreys of Ware Priory, Herts, who has so often lent me his valuable assistance; and a few sheets of dried plants, after being inspected by my friend and fellow-traveller, Dr. Carlo de Marchesetti of Trieste, were transmitted to Professor Balfour of Edinburgh. The photographed inscription found on the march to the "White Mountain" was submitted to Professor Sprenger, to Dr. Socin of Bâle, and to Mr. C. Knight Watson, of Burlington House. Finally, Mr. Reginald Stuart Poole, Keeper of the Coins at the British Museum, obligingly transcribed for me the Kufic inscription upon the glass piece bought at Burj Zibá. My many other obligations have been acknowledged in the following pages; and, if any have been neglected, I would here offer an apology.

The matter of the volume may be considered virtually new. After the return of the Expedition to Egypt a few brief and scattered notices appeared in the Press of England and the Continent. The information had been gathered by "interviewing," and nothing appeared under my own name. For this mystery there were reasons which now no longer exist. I therefore place the whole recital before the Public, without reserve or after-thought, merely warning it that my volume begins with the beginning of a subject which will probably go far.

When these pages shall be in the reader's hands, I shall once more be examining the "Land of Midian;" attempting, under the auspices of His Highness the Viceroy of Egypt, to investigate the particulars of which the generals are here described;

to trace the streams of wealth to their hidden sources; and to begin the scrutiny to which all such exploring feats should lead. I have therefore left the MS. in the hands of my wife, who has undertaken to see it through the Press.

PREFACE.

Dear Reader,

Captain Burton is in Arabia, in the Land of Midian, once more, and I am left behind—much against the grain—in order to bring this book through the Press, that you may know what was done last year; and besides the hopes of pleasing you, the thought that I am contributing the only service in my power towards his great undertaking makes me bear my disappointment quietly. My task will be finished in a few days, and I shall then take the first steamer from Trieste to Suez, where I hope to be allowed to join the Expedition.

The volume you are about to read requires but little explanation. Captain Burton, in his old Arab days, wandering about with his Koran, came upon this "Gold Land," though I remark that in his recital he modestly gives the credit to others.

He was a romantic youth, with a chivalrous contempt for "filthy lucre," and only thought of "winning his spurs." So, setting a mark upon the spot, he turned away and passed on. A foreigner will exclaim, "How English!" when he reads that he kept his secret for twenty-five years, and that when he saw Egypt in distress for gold, the same chivalry which made him disdain it before, made him ask leave to go to Egypt, seek H.H. the Khediv, and impart the secret to him, and thus act like a second Joseph to the land of Pharaoh. His Highness equipped an Expedition forthwith to send him in search of the spot; and this year he has again obtained leave, and has gone to finish what he began last year. I pray you now to read the account of his labours in 1877; and you may probably hear more of them, as he tells me that the discoveries of metals have thoroughly satisfied him.

ISABEL BURTON.

Trieste, January, 1878.

CONTENTS.

CHAPTER I.
	PAGE
AT ALEXANDRIA	1

CHAPTER II.
| THE CHANGES AT CAIRO ... ... | 28 |

CHAPTER III.
| TO SUEZ AND HER SANITARIUM ... ... | 63 |

CHAPTER IV.
| DEPARTURE FROM SUEZ, AND ARRIVAL AT EL-MUWAYLÁH | 94 |

CHAPTER V.
| FROM EL-MUWAYLÁH TO WADY AYNÚNAH ... ... | 122 |

CHAPTER VI.
| FROM WADY AYNÚNAH TO THE WADY MORÁK IN THE JEBEL EL-ZAHD ... ... | 148 |

CHAPTER VII.
| MIDIAN AND THE MIDIANITES ... ... | 174 |

CHAPTER VIII.
| FROM AYN EL-MORÁK TO THE WHITE MOUNTAIN; THE INSCRIPTION AND THE NABATHÆANS ... ... | 206 |

CHAPTER IX.
| HOW THE GOLD WAS FOUND IN MIDIAN: THE GOLD-MINES OF ARABIA ... ... | 242 |

CHAPTER X.

THE RETURN FROM THE WHITE MOUNTAIN TO EL-MUWAY-LÁH, *viâ* WADY SHARMÁ AND WADY TIRYAM: NOTES ON BOTANY ... 265

CHAPTER XI.

THE CRUISE DOWN SOUTH: SULPHUR AND TURQUOISES: NOTES ON FISHES AND SHELLS ... 299

CHAPTER XII.

THE CRUISE NORTHWARDS TO MAKNÁ, CAPITAL OF MADYAN ... 317

CHAPTER XIII.

RETURN TO CAIRO, ETC.: THE "PROCÈS-VERBAL" ADDRESSED TO HIS HIGHNESS ... 370

CHAPTER XIV.

DEPARTURE FROM EGYPT ... 380

CONCLUSION ... 390

APPENDIX I.

A.—LIST OF SUPPLIES FOR A DESERT EXCURSION, OF SIX TO TEN PERSONS, LASTING SIXTEEN DAYS, AND A CRUISE OF FIVE (TOTAL, TWENTY-ONE DAYS) ... 393

B.—LIST OF EXPENDITURES MADE DURING THE EXPEDITION 395

APPENDIX II.

LIST OF CAPTAIN BURTON'S "LAND OF MIDIAN" PLANTS ... 396

APPENDIX III.

LIST OF INSECTS... ... 397

APPENDIX IV.

SPECIMENS OF REPTILES PRESENTED BY CAPTAIN BURTON TO THE BRITISH MUSEUM ... 398

THE GOLD-MINES OF MIDIAN.

CHAPTER I.

AT ALEXANDRIA.

At last! Once more it is my fate to escape the prison-life of civilised Europe, and to refresh body and mind by studying Nature in her noblest and most admirable form—the Nude. Again I am to enjoy a glimpse of the "glorious Desert;" to inhale the sweet pure breath of translucent skies that show the red stars burning upon the very edge and verge of the horizon; and to strengthen myself by a short visit to the Wild Man and his old home.

And this visit was brought about as follows: His Highness the Viceroy of Egypt having heard, from a common friend, that many and many a year ago the site of a gold-field had come to my knowledge, honoured me with an invitation to report this matter in person. I applied for a month's leave of absence, which was obligingly granted to me by H.B.M.'s Foreign Office, in consideration of a ferocious winter, all Bora and Scirocco, spent in the "trail of the slow-worm," at Trieste. On March 3, 1877, I found myself, despite the awful predictions of the late Mathieu de la Drôme, and the words of wisdom poured by wifely lips into the obedient marital ear, boarding the Austro-Hungarian Lloyd's *Aurora*, Captain Markovich.

The trip of twelve hundred miles was more than usually pleasant, along those picturesque coasts of Istria and those Highlands and Islands of Dalmatia, which War, the Regius Professor of Geography, has now introduced to the Wandering World. Beyond the romantic Bocche di Cattaro, Bosphorus of the West, we had nothing to fear from foul weather; and we could gaze without apprehension at the ice-revetted peaks, and the snow-powdered slopes of the grand Cunariot range: the far-famed Acroceraunians, of late years known only for flint-knapping. It was, as usual, black night when we anchored off the citadel and forts of Corfu; once the most charming of soldier stations, and ruined, since the sad year 1864, in the cause of Independence—unwillingly, too, as was shown by the rising in 1873, the object of which was to hoist once more the British flag.

Past the breakers that swarm up Leucas or Sappho's Leap, still purple with her blood; through the far-famed *Canale* with rugged Theaki (Ithaca) to port, and lofty Cephalonia to starboard; hard by Zante, whose lovely slopes and castled white town have made her the flower of the Levant; across the gulf of Patras, and the town of Katakolo, with old Poudiko Kastro, the Venetian fort, towering high over the currant-grown lowlands; past the German-haunted Alpheus of Jupiter Olympius; along that rude and rocky and windwrung Arkadía, which so strangely gave birth to soft Arcadian tale and song; under the savage walls of strong Peloponnesus, a fair specimen of the land in which Europe has imprisoned the Greek, expecting him, withal, to beget Homers and Herodotuses, Aristides, and Themistocles; across historic Navarino Bay and its ruin-crowned breakwater, to Sphagia Island;—past all these memorious sites we steamed, and we awoke, on the morning of the fourth day, when coasting along the southern shores of Crete, which men need no longer call Candia.

The long thin island, whose lines and blocks of silver-tipped peak and pinnacle, some rising upwards of 8000 feet, and acting as condensers to the rain-winds that rush through the frequent gaps, was the last land visible upon our course; and, although Candia mostly exposes her beauties to the North Pole, still nothing can exceed her Alpine charms of bright sun and sparkling snow, gold-dust rained upon the purest ermine, and the whole set off by the true Mediterranean blue, the sea dancing to the music of the winds. With a heartfelt wish that Crete—annexed in A.D. 1680, by Mohammed IV., the last Sultan who took the field in person—may find herself, in the evening of her days, made happy by re-union with Christendom and the flag of St. George, we bade her a fond farewell, and marvelling to see the way of sea so desert of ships, we cast anchor on March 8th, in old Eunostos, the new harbour of Alexandria,*—a noble work, worthy of Egypt's greatest days. We travellers now look forward only to a baggage-landing company, which

* The harbour improvements are estimated to cost £2,000,000; and blasting the Bugzaz, or pass between the shoals into the harbour, will add £70,000. It is now proposed to fill up the Eastern, or Back Bay—called the " New Port," probably because utterly unfit to harbour a ship—between Forts Farrilon and Caffarelli. The latter is undoubtedly built upon the site, and partly with the materials, variegated marbles, of ancient Pharos. The engineering operation would be made easy by running a tramway from the old Necropolis and quarries of Maks (Mex) beyond the obsolete Tábiás, or batteries, and the bulbous ruin-Palace of Said-Pasha; but the financial part, which also demands £70,000, is a very different matter. The forts have sensibly been allowed to fall to pieces. What is the use of attempting to defend one end of a city? The works on the land side are now riddled and levelled for railway lines and stations. In fact, the days when Alexandria wanted such defences are gone by: she can renew them when these times return. In my "Pilgrimage" I mistranslated Ras-el-Tin "Headland of Figs" instead of "Headland of Clay," the latter being still used to make "gullehs," or *gargoulettes*.

shall save us from the mortification of the jarring boatman and the rapacious dragoman.

The "Lybian suburb," the city of Prophet Daniel, of Alexander the Great, and of Mark the Apostle, is no longer, as in 1853, "a city of misnomers, whose dry docks are ever wet, and whose marble fountain is eternally dry; whose 'Cleopatra's Needle' (why not call it the Obelisk of Thothmes?) is neither connected with Cleopatra, nor is it a needle; whose 'Pompey's Pillar' (why not boldly say the Column of Diocletian?) never had any earthly connection with Pompey; and whose Cleopatra's 'Baths' are, according to veracious travellers, no baths at all."

Yet it is her unlucky fate to be abused by every traveller. Never a tourist of a few hours spent at Abbat's or at the Hôtel de l'Europe, but throws his little stone, his *critique malveillante* at her. I have even heard her charged with the "vulgarity of the West." Viewed from the sea, the great emporium commands a respect which we indignantly refuse to Karáchi; and yet the essentials and even the accidents of Old Egypt and Young Egypt bear a family, nay a sisterly, likeness.* The failures, called "improvements" in other Mediterranean ports, notably at Trieste, turn to the benefit of Alexandria. The difficult and dangerous

* The curious reader will consult "Sind Revisited"—*passim*.

entrance of yore is safely buoyed; the anchorage-ground, formerly exposed, is now land-locked; the noble breakwater, guarding the sea-front, wants only a better lighthouse at the Point: the interior of the old Port is provided with moles and docks; the landing-place is being deepened by filling up, perhaps too much, the inshore shallows; and, finally, broad, slab-paved quays along the Marina will presently facilitate transit and traffic. "Semper Libya novi aliquid parit," said the historian; and Libya has never brought forth anything better than the new Harbour.

The "improvements" which, at Alexandria, really deserve that much-abused term, culminate about the Place de Consuls, now named Place Méhémet Aali. In 1853 this big oblong square or Place, the base of the T stem representing the shape of the modern city, was a bald, wind-wrung, and barren wilderness, alternately light dust and dark mud. Since Europe took the matter in hand, it has become a highly respectable square, surrounded by pavements and *trottoirs* of stone. The inner space reserved for promenaders, where the turbaned Napoleon * sits his Arab steed, in the presence of growing trees and flowing waters, is girt by posts and by chains which sin only in profusion of metal: they are massive enough for

---

* The *Saturday Review* erroneously places Méhémet Aali's statue, instead of Ibrahim Pasha's, at *Cairo* (April 20, 1877).

the sheet-anchor of an iron-clad, and the tall spikes remind you creepingly of the Mamlúk Beys, and of their pet punishment which, *pace* Musurus Pasha, is not wholly obsolete.* The round white basins no longer lack water : there are Kiosk band-stands whence music enlivens the lovely summer nights : the English Church is less homely-hideous than she is wont to be ; and the light-blue Palazzo Tositza, at the east end, makes a satisfactory Municipality and Court-house. Though it is the British fashion to live out of town, the old north-fronting *palazzi* are large and comfortable, catching the sea-breeze and escaping the sun.

But Alexandria, like Damascus and all such places, is more appreciated by the land-traveller coming the other way ; by the homeward-bound who enter it from the south. The Cairo railway-line is far superior to all others : even the omnibus trains are punctual ; and the mail-trains cover their 131 miles in four hours and a half. In the warm season the first whiff of the sea-breeze is enjoyable as the first glass of Nile water. The aspect of

* On this vexed subject of "man *versus* bean-log," see p. 259, " Through Syria and Herzegovina on Foot,"—an excellently written account of a bold adventure by Mr. Arthur T. Evans, etc. —2nd edit. London : Longmans, 1877. The argument of the Greco-Turkish diplomatist, opposed to eye-witnesses, was convincing : " Turkey has abolished the stake by law, consequently men are never impaled." Yemen, in Southern Arabia, could tell another tale.

Mareotis, Eastern and Western, cools the eye that has suffered from the glare of Cairo and the Desert. The *gare*, with its shed of corrugated metal, is more roomy and less "ramshackle" than anything of the kind in Egypt. The main streets are also paved, after the fashion of the Italian towns, with the large slabs of that eocene sandstone in which Trieste still drives a roaring trade. The houses are numbered, although the thoroughfares are not named.

The European shops are something like shops, not the miserable Frankish booths of the capital, where for third-rate articles you are charged first-rate Parisian prices. "Shopping," indeed, is throughout Egypt an expensive and unsatisfactory pastime: at Ebner's Library, Cairo, I was relieved of ten francs for Brugsch Bey's last pamphlet, which Leipzig sells for one thaler and a half (5 fr. 50'); while the Pharmacie Centrale charged me four francs for an eye-wash, half a pinch of borax in a wine-glass of rose-water.

The "Canal of the Two Seas" was the first blow to Alexandria, once so confident in her pride of place as the port-capital of the Levant, the successful rival of Algiers and Smyrna, and the last and best of the new births which Africa ever bears. This was succeeded by another shock on April 19th, when the sweet-water line, "El Ismaelíyyeh," that connects the Nile at Cairo with Lake Timsah, reduced the area of her imports and exports to the very smallest radius. She is poor, and her poverty is of the ever-increasing order.

Nothing remains for her but to make feverish Lake Máryút (Mareotis) exchange the fish for corn, wine, and oil; as more than one English company has proposed to do. But the injury to the passenger-traffic renders the hotels far more pleasant and comfortable than of yore. Yeck's old "Orient" has gone down in the struggle of life, and Abbat's, in the triangular Place de l'Eglise, dating from 1868, is mostly preferred by summer visitors. The Hôtel de l'Europe, to which the Khediv* sends his guests, has now taken the lead; and the terms are moderate, fourteen francs per day, when you pay sixteen shillings at the Suez Caravanserai.

This prospect of bankruptcy has not tended, I need hardly say, to keep up the spirits of the Alexandrians. The "Arabs," as the Egyptians are

* I cannot understand why we have naturalized the debased corruption Khédive, or Khedivé of the French, who ever love to pepper the last syllables of Oriental words with their barbarous accents; and worse still, Kedivé, as an English author further degrades the title. The good old Persian word, Khadív (Khediv), Khudiv, or Khidív, means a prince, a king, a great sovereign, as Khedív-i-Hind, the Monarch of India. It is etymologically connected with Khúd (self), and with Khudá (the Self-existent, *i.e.*, Allah).

called, probably because they have so little Arab blood in their veins,* are surly ; and the turbulent tribe of Levantines is still surlier. Here, in case of a Jéhád or religious war, and the threatening unfurling of the Khirkah Sheríf, that Holy and Apostolic flag, the Moslems will require protection against the Christians. Cairo has ever been indifferent; and Suez continues to be fanatically " Faithful."

The new Police at Alexandria has done something towards abating the nuisance of which every stranger complained in the " mournful and heartoppressing city" of 1825. When commerce in cotton and cereals enriched the port, it became a den of thieves, the common sewer for all the scum and offscourings of the Mediterranean. Energetic measures were fitfully applied to those Greek and Italian *prolétaires* with their ready knives : they were often deported, but they always succeeded in

* On this point, with full knowledge of the danger, I must differ from Lane, our greatest modern authority. The Egyptians are not one race, but many : even descendants of the Hyksos are suspected to exist in the eastern parts of the Delta by the learned and experienced Professor Owen (Ethno. 1. of Egypt. *Journ. of Anthrop. Inst.*, April—July, 1874). My conviction is that the tradition related to Herodotus some twenty-three centuries ago was true ; and that the substratum of population is African, Negroid, *i.e.* Semito-African, but not negro. The most superficial glance at the Egyptian Fellah, and at any given Arab from El-Hejaz will supply the measure of the ethnic difference.

finding their way back. During my last two visits I noticed an evident improvement; and doubtless Time will do his work well.

The influx of foreigners may have its drawback; but we must not close our eyes to the other side of the picture. Contrast Egypt's improved capital and splendid port, her maritime and sweet-water canals, and her fifteen lines of railway,* with that unhappy Syria, whose Bayrút is still a mere country-port, and whose capital, Damascus, the "Eye of the East," has become a ruinous heap. Since the days when Ibrahim Pasha's civilizing career of conquest, reform, and progress, which Lord Palmerston, unwittingly the cat's-paw of Russia, thought proper to arrest while threatening to "chuck Mohammed Ali into the Nile," the Holy Land cannot show a single important public work, except what was bequeathed to her by the Egyptians. Had the latter enthroned themselves at Stambúl, Turkey would not now have been a hopeless bankrupt.

The one carriage-road of Syria, connecting capital and coast, was built and is held by French specula-

* Before 1863 there were only two lines, with a total of 155 English miles. Between that year and 1872, nine lines and six branches have been added, bringing up the figures to $581\frac{1}{2}$, not including the doubling of the rails, or to 1,112 miles comprising the whole of the works. Moreover, the latter are still in progress; and, under the experienced eye of Mr. U. P. Le Mesurier, formerly of Bombay, they have every prospect of success.

tors, on terms highly injurious to the country—a concession of ninety-nine years. The route between Jaffa and Jerusalem, with its stiff gradients and its deep holes, is one of the most dangerous bits of riding from Dan to Beersheba. Railways have been talked of for years, but not a yard of iron has been laid down; and, when the Khediv of Egypt proposed to connect Port Said with the harbour of the Holy City, the works were abruptly stopped by orders from Stambúl under Aali Pasha, the last and the worst of the "Grand Viziers."

The principal excitement at Alexandria, even when the Russians crossed the Pruth (April 24th) was the Great Needle Question. Mohammed Ali Pasha, in 1801, had presented to England the companion Obelisk to "Cleopatra's Needle," that once adorned the Temple of Tum, the setting sun, at On (Heliopolis);* but England, afflicted with Liberal ideas of economy, and too poor to pay £10,000, had refused the gift, which consequently became null and void. The offer was repeated through Sheríf Pasha, under the present viceroy,† and has been accepted;—although

* Both were removed to adorn the water-gate of the Alexandrian Cæsareum, in the time of the Egyptian Circe (*ob.* B.C. 30) it was imagined, and hence the popular error. As will appear, the obelisk dates from the reign of Augustus (B.C. 22); not of Tiberius, nor "one of the Cæsars," as Wilkinson said ("Hand-book for Egypt").

† Sir James Alexander, the traveller, again brought the affair forward; Dr. Erasmus Wilson offered £10,000 for expenses; Mr.

the upper face has been quite effaced by the wear and tear of 3500 years, and, on the side exposed to the North, only the cartouche of the King (Thothmes III.) is well preserved * Of the under-surface in contact with the ground, a local legend declares that the earth was scraped away, and that a Royal Highness, creeping under the "ugly old boulder," as an English paper profanely calls it, ascertained that it had not been seriously injured by damp burial; besides which, is not Dr. Richard Lepsius ready to restore any amount of obeliskal defacement? In early 1877 the peculiar phase of the Great Needle Question was the right of property. M. Giovanni de Demetrio, the antiquary, had asserted a claim to it, and had been nonsuited in the local court. He behaved, however, very liberally, and in deference to the English Government, he ceased further obstruction. This would not have been the case a few years ago, when Egypt was the happy hunting-ground of the Western barbarian. It is

Waynman Dixon, C.E., took the contract, and Mr. Carter, C.E., came out to Alexandria as his representative.

* In the standing obelisk, which should also be called after Thothmes (III.), the southern and eastern faces are much damaged by the sand-laden winds, they say. It is now too late to protest against the modern absurdity of single and bare-headed obelisks, which should be double and metal-capped. But what anachronisms they appear in a modern European city—grandpa's old turnip of a hunting-watch dangling at the *châtelaine* of a modern squire!

related of Said Pasha—a witty Prince, fond of his joke—that when a certain well-known "claimant" made *chapeau bas* in the presence, he exclaimed, "*Monsieur, couvrez-vous! Si vous attrapez un rhume, vous me demandrez une indemnité.*"

Shortly after my departure from Egypt, Mr. Dixon (June 20, 1877), urged by a laudable curiosity, obtained leave to uncover the base of the standing obelisk, "Cleopatra's Needle."* He had remarked certain "peculiar notches" in the base of its fallen sister, and mysterious bronzes in the antique model preserved by the Madrid Museum. He found that the four angles of the base had been chipped off, exposing a bar of metal let into the shaft, and connecting it with the granite *socle* by means of bronze feet representing crabs, remarkably well-worked. Originally the animals only were visible, and fortunately the southern one remained, showing two important inscriptions. That on the outside bears, in legible letters, five-eighths of an inch high—

  Η ΚΑΙΣΑΡΟΣ
   ΒΑΡΒΑΡΟΣ ΑΝΕΘΗΚΕ
   ΑΡΧΙΤΕΚΤΟΝΟΥΝΤΟΣ
   ΠΟΝΤΙΟΥ.

---

* Mr. Waynman Dixon gave an account of his find in the *Athenæum* of July 7, 1877, and an illustration from the photograph in the *Graphic* of the same date. The *Phare d'Alexandrie* (June 21, 1877) also contained an able notice from the pen of the learned Greek scholar, Dr. Néroutsos-Bey.

And on the right side or south-south-western inside claw, we read—

>ANNO VIII
>AVGVSTI CAESARIS
>BARBARVS PRAEF
>AEGYPTI POSVIT
>ARCHI TECTAN TE
>PON TIO*

For this information, and for the accompanying sketches, I have to thank Messrs. W. E. Hayns and Willoughby Faulkner. They add that all the feet of the remaining crab have been mutilated, and that the place of at least two of these supports has been supplied by rubbish of rough stone, set in mud and bad lime. As the obelisk is raised some eight inches clear of the *socle*, the whole weight rests upon the masonry and the metal support;† hence the needle has a "cant" seawards, or to the north and west; the stone props are cracked, and the venerable relic will presently fall unless steps are taken to arrest and repair damages. Let us hope that it will not share the fate of the old Orotava Dragon-tree, in Teneriffe, whose proprietor, worried by perpetual and conflicting advice, did nothing to save it.

---

* In South European inscriptions these enlarged T's would represent a date. Mr. Hayns holds them to result from mere clumsiness on the part of the workman.

† Neither my correspondents nor Mr. W. Dixon make it clear whether two crabs or only one crab remain.

16   *THE GOLD-MINES OF MIDIAN.*

According to Mr. Hayns, the wall adjacent to the obelisk yielded, when destroyed, a cippus or

[*From the Photograph.*

section of a column containing a fragmentary Latin inscription in a frame. It seems also to date from the days of Augustus Cæsar, and thus confirms the writing on the crab. We read upon the top E I Λ

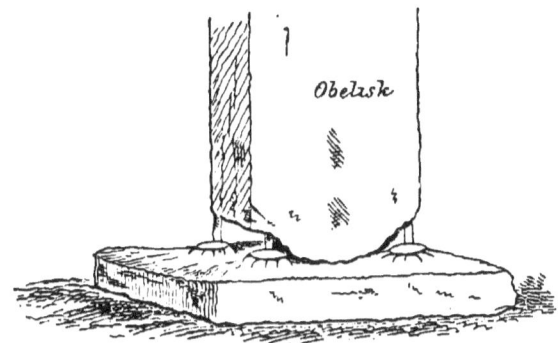

followed by some undecipherable letters, and at the base AVG LIB.

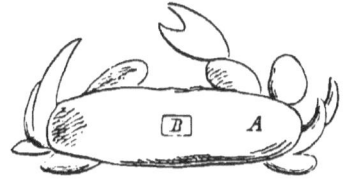

One of the first wants which the traveller remarks at Alexandria and Cairo are Humane Societies. The people generally are neither savage nor brutal, as are certain of their northern neighbours, but they are thoughtlessly cruel, like children, who inflict pain without knowing it. The hack-carriages and cattle are here notably superior to those of Cairo; and wherever Europeans are numerous, even the Hammár (donkey-boy) has learned that the Infidel generally prefers an ass with the least possible amount of "raw," and a four-legged to a triped carriage-horse; yet, even here, we often see needless thrusts and blows, which disgust the least humane; and the use of the whip, especially when the driver appears in the semi-bestial negro shape, is universally excessive. Many amateurs, especially ladies, have proposed to check the abuse by legal means. His Highness has expressed approval of the undertaking, and his officials are universally in favour of establishing civilised societies. Yet nothing has been done. The steps evidently required are to send round a subscription list; to apply for a delegate from London—a professional man of experience, who would reside in Egypt for a time; and to obtain orders that the police should arrest, and summarily visit with corporal punishment, all scandalous cases of cruelty to animals, brought to their notice by residents who are known to be of good repute. After a short course of such training, we should see evident improvement amongst a people who are docile as they are intelligent.

The Europeans, and especially the English, of Alexandria are fortunate in having their own station "Ramleh" (the Sand-heap). This was old Juliopolis and Nicopolis, the Roman Camp, and it is now separated only by four short miles of unoccupied ground from the city, which formerly extended some four leagues eastward to the Cape Zephyrion of Abú Kír

(Aboukir), and which, we can readily believe, lodged three millions of souls. A railway, working between early morning and midnight, runs parallel with the Roman chariot-road, passing over a heap of ruins which now serve as stone quarries; and winding through pottery mounds, *montes testacei*, the *Kerámia* of the Greeks. Few finds have been made, probably because there has been no regular search; and what is found is not preserved. For instance, the little Doric Heröon, an *ædicula-in-antis* upon the Ramleh shore, cut out of the sandstone rock and cemented with the hardest shell-mortar, has been reduced from eleven to three columns; whilst the funerary Christian chapel of the fourth century, sunk in the southern flank of the Karmús-plateau, at the other side of Alexandria, has been hopelessly despoiled.*

The French occupied the highest levels of the Ramleh Railroad, "on the memorable first of March, 1801," and made the fatal mistake of abandoning a position of command, strengthened with batteries, whilst the English were disadvantageously posted upon "Cæsar's Camp," between Casa Grace and the Station. The battle was fought upon the strip of loose sand parting the sea and the pretty lakelet El-

* Editors of new guide-books—especially the coming " English Bädecker"—will consult the two admirable papers by Dr. Néroutsos-Bey, in the *Bulletin de l'Institut Egyptien*, 1874-5, No. 13, Alexandrie, Mourés, 1875. In p. 20 there is a ground-plan of the funerary chapel.

Khazrá, an eastern continuation of Mareotis. The Rev. Mr. Davis, chaplain at Alexandria, denies that the English here let in the sea and ruined the land. He contends that all that they did was to cut the sweet-water canal connecting the two neighbouring Nile-arms; moreover, that the deepest parts of Mareotis, being below the level of the Mediterranean, were always flooded by percolation. The blunders on both sides were more conspicuous than in most battles : we might have avoided severe losses by marching along the lakelet, and by turning the enemy's flank. It is not generally known that Abercrombie, after receiving his death-wound, was carried to the little Mosque of Ramleh. We can hardly expect to find the humble monuments of our gallant countrymen, where the "Soma" of Alexander and the Sanctuary of Saint Mark are forgotten : the Evangelist, as is well known, was removed to Venice, neatly packed in a bale or barrel of pork.

The trains passing the *abattoirs*, where the Pariah dogs are not safe, especially at night and early morning, halts at one of the Palaces which now stud the length and breadth of Lower Egypt. The Court never visits it on account of its being the scene of domestic bereavement. It was burnt down, and, between building and rebuilding, it cost, they say, a million sterling. In 1853 visitors to

Ramleh still pitched tents on the sand-ridge overlooking the cool, soft blue sea; and presently they began to build the broken line of bungalows on the cliffs, which are now threatened with destruction by the waves. The land belonged to no one, but some fourteen tribes of wretched tent-dwellers, one-part Bedawin and three-parts Felláhín, smelt piastres and, as is the universal custom of these people, managed to make out a title. They are still employed to act as "Ghafírs," or guards; whilst the Ramosi, the Paggi and other clerks of Saint Nicholas, formerly paid to refrain from robbery, have died out of Bombay. Ramleh has her little wooden station, apparently of Japanese style, her haunted house, her "Folly," and her hotel, the Beauséjour, which has thriven since poor Bulkeley's death; and she still maintains the traditional hospitality for which Alexandria, unlike Cairo, has ever been famous.

The lesson which we learn at Alexandria and repeat at Cairo is, that the more foreigners are employed in Egypt the better for her interests. In 1840, there were 6150; in 1871, 79,696; and in 1877 we may safely lay down the total as over 80,000. The Rev. F. Barham Zincke, in his sensible volume with a corrupted title, pointedly observes that the Nile-Valley, between the days of the Pharaohs and the Khedivs, has never flourished except where autonomous; such being the logical effect of her peculiarities in position, her formation and population. I will go still further, and assert that to complete Egypt, Syria should be restored to her. Let me hope that she will soon achieve her independence, and express my conviction that when she regains her birthright— Liberty, her progress and development, now arrested only by subjection to Stambúl, will surprise the world. She has outlets for her population, not only in the rich lands of the Isthmus, whose type was and still is "Goshen," and in the Upper Nile region; but also westward throughout Dar-For, Waday, and the Somali Coast about Zayla' and Berbera; and she has occupied Harar, which will speedily become an important station on the Main-trunk-road between the Red Sea and the Lake Regions of Central Africa. A land whose winter climate is delicious, and whose air brings out latent gout, should appeal strongly to the British heart.

The run between Alexandria and Cairo shows a country marvellously like the Surrey plains. Both towns and villages retain signs of the prosperity which was forced upon them in 1820, by the great Mohammed Ali, a Prince whose memory will grow brighter with every generation. At Birket el-Sa'ab, the station between Tantah north, and Benhá south, I inquired about the Kutn el-Bárniyeh (hibiscus cotton), there discovered by a Copt about 1873; brought forward in 1877; and likely to affect the market in 1878. The Arab name denotes their theory that it is a hybrid between the cotton shrub and the hibiscus. This is evidently impossible, and yet the experiment of planting them together is being seriously tried. Sometimes the "mallows cotton" is a straight single stem twelve to seventeen feet high, bearing from thirty to sixty, and even to ninety pods. It is planted in March, and uprooted in September, and yielding per *feddán*,* or small Egyptian acre, eighteen to twenty-eight kantár (cwts.), instead of four to five of El-Ashmúní, hitherto held to be the highest quality. The dry specimen, shown to me by Mr. Vetter, of Zagázig, had four stems; and in the flower and the pod I at once recognized the common arboreous *gossypium relligiosum*, with the loose black seed, and the fine long-stapled lint of Unyamwezi. The variety has, doubtless, found its way from Central Africa by accident, and possibly before the acute Copt thought of collecting it. At Trieste it was carefully examined by my learned friend, Cav. de Tommasini, who agreed with Dr. de Marchesetû in identifying it as above.

Hitherto the new discovery has proved a failure.

* The Feddán, an agrarian and superficial measure, represents 4,200·8333 square métres. The Kantár or Quintal (100 Ratls or 36 Okes) is = 44·5458 Kilogs.

In the specimens sent to me by Mr. Clarke, the cotton in seed from the lower stem was good; and it became worse and worse as it approached the summit, where it was quite spoilt. Growers have tried to prove mistake in season of planting, bad management, unfavourable weather, and so forth; but the excuses are not valid. The tall shrub thrives under the humid skies of Unyamwezi; but in arid Egypt it yields a poor staple, hardly equal to the coloured native growth, although the contrary was asserted. Moreover, the luxuriant growth exhausts the ground, and demands more manure than the Fellah, who is compelled to use cow-dung for fuel, can well afford. The experiment remains of planting it earlier in the season upon the richest soils fertilized by the great Father.

The Lower Nile remarkably confirms the law of rivers, first detected, I believe, by the Russians. The stream is deflected westward by the earth's rotation, modified by its difference at every stage along a meridianal line trending north-south or south-north. The observations made by me upon the Indus * are confirmed by the engineers of the old French expedition. They predicted a shrinking of volume in the Delta's eastern arm, and now we note that

* In "Sind Revisited." But the deflection was made eastwards instead of westwards. For this carelessness I was duly and deservedly rated by the reviewers, who were, however, unduly sceptical upon the subject of the law.

the water is gradually diminishing and that the Damietta branch bids fair to be silted up.

STATISTICAL NOTE.

The old idea that Alexandria, the second city in the Nile-Valley, with her damp heat, and her fever-breathing neighbour, Mareotis, has an essentially unwholesome climate, and an annual death-rate of 40 per 1000, was not founded on error. The copious statistical tables, published by the Minister of the Interior,[*] would prove, however, that whilst upon a registered total of 212,034 souls at Alexandria, *one* death occurs annually in 24·40, about equal to that of St. Petersburg and Madrid; Cairo, with 449,883, has 1 in 21·40. This is a very high figure, far exceeding that of Trieste (varying from 30 to 42 per 1000), which ranks second in Europe, in fact after Rotterdam. The whole country, with 5,250,000 souls, has 1 in 37·88; somewhat less than that of the Netherlands. The proportion of male deaths, formerly so abnormal, tends, however, to diminish; while that of male births maintains itself, showing an improved condition of the labouring population, while the reduced number of infants born dead compares satisfactorily with that of other countries. It is especially difficult to account for the mortality of Cairo, favoured, as she is, with an exceptional climate, with a pure sky, with constant ventilation, and an atmosphere whose dryness and salubrity attract visitors from every part of Europe. It must be referred to local considerations; the rough treatment of infants; the diseases of the Súdán negroes, who suffer from the comparatively sharp winter; and the deaths of Egyptians who, like the Romans, flock to their capital to breathe their last.

Meanwhile it is believed that, between 1872 and 1877, the sanitary improvements, such as the abolition of rookeries, and the opening of wide boulevards, both at Alexandria and in Cairo, have changed matters for the better. The death-rate of Europeans is

[*] *Statistique de l'Egypte;* Année 1873-1290 de l'Hegira Le Caire Mourès, 1873: the figures are the work of H. E. Ede. Règny-Bey, Chèf du Bureau Central de Statistique. The *Neue Freie Presse,* which gives a hebdomidal table of mortality, and sums up at the end of every half year, assigns for June 30, 1877, to London, 19·2; Vienna, 27·4; Trieste, 30·6; and to Alexandria, 40·9. It neglects Cairo, probably because there are no statistics.

certainly low at the great Port; and it is generally held that about one-third of the enormous total shown in the tables is represented by babes and children of tender years. On the other hand, this Spartan treatment of the young accounts for the vigorous manhood of those who attain puberty; and it is a serious question how far the scientific preservation of weaklings will, in course of time, injure the peoples of civilised lands.

An idea demanding correction is the popular fancy that the frequency and quantity of rain in Egypt have increased of late years by the planting of trees. Clot-Bey and M. Jomard declared that, despite the vigorous measures of Mohammed Ali Pasha, who alone laid down three millions of mulberries, the fall measured what it did forty years before, and had probably remained the same for many centuries. The Meteorological Tables, for the three years of French occupation, drawn up by M. Coutelle, compared with the recent observations of Mr. Destoviches, show no sensible variation. Between A.D. 1798 and 1800, the rainy days averaged fifteen to sixteen; while, during the five years between 1835 and 1839, it diminished to twelve—thirteen. The Abbasíyyeh Observatory registered (1871) nine rainy days at Cairo, with a total of 9·08 hours; and thus it gave a rainfall inferior to that witnessed by the beginning of the century.

Finally, a few figures upon the material progress of the Nile-Valley. The passing stranger, who casts an incurious look upon the land, and who is apt to compare it with his own type and model of perfection, unduly underrates the amount of development. Not so we Mediæval Egyptians, who date, we will say, from 1850, and who can place actual Egypt by the side of her former self. Our conviction is that the amount of general improvement is highly satisfactory. For instance : the total of cultivation in 1870 amounted to 3,218,715 feddáns; in 1872 it had risen to 4,624,221; and in 1877 we may readily rate it at 5,000,000 (=21,000 square kilomètres) out of a total of 7,000,000 (=29,400 sq. kil.) The latter figure, the amount of land cultivated in the palmiest days of Egypt, is about equal to that of Belgium, the smallest State in Europe (=29,455). Applying to the 29,400 square kilomètres of Egypt the usual figure which the population claims, 5,250,000 souls,[*] we have thus 178 per square kilomètre;

---

[*] Mr. J. C. M'Coan, in his valuable work, "Egypt As It Is" (London: Cassell, 1877), assumes the population at 5,500,000.

to 173 in Belgium; 101 in England; 58 in Austria, and 33 in Spain.

As the country is entirely self-supporting, and as, instead of favouring emigration, it attracts immigrants, the population of the Nile-Valley doubles itself in seventy-four years, and may presently do so in sixty. During the decennial period between 1862–1871, the births were 1,811,627 to 1,342,655 deaths, thus showing an annual average increase of 46,902, despite an abnormal attack of typhus, and the choleraic epidemic of 1865, which cost 61,189 victims. This is a sufficient answer to the many who look upon the Egyptians as a decrepit people. In 1800 they numbered only two millions; in 1830 about two millions and a half; and before the middle of the next century, the census may show the total of the Pharaohnic days—seven to eight millions.*

The principal productions, cotton, sugar, and cereals, will ever find a market. The mining industry, hitherto confined to the natron of the Buhayral province, to the nitre and nitrate of potash in the Fayyúm and Upper Egypt, and to the Salinas of the Mediterranean and the Red Sea, will presently, I am convinced, assume gigantic proportions, or these pages will have been written in vain. In fact, Egypt, despite the " croakings " of philanthropists and the head-shakings of " humanitarians," who in justice should place her side by side with our wretched pauper province, Sind or the " Unhappy Valley," must be considered, as the regular increase of her population fully proves, one of the most successful of modern kingdoms. She has extended her frontiers beyond the limits known to the Pharaohs and the Ptolemies, and, as the " Greater Egypt," she is destined to spread commerce and civilisation throughout the heart of Africa. It is hard, indeed, to see any limit to her career when, numbering ten millions, she shall extend to the Equator, embracing the Northern Congo Valley and waters of the (Victoria) Nyanza Lake, and controlling the commerce of that African Amazons River and Caspian Sea.

* This figure will of course not cover the population of the new conquests: the southern basin of the Nile, and the wide western regions about Dár-For (the land of the For tribe), both unknown to the Pharaohs and the Ptolemies. Diodorus Siculus (1. 31) tells us that, in the days of the latter, Egypt numbered seven millions of souls, which Josephus increases to seven and a half millions. Champollion calculated that the Nile-Valley of his time could support six to seven millions. Lane proposes eight, and I confidently look forward to ten.

CHAPTER II.

THE CHANGES AT CAIRO.

My short stay at the capital began in the saddest way. Visiting it with the intention of reading a Paper before the Société Khédiviale de Géographie, I ordered a carriage and bade the dragoman drive to the quarters of the Marquis Alphonse-Victor de Compiègne, whose last letter lay unanswered in my pocket. "*Mais, vous ne savez pas qu'il est mort?*" was the reply, followed by an account of the needless untimely death in a duel on February 28th. It is vain now to dwell upon the singular combination of malign chance, the fatal mismanagement of "friends" who should never have allowed the affair to become serious, the declining health which made a shoulder-wound mortal, and the failure of the right man to find himself in the right place. It is only fair to notice that they were in error who attempted to apply a political complexion to the event, simply because it happened between a Frenchman and a German. Those best informed can find no fault with the conduct of Herr Meyer, who was subsequently condemned to three months' imprisonment in Prussia, and who manfully returned home with us in the Austrian Lloyd's S.S. *Flora*, to expiate his offence. Yet the perfect loyalty of the two concerned offers scanty consolation for the unhappy close of that young and promising life, which began so gloriously with exploration, and which, at the age of thirty, ended as it were by mistake,* the exit being the only act which did not become it.

Mr. Frederick Smart, one of the "Ancient Egyptians," whose ranks are now so sadly shrunk, kindly announced my arrival to His Highness, and I was honoured with an invitation to the Ábadin Palace next day. My reception by the Viceroy was peculiarly gracious; and the first audience taught me that this Prince is a master of detail, whilst in promoting the prosperity of the country he has been taught by experience to exercise the utmost vigilance and discretion. The Khediv, indeed, has hardly received from Europe the ample recognition which his high moral courage deserves. It requires no little strength of mind suddenly to give up all the traditions of absolute rule, or rather to exchange them for the trammels of constitutionalism, and,

* A most able *Notice Nécrologique* of M. de Compiègne has been published by Mr. C. Guillemine, Bibliothécaire-Archiviste de la Société Khédiviale. Le Caire: Dalbos-Demouret, 1877.

when the time-honoured policy and administration of a country prove inefficient or incapable, to invoke the aid and services of the stranger in race and creed. Upon this subject much more could be said: it is enough to point out the direction which public opinion should have taken, and which, some day, it will undoubtedly take.

* * * * *

This dear old Cairo! Once more I illustrate the saying of her sons anent drinking of the Nile. And what water it is! Sweet, light, and flavoured; differing in kind, not only in degree, from that of any other river. No wonder that the Hebrews grumbled when they lost it. The first draught of " Nile," which will presently find its way to London, with caravan-tea and desert-mutton, is a new sensation; a return to it is a real pleasure. And now it is early March before the Khamsín * or Fifty-

* In popular parlance the name of the wind is confounded with its period. Coptic astronomers divide the year into four "Khamsín" (fifties) and four "Arbáín" (forties), a total of 360 days: the first of the former begins on the Sunday following the full moon after the Equinox, thus having a maximum variation of twenty-nine days. On the Monday is their Shamn el-Nasim, or "breathing the zephyr," which has become a general *fête*. The Khamsín therefore opens in later March, and closes about mid-May. It is called *Merís*, because it blows from that country, better known as Dongola; and *Shara*, from its *raffales*, or violent gusts. Lane (Introduction, and vol. iii. chap. xxvi.) is, I believe, in error when he writes the word "Khamáseen" (in the plural), and explains it only as lasting "during a period of somewhat more or less than fifty days." Moreover, it is not a "southerly wind;" it

days' period of local Scirocco, which the Arabs, especially in El-Hejaz, call *Samûm* (Simoon), has set in; and the water, like the mornings and evenings, is bright and cool. During April, the spring-end, and May, the harvest-home of Egypt, we shall hardly find Cairo so pleasant, though the climate recovers itself in June, and the "Ancient Egyptians" enjoyed the summer. One draught more, and we will set out to gather first impressions of the City of the Khediv, and to prospect the changes with which the last quarter of a century has visited the capital of Mohammed Ali. New Vienna as opposed to the dull little old "Hof," which still lingers through decrepit age, dates her birth, we may say, from 1857; and about the same time New Cairo began to be.

When, at the close of the great Napoleonic wars and the dreadful battles of the dragoman hosts, headed by Salt the Britisher, and Rosetti the Frenchman, a *modus vivendi* was tacitly established; and when France, contented with supplying the *personnel*, kindly left the *matériel* to England, the boldest of forecasters would have hesitated to predict that a bit of Paris, a bran-new spick-and-span Gallican city, with its Places, its Boulevards, and its Rond Points; its Opera, Théatre Français and

mostly begins in the morning from the east, and waxes stronger as it veers to south-east; about noon it is a souther, and it ends the day as a south-wester.

two Hippodromes, its Rues Castiglionis, and its Grand Hôtel, would have arisen upon the north of the squat and solid parallelogram which here terminated the City of Mars.* And never did the sober Moslems dream, when they permitted a Frankish quarter in their capital, that it would so soon threaten to swallow up the whole. A glimpse at the embellishments between the west-end of the old Muski, or semi-European bazaar-street, and the beginning of the Shubra Road, will suggest what our descendants may expect to see within the coming fifty years.

The core and focus of modern improvements is the Ezbikíyyeh, the old marshy camping-ground of the Uzbegs, which the present Suleyman Pasha, better known as Linant-Bey, converted, by order of

* The critical *Saturday Review* (April 20, 1877) translates the very vulgar "Masr-(for 'Misr')-el-Káhireh," or the "*Victorious City*." The word means "City of Mars," in Arabic El-Káhir, or the Conqueror; and the name commemorates the fact that the capital was founded by Janhar-el-Káid, general to El-Moezz, the first Fatimite Khalífeh, in A.D. 968, when that planet was in the ascendant (Richardson, *sub voce* " Káhirat "). Mr. Edward T. Rogers, the Arabist, has ascertained, from El-Makrízi and others, that Janhar bin Abdillah (a convert's patronymic) El-Rumi (the Greek, or of the Greek faith) was a bought slave (not a eunuch) of El-Mansín, father of El-Mu'izz-li-dín-illah. He founded Cairo, and on Jamádi el-Awwal 6, A.H. 359, he founded El-Azhar, the first Jámi' or Cathedral Mosque in Cairo, which was finished three years afterwards (Ramazan 9, A.H. 361).

The works of the New Hasanayu Mosque are charming in detail; and, considered as a whole, mean.

Mohammed Ali the Great, into a public garden, used for miscellaneous and promiscuous purposes. Twenty-five years ago it was an unenclosed *Jardin Anglais*; wild, picturesque, and essentially Levantine in all its accessories. Here fairs were held, and the worshippers' backs were ridden over.* Here Kara-gyuz, a naughty Punch, so scandalized the Consular corps, that complaints poured in police-wards once a month ; here " Howling Dervishes," as they are politely called, grunted *Allah-hu ;* and here the evening air rang with " shoutings " for *sciroppo di gomma*—the cough-loosing mixture being the fashionable euphuism for a dram of forbidden *Raki*. Under Grand-Bey, it has lost this family *cachet :* we recognize nothing but the old mansion of the late Kyámil Pasha, and the fleas that haunt the benches. It has become ultra-civilised ; the veriest *badaud de Paris* would here find himself "in his plate."

The glorious Lebek-trees (*Acacia Lebbekh*), whose white-yellow blossom-bunches and large golden pods won for them the name of Dakn el-Báshá (Mohammed Ali), " Pasha's beard," and whose perfumed extract was not unjustly called, from its Cytheræan effects, "fitneh" or "trouble,"

---

* The well-known ceremony " El-Dosch," which should be written " El-Daaseh." It is not confined to Egypt, and may be seen on a small scale in the Syrian Buká'a.

have made way for a Hyksos invasion of outer barbarians, especially the ugly and shadeless "bluegums" of Kangaroo-land. The Birket (tank) is now shrunk half size, converted into a pear-shaped pool, and surrounded by a railed octagon of garden.

The latter, also sadly reduced to serve for building purposes, is approached by gate-keepers' lodges of the châlet-type; the pleasure-water is provided with boats and with wheel-canoes paddled by the feet; the turf is irrigated by metal pipes, and the grounds are diversified by a canal and a cataract, by coffee-houses and "Kahwehs," the latter intended for the "native," by kiosks and band-stands, by a hippodrome and a merry-go-round, wooden horses, boats and all. Moreover, a mountain, some twenty feet high, is crowned with a rustic double-storied summer-house which, entered by a rural bridge, is based on a grotto wherein you eat ices and play dominoes.

Lastly, there is a French restaurant, of which I would speak respectfully, on account of its wines and its lamb-cutlets, so appreciable after a course of that melancholy and monotonous institution, which our fathers called an "ordinary," we a *table-d'hôte*. The restaurant is at any rate more appropriately placed here than at the Hierosykosninow, the Holy Sycamore of Isis, the Virgin's Tree at Mataríyyeh (Heliopolis). Shortly before sunset the turnstiles are manned by white-coated policemen—who should wear brown holland—demanding, by way of entrance-money, a piastre, or twopence-halfpenny. The object is not municipal economy : the tax is intended, and fondly supposed, to prevent the black-bloused Fellah and the hog-faced eunuch from affecting the nerves of young Cairo. Here we see both sexes promenading, one in French millinery, and the other in that collarless "Constantinople coat" whose one merit appears in that it is at once dress and undress.

New Cairo, lying around the Ezbekíyyeh, is, like all such modern adjuncts or excrescences, a city of magnificent distances, in a high state of unfinish ; a fresh-from-the-band-box Franco-Italo-Greco-Hebraico-Armeno-Yankee-Doodle-niggery sort of suburb. The modern thoroughfares, of vast length and huge breadth, bear trees planted at the sides, whereas they should have been laid out in central avenues and *trottoirs* for pedestrians, and outer exterior pavements for carriages, as in the *Via dell' Aquedotto* of Trieste. The growth is still in a state of babyhood ; and the only bit of shady walk is represented by two hundred yards, or so, at the south-eastern corner of the New Hotel. The grumbling stranger, afflicted by the dust of the Nile, which is as fine as its water, dwells upon the unwisdom of the Egyptians and compares their ways with those by which Nero was accused of spoiling Rome. Certainly the damp-dark alley seems best suited to these suns: on the other hand the broad and breezy boulevard has already done something towards abating the inordinate mortality of Cairo. Gas is still a local luxury. The new thoroughfares are not named. The detached and semi-detached villas are not numbered, making it as difficult to find out a friend, as on Malabar Hill, Bombay.*

The new Boulevards, Ábidin, Abd-el-Aziz, and Fawwálah (the bean-seller), with their neat slips of garden, mostly affect the north-western and the western parts of the parallelogram. One, however, the "Boulevard de Méhémet Aali," has been run through the vitals of the old city, disturbing many a rookery. It debouches upon the Mosque of Sultan Hasan, by far the grandest of the Cairene Mosques, since those of Taylún, fashioned after the Haram of Meccah, and of El-Hákim, the Druze-God, still so picturesque under moonlight, have been left unrepaired. The noble Egyptian architecture of Sultan Hasan, with the huge cornice capping those immense unbroken walls, gains dignity by confrontation with the new Rufá'í mosque, the big

---

* This is the case also with the intricate labyrinthine "native-town" of Bombay, where a small house-tax might profitably be devoted to the diffusion of moral literature, as is the fashion in Damascus.

pile still building, and showing in every line traces of the European hand : the best we can say of the latter is that it will be a renaissance of art compared with the alabaster Greco-Turkish horror in the Citadel. The boulevard ends at the Kara-Maydán (black plain), the classical Rumayleh of the Mamlúks, where the *Jeríd* was played, and where criminals, brought out of the Gate of Punishment, were decapitated over a tank used for peculiar purposes. What would Abyssinian Bruce say to the bald parallelogram of modern days which also, after a truly Parisian fashion, has changed its name to " Place de Méhémet Aali " ?

In the native town, the main thoroughfares have been widened by pulling down the houses, and replacing them with "dickeys." They are now provided with squares of highly irregular shapes, and have been prolonged to the enceinte-wall : the Muski, which cuts the city from east to west, becomes in the former direction the *Rue Neuve*. The Ezbekíyyeh still preserves traces of old rusticity : the dingy claret-case of a Zabtíyyeh, or Police-office, contrasts with the neat red buildings that now represent the " Karakol " (Guard-house) ; and the Diwán el-Murúríyyeh, or Transit-office of the forgotten Suez-vans, has been turned into a Frankish-oriental market.

The " green threshold " (Atabat el-Khazrá),

where Ibrahim Pasha, the gallant father of the present Viceroy, with right hand pointing to victory, rides his bronze charger, is still a place of punishment to pedestrians. The donkey-boys, once the only cabbies of the land, are urgent as the sedan-chairmen of Bath before the days of Beau Nash; and the charioteers of Egypt are fond of driving furiously in places where the *trottoir* is a strip, and where the street, some five yards of maximum breadth, is crowded with humanity, jostling and hurrying to and fro. The running footmen, who precede the grandees at a long trot, crying *O-â!* in the loudest voices, do not use their long canes freely as of yore; they are mere survivals, especially in the broad-streeted new city, and the sooner these victims to *Raki* and heart-disease disappear from the world the better. All orders are kept in tolerable discipline by the new police, but cruelty to animals is still the rule. A benevolent person of my acquaintance proposed, after a few days at Cairo, the establishment of :—

(1) A society for abolishing donkey's raws;
(2) Ditto for moderating coachmen's whips;
(3) A home for dissolute dogs; and
(4) An anti-bullock-tail-twisting association.*

* In the Book of " Teukelúshá of Babylon," supposed to have been written about our first century, we read : " Hurt not a dumb beast, nor do aught to damage it, nor load it beyond its strength. If thou do otherwise thou art accursed before the (planet)-god

The Muski, type of the improved inner thoroughfare, has still many a want. The paving of foul black earth, the decay of vegetable and animal matter, is made, by watering, muddy and slippery even in midsummer: it forms heaps which must be levelled with the hoe, and it is ever rank with the rush and reek of man and beast. What the pavement should be, I hardly know. Either wood or some form of concrete, like the *pozzolana* used at Alexandria, would suffice for the very light traffic. In the branches of the main trunk, the steam is less *piquant*. Dust, the *débris* of loose sandstone, supplants mire, and the mounds are higher, tilting up wheels at an angle of thirty degrees. Again we wonder to see Automedon canter his lean nags down a crowded lane hardly six feet broad, and double, without drawing rein, the sharpest corners, whence the old women must hurry away with their baskets of *chow-chow* or risk absolute ruin.

Evidently—

"Le superflu, chose très nécéssaire,"

as the epicurean held, has won the day at Cairo. The building-plague rages here, as in Vienna; but it

Jupiter, and before the god (gods?) of the Sun; and whoso is accursed he is rejected; and whoso is rejected is removed; and whoso is removed becomes like a brick; whose earth is first drowned in water to make clay, then dried in the sun, then burnt in fire, and lastly set in the wall where it is oppressed from above and below" (p. 160, Prof. Chevolson, quoted below).

expends itself on mansions of lath and plaster without, and gingerbread within. Happily the frontages are not very solidly built, and a dozen years or so will give frequent opportunities for "ædile" improvements. The city-plan shows 279 principal mosques, and a total of some 400 : still more mosques are wasting money in stone and lime, and the "Church improvements" are notable as amongst ourselves. The façade of the venerable Azhar, the head-quarters of Moslem learning, now bears inscriptions, *or* on a *field azure*.

The noble Hasanayn which, like the 'Amawi of Damascus, shelters a head of the Apostle of Allah's ill-fated grandson, has become a manner of Greek cathedral : the tongue-shaped battlements are stepped, and these grades break the tops of the buttresses that stunt, and do not support, the outer shell. The windows are parallelograms in the ground-floor, and two-light ogees in the upper part; and the unfinished minaret is in the most civilised style, a fluted pillar, crooked withal, based upon a lofty pediment. Nothing can be nobler than the campanile-like square towers attached to the old mosques; nothing meaner than the candles bearing extinguishers, the latest borrowings from Constantinople. There are some half a dozen different models of minarets, each the expression of its own age, from which the architect might have borrowed; but he has preferred his idiosyncratic conceit, and the dragoman glories in the "improved" Hasanayn, because it contains fifty-four columns of white marble. The French in Algeria are repairing the monuments of former days; Haydarábád in the Dekhan is patching up the tombs of the Golconda Kings; and Cairo should not allow the beautiful Mausolea of the Mamlúk Beys, upon which Europeans have conferred the mistaken name of "Tombs of the Caliphs," to sink into mere wrecks, or to become Jubbeh-Khánas (gunpowder magazines), which, moreover, threaten the city with sudden death.*

In the new houses the only traces of local colouring are the projection of the upper stories, and the denticulation of the façades; each window being disposed at an angle to its neighbour, with the object of catching every stray breeze. The Rue des Coptes, especially the southern line fronting the new street and square, has been left almost untouched, except that the cool, comfortable, and picturesque lattice-work, so dear to the collector, has been removed. Of this we cannot reasonably complain, as it harboured vermin and greatly increased

* The papers lately contained some project for restoring, by subscription, these "Tombs of the Caliphs," which should be called "Tombs of the Sultans," or, better still, "of the Soldans." The three chief items mentioned were Malik el-Ashraf, Sultan Barkúk, and Kaid-Bey, who gives the native name to the group. Of this plan nothing was heard at Cairo.

the danger of fire; but glass windows in these latitudes are as barbarous as drinking Nile-water from a tumbler instead of a gulleh (*gargoulette*). The blocks looking upon the Place de l'Esbakié are faced with arcades like the Rue de Rivoli: the only objection to this most sensible of innovations is the narrowness of the covered way. The Municipality, so sharp in the matter of piastres, should determine and insist upon the proper dimensions.

And now of the Travellers' Homes. The "New Hotel," built by an English company, was probably copied from a railway *gare*, and is generally supposed by fresh arrivals to be a Vice-regal Palace. It is crowned in front by a false tympanum; it is unfinished behind, and, like the monsters of the United States, it is honey-combed inside into stuffy little bed-rooms, which contrast queerly with its fine hall, with its grand marble staircase, and with its huge public saloons. If Cairo will only listen to the voice of the charmer, the actual representative of the late M. Blanc, the Hotel may see better days, and the Home worse.

The other three establishments, known to us of yore, are still confined to their respective nations— French-cum-Greek, German, and English. The old red Hôtel de l'Orient,* alias Coulomb's, facing the

* The good old Hôtel de l'Orient, of Cairo, *alias* Coulomb's, now under charge of a Greek, may be left out of the list of hotels; and the French are scattered abroad.

new Place de la Bourse, and now kept by a Hellene, charges " Mossoo " and " Kyrios " sixteen francs per diem, instead of as many shillings. The ordinary of the Hôtel du Nil (Herr Friedmann) is preferred by residents ; but, unfortunately, the approach to the flimsily built house is a long lane leading from the Muski, and you hear your next-door neighbour snore. Shepheard's has become Zeck's. Formerly the door debouched upon the gardens, now it fronts the queerest article ever devised by mortal man, a block of masonry, whose façade seems imitated from a mould of vermicelli, or a swarm of caterpillars, and yet which is not wholly hideous.

I cannot pass Sam Shepheard's old home without a few words upon the subject of its first owner, a remarkable man in many points, and in all things the model John Bull. The son of a Warwickshire peasant, born upon the V—— property, which had belonged to an old county family for generations, he felt a soul above the plough, and determined to push his fortune beyond the fields. He took service with Mr. Walker, a pastry-cook at Leamington, like the first of the Menschikoffs, as baker's boy, and in happier times he sent for his old master, who had failed at home, and, with characteristic generosity, opened a shop for him in Cairo.

As cabin-boy on board the barque *Bangalore*, Captain Smith, he landed at Suez in 1840, when

Waghorn was organising the transit. Here he was supplied with the sinews of travel by the passengers; and my old friend, Mr. Henry Levick, still holding the English post-office, introduced him to Mr. Hill, Mohammed Ali Pasha's Arabazíbásh (head coachman), who then kept a small inn in the Darb el-Berábereh, Cairo. After driving the Suez vans for some time on £5 per mensem, he married the good wife who survived him only about a year; and he soon gained coin and credit enough to open business on his own account. At what time he conceived the *idée fixe*—not always a symptom of madness—that he was born to buy the V—— estate, I cannot say. He certainly was possessed of the idea between 1840 and 1845, and he made no secret of it to his customers, including my late friend and kinsman, poor Sam Burton. Uneducated, he began to fit himself by reading for the position he was destined to hold; and, though he was weak in the aspirates as a Lancashire squire of the last generation, he wrote *vers de société* which had a local vogue. Methinks I still hear him reciting—

"Come to the Desert, come, Polly, with me!"

His Arabic was ever uncouth: with him a Tarbúsh was nothing but a Tar-brush.

There are wild stories accounting for his rise to fortune, a process natural to the genus hotel-keeper everywhere, and especially to the species hotel-keeper in Egypt. For instance, he was entrusted by Mohammed Ali with making ham-sandwiches (!), which he carried to the Palace in a double-locked silver box; one key being kept by him and the other by the consumer. The truth is that he became a boon-companion of the late Khayr el-Dín Pasha; and this chief of the old Transit-office, who delighted in billiards and in strong drinks, gave him a contract for supplying provisions to the passengers of vans and Nile-steamers, a lucrative affair when we paid £12 a head. No one repined at his good star: he was large-hearted and open-handed as he was prosperous; his acts of kindness were innumerable, and his independence of mind and manner that offended the few, secured him many friends. He has turned bodily out of his doors a Prince who would not behave like a gentleman, and once I had some trouble to save him from the ready fists of an irate Anglo-Indian major.

At length, contracts for rationing our troops in transit, during the Crimean War and the Sepoy Mutiny, filled his pocket with gold: despite his profuse liberality and his generous living, he became, they say, master of a "plum." He hurried off to Warwickshire; he bought at once part of the coveted estate which, curiously enough, was in the market; and the whole was gradually falling into his hands when he died.

I have a pleasant remembrance of my only visit to "Squire Shepheard;" of the drive in the comfortable brougham, furnished with all the material for assuaging hunger and thirst; and the long chat concerning old faces and old places. He had become a favourite with all his neighbours. He rode like a sack of corn, always slipping off at the first fence; but he rarely missed a meet, and his friends were always welcome to his shooting and fishing. He had not forgotten his humble days, but impecunious aristocratic connections were cropping up as they will do when a man grows rich; he was becoming related to a baronetcy, and his only sorrow was not having a son to succeed him and found a family—a truly English idea and rather praiseworthy than blameable. Briefly, few men have led happier lives, or have done more good, or have died more successful than kind and honest Sam Shepheard. R.I.P.

This talk of bygone times recalls to my mind another veteran dweller on the banks of the Nile, the late Mansúr Effendi, Mr. Lane. His "Modern Egyptians" is as necessary to the student as Wilkinson's "Ancient Egyptians;" but the experiences of 1835-42 now no longer suffice. A considerable part of the work, especially the first volume, requires the pruning-knife; retaining, however, the flowers and the fruit—the anecdotes so characteristic of the times. Some ripe and practical Arabic scholar, like Mr.

Consul Rogers, should be allowed to modernise, and to supplement the work with our later knowledge. Much that has been cursorily treated should be carried out to full length : for instance, the prayers should be given not only in the vernacular, but also in Arabic, as well as in Roman characters. Chapter IX., on Science, should be wholly re-written ; and other interesting subjects should not be sacrificed in deference to the prejudices and to the ignorant impatience of the general reader, such as he was forty years ago. Baron von Hammer-Purgstall and other Orientalists have pointed out a host of deficiencies ; and the learned author's excuses for his superficial treatment, and for his frequent sins of omission, can no longer be looked upon as valid.

Egypt has now two Scientific Societies : neither of them, however, being by any means patronised to the extent it deserves. The elder is the *Institut Égyptien* which took the place of the ancient *Institut d'Égypte*, under Said Pasha, in 1860. Its headquarters and Library are in the Health-office of Alexandria, where we shall visit it on our return ; and its Bureau is composed of an Honorary President (Marriette Bey) ; a President (Colucci Pasha) ; two vice-Presidents (Dr. Gaillardst and Mahmud Bey) ; a Secretary (M. A. Gilly) ; an Archivist (M. G. Pereyra) ; a Treasurer (Dr. Abbate-Bey) ; and a Librarian (Dr. Colucci Bey) ; with M.M. Gatteschi,

Dr. Néroutsos-Bey, and De Régny-Bey, as Publishing Committee. Its last bulletin, No. 13, issued in 1874-5, contains matter most valuable to the local and even to the general student.

The Royal Geographical Society of Cairo is entitled *Société Khédiviale de Géographie*. An unfortunate occurrence deprived it of the learned services of Dr. Schweinfurth, botanist and explorer; and H.H. Prince Husayn Pasha, the second son of the Viceroy, and Minister of War, has, ever since the regrettable resignation, been spoken of as the future President. Of the sad fate of its energetic *Secrétaire Général* I have already spoken: under his charge the first number of the *Bulletin Trimestriel* appeared in February, 1876,* and a very good number it is. The last itinerary of poor Ernest Linant de Belleferends would be welcomed by any Geographical Society in Europe.

The Standard Alphabet of Dr. Lepsius has been uncompromisingly adopted; and now the venerable Sheikh or Shaykh disguises himself as Šeχ. When I left Cairo there was a report that an Englishman had volunteered to lend his services gratis as Secretary for a couple of years. The berth is not unpleasant; sessions take place during "the season," leaving the hot weather for holidays. The Society is admirably well-lodged;

---

* Typ. Française, Delbos-Demouret et Cie., Le Caire.

books are accumulating, slowly it is true, because money is scarce, but surely withal; and the number of highly educated American officers, reporting from the African interior, to their excellent Chief of Staff, General Stone (Pasha), will supply a quantity and a variety of original matter. The *Société* also proposes to assist with advice, maps, plans, and other necessaries, the travellers of all nations, who propose to pierce the heart of Africa. This is evidently the most important of its functions. Would-be monopolists will of course be found; but let us trust that they will ever be found in the minority.

At Bombay, the Asiatic and Geographical Societies, now combined, form one strong body instead of two weaklings. Should not this good example be imitated by Egypt, where a subsidy of 5000 francs per annum suffices for a single learned body, not for a pair, and where the united libraries, one of old, the other of new books, would complete each other? But the difficulties, apparently small, are really great; it requires a Cavour or a Bismarck to unite, when almost any Thersites suffices to disunite a Kingdom or a Society.

At the Capital we miss the convenient old public Reading-room in the Coptic quarter, whence the rare and valuable books have been transferred to the Central Library of the Ministry of Instruction,

E

under Professor Spitta, in the Darb el-Jamámíz. It would be egotistical to regret the change, which has already done so much good; and I was fairly surprised to see the number of native students and copyists that frequented the well-lighted and comfortable rooms. The Bulák Museum of Egyptian Antiquities, all, except a few articles bought from M. Consul-General Hübner, the produce of excavations by M. Auguste Mariette of Boulogne, is too well known to require description. Last year it issued the sixth edition of its *Notice des Principaux Monuments*, &c. (Le Caire, Mourès), a volume of valuable matter in the *Catalogue raisonné* style, and numbering 300 pages. The only want of this noble collection is the planned and promised building. At present it occupies the old Bulák Station of the Nile steamers, including the *Little Asthmatic*, and the walls appear to be barely safe.

Times in Cairo are almost as "hard" as at Alexandria, and remind the collector of a certain old saying concerning ill winds. Of late years Birmingham has flowed into the Nile, like Orontes into Tiber; and the deluge of shams and shameless imitations ended by almost abolishing the buyer: hardly a tourist dared to look seriously at a scarabæus or a statuette. The "Antíká-hunter" has been tolerably safe during the last two years. It is cheaper for the peasant to find real relics than to risk his coin on forgeries. Yet I should always advise the wealthy amateur who intends to buy such matters, or to invest in ancient armour and "Damascus" blades; in turquoises, and in attar of rose; in Persian tiles, in coins and in all that genus, to secure an introductory letter for some first-rate local authority.

"Doing Cairo," under the normal dragoman, has become as much a matter of routine as the course prescribed to the country-cousin bent on enlarging its mind in Westminster Abbey, or in St. Paul's. The inevitable trips to the environs; to Shubrá Palace, to Mataríyyeh, and to the petrified Forest; to Rodeh (Nilometer), to El-Jezírah (Zoological and Botanical Gardens), to Old Cairo and Memphis, to Sakhára and to the Pyramids, not to mention any but the chief, have been made easy in one way, difficult in another. The Shubrá Road, for instance, still the "fashionable" evening drive, begins well, and ends in inequalities which threaten the carriage-springs.

Moreover, to enter the Palace-gardens, formerly open to the public, you must now obtain an order from your Consulate. This official pass is also required for the Establishments at El-Jezíreh, and for certain of the mosques where formerly your Kawwás (janissary) had only to pay "bahkshísh." The old picturesqueness and the funny accidents of travel are now no more. You hire a carriage, you cross Father Nile by a grand lattice-bridge, which cost only 1,800,000 francs ; a second passes you from El-Jezíreh to the Lybian shore, and lastly a broad, loose, and dusty embankment, avenued by young trees, spanning the fields straight as a highway in Normandy or Canada, and ending in a " Frere Road," a manner of sketch or outline, lands you, after two hours, at the base of the shelf which bears the Ghizeh Pyramids, the last houses of Khúfú (Cheops), and of Kháfrá (Caphren).

Hitherto your mind has been making *mauvais sang*. There is a lack of fitness, a whiff of the *voirie du Caire*, in this trim, modern *chaussée* leading to yon piles of awful ancient majesty, the first-fruits and the foremost of wise Egypt's works, the legacy of a race that looked upon the Greeks as little children, petulant withal and pert. But now your spirit breaks into open revolt. That masonry-ramp, already half buried in the Sands of Typhon—by Him who sleeps in Philæ!—what does it here ? Is it the importation of some Rock-Scorpion from Gib, classic Region of Ramps ? And that Cockney *châlet* which, sitting at the very feet of the Great Pyramid, profanes the cool violet shadows of evening, and pollutes every photograph, is it a practical joke upon the nineteenth century ? or is it a measure of the difference between us grubs of A.D. 1877, and the giants and demi-gods of B.C. 3700 ?

The next step must, evidently, be "improvements" applied to "Khut" (the Splendid), and to "Ur" (the Great). We shall presently find a flight of comfortable steps, with its zigs and its zags, running up the northern and down the southern faces of Khúfú's and Kháfrá's marvels; provided with a neat iron *garde-fou*, or railway by M.M. Cérisy et Cie. de Lyons, and painted, for picturesqueness and economy, a lively pea-green. The surveying post, which now decks the apical platform, robbed of its "rock of offence," will make way for a trim café-kiosk, where, amongst other things, there will be *consummation* of *Pelel* and of coffee-cum-chicory, to say nothing of the lively and exciting *Constitutionnel*, and the honest and genial *Saturday Review*. The interior will be provided with easy inclined planes of battened plank, and with the rustic bridges which decorate the desecrated Cave of Adelsberg—the venerable Aræ Postumiæ. And perhaps we may even expect to see the *châlet* improved off in favour of an *Hôtel des Pyramides* with *chèf*, and *sommeliers*, and *garçons*, habited in the ancient garb of Kemi, the Black Land.

These manifest modernisations will, verily, form a notable contrast with the tenets of the New Faith, with the symbols detected by the Pyramidists, Filopanti, John Taylor, Abbé Moigno and C. Piazzi Smyth; and with the "triumphs of coincidence" according to the common-sensists; in "the greatest, oldest, best built, most mathematically formed, and most centrally placed building (N. lat. 30°) geographically, to the lands of the whole earth." *

Meanwhile, the learned Egyptologist, M. H. Brugsch-Bey, who has made such havoc with the received version of the Exodus, treats the Pyramids in his own novel and ingenious way.† Finding no hieratic word to represent "pyramid," he can only suggest a metathesis of *Abumer* (a "great tomb"), corrupted to *Aburam, Buram,* and Buram-is. Usually we suppose that the Coptic "Piramis" embalms the *Haram*, still popular amongst the Arabs, with the Egyptian, Pi, Pui, or Pa prefixed, and with a Greek suffix by way of making it decent; Pe-haramis, Pyramis, while others find it in "Pi-re-mit," the "tenth of numbers." He rehabilitates, after the fashion of the age, the memories of Cheops and Caphren, who, since B.C. 450, have represented the model tyrants: Herodotus, it appears, was deceived by his dragoman as completely as any elderly damsel of the nineteenth century that admires the picturesqueness of gold-laced jacket and big bags.

* Such are—to quote only the most vulgar—the cubit, the foot, and the inch. The pound and the pint, "which bring back for the country hind his old rhyme with enlarged truth—
  'A pint's a pound
  All the world round.'"

† P. 52, "Histoire d'Egypte," Première Partie. Leipzig: Heinrichs, 1875.

Inscriptions which in Egypt do not lie, even when treating of the Per 'ao,* the Pharaoh, officially assure us that the activity and the valour of these two kings had merited apotheosis. Consequently Rhetoric, once more put to flight by History, must part, perforce, with one of her favourite and venerable commonplaces, the "enormous cruel wonders" of "Cheops' Folly;" and the vain pomp and pride of these ancient despots. Building the piles was evidently the most religious of pious works, a lesson and a lasting example to the lieges of Tesher, the Red Land.

Cairo also has attempted a Sanitarium upon a small scale, and hardly likely to become a Ramleh. It is used chiefly by rheumatic patients, and by strangers in the cold season, especially as a sleeping place for those visiting Sakkárá. Helwán (*les Bains*), fifteen miles and a half south of Cairo, on the right bank of the Nile-Valley, and about two miles and a half from the river, is connected by its own railway, and offers peculiarly offensive sulphur-baths with a temperature of 86° (F.) Moreover, it lies 120 feet above the stream, about the height of the tallest minaret in the Citadel; and thus the air is considered a pleasant change. A few outlying bungalows lead

* Literally the Great House, the Sublime Porte. I have elsewhere noticed the Krophi-Mophi of the Father of History, which, apparently the "chaff" of an Egyptian scribe, led indirectly to the death of Dr. Livingstone.

to the Établissement, a large hollow building, with a central court-yard which, unprovided with díwáns and sofas, suggests, when closed for the night, the idea of a pretty Queen's Bench. The *table-d'hôte*, however, is tolerable; the manager is civil, and there are such conveniences as a post-office and a telegraph.

The plain of Helwán shelving up from the modern bed of the Nile towards the eastern hillock

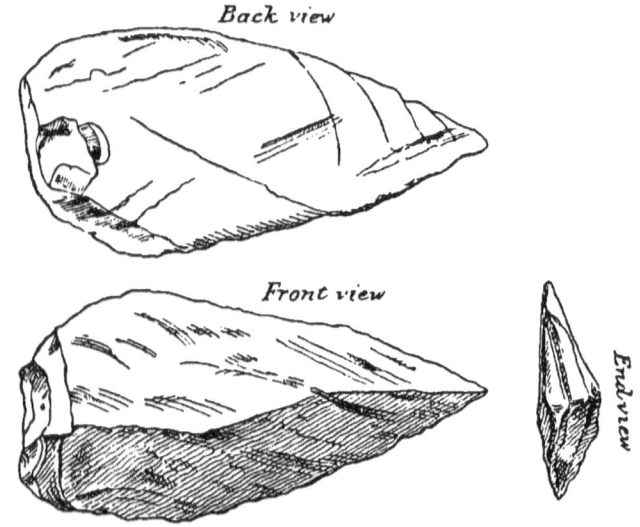

WORKED FLINTS FROM HELWÁN.

range which defines the ancient river-valley, has two centres of silex-production, suggesting, possibly, prehistoric manufacture, especially as worked flints are found three feet and more below the surface. One lies around the last well north of the Helwán Hotel and west of the Railway. Here Messrs. Brown of the Geological and Hayns of the Numismatic Society, guided by Dr. Reil, picked up a flint-saw and many flakes. The other is about two miles south of the Hotel, upon the slopes of a basin which drains to a large and open Wady, and which after rain carries its waters to the Nile : the stiffly standing cliffs of a harder stone. Here fragments are again abundant, and the shapes at once distinguish them from the dark limestones scattered around.

I was supplied by M. Lombard, Manager of the

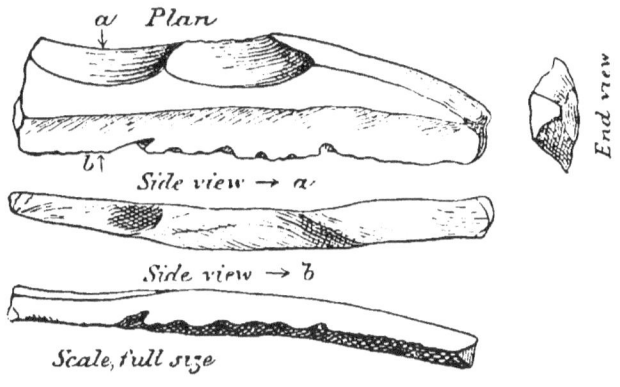

Helwán Hotel, with fine specimens of saws and toothed flints ; but—travellers beware !—they are now " knapped" by the Egyptians. On the western side of the Nile, at Záwiyet el-Uryán, Professor Lewis of the London University found a saw, and Mr. Hayns subsequently a scraper. The learned world is divided, as often happens, into two camps. The thorough-going Egyptologist, who holds, despite Herodotus, that " Art had no infancy in Egypt," has a personal aversion to a prehistoric stone-age; and he readily accepts the theory of Dr. Schweinfurth, Herr G. Rohlfs, and Dr. Zittel;* namely, that sudden and excessive changes of temperature have produced what is attributed to early handicraft. On the other side the naturalist considers the question settled. Sir John Lubbock and others discovered palæolithic silex-types in several places, especially at Thebes and Abydos.

Dr. Gaillardst mentions also Assouan (Syene), Manga, and the crevices of Jebel-Silsileh; and this savant finds no reason why man should not have been co-eval with the powerful quarternary vegetation of the Nile-Valley. The highly distinguished M. Auguste Mariette-Bey is reserved upon the subject, because he will speak only of what he has seen when working the ground. M. Arcedin has published in the *Correspondant* of 1873, "La Question Préhistorique," and has replied to objections in "*L'age de la pierre et la classification préhistorique d'après les sources Égyptiennes.*" The silex-knives of the Ancient Egyptians are well-known: they are divided by Wilkinson (vol. i. 7) into two kinds; one broad-flat, the other narrow-pointed; and he translates the "Æthiopic stone" by "flint" (obsidian?). Moreover, the important march made by Messrs.

* See note at the end of this chapter, and the Bulletin of the Inst. Egyp., No. xiii., pp. 56–64.

C. F. Tyrwhitt-Drake and Palmer through the Desert of the Exodus and the Négeb, or South Country,* practically settled the question by finding (p. 197) numbers of flint-flakes near the monuments of Surábit el-Khádim, used, as M. Bauerman had suggested, to sculpture the hieroglyphic tablets. Shells and worked flints (p. 254) again occur, with the skeletons doubled up, in the quaint beehives called Nawámis (mosquito-huts); and lastly, flint arrow-heads (p. 312) were observed lying about a hill fort (?) near Erweis el-Ebeirig (Kibroth Hattaavah, the Tombs of Lust?).

The changes of Cairo, the Capital of the Khediv, have, I fear, affected my temper. But the city of the Fatimate Caliphs is not yet thoroughly Hausmannized; and it will be long before the modern improvements eat into her heart. Except in the great Boulevards they are skin-deep, not extending beyond the street fronts. Wander about the Bab el-Nasr, during the moonlit nights, and the back alleys and *impasses* will still show you the scenes which I described in the year of grace 1853—views so strange, so fantastic, so ghostly-weird that it seems preposterous to imagine how human beings like ourselves can be born in such places, and live through life, and carry out the primal command "increase and multiply."

* London: Bell & Daldy, 1871.

I did not fail, when returning to Cairo with my old friend, Haji Wali,* to visit the place where we first met. This was the Wakálah Siláhdár, so called from the "armour-bearer" of old Mohammed Ali Pasha, in the Jemalíyyeh or Greek quarter. The sight of familiar objects revived me much. Hard by the little shop of my Shaykh, Mohammed el-Attar,† or the druggist, had fallen to ruins—this was in the fitness of things. Outside the entrance door, hung with its heavy rusty chains, sat or squatted the same old bread-seller who had supplied me nearly a quarter of a century ago; and the red-capped Shroff in the stifling rooms on the first floor to the north had apparently been gazing out of his window, smelling the air, ever since. Not an object was altered inside. The *patio*, or hollow square, was still cumbered with huge bales of coffee, gums, and incense, whilst from the two rooms which we had occupied, on the south and the east sides, issued the same grating and guttural accents of traders from Hazramaut and El-Hejaz.

A great repose fell upon my spirit. I once more enjoyed the soothing sense of the unchangeableness of the East.

* See "Pilgrimage," chap. ix.
† "Pilgrimage," vol. i. pp. 98–102.

NOTE ON THE FLINTS OF HELWAN.

Mr. W. E. Hayns informs me that the exact site of the " find " is the stony tract about the Sulphur and Soda Springs of Helwán, extending two or three miles along the right side of the Nile. Prof. Lewis, when walking over the grounds some three years ago, came upon a fine specimen of a saw, about $2\frac{1}{2}$ inches long. Flakes and roughly shaped spear-heads have also been collected on the opposite river-bank. Between Záwiyat-el-'Uryán, the Chapel of the Naked Shaykh,* about ten miles above the Pyramids of Gîzeh, and the platform of the " Reegab " (?), in Arabic " Haram Abu-Torab," a similar feature now ruined, Mr. Hayns lately picked up a flake which appears to be a scraper. Near the place where the saw came to hand, and about a mile and a quarter south of the Hotel, amongst a great number of flakes, scrapers, and small implements, he further secured one undoubted arrow-pike, or spear-head; and he intends to go further afield in the hunt for Celts.

The collection in the Bulák Museum (*Salle de l'Est Vitrine* A Y), mostly palæolithic, is divided into the following five parts :—

1. Pierced agate, etc., rough spear-heads and flakes, from the plateau-summit of the Bíbaú el-Mulúk, the Valley of the Kings at Thebes.

2. M. de la Nove's finds (chiefly rough flakes and cores) at Jebel-Kalabiyyah, near Esneh.

3. The collection of the same geologist from Girget or Girgeh (only cores).

4. The flints of Halwán, presented by Dr. Reil; and

5. Miscellaneous finds from the Necropolis, especially the tombs of the Greek epoch,† consisting of four polished stones and six flakes, the central winged and fanged arrow-head.

M. Mariette remarks (*Notice*, etc., 6th edit., pp. 81-2): "The

---

* According to Howard Vyse, " *Zowyet el Arrian*, called by the Arabs *El-Medowareh* (El-Mudawwareh, *i.e.* the circular), takes its name from a sheikh's tomb in the vicinity, and is ten miles from Gizeh up the Nile." It is evidently derived from *zawiyat*, an angle, a corner, or a small place of worship; and 'Uryán, a nude man, the Adamical costume being a favourite with certain of the Derwaysh. Mr. Hayns is quite unable to explain what " Reegab " means.

† Mr. Hayns has not yet been able to discover what Cities of the Dead are alluded to.

question of a Stone-age in Egypt is not yet resolved. Our collection, though certainly showing signs of the human hand, gives us no right to conclude, as so many have done, that these remains belong to the remote period vaguely characterized as prehistoric. Before pronouncing upon this point, we must carefully investigate the peculiar circumstances under which the monument was found. If the flint be taken from virgin ground where time has imprisoned it, the problem may be considered solved. On the other hand, when the silex is superficial, the marks of art have evidently no significance : in the most flourishing epochs of Egyptian civilisation flints may have been used as lance-heads and arrow-piles, or even as knives to incise the dead for mummies ('Herodotus').* Now, the latter is the condition of all the objects in the glass-case AY ; they were found on or near the surface, and consequently it would be rash to date them. Under the burning suns, and during the dew-drenched nights of Egypt, the *patina* is so easily formed that it is no proof of age ; the flints may belong to the Pharaohnic eras, to the time of the Greeks, or even to the Arab epoch. We do not, therefore, exhibit them as prehistoric remains : we simply collect and prepare the elements for discussing a question which is still *sub judica*."

* The same prejudice in favour of ancient and primitive custom perhaps induced the Israelites to retain the flint circumcision-knife till a late period of their national life.

CHAPTER III.

TO SUEZ AND HER SANITARIUM.

THE Land of Midian is Egyptian, in a region inhabited by Egyptian tribes, and held by Egyptian garrisons. I was at the right spot at the right moment, so I made no mystery of my long-guarded secret,* but placed all the particulars then known to me at the disposal of the Khediv, leaving him to recognise my services as he might think fit. His Highness at first appeared satisfied with the simple information that gold had been picked up by a pilgrim near the second or the third caravan-station on the way from El-Muwayláh to El-Akabah. From Suez to El-Muwayláh the distance is 229 geographical miles. As at that time I had never heard of the Mining-cities, my hopes of finding an Ophir,

---

* The only allusion to it ever published was the following statement in the Tauchnitz Edition of my "Pilgrimage" (vol. ii. p. 218): "This country may have contained gold; but the superficial formation has long been exhausted. At Cairo I washed some sand brought from the eastern shore of the Red Sea, north of Wijh (El-Uijh), and found it worth my while."

a California, were comparatively humble. I expected only a few "placers" which might, however, as gold formations are rarely sporadic and isolated, lead to an auriferous region.

Presently, about latter March, as I was preparing for the return voyage to Trieste, the Viceroy changed his mind, and on the 25th he formally invited me to lead an excursion, or rather an expedition, to the place where the metallic sand had been gathered. Refusal was out of the question. A Government vessel was promised for Thursday, the 29th, and it was actually ready on Saturday, 31st. In other parts of the dilatory East, and perhaps, under other circumstances, even in Egypt, this operation might have been delayed for a month.

I left Cairo for Zagázig, where Haji Wali and Mr. Clarke were awaiting me. When we parted in 1853, I described my friend as a man of about forty-five; of middle stature, with a large round head, closely shaven; a bull neck; limbs sturdy as a Saxon's; a thin red beard; and handsome features, beaming with benevolence. The lapse of so many years had affected him. The figure had become stouter and the face more leonine; but the change was not sufficient to prevent my recognising at once the well-remembered features and the cheery smile. We embraced with effusion, and, in the few words of conversation which followed, it was pleasant to find that his memory, tenacious as of old, had not forgotten the least detail. This inspired me with a perfect confidence that he would lead us directly to the place where he made the discovery.

We talked of his enemy Mohammed Shafi'a, the slaver so impudently protected by Dr. W——, of the British Consulate, who died at Stambúl after a three-days' debauch of "Hashish" (Indian hemp); of my host Miyau Khudabaklyh, the Hindi, now settled, I was told, at Bombay; of Khwájeh Anton Zavanire, whom I afterwards found a thriving father of a family with the handsome *Sitt* and many olive branches, Senior Dragoman to the Consulate of Alexandria; of the pretentious little Mirza Husayn, who by virtue of his dignity as Shah-bandar (Consul) once ranked amongst the dozen little quasi-diplomatic Kings of Cairo; and of my old Shaykh, Mohammed El-Attár,* whose constant exclamation, " Be-taktub ay ? be-taktub ay ? be-taktub ay?"—" What *art* thou writing ?"—again rang in my ears.

During the whole of our excursion nothing amused the Haji more than to address me as Derwaysh-bábá (Father Dervish), the name which he had at first applied to me when we were passengers together on board the *Little Asthmatic;*

---

* All these personages appear in the first five chapters of my "Pilgrimage."

and he smiled slyly, when I reminded him of the carouse with Ali Agha, the Bulukbáshi or Captain of Arnaúts, and of the hidden bowl brimful of lemonade. Formerly a Persian *protégé*, he has now become a *Mosko* (Russian); his is a strange fate for a pious Hanafi-Sunni with a due horror of the heretic and the Infidel. He at once agreed to accompany me; of course with the implied condition of all his expenses being paid, and of leaving a few *bent* (Napoleons) to support the family during his absence; and he began by charging his donkey's hire, which was a hint that the ancient thrifty habits had not abandoned him.

Mr. J. Charles J. Clarke, *Directeur des Télégraphes*, kindly received me in his house at Zagázig, far more comfortable than the Greek inn which usually lodges the few tourists to Bubastis. Zagázig, properly Zakázík, meaning certain small fishes (Zagzug*), is hardly noticed by the Hand-book of 1858, which, by-the-by, forms a fair starting-point for estimating the amount of change produced in Egypt by a score of years. Since the U.S. war, the capital of the Sharkíyyeh, one of the largest cotton districts in the Nile-Valley, has become a large and flourishing town, where five lines of railway meet, contain-

---

* Some Europeans erroneously derive it from Zagzag, the bag of a bag-pipe. The Zagzug is probably the "Sacksulk" or Cyprinus of Seetzen, who gives measurements ("Collected Works,' ' iii. 496).

ing 28,000 to 30,000 souls (in 1858, 12,000), and thirteen ginning factories, of which nine are worked in the season between September and March; there are also four steam flour-mills which never rest. The approach on all sides is made pleasant and picturesque by the unusual quantity of wood and water; and the view of the town from raised ground is admirable—always considering that we are on the verge where the Delta and the Desert meet.

At Zagázig I heard much concerning the want of an English Consular Agent, to protect the British community from the local *avanie* which in numbers rank after the Greek and before the French. Of course all European nations are here represented but ourselves. Whilst the Spanish Vice-Consul has one individual to protect, and whilst the Prussian and Brazilian Agents have none, we allow our subjects, Maltese and others, to look after themselves when alive, whilst there is no one to look after them when they cease to live. The last who died at the Naffísheh Station was a Miss B——. The body was sent by a cattle-truck to the nearest Zabtíyyah (police-court), and it was on the point of being hid by the native constables in a hole, with the shift worn during life. Thereupon M. Rempler, a German, cried shame, and generously paid the bill for a coffin and other decencies of death. He has, however, been repaid for his outlay.

The Zagázigites are rapidly becoming civilised as far as the ripest trickery goes. Soldiers being stationed on the several roads to levy the *octroi*, the innocent Fellahs have organized smuggling-funerals. The biers, instead of containing human matter for Paradise, are stuffed with taxable cheese, butter, and other creature comforts for the living. The women dress up skins like two-year-old children, fill them with forbidden goods, and carry them upon the shoulder, patting and prattling with them till the guard is safely passed. Nothing 'cuter could occur to the Parisian mind; evidently a high future awaits this very ingenious race. Moreover the "Bámiyah Cotton" has caused a vast development of unfair play. The Copt who first grew the plant gave the bolls for ginning to certain Greeks, who at once sowed the seeds for themselves, returning the ordinary produce to the Copt: the latter, however, found out the trick, and now lays claim to half the yield. The same sons of Hellas also, noting that prices ran high last year, mixed the Bámiyah with any common seed they could find; consequently there will be immense trouble in "picking."

Next morning, whilst awaiting the Suez train due at 1.30 p.m., we walked to the famous Tells, which begin at the Railway Station, and which show their largest masses to the south of the modern town. The ruins called Tell-Bastah have been generally identified with Pe-Bast, or Bubastis; * although the eminent Egyptologist, M. Chabas de Chalons, prefers to place the great Diana at Pe-bailes. His insufficient reason for disturbing the tradition of centuries is, that the stranger goddess Bailes, or Baalis, was a form of Sekhet or Sokhet, and was probably the same as Bast.

A dozen years ago the remains were looked upon as haunted, and no Fellah would have dared to cross them by night. Now, however, familiarity has done its usual work. The people have obtained permission to dig, and to use as compost for their vegetables the dark-brown *débris* dust, which is impregnated with animal and vegetable matter, and with a little lime. It is invariably sifted, and thus a quantity of small antiques, especially scarabei, statuettes, and amulets for necklaces, are found almost every day. At times there are more valuable discoveries, especially life-sized bronze cats, the very sacred animals which the Egyptians copied with most art, bearing the collar and symbol of Bast.

Of the famous temple nothing now remains but two heaps of the finest pink-red syenite. They

---

* Pi-Bast (City of Bast) or Bubastis, where Bast (Pashr or Diana), that is, Isis with the head of the tabby-cat (Bast = Vissat in Modern Arabic), had her head-quarters; whilst Osiris, her husband, assumed the form of Bas or Bes (Arab. Biss), the tom-cat. (Brugsch, *Geschichte*, p. 200.)

occupy the midst of a kind of amphitheatre, whose ruin is composed of the normal adobe (unbaked brick) now weathered back into the original clay. The Tells, distinguished by their bald bare polls, swelling, rounded out of the rich velvet green of the fields, extend for at least ten miles southwards to Abu Hamad, along the Suez Railway. I can only hope that a careful plan of the ground will be made before these mounds are bodily removed.

We saw Haji Wali comfortably seated in the train, and after the normal five hours and a half arrived at Suez. The country traversed is highly interesting. The old land of Goshen,* pastoral, whereas Tanis (Sau) was agricultural, appears to be reviving under the influence of the sweet-water canals. A few years ago it was a howling waste; now it is patched with tracts of emerald verdure. A little farther south are the gardens of Abu Bulah, the fine estate belonging to His Highness's mother, which have seen only three floods. The well-grown trees, mulberries and vines, admirably illustrate the all-might of water in these regions. It was visited and surveyed in 1872 by Colonel now General Purdy, the American Staff-officer who has lately been doing such good work in Dar-For.

* The Arabs call it Bilád-el-Gesh, or El-Rabí'a (the pasture); the popular term is now El-Wady: it is the Gesem of the old Egyptians, and the Kesemet of the Copts.

At the Naffisheh Station we inspected the collection of M. Vannini, of the refreshment rooms, whose sign-board is the Manx coat of arms supplied with a central eye, and whose wife, a Bolognese, was delighted to chat with one so lately from her grand old home.

From Maffisheh a small branch line leads to Ismailíyyeh upon the Timsah or Crocodile Lake. I have assisted at its birth, and predict for it the highest destinies. The situation is charming; the climate excellent, fanned by the sweetest of Desert airs; the soil extra fertile, the bathing first-rate. Viewed from the lake southwards, it shows a huge pile of building with fine gardens, the Vice-regal Palace extending left to the *Pompe-à-feu* works, while a number of flat roofs rise from the dense clumps of verdure, and crown the surface of a tawny land. Already, in 1876, it contained 2000 souls, and it hoisted nine several flags. The land-approach, with its mean mosque and small huts, its big-tiled houses, its three *cafés* (*bière en chope*), and its suburbs of stone, mud, and thatch, is by no means so pleasant. But presently esplanades, quays, and moles will be built; and tall ships will load direct for Europe. Besides the *Canal des Deux Mers*, that Egyptian Bosphorus connecting the far West with the outer East, the sweet-water Ismailíyyeh, will transport the produce of the Upper Nile. Thus the babe which bears the name of its founder, the present Viceroy, is apparently fated to become a giant in the land, to take the place of Alexandria, and to represent the one great Emporium of Egypt. Were I settled in the Nile-Valley, my first speculation would be to buy up every purchasable acre in and around Ismailíyyeh. Perhaps I might be too late.

Unfortunate Suez! When I last saw her, in 1869, she had taken a fresh lease of life; but her career was fated to be short as it was fast and brilliant. The Khedivíyyeh, or *rigole* of sweet-water, had brought with it Hammáms and coffee-houses, where the decoction of Mocha did not taste as if flavoured with Karlsbad salts. The tumble-down walls and gates had been swept away like cobwebs; a lusty young growth of houses and villas had sprung up outside the enceinte and along the creek; the Pasha had built a kiosk upon the ruins of the old town ; a casino-cum-gambling-house, where the ill-fated Captain A—— of the 16th Lancers lost his life by a treacherous stab,* had been opened to the " gay world " by two Italian ruffians ; business throve as well as pleasure, and, briefly, everything was jollity and prosperity.

The completion of the Lesseps Canal (Jan. 1, 1870) changed all that. As if by magic, the traffic and transit which had passed through Suez old road

* The murderer was sent to Italy, tried, and duly acquitted.

made for themselves wings, and flew to the new cut; and, behold! after a short seven years she finds herself temporarily ruined. No wonder that the passing traveller calls her a "dreary town." I use the qualifying adjective with intention. The Gulf-port has suffered from the Canal, like Trieste from her railway, the Süd-bahu; but these accidents are temporary and transitory, whereas the power of position is essential and permanent.

The causes assigned to the Canalists for building a Port distant three miles to the south, instead of passing close by the town, are various. Some declare that the waters south and south-west of Suez are shallow, and that the borings come upon rocks, as was the case at "Petit Chalouf;" others that the Suezians, resolved to make sudden fortunes by exorbitant demands, so offended the son of the biographer of La Pérouse* that the proposed Duc de Suez swore they should never see a centime of his money. The truth is that the "Universal Company" built large expectations upon their three miles of ground on either side of the waterway, and this tract would not have included

* *Journal Historique du Voyage de la Pérouse* (1790), and *Voyage de la Pérouse* (1831), by Baron Jean-Baptiste Barthélemy de Lesseps; born 1765. He had been sent home to report the details of the expedition to Louis XVI. He was, I believe, the only officer who escaped with life, and he died Consul de France at Lisbon in 1834. His more famous son was born November 19, 1805.

the town. But the grant has long ago been given up for a consideration; and the fact remains that, by the selfish tactics, much money has been spent, and poor Suez wears the appearance of a Red Sea settlement lately bombarded and not yet repaired.

But Suez, the latest representative of so many historical towns, will presently have her revenge. Already the engineers are speaking of a double canal, one line for the northwards, the other for the southwards bound, and both communicating by locks. This supplement would not cost half the sum (say £20,000,000 sterling) swallowed up by the original, and, all things considered, making it would probably be found cheaper than widening the actual channel. It is expected that the successor will reverse the proceedings of its predecessor, and run as it easily can, down the town-creek. Apparently, it has been the fate of the Vermiculus, the "wormlet," * ever to keep moving, to creep down from north to south.

* In vulgar Arabic Suways (Suez) is the diminutive of Sûs, a worm, a weevil, not a "moth" as Wellsted supposed. This can hardly be accepted, as the name is found in the Abyssinian "Sos," a shepherd, a pastor, which also survives in the hated and historic Aramæan Arabs, called Hyk-Sos. It may be "little Sûs," as towns of the latter name are found in "Susa" of Khuzistán, in Morocco, in Tunis, and in other places. Stephanus (*sub voc.* Σοῦσα cccclvi., vol. ii.) associates Susa with the Grecised Persian word σοῦσον, a lily, which he states to be of Phœnician or Phrygian origin, and the Arabs still term it Sûsan, whence Susannah. Others derive it from the old Persian Shús, pleasant (Col. Kinneir's "Geographical

The tradition of the people is that in the early Christian ages the site was occupied by fishermen and smugglers. Some six centuries ago, a Shaykh from Sús in Morocco, returning from his pilgrimage, took up his abode on the sea-shore about a hundred yards west of the English hotel; his sanctity caused him to become famous as El-Súsí, and the place was called after him El-Sús, and afterwards El-Suways. His tomb is still shown and venerated as the founder of the port-town.

The Heröopolis which named the Heröopolitan Gulf, and which Ptolemy (iv. 5) places in N. lat. 29° 45', can hardly have been far from Suez, and is generally supposed to be the Ajrúd Fort (Shaw, ii. 2). Arsinöe or Cleopatris,* built by Ptolemy Philadelphus, and named after his sister in the third century B.C., and existing as a town in the second century A.D.—a life of more than 400 years—has been identified by H.M.'s Consul Mr. George West† with the

---

Memoir of the Persian Empire," p. 100, *et seq.*). Finally, in 1412, the geographer, Abu'l Rashíd-el-Bakuy (vol. ii. p. 243), calls it Suways el-hajar (Suez of the stony-ground), as if to distinguish it from others of the name. See Ayrton's note upon Wallin, p. 340, *Journ. of R. Geog. Soc.*, vol. xx. of 1850.

* Strabo (xvi. 4, § 24, and xvii. 1, § 26), Pliny (vi. 29), and Ptolemy (*loc. cit.*), who places it in 29° 10'.

† Consular Reports "on the Trade and Commerce of the Port of Suez for 1872." Mr. West well explains the reason of the several migrations of the town by the successive siltings-up of the several anchorages; and he believes that " the existing site of Suez, including the land recovered from the sea, south of the

Tell el-Klismeh (Clysma), a mound about seventy feet high, at the head of the creek, where the late Said Pasha built his Kiosk. In Ptolemy it lies twenty miles north of the Clysma Præsidium * (N. lat. 28° 50'), whence it is supposed the Arabs derived their "Kulzum." Of the latter town Yakrút el-Hamawi, in his " Mu'ajam el-Bildán " (" What is known of Countries "), written at the beginning of the thirteenth century, states (*sub voc.* Kulzum), "it was then a ruin, with a gate ; and a place near it, called Suways, had become the port, and it also was like a ruin, and had not many inhabitants."

Suez, at present only a " patch " upon Port Said,

settlement as far as the new port, will, for any period of time we can practically contemplate, be that of the Egyptian Red Sea *entrepôt* best suited for the trade between Egypt and the countries about the Red Sea and beyond it." M. Linant de Bellefonds ("Mémoires sur les Principaux Travaux d'Utilité Publique," etc. Paris: Bertrand, 1872–73) would place Arsinoë or Cleopatris at the so-called Serapium Plateau or Lake Timsah, then the terminus of ship-navigation.

* Bochart (Phareg *sub voc.* Clysma) supposes the port to have sent a bishop to the Council of Chalcedon in A.D. 451. Vincent ("Commerce, etc., of the Ancients," i. 522) considers Kulzum an Arabic corruption of Κλύσμα, which seems to imply a place by the sea-shore ; although Bochart (*loc. cit.*) had suggested that it ought to be written Κλίσμα or Κλείσμα, from κλείω, to shut, in reference to its assumed position as a port at the entrance of the famous old Isthmic Canal (Strabo, xvi. 4, § 24). Mohammed ibn Ya'akúb el-Firozábádi (died A.D. 1414), author of the " Kámús (or Ocean) Directory," and other worthies, derive the name of the town and its adjacent sea from its Arabic sense to "swallow up," alluding to the destruction of " Pharaoh and his host " near the spot.

may be described in 1877 as exactly the reverse of what I described her in 1853. True the old hotel remains, with its bad dinners and its unclean and sulky Hindi-Moslems, who never forget their creaking shoes, nor remember their turbans and waistbelts. To the experienced eye these latest developments of the óran-útan, or man of the woods, are pleasant as would be an English waiter in waistcoat and turned-up shirt-sleeves.

But behind the Caravanserai there is a Roman Catholic Church, with tall steeple and jangling bells; whilst priests, nuns, and pigs promenade the streets. What would that large old Turk, Giaffar Bey, have said to these abominations? The original English cemetery upon the Creek-islet shows rents and tears in all its buildings; and the Wakálet Jirjis, the "George Inn," survives in the last state but one of dilapidation and decomposition. The Farzeh Daur, or rotation system,* so ably denounced by Mr. Henry Levick, formerly Vice-Consul, and still British Postmaster for Suez, has completely died out; and the shipping has changed from sail to steam.

I found quarters at the Hôtel de l'Orient, in the Boulevard Colmar, formerly Súk el-Nimsá, the Austrian Bázár. Early on the following morning

---

* "Pilgrimage," vol. i. pp. 250–52. By a curious misprint the word generally appears as "Fazzeh."

(Friday, March 30th), M. George Marie, C.E., called, and gave me the following letter, bearing the signature of H.H. Prince Husayn Kamil, Minister of Finance.

Le Caire, 29 Mars, 1877.
"Monsieur,

"J'ai le plaisir de vous annoncer par la présente les dispositions que j'ai prises relativement à l'excursion que vous vous proposez de faire.

"Les officiers de l'Etat Major Egyptien—Amin Effendi Ruchdi, Hansan Haris, Abd-el-Kerim Izzet; ainsi que l'Ingénieurs des Mines, M. George Marie, ont été désignés pour vous accompagner; en dehors de ces Messieurs il y'aura encore environ une dizaine* de soldats du Génie qui iront avec vous.

"Les susdits officiers ont des tentes, ainsi que tous les instruments nécéssaires pour faire les cartes géographiques; M. Marie aura à faire le rapport sur les mines.

"Tous seront à Suez après demain (Samedi) matin.

"J'ai donné l'ordre par écrit au Gouverneur de Suez, pour qu'il soit à votre disposition pour le cas, où vous auriez besoin de lui; si par exemple vous voudriez quelques guides pour vous accompagner, vous n'avez qu'à les lui demander.

"La Frégate Égyptienne *Sinnar* partira de Suez Samedi; et j'ai déjà donné les ordres necessaires au Commandant des bateaux stationnant à Suez pour que le Capitaine de la Frégate vous porte dans le port où vous voudrez aller, et qu'il reste autant que votre excursion l'exigera.

"Enfin j'ai donné aussi l'ordre au Gouverneur de Moelh (El-Muwaylah) pour qu'il vous donne des chameaux, guides et toutes autres choses, que vous voudriez, pour pouvoir faire votre excursion.

"Agréez, Monsieur, l'expression de ma plus haute considération.
                      (Signed)   "HUSSEIN KAMIL.
"Monsieur Le Capitaine Burton."

Nothing could be more satisfactory. The three

---

* There were twenty with the Sháwísh (chaush or corporal) Ali.

Egyptian officers were introduced to me, and I formally took command. We then called upon the Muháfiz (Governor) of Suez, H.E. Sa'íd Bey, to meet the Captain commanding the corvette, and to settle the time and way of embarkation. Sa'íd Bey is an old captain in the Egyptian navy, a fervent Moslem, born in Candia (Crete)—a man of energy, activity, and full of friendly feeling towards Europeans. M. Marie kindly undertook to become caterer, and Mr. Clarke, who was on "sick leave," to act as my secretary. All was ready; the officers had their surveying-gear, but the engineer had brought only a few bottles of acids for testing metals; and he afterwards assured me that he looked upon the whole affair as one of those *Carottes* which periodically sprout up with peculiar luxuriance in Egypt. Incessant work was required, during the short space of twenty-four hours, to collect the provisions and furniture; camel saddles, water-bags, large and small; *batterie de cuisine*, eating-gear, and the manifold other requisites for a three-weeks' cruise and desert-trip.

However, by the good aid of Mesdames Chiaramouti, a ship-chandler and general dealer established at Suez, and Isnard, proprietors of the Hôtel de l'Orient, we did pretty well.* The latter also entrusted to us her son, Marius Isnard, a youth of

* See Appendix I.

twenty, who was to act as *chef*, together with an assistant, whom I shall call Antonin Rosse. He was a Southern Frenchman, and not very strong. He died at Suez December 9, 1877. Had I known what was before me, the least expensive and the best plan would have been to engage a dragoman, with a cook accustomed to the Desert, under contract to supply us with bed and board, with riding donkeys, and, in fact, with the wants of a common tourist-party. On such journeys the dromedary is a nuisance, because of the loss of time in mounting and dismounting to collect specimens.

I saw as much as possible of my old friends, Mr. and Mrs. West, and the Levick family, who had been stationed at Suez long before the days of my Pilgrimage. Our mission was, of course, kept a profound secret. The excellent correspondent of the *Times* at Alexandria (May 14), says that "there never was any real necessity for the mystery:" let me advise him, should it be his fate to have anything to do with gold in Arabia, to be quite as reticent as I was. Lastly, the good Haji Wali gave me endless trouble. He would not go to bed; he would eat only a bit of meat and drink a drop of soup; he had told me everything, and now he wanted to go home; he was an old man who could not stand the fatigues of a march; he had pains in his head, in his side, in his knees, and so forth. A doctor was sent for, and requested to supply him with a flask of the most nauseous gout-mixture. Mr. Clark was told off to keep him well in hand: I really feared that he would break loose and disappear. He afterwards owned that it was all "funk," and two bottles of bitter ale a day proved even more efficacious than the gout-mixture. Yet it was a serious step; to take, as it were, a man of eighty-two, by the neck, as he said, and to carry him off into Arabia. I felt relieved of considerable responsibility when he returned to his family in better condition than when he left it.

This chapter may end with a sketch of the Sanitarium proposed for Suez, and, indeed, for all Egypt. Much has been written about the change of climate in the Isthmus, caused by the *Canal Maritime;* and pilots agree that not only fogs and clouds now appear in a sky that was once of brass, but that the water also draws with it a wind from the north, in fact the sea-breeze of the Mediterranean, the Etesian gale of Herodotus, which regularly assisted those sailing up the Nile.

At Suez, formerly so stagnant, this cool indraught is perennial, even during the season when the Canicule rises; and three winters ago Jebel Atábeh and its fronting range of Asiatic mountains were, during forty-eight hours, powdered with snow—a portent which not a little astonished the oldest inhabitant.

In early January, 1876, two violent showers fell over the northern part of the Red Sea; and I found that the notable change for the better at Jeddah was popularly attributed to "the Ditch." It certainly has some effect.

The evaporation from the Bitter and the Crocodile Lakes is enormous. A gallon of water in the hot season gives thirteen grains of salt, the Dead Sea yielding eighteen. There are many species of fish which cannot exist in such a medium, and at times the shores are strewed with their dead. But Mr. Andrews, of the P. and O. Office, who since 1869 has taken meteorological observations at Suez, distinctly denies that the Canal has exercised any effect upon the rainfall of the Isthmus. He holds the snow and the showers to be accidents, and his objections are borne out by the winter of 1876–77, when there was literally no rain. However, one must modify all extreme statements upon this subject, as some declare that it has not, and many that it has totally changed the climate. It would therefore appear that there is a change, which affects persons differently according to their respective temperaments.

Ramleh and Helwán (les Bains) are, I have shown, the only spots in the whole land of Egypt which offer anything like a change of air to the burnt-out denizens of her cities, while neither of them can claim the title of Sanitarium. The main climatic disadvantage of the Nile-Valley in Northern eyes is its distance from the *Sommerfrisch*, the cool *villegiatura*. Libanus, the nearest, wants every comfort of civilised life ; and that next removed would be cocknified Bagni di Lucca. There is, therefore, permanent local interest in the *reconnaissance* south of Cairo, made during early 1876 by Doctors Schweinfürth and Güssfeldt, both African travellers of credit and renown. The papers* contained passing and very superficial notions of their " attempt to unravel the mysteries of that region of mountains and depressions, which extends from the Arabian chain to the Red Sea ; " and even the explorers seem by no means to have realised what may be the results of their exploration.

A few details concerning these mountains of the Lower Thebais, as Shaw calls them,† a block which promises so much. The Jebel-Galálah (Khelál), now proposed as a Sanitarium, was visited in search of coal, and to cure an obstinate ophthalmia, some thirty years ago, by the well-known engineer, Hekekyán Bey, uncle to my friend Yacoul Artin

* The *Academy* (p. 511) of May 27th and of June 3rd (p. 534). Dr. Paul Güssfeldt began in July 7, 1877, a formal description of his trip in Herr Petermann's " Mittheitungen."

† I have consulted only the " Voyages de M. Shaw;" the noble French translation is two vols., folio. La Haye ; Jean Neaulme, 1743.

Bey: he spent nearly twenty-four months there, and he left his name cut on a rock, which the travellers have called *Hekekyán-fels*.

The plateau lately surveyed by Col. Purdy and other Anglo-American officers, under orders from their energetic Chief of Staff, General Stone (Pasha), averages three thousand feet high, and measures in round numbers fourteen geographical miles from east to west, by forty north and south. Composed of white and yellow limestones and sandstones overlying granite, it seems to prolong in Africa the Sinaitic foundations split by the Red Sea; and a broad band of primary formation, along which we shall steam, offsets from the south-eastern extremity, and subtends for a considerable distance the African shore of the Suez Gulf. The great (African) Wady el-Arabah, trending from north-east, on a parallel with the Zá'aferáneh Light, to south-west, and averaging in breadth six hours of march, separates our block from the barren Jibál el-Humr (Red Mountains) which buttress the right bank of the Nile opposite the railroad station, Benir-Suéf (Suwayf.) This African Wady, which must not be confounded with the Asiatic Wady el-Arabah * (of

---

* "Arabah" (Heb.) means a desert, from "Arab" (to be dry), and relates to its physical qualities; while Midbar describes the waste in relation to its use by man. Wady el-Arabah is not an uncommon term in Arabia; all, however, are features of inferior importance to the north-western, which Deuteronomy (i. 1, and

the Arabs), the southern prolongation of the Dead Sea depression, has been incorrectly rendered "watercourse of the chariots," Pharaoh's heavy-driving wheels probably haunting the interpreter's brain.

The vegetation of the block is mostly gramineous; sun-burnt and wind-dried in August and September. Trees, especially the short and thick-trunked acacia, grow only in the valleys, and Dr. Schweinfürth found to his surprise not only Asiatic plants, but one held peculiar to Siberia. No antelopes were seen; the game is principally steinbok (*ibex*) in the high lands, and hares in the low levels. The scanty population is partly settled—partly nomad. The former comprises the reverend inmates of the two convents. Dayr Már Antonios (of St. Anthony), one of the most ancient, if not the oldest, in the Christian world, stands upon the southern lip of the Wady el-Arabah, about 4750 feet high, and not visible from the sea, whence it is distant thirty-five miles. It is reached by Sambúk (boat) from Suez to Za'aferáneh Lighthouse, a run of fifty miles, easily covered in a day, or even

ii. 8) calls the "plain over the Red Sea" (read "at Arabah in Yamm Súf, or the Weedy Sea"); and "the way of the plain from Elath" (for "the road of Arabah from Elath"). In the former place the LXX. has πλησίον τῆς ἐρυθρᾶς θαλάσσης; and the Vulgate "in solitudine campestri contra mare rubrum." The second is rendered respectively παρὰ τὴν ὁδὸν τὴν Ἄραβα and "per viam campestrem de Elath."

in eight hours of northerly wind. The thirty-five miles of land-route must be done on horse, ass, or camel-back.

At a distance it appears a long wall of masonry, the well-built enceinte of a quadrangle, containing lodgings for fifty monks, and huts for the people attached to them, with gardens and other conveniences. In the middle rises a tower with converging sides, the blunt section of a cone. There is no open gateway, and the visitor, as at Sinai, is hauled up by a rope. Már Búlos (St. Paul's), separated from its neighbour by the main ridge of the Galálah *massif*, lies some fifteen miles southeast by east : it is visible from parts of the Gulf, and its shape resembles that of its brother. The nomads of the mountain, the Beni Ma'ázeh, of whom we shall presently hear more, are said to number 3000 souls, although not more than thirty are visible. They are a fine race, and treat their strangers with courtesy. The chief camp lies to the west and south-west of the *Hekekyán-fels :* elsewhere the necessary water must be carried on donkey-back.

There are two lines from Cairo to the Jebel-Galálah. The first, by Suez and Zá'aferáneh Point, has already been mentioned : the second, by the Upper Egypt Line (Rodeh Station), places you in four hours thirteen minutes at the *gare* of Beni-Suwayf, distant from the capital fifty-five direct geographical miles. You engage camels at the village, and you cross by ferry to the right bank. Here several small settlements are scattered around Bayázel-Násará, a Coptic church now being rebuilt. This stage will take about two hours and a half, and the same must be allowed for the ride over the river-valley to the nearest spurs of the Red Mountains.

When the "Champagne air" of the uplands, perpetually poured on by the pure dry winds of the Desert to the north and south, and by the salt breezes of the Kulzum Sea to the east, with the Nile-draught to the west, shall be duly appreciated, a tramway will shorten the transit of the plain; even now the short space of ten hours removes you from the rank reek of Cairo to the future Hill-Station.

I will borrow the travellers' *vivâ voce* version of their trip, assisted by lithographed sheets issued at Cairo (May 20th, 1876). Doctors Schweinfürth and Güssfeldt went with a multiplicity of objects—to collect botanical specimens, and to rectify previous flying-surveys by an exact topography. They also proposed to fix the age of the sedimentary rocks by studying the palæontology; and to determine the astronomical positions, the altitudes and the magnetic intensity, inclination and declination.* On

* Their instruments were a pocket-chronometer (makers, Har-

March 19th they made the church village " Bayáz el-Nására : " hence skirting the northern slopes of the Jibál el-Humr, where nine several valley-systems were laid down, they reached the spring El-Arayyideh, on the nearer bank of the Wady el-Arabah before mentioned.

The greater part of the surface, especially the nummulitic plateaux between N. lat. 28° and 29° 30', was bare of vegetation, or dotted with the whiteblossomed broom (*Retama Raetano*, F.); some of the valleys bore a rather abundant growth, whose characteristic was the absinthium (*Artemisia Judaica*, L.). Immense quantities of silex, like those that cover whole tracts in the Libyan and Arabian Deserts, strewed the Wady Senúr (No 4): the cores had been split to prisms by the abnormal variations of temperature, and though none were

burg and Weill) whose maximum variation was + o' 9, and two watches, a six-inch sextant, the magnetic apparatus already used by Dr. Güssfeldt in Western Africa, a travelling barometer (Fortin), and two aneroids (Beck) for simultaneous observations at Cairo. The longitude was determined by careful chronometric work at Beni-Suwayf; and a meridional difference of 4' 52". 7 was found between that station and Alexandria, or rather the observatory of M. A. Pirona, a scientific merchant long settled on the sea-board. The following table was brought home by Dr. Güssfeldt, who had not finished his calculations of magnetic intensity—

		Declination W.		Inclination N.
March 12.	Beni-Suwayf	5° 42' 4"	...	39° 2'
April 1.	Dayr Már Antonios	5° 16' 8"	...	39° 1'
,, 8.	Dayr Már Bulos	5° 17' 6"	...	38° 7'
,, 21.	Beni-Suwayf	5° 38 8"	...	39° 3'

worked, the cleavage was clean as in our museum specimens of stone-age weapons.

The travellers crossed the Wady el-Arabah, well known in the days of Mohammed Ali, from west-south to east-north-east. This valley, and its secondary or branch, Wady Herkes, supplied the Great Pasha with alabaster for his mosque in the Citadel. The material also forms the mosaic pavements in the older places of prayer; and it yields red, yellow, and flesh-coloured marbles, with blue veins; orange-tinted, like that of the Mosque El-Ghori; and black from the rocks about Saint Anthony.

The general aspect resembles the vast oasis-depression of Khargeh, both being bounded by similar steeps of eocenic chalk, evidently an old sea-coast. The southern bank is formed by the northern steeps of Galálah (1000–1100 mètres). Seven branch-valleys mouth into and traverse the main stem. Two of these, Wadys Natfeh and Askar, were carefully examined, and gave a comprehensive view of the whole formation. The head of the former is distinguished by a cavern, rich in the maiden-hair fern (*Adiantum Capillus Veneris*), wholly absent from the Egyptian Desert; and the roof stalactites, twenty feet long, are clothed with mosses. A stream, gushing from the cliff-sides, here about 1,200 feet high, forms two kieves, or basins, about 125 feet in diameter; and the rocky steps and mossy ledges, over which the water rushes, are fringed with figs (*F. Palmata*, F.) fifteen feet tall, wild palms, and the richest verdure. The large Wady Askar is also rich in camel-pastures, and even more so in the variety of its flora.

After winding through the picturesque precipices forming the bed, our explorers came upon the only path practicable to camels; and thus reached the Galálah-crest, where the Bedawin camp with their flocks and herds. Here the vegetation was of a type totally differing from that of the Wady. The rolling surface was clad with dense herbage, and at the altitude of 1000 mètres, unexpectedly appeared several plants, hitherto found only on Mount Sinai and in Inner Palestine; whilst not a few belonged to Persia and Afghanistán. The prevailing type was that of the Sinaitic Peninsula, mingled with the Mediterranean coast-growth about Alexandria. There was an abundance of the edible root Scorzonera [*] (*mollis*), and of Malabaíla Sekakul (R.): the Artimisia bore a parasite, the characteristic *Cynomorium Coccineum*.

The travellers, having rounded the north-eastern flank of the Galálah, reached the Convent of Saint Anthony, where they were hospitably received by the Coptic monks. Organic remains on the southern, were as rich and various as the vegetation of the

[*] It is also common on the Midianitic coast.

northern region : a fine booty of petrifactions was sent to the Palæontological Museum of Munich.

Near St. Paul's, where they were treated with equal kindness, appeared three strata of middle chalk, which, on the northern flanks, is disclosed only by the deepest valley-cuttings. They ascertained that the Upper Galálah consists of nummulites, whilst the lower levels and the foot hills are composed of exogyra (*Mermeti Glabellata*). The marly strata intersecting the latter abound in echinites, spharolites, and especially in ammonites of three several species, which sometimes measure a foot and a half in diameter. The fossil beds, 500 feet thick, underlie the sandstones which, about St. Paul's, appear in the lowest valley-sections : the latter, wholly destitute of fossil-remains, seem to be connected with the Sinaitic Peninsula and Palestine.

Some hours' journey south of St. Paul's, in N. lat. 28° 40′, the sandstones are seen, for the first time, to rest upon a confused primary formation of hornblende, granite, diorite and porphyrite, thus suggesting that it is a westerly prolongation of Mount Sinai; and that both were once a single range. We shall presently see the same on the eastern shores of the Akabah Gulf, and in the regions immediately to its south. The travellers noted that the upper chalk of the Ananchytes, so highly developed in the Great Oasis, is here wanting ; and, as they found no sedimentary beds older than the middle chalk, it was in vain that Dr. Cav. Antonio Figari Bey,* some years ago, sank a shaft to strike coal.

Passing the southernmost offsets of the Galálah, the primary region, of which Umm el-Temásib is the northern block, the Wady el-Ghazáleh, and the Wady Murr, where the chalk is extraordinarily rich in ammonites, the explorers reached the great natural basin, or cistern, Mghátá. This place was visited by Raffenan-Délile, the celebrated botanist of the French expedition, in the early part of the present century. Its formation is here unique. The eocenic chalk is so full of silex-masses, rounded and melon-shaped, that water cannot find a free passage. Similar and equally regular forms clothe parts of the Libyan Desert-plateau.

From Mghátá the return route to the Nile, with a general west-north-west rhumb, ran first over waste tracts of sand-heaps, and then struck the Wady el-Gos, unknown to our maps. After watering at the abundant spring of the Fiumara el-Kamr, the travellers crossed the naked upper eocene, and, forty kilomètres from the river, they found the snail

---

* This chemist, who amused his leisure hours with geology published a geological map of Egypt, full of errors, according to Schweinfürth and Güssfeldt, but called *belle carte geologique*, by Issel (part 1. p. 24). For a notice of the latter, see chap. xi.

(*Helix Desertorum**) of the Mukattam mountain, the block lying south and south-east of Cairo. These molluscs extended as far as the stream.

On April 22nd, after thirty-five days in the "Jebel," our wanderers returned to civilisation. Dr. Schweinfürth was so pleased with his fossils and botanical specimens, that in March, 1877, he made a second excursion.† He was still absent when I passed through Cairo homewards; he did not return to Cairo before early June, and we failed to meet on his way home. Dr. Güssfeldt, who had accurately determined twenty stations for the benefit of future travellers, was kind enough to call upon us and "talk Africa" at Trieste. Neither of them appeared to appreciate the importance of their undertaking. This *reconnaissance* of the Jibál el-Humr and the Galálah may lead to the establishment of a Hill-Station, a vital want, like those of India, for the country of the Khedivs. In thirty years, as has been shown, the European population of Egypt grew from about 6000 to 80,000. It will presently number hundreds of thousands; and many of them will be grateful to find this healthy range of mountains so near at hand.

* Mr. R. M. Redhead (*On the Flora of Sanai:* read before the Linnæan Soc., April 6, 1865) found the dead shells of the same Helix, indicating an approach to vegetable life, near No. VI. Station on the Cairo-Suez van-road.

† Dr. Schweinfürth has just published an illustrated paper, *Die älteste Kloster der Christenheit*, etc., enlarging upon the results of his two trips.

CHAPTER IV.

DEPARTURE FROM SUEZ, AND ARRIVAL AT
EL-MUWAYLÁH.

SOME twenty-four hours of incessant work enabled us to pronounce the arrangements complete, after a "scratch" fashion; and at six p.m. on Saturday (March 31st), just as a hasty telegram from Cairo asked if it had started, the party embarked on board Steam-tender No. II. We were accompanied by H.E. the Governor, Sa'íd Bey, and by the two Messrs. Levick, after receiving the God-speed of my old friend West, and of my brother "wanderer," Major R. Adeane Barlow. Suez saw us depart with the settled conviction that we were in search of —*absit omen!*—"gas," that is, petroleum; of salt, of sulphur, and of ruins. To the latter conjecture, however, a pair of fellow-countrymen offered, within my hearing, the liveliest objections in the purest vernacular.

The usual hour of steaming placed us at the New Port, when we were received on board His

Highness's steam-corvette, *Sinnár*, Capt. Ali Bey Shukrí, and by the Acting Harbour-Master Ra'íf Wakíl el-Komandamiyyeh, or Assistant-Commodore of the station. Having reported to head-quarters the kindness and courtesy of all these officials, and having managed in the gun-room, *tant mal que bien*, a hasty dinner for twelve mouths, I requested that no delay might be made. "Allah yahfazkums!" (Allah preserve you!) were exchanged, and at ten p.m., as soon as the moon served, *Sinnár* steamed out of dock, and slowly passed the large floating light-ship of Suez.

The *Sinnár* is an English-built ship, a sister of the *Khartúm*, solid as the wooden walls of the olden day, armed with Armstrongs, and carrying a crew of 120 men. Her horse-power is ninety; and she makes from seven to eight and a half knots per hour, with a daily expenditure of sixteen tons of coal. Her captain is one of the best sailors in the Egyptian navy; and we had reason to admire the style in which he and his officers threaded the dangerous shoals fringing the eastern shores of the Red Sea, which the Egyptians called *Ket* (circle); *Sekot* (to encircle); or Sharr (a barbarous insignificant word); headed in Moses' day probably at Lake Timsáh, possibly at El-Kantarah, where the meeting of the Northern and Southern Mediterraneans caused dead water, depositing the silt, and built the first natural bridge that led to Phœnicia and Syria. Nothing can be stranger than the language in which the words of nautical command are given. Whilst the Egyptian soldier uses the high-sounding Turkish, his sailor brother talks Babel, borrowing from every dialect of the Mediterranean, not neglecting, withal, duly to acknowledge the merits of our English vocabulary.

During the night we passed Moses' Wells ('Uyún Músá),[*] the scene of our pleasant picnic in 1876; and dawn saw us a little south of Point Za'aferáneh and its lighthouse, with the brother blocks Abu Deraj (the Father of Steps) and Jebel 'Atákeh (the Mountain of Deliverance),[†] forming northern backgrounds on the bare and barren African shore. Between the first and the second chain lies the Wady Músá, whose mouth opens within sight of Suez. It is evidently so named by Christian pilgrims, because the great Deliverer thence marched upon the Red Sea,[‡] whereas the latter in Moses' day

---

[*] In a popular book I find the "Wells of Moses" included amongst "hot springs;" and described as boiling up three or four inches above the surface. If this was ever true, and it is vouched for by Shaw, the waters are cooling like the "Great Geyser."

This Jebel 'Atákah must not be confused with the "Sit Atákah" (Land of 'Atákah) in Midian (p. 594 *et seq*. "Geschichte Ægyptens," Dr. Heinrich Brugsch Bey. Leipzig, 1877).

[‡] The reign of Menephtah (Menephthes I.), the Pharaoh of the Second Book of Moses, was not happy. Besides the comparatively small and unimportant movement of the Jews, his reign

certainly extended to the Bitter Lakes, and probably headed at Lake Timsáh. Authors like Keith (on Prophecy) used to quote the names as evidence that the Arab tradition is "fossilized" in Arab nomenclature, and that the people have preserved the memory of the Mosaic Exodus. But the slightest acquaintance with pre-Islamitic history would have taught them that in the "Days of Ignorance" Moses was a name known to the Arabs only through the uncritical Jews and the Coptic Christians, from whose pilgrimage to Mount Sinai, in the third and fourth centuries, the modern Bedawin and Egyptians have picked up these monkish legends, and still deceive themselves and others by a conviction that the "Arab tradition" descends from historical times.

saw the great league of Libyans and Mediterranean peoples; Siluli from the Peloponnesus; Sardunas from Sardinia (and Sardia?); Etruscans from Lydia; Acheans, Pelasgi, and other Middle-Sea peoples, who, making an Exodus which possibly was national, fell upon Egypt and laid it waste. Many Egyptologists declare positively that the Hebrews are nowhere mentioned in the hieroglyphs. Vulgarly they are identified with the *Apuri*, or *Aburi;* but Brugsch Bey would make this word (*Apur*, plural *Apurin*) signify the "Red Man" of the Desert lying to the west and northwest of Suez; and from it he would derive the "Erythræan Sea." Thus *Apur* would bear the signification of "Ophir." Manetho, to the disgust of Josephus, narrates that the Hebrews, an impure tribe of strangers, were expelled the pure country because they spread leprosy among the people. Strabo (xvi. 5, § 25–26) does not allude to this fact in his excellent sketch of Jewish history, where Jerusalem is described with realistic force "a spot not such as to excite jealousy; for it is rocky, and although well supplied with water, it is surrounded by a bare and droughty land."

Here we see a fair illustration of my doctrine concerning the secular migration of Biblical sites and Holy Places. The Arabs who, like the Christians, suppose the children of Israel to have set out from Memphis * at the head of the Delta, instead of from Goshen on its extreme east, and to have marched down the Wady El-Tíh, which, like its brother north of Sinai, is translated, " Valley of *the* Wandering," instead of "Valley where man *may* wander," send the fugitives down the Gulf as far as Tor.† During the ages between early Christianity and the first half of the present century, universal Europe, with the exception of Lord Valentia,‡ placed the passage of the Red Sea somewhere about Suez. When the Canal began, the ford migrated north, *viâ* the Bitter Lakes to Timsáh; whilst in the last few years the learned Brugsch has transferred the same bodily from the Suez Gulf to the swamp bordering upon the Mediterranean—in fact to

"that Sirbonian bog,
Betwixt Damiata and Mount Casius old,
Where armies whole have sunk."

The venerable legend, however, explains the

* Strange to say, this departure from Memphis or its neighbourhood is still urged by so well-read a scholar as Professor Palmer (p. 270, "The Desert of the Exodus").

† See my "Pilgrimage," vol. I. chap. x. To "Tih" is sometimes added, "Beni Isra'el," but what is the date of the addition?

‡ "Travels," III. p. 356. London, 1809.

frequent ruins of Coptic convents and hermitages which stud the lowlands about Wady Músá. I visited them all in 1853, after returning from my Pilgrimage, and found nothing of importance. In 1876 it was said that the traveller must not trust himself amongst the Bedawin without a pass from their Shaykh Abu Shadíd, who is gently compelled to make Suez his head-quarters.

Za'aferáneh Lighthouse, a stone-built tower, marks the site of the two convents mentioned in the last chapter. We remark the notable contrast between the African and Asiatic shores along the length of the Suez Gulf. To the west rise sharply out of the desert-sand detached and primary ranges prolonging the Gelálah (Khelál) block southwards.*
Their wild grim nature is well explained by their hydrographic names, Sharp Peaks, Jagged Razor Hill, the Sugarloaf, and the Saddlebacks. They subtend the Ghárib light, an open frame-work, and the bird-cage of Ashrafi;† and they extend to the Jebel el-Zayt, in the map called "Zeiti Hills," that comb-like wall, behind which petroleum, supposed to be derived from buried molluscs, oozes from the ground. The rock-oil has supplied for ages the two convents with light, and its overflow still

---

* See chap. iii.
† For an excellent description of these lighthouses, see Mr. Consul (George) West's "Report on Suez, for 1872."

iridizes with opalescent colours, like mother of pearl, the sky-blue surface of the calm sea.

Despite adverse intrigues and evil predictions, which are never wanting in Egypt, the Viceroy has determined to strike the oil by deep borings; and at the date of my visit he had proposed to place them under charge of Colonel Middleton, an officer whose mining experience extended from Philadelphia to California. The Zayti Point, now nameless in the Admiralty Chart, is the old Drepanum Promontorium. Further south lies the Ghabbat, or Bay of Gimsah, and the Sulphur-diggings made celebrated in local legends on account of the indemnity claims, said to reach 19,000,000 of francs, put forward by the Marquis de Bassano. It directly fronts Jobal Island, naming the Suez "Bugház," or Strait. "Jubal" of the Chart is one of the many reefs and rock-lumps projecting above the shoals, which threaten to "dry up the tongue of the Egyptian main." The slow growth of corallines is gradually blocking the entrance and converting this north-western fork of the Red into a second Dead Sea.

On our return we passed the night in a snug bay, east of Tawílah or Long Island, forty miles from Tor, and sixty from Suez. A party set out to search for guano; and they found a small quantity of brown matter, much weathered, and rain-washed till it is hardly worth the expense of transport. The Arabs, who decline to use the impure substance, declare that it is deposited only in the smaller isles and islets of the Gulf; while certainly all the larger features which we examined did not justify the Peruvian reports spread throughout Egypt. Our fishermen, amongst whom Captain Ali Bey was ever the keenest, again supplied us and the whole crew with excellent rock-cod. The clear waters appeared full of life, the reason being doubtless the weedy bottom, which I saw here for the first time ; but the fish would bite only for a couple of hours after sundown, when the moonlight did not suffice to show the line.

The opposite or Sinaitic shore, so dull and uninteresting when viewed from the east, is here one grand *massif*, and very properly called the Shur or Wall, an offset from the great chain which begins north with the Libanus, and which extends southwards to Aden Point. This mountain-rampart, grandly swelling from the low and sandy plain, El-Ká'a, an uncompromising bit of Arabia Sterilis, runs almost parallel with the Gulf till it breaks and sinks to mere papillæ at the bold tongue-tip Ras Mohammed, which some have identified with the Poseidium or Poseidon Promontory[*] of the

[*] Strabo (xvi. 4. 18), however, places his Poseídeion within the *Alanatic* Bay, which is here supposed to be a clerical error for the *Heröopolitan* or Suez Gulf. It derives its name from an altar (Diod. Sic. III. 42) erected in honour of Neptune, by Aristo-

Ancients. Its splendid monotony is relieved by the lone and castellated domes and peaks of Jebel Serbál (Mountain of the Skirt), and by the comparatively rounded outlines of Jebel Katerina and Jebel Músá, the true Sinai. Behind a dark projecting point nearly opposite the Ghárib light, and 120 miles from Suez, lies the little horseshoe-shaped port of Tor, whence pilgrims make the convent in two or three days. The Greek *Phœnicon* * still shows detached clumps of dates clustering, as at Ayn Músá, wherever brackish springs ooze from the sandy shore. Since El-Wijh (Wedge) † was given up as a quarantine station—the harbour being bad and the water worse—unhealthy, miasmatic, marshy Tor has taken its place; an unfortunate Italian—Dr. Bianchi, the Deputato di

creon the Greek, whom Ptolemy Philadelphus or Lagi sent to survey the Red Sea. In Agatharkides (Diod. Sic. III. 42) Neptune's altar appears to be upon the Sinaitic coast near Pharan (Wady Firán) and north of Tor. Ras Mohammed is probably Strabo's unnamed "promontory which extends towards Petra."

* It must not be confounded with the *Phœnicum Vicus* or *oppidum*, south of El-Muwayláh, which Sprenger places at the modern Salina or Kufáfal, and others a little south of El Wijh. Of course ροινιμῶν (*palmetum*) would be a common term in these regions where every strip of watered ground bears its palms. The genuine Greek name for the palm is supposed to be derived from a district called *Phœnicus;* and Sir Charles Fellows ("Discoveries in Lycia." London: Murray, 1841) thinks that he discovered the latter in "Phineka."

† Described in my "Pilgrimage," vol. I. chap. ii.

Sanità—being compelled to live under canvas, and to endure all manner of discomforts, when he might easily be allowed to pass the greater part of the year with his family at Suez.

In memory of my first visit, I walked across the plain of dried mud, the Jabkhah (salt-plain), and the sand-heaps, to the "Nakhl el-Hammám" —"date-grove of the Hummums"—north of the squalid Christian village and the ruined (Venetian?) forts. The palms, plentifully irrigated, are luxuriant, and the small yellow fruit is delicious, as of yore ; but the Convent, to which belongs the property, annually worth some five thousand dollars, has allowed the enceinte wall to become a system of gaps, whilst the house of the white-bearded old guardian is in ruins.

Worse still, the "prim little bungalow" built by Abbás Pasha, who, by the advice of his physicians, seems to have delighted in Desert air, had been gutted by the plunderer. Here the Torites camp out during the hot season. Two mangy lads crept from the impure cistern ; the guardian had disappeared, and with him the Kahwahji, who used to supply pipes and coffee. The village-port has risen to the dignity of a station, with a Muháfiz, or governor, and a garrison of some twenty men. The hovels of mud-cemented stone are still occupied by a hundred souls or so, the descendants of the old Jebelíyyeh Nazarenes, Wallachian and Egyptian slaves, stationed by Justinian in the sixth century to guard the Holy House.* They send wood and charcoal to Egypt; they fish; they convoy pilgrims, and they seem to have a tidy idea of trade. They are headed by Khwájah Kostantin, the Wakíl, or Agent, of the Monastery, and they charged us a franc for a small tumbler of Rakí (raisin-brandy). Moreover, it was poor stuff, whereas that made by the jolly and dirty old men of the mountain is so good that it has fuddled and floored many a thirsty traveller.

The "Bugház" (throat) of Jobal ends at infamous Shadwán,† where many a good ship, including the P. and O.'s *Carnatic*, in 1869, has come to notable grief. Thus far the Gulf is well supplied with lights; there are four between Suez and the Ashrafi Islands, both included. Beyond this, with the sole exception of the Brothers (north and south), and the Abu'l Khísán, or Dædalus Light, the Red Sea, as far as Perim, is one succession of dangers; Shadwán Island and Ras Mohammed on the opposite side, taking high rank amongst *famosæ*

* I cannot explain the popular Moslem belief that a colony of Jews is still settled near Tor.

† The Island of Seals (φωκῶν νῆσος) in Strabo (?), the Ptolemeian "Saspeirene," or "Sappeirene," insula in the "Kolpos Arabios" (iv. 5, § 77). Others make "Jobal," *Saspeirene;* and Shadwán *Scytale* of Nessa, the Seals Island of Agatharkides. Notice will be taken in chap. vii.

rupes. What has been done has been well done, and under McKillop Pasha, Controller-General of Ports and Lighthouses, everything works like clockwork. But it is hardly fair to expect that Egypt should make any further outlay; and presently an International Committee will fix upon the points and raise the money required.*

The same should be the case with the campaign against the slave-trade in the Red Sea. If we are determined to cut off the exportation, we should provide these shores with a "Coffin-Squadron," at least equal in number to that which for years blocked the Guinea coast and the two bights of Western Africa. Even then I should hardly predict success, where every baylet is a port, where every native craft is a slaver, and where every man's religion, as well as his interests, points to the capture and to the sale or barter of Pagan flesh.†

---

* It is the more necessary to make this observation, because on the occasion of an English ship being lately wrecked off Cape Guardafui, H.H. the Khediv was waited upon by a zealous official, with the modest request for a lighthouse, to be built at the expense, not of the British, but of the Egyptian, Government.

† I take the following extract from one of the interesting "Letters from Pantellaria," published by the *Times of India*, overland, March 12, 1877. " Even the Press of England begins to suspect Mahomedans of a vague impression that England owes allegiance to the Sultan. The home public will not believe, the Anglo-Indian will, that according to Turkish idea, fixed and ineradicable, every European Power is simply tributary to the Porte ; and that the recusants are all Yâghî, or mere rebels. Islamism

At night steaming past Ras Mohammed, the *ultimum Continentis promontorium*, a bluff and a long, low point, as usual outlined by dark reef and leek-green shoal, we awoke on Easter Monday with cliffy Yubú'a * islet, bare and yellow, on the port- bow, while fronting us, clad in gold, blue and gorgeous purple, towered the kingly Mountains of Midian, a surprise and a delight to the traveller's eye after the flatness and meanness of the Suez coast.

classes mankind in three : the Moslems ; the Káfirs, or Unbelievers, who are Peoples of the Books (Ahl-el-Kutub), such as Jews and Christians; and finally, the Pagan-heathenry, like the Hindus and the Chinese, whose Scriptures are thus ignorantly ignored. The Moslem, who inherits the earth, is enjoined to bear with the first order of infidels, provided that these become his subjects; paying their taxes as unbelievers ; and that the non-Mahomedans, who form their own States, supply tribute and add to the *arrière-ban*. Thus all the wars with infidels are merely caused by the revolt of these headstrong vassals, who dare to oppose the 'Grand Signior.' *As regards the third category, the pure heathen, the Moslem is bound to eternal war with them : hence the slave raids in Africa are sanctioned by the Faith.* To the doctrine that the Khan and Sultan of the Osmanli is Lord of the Earth, a single exception may be found in Morocco, ruled by a direct successor of the Western Khalifat of Toledo ; but this is a very disputed point. Algeria and the French are directly tributary." The doctrine which makes the hereditary Osmanli Sultans represent the elective Caliphs, is, I may observe, a legal fiction at least as violent, *pace* the Rev. Mr. Badger, as that which derives the Czars from Cæsar Augustus, through Rurik, and which attributes to the Romanoffs all the rights of the Byzantine Emperors, their forefathers.

* The older charts call it Jeboa, Jobah and Juba, the northern "Yuba :" so Wáleh, the flat shoal to north, still rejoices in the name of "Wyler" in Berghan's "Wales."

I shall describe these noble forms more particularly during our cruise along the coast to Aynúnah,* when, however, they had lost to us all the charm of novelty. The first aspect of Midian is majestic, and right well suited to the heroic Bedawi race that once owned the land. Beyond the golden cushions which, embroidered with emerald green, line the shore, rise flat-topped sand-banks and peaky hillocks of arenaceous stone, both formations sprinkled and revetted with dark primaries and, especially, with weathered fragments of ruddy porphyry. Inland they become fort-hills similarly metalled, but painted purple-brown by the intervening atmosphere. The picture's towering background, amethystine with blue aerial distances, here lit up with golden glow, there shaded with violet stripes; naked and barren, still gorgeous and beautiful as each feature stands clear, distinct, and fantastically cloven against the bright plain of the cloudless sky, is a wall, apparently continuous, ranging between 6000 and 9000 feet above the sea-level.†

* See chap. v.
† So the hydrographers, and we had no time to control them by measuring a base. Wellsted (ii. 176) who describes them briefly but well, assigns 6500 to "Mowflahh High Peak," the most elevated. The maps which accompanied us were—
1. The Stasimetric Chart of the Red Sea, by R. Moresby and Carless in the *Palinurus*, 1830-34; 2. Sheet I, the Red Sea, by Captain (now Sir) George S. Nares, 1871-2; and 3. Keith

Nothing can be more picturesque than the shapes of these "Alps unclothed," these giants, which the Hebrews of old provided with ears and teeth, ribs and loins. Their Titan shoulders, bared to sun and wind, support domes and towers, " organ-pipes," peaks and pinnacles ; and, fresh from the dolomites of the Tyrol and Dalmatia, I gazed upon them with dismay. What could be expected from fire-bleached limestone ? M. Marie was not so easily imposed upon, and, like a true Parisian, he backed his opinion, that the mass was schistose, with *un déjeûner* at the *Café Anglais* by way of wager.

At 11.30 a.m., *Sinnár*, which had threaded her way cautiously between the outlines of Yubu'a, to the north, and the low coral-reefs of Siláh,* southwards, ended her 220 miles, measured along the course, and cast her anchor in the open and dangerous roadstead of El-Muwayláh,† which has

Johnston ; the latter preserving Moresby's spelling, which is truly terrible.

* The Sela of the Classics (see chap. xii.), not to be confounded with the Siláh Station on the mainland (Wady Tiryam ?). This place may derive its name from a glaucous and prickly plant (*Zilla Myagroides*).

† In charts and travels Mowilah, Mowilahh (Wellsted), Moilah, Moïleh, Mohila (Rüppell), Mueileh, Mueilih (Zehme), Muwéilih, Moelh, and other corruptions, lying in N. lat. 27° 39 and E. long. (G.) 35° 34'. Sprenger (p. 23) is certainly not right in preferring "al-Mowayliha." The word is the diminutive of Málih, salt. In the Sinaitic Peninsula there is an Ayn and a Wady El-Muwayláh, famed for cairns ; the traditional Hagar's

an inner cove for the accommodation of native craft. The first ship of war ever seen in these waters, she fired a gun, which sent the few idlers flying in terror from the shore, and despatched her gig to bring off the Governor and the Civilian Accountant of the port. The former, poor man, was in agonies of terror, frantically inquiring, whilst he returned the salute with a pop-gun and flew his red flag, what *could* have happened. Presently, when he found that all we wanted was his assistance in procuring camels, the revulsion of joy brought on a short malady.

El-Muwaylâh means the "little salt," alluding to its walls and water-pits; hence the Arab saying, "*Ant fi Muwayláh*," *i.e.*, "Thou art athirst." Evidently an old site, it is now one of the fortified Manzil, or stations, of the Cairo Hajj * (Pilgrim

Well, transferred by the Moslems to Meccah; and probably in after years one of the "Cities of the South" destroyed by the Israelites. Vance and D'Anville identify it with the *Phœnicum oppidum* of Ptolemy (El-Wijh?): Niebuhr ("Description de l'Arabie," p. 325), Müller ("Geog. Gr. Minoris"), and Sprenger, who evidently assume Ptolemy's latitude, with the Modíana of the same geographer. Popular writers confound it with Lenke-Korne, El-Haurá or Hawará, far south in N. lat. 25°; while Wallin holds it to be a modern place.

* In Heb. חג, primarily denoting circular form or motion, a circuit, a circle; secondarily, a pair of compasses to mark out circles; and, thirdly, the celebration of religious ceremonies, of circular or rotatory dances: for instance, Exod. x. 9, to "hold a Hagg (festival) unto the Lord." It is well applied to the Moslem Pilgrimage, one of whose principal rites consist in circumambulating the Ka'abah or Cube-House.

Caravan), distant five days' march from El-Akabah. These two points define the north and south of the Tihámat Madyan, the Low-lands of Midian.* The fort was originally built, as an inscription in the Sulsi character, set over the large and complicated main entrance, tells us, by Sultan Selim, the loser of Lepanto in A.H. 968 (=A.D. 1553-54); when he conferred the right of way, and the government of the country, upon Egypt. It was allowed to fall in ruins by Abbas Pasha, destroyed by Said Pasha, and, finally, it was restored and strengthened by the present Viceroy shortly after his accession in A.H. 1281 (=A.D. 1863-64).

Looking small from afar, a simple parallelogram of masonry, with plain curtains connecting round towers at the angles, where the old guns have been remounted, it is a spacious enceinte,

* Arab geographers generally divide the peninsula, says Golius (*Notæ in Alfragano*), into five districts : 1. The Tihámah, or lowlands, on the Red Sea, especially the southern part of El-Hejáz. 2. Nejd, the northern plateau. 3. El-Hejáz (the colligated by mountains, the *Mittelland*, or the Separator, *i.e.*, between Nejd and Yemen). 4. El-Yemamah or El-Arúz, the "oblique," because so situated with respect to Yemen, the Land on the right hand (facing the east), and Shám (Syria) the Land on the left hand ; and 5. Yemen or Southern Arabia. The Jezirat-el-Arab proper (Arabian island, that is, peninsula) originally extended from the town of Ayla (Allabat Ayla, the Elána of Ptolemy) in N. lat. 29° to where the confines of El-Yemen meet those of El-Hejáz. The mediæval and modern geographers confined it to the south of an imaginary line drawn from Ras Mohammed to the mouths of the Euphrates.

containing, besides quarters for the men, a well of brackish water; a mosque, and the tomb of a holy man, Shayhk Abu el-Umrah. The garrison consists of twenty-four infantry, with Bulukbáshi (captain of irregulars), and of six gunners, with an Oubáshi (corporal), all under the Yuzbáshi (captain) Abd el-Wáhid, who has been Governor for two years, living *en garçon*, and leaving his family at Suez.

The rest of the settlement, which occupies the regularly terraced left bank of the Wady Surr, the great Fiumara dividing the Monarch of Mountains behind El-Muwayláh from its northern neighbour, Umm Jedayh, consists mostly of ruined houses, and a few inhabited square boxes of rough stone and mortar, with wooden shutters—in fact, the regular coast-settlement. The tenements may lodge some thirty souls at the dead season, that is when the pilgrims are not passing; and the only tolerable house is that of the Kátib, or civilian who acts as steward or accountant.

The latter is the Sayyíd (Hasani) Abd el-Rahím, a native of El-Muwayláh, cousin to Abd el-Salám Bey el-Muwayláhi, a well-known member of the Majlis at Cairo. He is highly respected by the Bedawin, and he proved exceedingly useful to the expedition, which, as will be seen, he accompanied to the last. The large clump of palms is fed by shallow holes and pits of tepid brackish water, including four masonry-revetted wells to the north-east and the south-east, these being Government property. There are dwarf fields of garden stuff and durrah (*Holcus vulgare*), while limes and pomegranates are not wholly wanting. The growth must depend upon irrigation, as only a few showers fall between October and April.

The tomb of another holy man, Shaykh Abdullah, in the shape of a dwarf tower, lies to the north of the settlement, where a parallel reef of coralline, subtending the shore-line, keeps out the " sea-dog "* (Kalb el-bahr, or the shark), and forms a charming bath. I have been minute in describing El-Muwayláh. As I have before remarked, it is 229 geographical miles from Suez; it *has* been a place of considerable trade, and it *will* be one of the headquarters of commerce, when the mining-industry shall have been resuscitated.

The cove under the Fort is much affected by the Sambúks of the Juhayni fishermen,† broad-beamed craft, descended from the "light ships" of the old pirates, carrying from ten to twenty tons, built of Indian planks bearing the brand of the Gujrátí merchant, with knees of native woods, especially

---

* Strabo (xvi, 4, § 7), speaking of the opposite African seas, says, " Even trees (corallines) here grow from under the water, and the sea abounds with sea-dogs."

† See chap. v.

tamarisk. Half covered with a small deck, they carry a large lateen sail. Of these boats some sixty to one hundred anchor at El-Muwayláh when returning from their cruises. Besides fishing, they search the shoals for "Sadaf," or mother-of-pearl, in most primitive style, the diver bringing up one at a time, and not unfrequently falling a victim to the sharks. The produce is sold by the hundred to the trader, who takes them on spec., as it were, sometimes finding a seed-pearl, and regularly selling them for the inlaid work of the Egyptian and Syrian cities, and for the rude devotional and other ornaments of which Bethlehem is the Birmingham.

The two officials, military and civil, came on board, and after reading the letter conveying the viceregal orders, undertook to supply us with fifty camels within three days. This delay, which we could ill afford, was caused by the Bedawin being at this season "Fauk," that is, in the interior. During the short chat after coffee, we heard for the first time of "Buyút el-Nására" (Christian's houses) at Aynúnah* and at other places. The good tidings filled me with new hopes. The Arabs, both Bedawin and

* Keith Johnston has Ain Ooneh, classically correct, but not used; and the Hyd. charts here place, "Ruins of a town and aqueduct, called by the Arabs Eynounah." But the Wady is wrongly laid down; the aqueduct is run in a straight line from north to south, and the "fertile valley, with stream or water," is placed some four miles from the coast, and distant from the Wady, instead of being at the head of the conduit.

I

settled, apply the term Nazarene to all the former inhabitants of all the lands which they now occupy, holding themselves immigrant conquerors from Arabia Proper. I at once ordered a Sambúk for a reconnaisance northwards; and the first craft which came in, coursing gallantly before the stiff south wind, was duly impressed and made fast with a cable to the corvette's stern. But the Juhaynah, like other tribes of the coast, have an utter inbred contempt for discipline. As soon as the head of the sentinel was turned, one of the crew quietly whipped out his whittle, and silently sawed through the rope; whilst the other three as leisurely shook out the broad sail, and hoisted it in the gay breeze.

It was amusing to see the contrast of this sedate coolness with the scene of turmoil and wild abuse and outcry on board. At length, after ten minutes, a boat full of armed sailors started in vain pursuit; and when the chase had lasted over a mile or so, the Arab winning easy, a cartridge was found, and a shot was fired in the air. The last we saw of the Sambúk was a patch of white, hovering like a gull's wing over the horizon, where, rejoining her fellows, she had probably reported, "They are seizing the boats."

"Once a philosopher, twice a fool," says the Eastern proverb, equivalent to our "Once bitten, twice shy;" and we took care to place strong guards upon the next two boats which we towed. As the shoal-fringed roadstead of El-Muwayláh is dangerous in rough weather, our captain prudently determined to anchor in Sherm (bight) Yáhár, between four and five miles down south, a run easily made in an hour. These refuges are common upon the Arabian coast of the Red Sea; they are wanting on the African shore, where Masawwáh is the nearest harbour to Suez; and, as will be seen, they are not to be trusted in the Gulf of Akabah. Mostly they run deep into the land, extending either from west to east, or to north-east, heading in two arms, which form either a straight or a crooked T. The depth of water at the entrance varies from nineteen to twenty-three fathoms; and the anchorage ground shows on the charts seven or eight. The port is completely land-locked, like a dock, and the heaviest storms hardly disturb the sleepy water.

At the head are the Wadys, or winter-torrents, the Nachals of the Jews; the Cheimarrhoi of the Greeks; the Poteks of the Slavenes, and the Fiumare of Southern Italy. The shallows near the shore allow bathing without fear of sharks. In these places one generally finds a native boat laden with charcoal, and the crew enjoys cooking and sleeping upon the hard clean sand.

During the rest of the afternoon we made preparations for the next day's work, and indented upon our good captain for the articles most needed; an Egyptian flag, three mattresses, two Colt's revolvers, and other odds and ends. I summoned to the quarter-deck the Rais, or masters, of the two captive boats, who were crouching in despair amidships, and explained to them that His Highness, far from intending a *corvée*, had ordered that their services should be amply and even generously rewarded. We then proceeded to settle the hire. For the work of a single day they began by asking fifty dollars, which presently fell to three, the latter being the sum actually paid for boats to Suez, a voyage seldom finished under a week. Then they pleaded empty bellies, and were fed with ship's biscuit. Lastly, they begged that one of their number might be disembarked in order to inform their friends that they had not been subjected to imprisonment or ill-usage. This was, of course, allowed, and the messenger duly returned as he had promised.

In the evening some of the party who had landed were accosted by certain chiefs, including Shaykh Alayàn, of the large and important Huwaytát tribe. They promised to bring as many hundreds of camels as we pleased, but required a delay of five days—more than our flying visit could afford. The authorities of the Fort had resolved upon

FROM SUEZ TO EL-MUWAYLÁH. 117

applying to the Beni 'Rekbah, a small tribe numbering about fifty Nafar, or males, which claims the land upon which the Fort of El-Muwayláh is built, and which is usually encamped in the neighbourhood. These men, who have long been settled upon the coast,* own the land between Makná and El-Muwayláh; at least, they were owners of it before the more powerful tribes immigrated from Egypt and dispossessed them.

Being salaried to act as Ghufará, or Pilgrim-protectors, between El-Akabah and Dhobbá, their "Madrak," or beat, and to supply the Hajj with camels and provisions, they are considered servants of the Mírí (Government), and, consequently, safer than their less dependent Bedawin neighbours.

* They are noticed by Abú el-Abbás Ahmed ibn Abdillahi El-'Kalkashandi (ob. A.D. 1418) in his book, *Nihdyat el Adab* (not Arab) *fi Ma'arifat Ansáb* (not Kabáil) *el-'Arab*, "The End of Learning in Knowledge of the Genealogies of the Arabs;" by the author of *El-Masálik el-Absár fi Mamálik el-Amsár*, "The Ways of Sight in Territorial Dominions," the work of Shihál el-Dín Ahmed ibn Yáhyá (ob. 1348); and finally, by Ibn Khaldún, the author of the *Kitab el-'Ibur wa Diwán El-mubtadá w'al Khabar*, "The Book of Examples, and the Receuil of Subject and Predicate," printed at Cairò some years ago: he makes them extend through Northern Africa to Tripoli. The learned Arabist, Rev. G. Percy Badger, whose Anglo-Arabic Dictionary will be a blessing to students, says that Beni 'Ukbah or Ukbá has so many meanings that we find difficulty in the choice. "People of the Remnant" would be one of them. The tribes of Madyan were ranked among the οἱ ἔξω by the early Moslems, and ever treated accordingly.

In their appearance there is nothing remarkable; like the Huwaytát they tattoo with gunpowder a spot under the right eye.

The Beni 'Ukbah own as Chief Hasan ibn Sálim, a Shaykh upon a small scale. They are not pleasant companions, the pilgrims having taught them contempt for travellers; and their camels, as is mostly the case upon this coast, are miserably fed, light, weak, and stunted, besides being half broken to burdens. The brutes are startled by every new sight or sound; their accoutrements, saddles, bags and ropes are wretched; they are ridden without nose-rings, the halter being the only curb; and the facility with which they throw their loads, and start off at a giraffe-like gallop, breaking boxes and damaging bales, is prodigious. Fortunately for us, we had brought decent riding-gear from Suez, mine having been lent to me by Mr. Alfred G. R. Levick.

I have already expressed my opinion of the "Ship of the Desert;" and the experience of my last expedition has not tended to improve it. The so-called "generous animal," the "patient camel," whose endurance has been grandly exaggerated, is a peevish, ill-conditioned beast—one of the most cross-grained, vile-tempered, and antipathetic that domestication knows. When very young it is cold, grave, and awkward; when adult, vicious and ungovernable, in some cases even dangerous; when old it is fractious and grumbling, sullen, vindictive, and cold-blooded. It utters its snorting moan and its half-plaintive, half-surly bleat even when you approach it. It suspects everything unknown; it roars aloud, like a teeth-cutting child, as each pound weight is added to the burden: and it is timid * and sensitive to the footfall, to the voice, or even to the presence of a stranger.

This unsavoury beast, which eats perfume and breathes fetor, works well upon hard clay. Rock cuts its soles; it labours and suffers when trudging through sand, and mud throws it heavily, at times splitting up the arm-pits. Its vaunted docility is the result of sheer stupidity. It lacks even the intelligence to distinguish poisonous herbs. It wants the nobility and generous disposition of the horse; the sure-footedness and sagacity of the mule; the ponderous safety of the riding-ox; and the frugality, the intelligence, and the docility of the ass, so ably "rehabilitated" by Buffon. Finally, I have mounted the peevish dromedary for years, and, except in one case, a pony-camel from

* "Camels, animals not easily frightened," says Wellsted (ii. 25). I have ever found them more liable to panic than even horses and mules.

Maskat, I could never conjure a shade of affection for the modern representative of the Anoplotherium.

Let me end this chapter with the Arab explanation of why the horse hates the camel, an antipathy noticed by the Greeks as early as the days of Herodotus. It is well known to all the world that Allah, determining to create this noble animal, called the South Wind and said, " I desire to draw from thee a new being : condense thyself by parting with thy fluidity." The Creator then took a handful of this element, now become gross and tangible, and blew upon it the breath of life : the horse appeared and was addressed, " Thou shalt be for man a source of happiness and wealth : he shall render himself illustrious by mounting thee." * But the stiff-necked stranger presently complained that much more might have been done for him ; that his throat was too short for browsing on the line of march; that his back had no hump to steady the saddle ; and that his small hoofs sank deep into the sand, with many other grievances of a similar nature, somewhat reminding us of a certain King of Castile. Where-

---

* The Bedawi believes the horse, first tamed and ridden by Ishmael, to have been produced by the sneeze of Adam when awaking to life. So the cat is the sneeze of the lion, produced when Noah, offended by the number of mice in the Ark, tickled the nose of the King of Beasts.

upon Allah, like Jupiter who once threatened the dreadful threat of granting the silly prayers of mankind, created the camel. The horse shuddered at the sight of what he wanted to become, and from that hour to this he has ever started when meeting his caricature.

CHAPTER V.

FROM EL-MUWAYLÁH TO WADY AYNÚNAH.

At 6.30 a.m. on April 3rd, M. Marie and I set out in the Sambúk *El Mabrúkeh*, Rais Atiyyeh. We were accompanied by Lieutenants Hasan and Abd el-Kerim: the escort, ten soldiers, with the Chawush Ali and Marius, the *chef*, followed in the other boat. The remaining force, under Lieutenant Amir, with Mr. Clarke and old Haji Wali, remained on board *Sinnár* to hasten the levy of the promised camels.

I felt thoroughly at home on board the Sambúk, where the sailors at once rigged up an awning to defend us from the sun. The distance, thirty-five miles by sea, twenty-seven to twenty-eight direct geographical miles by land, or twelve to thirteen Sa'át (hours)* of caravan-marching and halting, is

* The "hour" is here reckoned at five kilomètres (5468 yards) or three statute miles and a bittock (5280 yards). The Arab mile is = to the English and Italian geographical = ten stadia = 1¼ Roman = ¼ German. The Sa'át thus corresponds

usually a day's boating before a stiff southerly breeze; this boon, however, Fortune denied us. The crew were Juhaynah Bedawin, descended from the Kahtaníyyeh or Joctanite Arabs.* The race has learned navigation, and supplies pilots to all our part of the coast. They are known by the Masháli, or gashes, numbering one to three, athwart the right cheek. Their habitat is south of El-Muwayláh, especially about the Jebel, or rather Istabl 'Antar. I had before met them at Mársa Damghah and at El-Wijh, where they are mixed with the scattered Orban Balíy.† They extend as far south as Yambú', and eastward to El-Tabúk: they are neighbours to and friendly with the Beni Ma'ázeh; and, like the latter, they may number 5000 Nafar (men and boys).

verbally with the Teutonic *stunde*, or hour's march, half a *meile* (four geog. miles), that is two direct geographical miles. The actual marching of a caravan would seldom exceed this distance. For further information, see chap. xii.

* The tribal, which is the same as the patriarchal name, is "Juhayní," in the plural "Juhaynah," but never *Jahaynah*, as I miswrote it in my "Pilgrimage" (i. 315). Wallin follows the Egyptian fashion "Guheiní"; Sprenger (p. 29) prefers "Gohayna," and makes the tribe, like the "Balyy," a branch of the "Jodhâ'ites," the great family El-Kudá'a. He borrows from El-Humdáni and Maltzan; and he gives an exhaustive list of their settlements which need not be repeated here.

† The Balíy are mentioned by Wallin in pp. 320 to 326. This Himyaritic tribe, claiming the whole of the Harrah country with the port-town of Wijh, is divided into a multitude of clans, as—
1. the Muwáhil, to whom the Shaykh's family belongs; 2. the Mu'ákilah; 3. the Arádát; and, 4. the Beni Lút. (See Sprenger on the "Balyy," pp. 30–1.)

Their land, as we could see by the ballast, supplies "harrah," or porous basalt, and some of their Kaliúns (pipes, dudheens) were of steatite, said to be worked at Makuá. As usual, there was a black slave on board to do servile work. "Marján" owned the usual broad grin, mother-of-pearl teeth, and yep-yep laugh, but he had quite forgotten Kisáwáhíli, with the exception, however, of the grossly abusive part which distinguishes that very free and easy African tongue.

The Governor of El-Muwayláh Fort had given, as a pilot and guide, a Muwallid,[*] or son of an emancipated slave, who called himself Sálih bin Mohammed, a Topji, or artilleryman, in the service of the Viceroy. He afterwards proved true to the instincts of his African blood, and his intrigues with

---

[*] Wallin writes the name "Mutawallid." He justly observes that these negroes not only fill whole villages, as El-Ríheh (Jericho), many parts of El-Jauf (the western hollow lying parallel with the Dead Sea), and the Súk-el-Shaykh; they also form large clans among the nomadic Arabs, leading the same pastoral and predatory life as their former masters, to whom, although freed, they generally remain attached from the true African feeling that once a slave always a slave. Genuine Arabs will seldom, if ever, condescend to take to wife a negress or even a brown-skinned Habashiyyeh (Abyssinian woman); so these blacks, intermarrying with their own race, remain in the nomad tents unaltered through long generations. With the settled tribes, however, the prejudice in favour of pure blood is not so strong; and the Muwallidín of the towns and villages mix and intermarry with the Arabs, "producing children in whose features it is quite impossible to recognize the African type" (?).

the Bedawin made him narrowly escape being sent in irons aboard the corvette. On the return-march to the Fort, he attempted to hurry us unpleasantly, because he had lately led home a second wife: in fact, his conduct was to be expected from the ignoble African strain. However, Sálih knew the land and sea by heart; and he aided us to name and catalogue the several items of the huge mountain-wall which subtends the Tihámah.*

These highlands are generically known as El-Shifah,† the lip, corresponding with the Hebrew Sapháh ‡—a lip, a language, an edge, a brink. Some are sharp and isolated cones, whilst others are represented to be the sea faces of extensive plateaux, and each feature has a character and a physio-

* We found this word, which, derived from Taham (*astus vehementia*), means a low unhealthy maritime region, as opposed to "El-Nejd," the salubrious uplands, generally used. Wallin calls the seaboard "Sáhil," or shore, allowing it an average breadth of twenty-four miles; and the maps write El-Ghaur, the hollow. The Tihámah would correspond with the Hebrew Ha-Shárún (Sharon).

† The classical form is El-Shafah. Keith Johnston has "Jebel-esh-Shefa," the first word being unnecessary. Wallin, who wrongly writes "Shefâa," calls its northern continuation El-Sherá', and considers our two longitudinal ranges as the western boundaries of El-Nejd. This Jebel el-Sherá'a must not be confounded with the range of the same name, the Mount Seir of the Hebrews, which forms the "rugged" eastern boundary of the great Wady el-Arabah, and in one of whose valleys Petra lies.

‡ Not to be confounded with Shephelah (whence Hispalis, Seville?), the term applied by the Hebrews to the hills between the Hor (mountain) and the 'Emeh (plain).

gnomy of its own. All the Bedawin agree in declaring that a second chain, the Harrah (volcanic?) range, runs parallel with the maritime mountains and slopes eastward into El-Hismá.* The latter they represent to be a tract of red sandy soil, a plateau broken by rounded hillocks, not mountains, and wanting water in the hot season.

The Shifah is the salvation of the Tihámah. The cold, bare, and stony heights, which act as barriers to the land winds, condense the warm and moisture-laden breezes from the Red Sea, and the heavy showers, sinking into the loose and sandy soil at the base, percolate underground, and presently reappear perennial in the mouths of the Wadies near the sea. During our visit the mountains tempered the nights, rendering blankets necessary; and about 7 a.m., when the sun's rays, with their beautiful vaporous effects, began to heat the plains, they sent forth a high cool gale, a local land-breeze, which does not appear even to reach the gulf. This Barri

* The word literally means a desert-flat with dusty hillocks. The region is described by Wallin as a vast level of the soft and comparatively fertile sand, of which the Nufood (Nufúz, *i.e.*, pure yellow arenaceous matter) "desert of Negd (El-Nejd) for the most part consists." He also speaks of the Hismá "gradually opening out into an extensive plain, over which a few isolated hills are scattered, having among themselves a north-westerly course." Finally, he corrects the author of the celebrated lexicon "El-Kámús," who explains the word as "a land in the Bádiyeh (Desert of Syria), with high mountains, whose elevated crests are generally enveloped in mist."

(land-wind) lasted through the morning until the Bahri, or sea-wind, * set in. During the winter the mountains are reservoirs of the " frigoric." Water freezes on the upper levels traversed by the raw and searching south-easter; the peaks must have icy fangs, and the churlish, chiding wintry winds become " Sarsars "—cold and shuddering blasts.

I must describe these blocks of porphyry, granite, and syenite with some detail. They have been carelessly laid down in the Hydrographic Charts, which, contented with determining the coast-line, often ignore correctness in the inner features, upon which the sailor sighting the shore is often forced to depend. The apparent wall is cut by broad Wadies, all of which, like the same features in Mount Sinai, are " Elath " or " Eloth," bearers of terebinths and palms (Elim) wherever water is superficial or lies near the surface; and we presently discovered that every greater Fiumara has its ruined settlement or settlements, each possibly, in days of yore, ruled by its own chiefs.

Beginning from the south is Mount Mowilah high peak, 9000. This splendid block, rising sudden and sharp from the flat sea-board, and invading the sky with its four giant arms, looks from

* The Huwaytát tribe has preserved the Egyptian names of the cardinal winds : 1. Bahri, the sea-wind, Etesian gale or norther; 2. Kibli, the south wind; 3. Sharki, the easter; and, 4. Gharbi, the Zephyr, or west wind.

afar more like a magnified iceberg than a thing of earth: the people call it Jebel el-Shárr, the director or land-mark, because it is first seen by the seaman. It *must* be the "Hippus Mons" of Ptolemy: no topographer or cartographer * could leave so remarkable a feature unnamed.† The mid-heights and passes are traversed in places by sheep-tracks; and the lower levels, as is the case with its neighbours, are furnished, they say, with fountains and palm-groves. The Shárr is separated by the Wady el-Surr, upon which El-Muwayláh is built, from its northern adjoiner Umm el-Jedayl,‡ a transverse lump which changes the north-south rhumb for north-west to south-east. The Wady el-Jimm, or Zojeh, parts this comparatively low mountain from the Jebel Dubbagh, one of whose items is a remarkable flat-topped tower, the Jebel el-Jimm, canted slightly southwards, and apparently inaccessible. The mass known as Fara' el-Samghi ends northwards in Abu-

---

* As Sprenger well remarks, Ptolemy is not a geographer, but a cartographer, or rather, as he would himself say, a geographer, not a chorographer.

† Müller (Map vi., Geog. Gr. Min.) offers a kind of hydrographic sketch of this splendid block, which the homely old English "Master-Mariner" Irwin, in 1780, called the "Bullock's Horns."

‡ Wallin gives "Umm Gudeilé" (Judayleh), and calls the mountains north of "Gimm" (El-Jimm), Sadr and Harb, words which we never heard applied to them. Sadr appears to be the name of a plain, and Jebel Harb lies far beyond and behind the coast-line.

Zayn, which probably appears upon the map as
"Sharp Peak 6330." Viewed from the west-northwest it appears weathered to a regular cupola, a
Puy de Dôme, a Funnel Hill like that of Bombay,
an Old Man of Hoy, a rounded cone resting upon the
two flat shoulders that form the base. Viewed from
the north the face separates into three distinct
features; and from the south it appears as if two
mighty slices of rock had been pressed together.
Indeed, the first objects which strike the traveller's
eye, and the last upon which it dwells, are the four
huge shoulders of the Horse-Mountain (El-Shárr),
the Jimm, the Tower-hill, and the *Puy de Dôme*.

Continuing northwards we find the wide, open,
and well-defined Wady Kuhlah, Wallin's "al
Kahalé" (Kahaleh), called, nearer the coast, "Wady
Tiryam," and separating Abu Zayn from its neighbour Jebel-Urnub. The latter, whose sky-line is
fretted with "organ-pipes," after bearing upon their
heads logan-like cap-stones of weathered rock, is
said also to have its sheep and goat paths, water
and inhabitants. We follow the Wady Kharís and
the Jebel el-Síg (Sík),* whose upper slopes, white
and glistening, demand exploration. The next block,
Arawáh, is reported to be the sea-face of a plateau,

---

* This word, the same as the "Sík," the narrow ravine or rocky defile, some two miles long, which forms the approach of Petra, means in Arabic "dust driven by the wind."

K

which suggests the table-land of Abyssinia—according to "Tommy Atkins," a table with the legs uppermost. A line of high land apparently connects it with "Jebel Eynounah, 6,090," more generally known as Jebel el-Zahd; the latter is easily recognized by its comparatively rounded forms and, seen from the south, by a deep nick or Brêche de Roland. The chart then shows a wide interval of lowland between the Zahd and the Jebel-"Tayyibat Ism, 6000;" it places, however, this "Mountain of the Good Name" some ten leagues inland, whereas the ridge extends, we shall see, to the eastern shore of the Gulf of Akabah, a few miles north of the old Midianitic capital, Makná.

Such was the range which came under our view, and which time forbade us to inspect carefully. It is not yet possible to lay down the upper and lower limits of this primary tract It is said to reach El-Akabah (N. lat. 29° 29'), where sulphur and lead have long been known to exist; and it may even prolong itself inland, along the eastern flank of the Wady el-Arabah, the Desert Valley of the Dead Sea, as far as Syria. Southwards it will probably extend to the northern frontier of El-Hejaz, in N. lat. 25°, thus giving a total length of 269 direct geographical miles. The general lie of the coast is much like that of California, and, as far as we have seen, it wholly wants the latitudinal lines of mountain which characterize Australia. Professor V. Vidal, *Directeur de l'Ecole de Droit*, and Fellow of the Khedivial Society at Cairo, would attach it to the Etna-Sinai circle of the learned Élie de Beaumont, and thus he would account for the east-west strike of the porphyritic dykes and the veins of metal.

The coast view, also, was by no means uninteresting. Passing the palm-orchards of El-Muwayláh, we saw the three valley-mouths all known as Wady Marer, and at 11.45 a.m. we doubled the yellow sandpit, backed by arenaceous hillocks and by hills of red porphyry, known as Ras Wady Tiryam,* with its green-mouthed water-course a little further north. Careful tacking through the verdigris-coloured reefs showed us the gap of Wady Sharmá, fronted by a long sandy island, unnamed in the maps, but called by the people Umm Maksúr.† During the dry season this island is connected by a ford with the mainland; and the damp surface produces a thin grove of Samur or Samgh (*Inga Unguis*) and Siyál (*Acacia Seyal*). Leaving to port Barahkán Island, a rugged heap of sandstone, and threading our way

* Rüppell has Deriam-Teriam; Wallin correctly writes Wady Teriam (Tiryam); Sprenger (p. 23) would change it to Taryam; others prefer Turiam (Adm. Chart). The two latter certainly do not represent the popular pronunciation.

† I would identify it with the Æni Insula of Ptolemy, whose latitudes are here too high; *e.g.*, Aynúnah, in N. lat. 28° 6', is placed in 28° 50'.

amongst rock-fangs, each occupied by its own cormorant, we turned eastward at 4 p.m. The Juhayní Rais, or captain, with the silly fears which imposed upon the travellers of old, here wished to anchor for the night, as the sun was low, and he could no longer sight the reefs and shoals. To this move we offered the liveliest objection. Sálih declared that there was a free passage for a frigate, with eight to twelve fathoms of clear water, bounded north and south by the beds of coralline and meandrine; moreover, we could already see the "tabernacles," or reed huts, on the shore, and inland the shadowy gap of Wady Aynúnah. At last, about 10 p.m., we came to anchor in the safe bight, defended on all sides by land and reef, with a long sandy point separating it from the mouth of the Wady; and we slept on deck through the cool and dewy night, preparing to camp next morning.

This is probably the "Kolpos," of which Diodorus (iii. 44) gives the following account: "The navigator passing these (grassy) plains is received by a bay, a paradox of Nature, which, bending to the deepest recess inland, extends to a depth of 500 stadia (600 st. = 1° = 60 miles), enclosed everywhere by rocks of marvellous size. The mouth is crooked and hard of passage, for a low reef hems in the way, allowing neither ingress nor egress. Amidst the onslaught of the current, and the changes of the wind, the billows boil tremendously, and are ever breaking upon the opposing stony shores. The people, called Banizomenes, live upon the flesh of wild beasts hunted with dogs. At that place is a most holy fane, held in highest honour by all the Arabs."* It is impossible not to believe that these fantastic, sensational, imaginary horrors, combined with the abundance of gold, were not fabled by the people in order to deter strangers from interfering with their monopoly. Yet Rüppell, the landsman, says Aynúnah Bay is full of shallows and quite useless for shipping; whilst Wellsted (ii. 162), the sailor, describes it as well sheltered from all winds, and assures us that under a good pilot a vessel might enter with every facility and safety.

Our first greeting was *Yá Pirán Pir! Yá Abd el-Kádir Ghilani!* ("O Saint of Saints! O Abd el-Kádir of Ghilán!")† pronounced with the true Hindi twang; and in the deepening shades we could dimly distinguish a dusky line of human phantoms ranged upon the Stygian shore. In reply to my question, they declared themselves to be Indian Hajis who, as usual, had been plundered by the Bedawin, and who were returning home by way of Jerusalem and Bagh-

* Possibly the Maghárat Shu'ayb, which will be alluded to in chap. xii., has succeeded to the honours of this pagan sanctuary. But the text evidently means that Aynúnah was the holy place.

† See "Pilgrimage," vol. i. chap. x.

dad. The party, six men and one woman, travelled on foot, lodging in the reed-huts, and often sleeping in the wilderness; yet, strange to say, none were in bad condition, and one fellow was positively fat. As they complained of hunger, I sent them some ship-biscuit, and afterwards gave them what alms we could afford. They blessed me with a Fátihah, the opening chapter of the Korán, asked for more, and finally declared that I ought to spare them the twenty days' march, *viâ* Akabah, by sending them in a boat to Suez. No sooner had these paupers cleared out, than they were succeeded by others in a similar condition. Apparently a string of stragglers passes along the coast during several months after the Hajj-season.

For long years * I have been vainly urging the Anglo-Indian Government to abate this scandal by binding the Moslems to abide by their own humane law. The Apostle of Allah, whilst making a single Pilgrimage to Meccah one of the ordinances of El-Islam, expressly forbade it to those who could not afford to leave money with their families, and to travel in a style befitting their rank. Nothing would be easier than to enforce the regulation by compelling every would-be pilgrim to show Rs. 500 before being allowed to sail. But that fatal Anglo-Indian apathy is the one sufficient obstacle. Meccah,

* See my "Pilgrimage," iii. 255–56.

the focus of Moslem intrigue, still points to living examples of what evils Káfir rule can work, and wretches are still allowed to starve in the streets of Arab towns, and to display the poverty and the nakedness of once wealthy Hind.

We landed early on April 4th, and passed five days in and about the Wady Aynúnah, awaiting the camels and inspecting the ruins. As this is the typical, and evidently the oldest, mining station seen by us in Midian, I shall notice it at some length, and thereby save the reader from *crambe repetita* by remarking only differences in the other ruins. The reason why this and other mining-cities were not better explored by travellers, and why the Pilgrim-caravans yearly pass by them without a visit, is easily explained. Even in Rüppell's day the Huwaytát rendered the land unsafe; many a straggler was murdered, and the Pasha of Egypt was compelled to pay each district chief a large sum in " blackmail" for permission of transit.

Aynúnah harbour lies in N. lat. 28° 2′ 30″. Directly upon its clean and sandy foreshore, a mile or so south of the Fiumara-mouth, and crowning the sand-heaps that overlie sandstones, stand the remains called El-Khuraybah, " the little ruin." The tenements, large and well-built, still show their bases; and on the ground are scattered fragments of sea-coloured glass varying in tint, like the Roman, from blue to green according to its thickness.* These fragments are found only upon the coast, where the wealthy enjoyed bathing; and never, as far as our researches extended, in the inland settlements. There are also rare sherds of a pottery finer than that picked up in the interior; the whitest are composed of almost pure kaolin. The ruins, like all others which we inspected, are reduced to mere foundations of unhewn stone, mostly coralline, bedded in excellent mortar, and nowhere are signs of architectural ornament. These maritime villas at Aynúnah are confined to the spot south-east of the sand-pit, and do not extend to the part of the bight where sharp rocks line the shore. Here they are succeeded by the 'Ushash,† or roofless huts of palm-fronds, the "tabernacles" of the Hebrews, mere temporary affairs, taking the place of tents; deserted and allowed to go to ruin in the cold season, and repaired in early summer. Such is the custom of the tribes extending far down the western coast of Arabia. The booths are usually divided into two compartments, for the separation

---

* The most solid fragment measures more than three lines: some bits are light, thin, and apparently modern, a fact easily accounted for where the Pilgrim-caravans pass.

† 'Ushsh, in classical Arabic, is applied to the nest of a bird building in trees. When more substantially made, and roofed with date-thatch, the huts are called Bakkár, in the plural Bakákír.

of the sexes, and many are fronted by rude porches with pillars of palm-trunk.

Water, made hardly potable by sulphur and Epsom, is found at Aynúnah, in a pit sunk in the sand; and near it is a draw-well partly coralline-revetted. On the highest level appears a small Hauz, a cistern regularly built with uncut stone bedded in cement, part of whose fine outer coating still remains. These plastered reservoirs, called Birket and Fiskíyyeh, are common in the Sinaitic Peninsula and in the Néjeb, or South Country. Here begins the aqueduct which, with a general direction from north to south, and skilfully conducted round the hill-sides, once supplied the thriving community. It is between four and five kilomètres, not a mile and a half, long (Wellsted), based upon the ground and supplied with a central and much larger cistern about mid-course. The material is again rough stone, compacted with the finest mortar, probably of burnt shells: it contains a quantity of pounded brick, an addition common to Roman cement and to that which, invented by the ancient Egyptians, has descended under the name of Humrá* to the moderns. The work is well and strongly made. In one place where the earth has been

---

* Powdered brick mixed with gypsum to make impermeable cement. "Kosromil" is earth and organic ashes calcined and united with lime to form the local pozzolana.

washed from under it, the unsupported masonry stands firm and solid as an arch. The channel has everywhere been lined with fine tegulæ, about eighteen inches broad, and turned up at the edges; of these, specimens were carried to Cairo. The fine ruin disappears at last along the left flank of the rocky gap through which the stream still flows.

The low undulating ground over which you pass is a comparatively modern conformation, backed, at a distance varying from two to five direct miles, by an ancient sea-cliff. This *falaise*, here about 200 feet of extreme height, is composed of argillaceous marl, of limestones, and of corallines, from which I secured the mould of a Venus and impressions of a Pecten.* Veins of carbonate of iron, apparently worked, appear in the lower parts; and the base is either upthrust granite and porphyry, or a deposit of hard conglomerate, the latter being the more general. At irregular intervals of some miles, this true coast is broken by "Bábs," or gates, which give issue to the waters of the Wadies, and these were the favourite sites of settlements, either single or in pairs; crowning the heights, lying upon the thresholds, and sometimes occupying patches of ground where the streams formed Deltas.

* Arturo Issel ("Malacologia del Mar Rosso. Pisa, 1869") treats of the Pectens of the Red Sea (pp. 102-3) and of the fossil Pectens (Australis Vexillum, Concinnus and Medius) in pp. 259-60.

The old sea-cliff is a highly interesting formation. It probably dates from the days when the Isthmus of Suez, that great bank of sand, lime, gypsum, sea-salt, and various testaceæ, still showing only eighteen mètres of maximum height at El-Jisr (El-Guisr), emerged from the waves; when the quaternary sea broke upon the Jebel Mukkattam near Terah; and when the African Sahará, a vast inland sea during the pleiocenic and post-pleiocenic periods, became dry land. So D'Abbadie (*Lettre*, etc., p. 121, "Bull. de la Soc. Géol. de France," 1839) observed that the whole Tihámah of Eastern Arabia is occupied by comparatively modern marine formations, the latter abounding in shells tolerably well preserved and gleaming white upon the surface of the soil. Finally, Rüppell found similar examples as far as N. lat. 26°, besides conchiliferous banks raised from four to five metres above sea-level.

The "Gate" of Aynúnah, about 200 mètres wide, has evidently been closed by a barrage, in order to form an upper lake for sand washing, and to supply the aqueduct. This flooded ground is now overgrown with a "Palmetum" and humbler vegetation. Two large blocks of masonry, the normal rough stone and mortar, still lie further down the bed. The builders had taken care to secure the best material for their dam. Their Makta' el-Hajar (quarry) is still open about four miles to the north, on the right bank of the Wady el-Makhsab. A low hill of argillaceous calcaire, fine and compact, runs from north-east to south-west. A regular incline can be traced up it. The crest which fronts the Wady has been all worked, and in two places the squared stones, tooled with a small pick, resembling that used in the great underground quarry called at Jerusalem "Tombs of the Kings," lie upon the ground. One slab puzzled us; it was shaped like the gravestones of a country churchyard, with a shallow circle in the upper third, measuring about a span in diameter by two inches deep, which seemed to want nothing but a cross to make it intelligible. It is impossible to forget that the Romans, when seeking the finest building material, had scanty regard for distance and labour.

Below the "barrage," and on the right side of the Wady, which is here lined with the normal conglomerate, lies the second or inland settlement, now called Dáo el-Hamrá, the "red house" or abode, and universally attributed to the Franks. It consists of two parts. The *basseville*, based on a hard conglomerate of the bed, the modern ground, shows a succession of small chambers, and a large heap or pile of rough rounded stones, which the Bedawin have named the Burj, or tower. A made zigzag, still traceable, leads up the stiff sea-face of the *falaise* to the *hauteville*. On the left of the path is a deep artificial hollow, striking from north-west to south-east, and the specimens of carbonate and silicate of copper which we carried off made us suspect that the people were right in describing it as a mine of Fayrúz (turquoises).*

The *hauteville* was the usual congeries of stone-huts, measuring some seven feet by four.† All were razed to the foundation, and they remarkably resembled the quarters in the Sinaitic Peninsula (Wady Mukattab) once occupied by the captive miners and by their military guardians. The walls are placed close together, and in one part we detected a line of street through the cells like a

* The Bedawin use this term, which is Persian. The old Egyptians called the stone "Mafka," and apparently were well acquainted with extracting it (Brugsch Bey, "Wanderungen Zu den Türkisminen"). We do not know if the ancients held the modern, or rather the Russian superstition, that the turquoise is a sovereign defence against mortal wounds. The tablet at Sarábit el-Khádim (the "Servant's Heights") says, "I (Har-ur-Ra, Superintendent of the ruins) ordered the workmen daily working, and said unto them, 'There is still Mafka (turquoise) in the mine, and the vein will be found in time,' and it was so; the vein was found at last, and the mine yielded well."

† The size and the disposition of these "cribs" reminded me of the *Casupoli* at Marzabotte, which Count Gozzadini determined, from their scanty size, to be tombs ("Etruscan Bologna," p. 129). So amongst the Kolarian Juangs, a leaf-wearing race in Western India, Colonel Dalton found the huts to measure about six feet by eight; and even this short allowance was divided into two compartments, room and store-room. (Page 100, *Journ. Anthrop. Inst.*, August, 1877).

"Laura." I picked up a quantity of rude pottery, and the half of an eared mortar cut in fine aragonite;* the guides spoke of a masonry-revetted well or cistern, but none could show us the way to it. A single tomb, or rather grave, amongst the huts appeared modern, and facing Meccah. All, however, denied that it was a grave, and they presently showed us the "Cemetery of the Nazarenes," a couple of hundred yards from the left bank of the Wady. The graves, ovals of rough stones, resembling those of the Bedáwin, but considerably larger, are ranged in two ranks along the modern Hajj-road, which probably dates from the most ancient times, and they form a barbarous Via Appia—the fashion of the olden world—for those approaching the settlement from the south. I dug six feet deep into the largest, known as the "King of the Franks' tomb," and utterly failed to find any remnants of humanity.

We came to the conclusion that the "Red Abode" was a settlement of workmen, most probably servile. Still continuing our investigations, we found in the conglomerate spine at the left side of the gate-threshold, and just below where the aqueduct heads, a line of some fifteen pits, varying in depth from a few inches to half a yard, and one

* Possibly the ὕαλος, calcareous or oriental alabaster, used, Herodotus says (Thalia xxiv.), by the Ethiopians as cases to preserve their dead. A fine specimen, the sarcophagus of Psammuthis, is found in the Sloane Museum.

of them still contained bark, pounded by the wild man to extract tannin. These were evidently mortars for stone-crushing, and as such we used them to treat our specimens.

Following up the left bank, and passing the upper end of the date-grove, where the Wady makes a great sweep from north to east, we were shown a road hewn in the rock, possibly intended for wheeled vehicles, and certainly a short cut for the workmen. It abuts upon the Wady, which here stretches from east to west, and shows in the latter direction a broad band of dark porphyry, looking as if a black sheet had been hung from top to bottom. A few yards beyond it on the right bank there is a valley which leads to Magharát Shu'ayb, the next Hajj-station, by a more direct line than that which the caravan prefers. It apparently heads in quartz, as we found at the mouth two massive boulders, very little weathered. On its proper right is another rock-hewn road, probably intended for wheels to fetch the metalliferous granite and porphyry from the adjoining mountains.

Presently the main valley splits, forming an islet of rock, upon whose southern slopes lies the third settlement, known as El-Kharábah (the ruin), or El-Bandar (the place of trade). Here the wall-girt Wady Aynúnah broadens and forms white spoil-banks of felspathic earth, a kaolin-like decomposition of granite. Hence the choice of the site for the " Afrán," as the people still call the smelting-furnaces. The fine large tiles lining the aqueduct were also made of this material. To the north, on the higher levels, are the ovens, double rows of some eight receptacles, the four to the west being almost unbroken : they are parallelograms of burnt tile, measuring a yard and a half by a yard. Evidently from the shape they were intended to smelt all the metals together; but whether the miners could afterwards separate the gold and silver from the tin and lead, can be determined only by careful examination of the scoriæ * brought back to Cairo.

To the south of the furnaces, separated by a sandy watercourse, a gentle rise had been chosen for the houses which subtended the work-places ; and, from the absence of scoriæ and vitrified clay, we judged that they had belonged to the slave-overseers. The Egyptian officers made a plan of the place, whilst we dug into the Afrán. They yielded no results, but the ground all about was scattered with bricks, in shape resembling the

* The celebrated chapter of Pliny (xxxiii. 21) shows the technological skill of the ancients, and notices the disengagement in the furnace of silver, which, volatilized by heat, takes the name of *Sudor*. In chap. xxiii. the historian treats of natural and artificial " electrum "—the alloy of silver with gold. The baser metals are easily separated by oxidation from gold and silver, a process extensively used at Kremnitz, the premier mint of Hungary.

European, and with fire-bricks partially fused and vitrified. We collected slag for laboratory analysis, some of it well-worked, and light as pumice, whilst other bits contained fibrous charcoal, evidently palm-wood. The plan also showed a broken cowrie,* and a quantity of pottery, but none of the glass which was collected in such quantities at the maritime settlement.

Such is Aynúnah, a word evidently composed of Ayn-Únah, the "fountain of Únah," the latter being the Ptolemean name.† Its water, the "Ayn el-

* For the twenty-two species and varieties of Cyprææ, see Issel (*loc. cit.* pp. 109–114). He makes the *Cypræa Moneta*, one of the most widely diffused of shells, common to the Mediterranean and the Red Seas (part 1, p. 32).

† In Lib. 1. chap. ii. "On the site of Arabia Felix," which is defined as being bounded on the north by the exposed southern flanks of Petra and Arabia Deserta, extending to the Persian Gulf; on the south by the Red Sea, eastward by part of the Persian Gulf and the sea washing the Syagros promontory (Ras el-Hadd); and west by the Arabian Gulf (Red Sea). We find the following names and positions on the sea-board going southwards from the Elaniticus Sinus.

	E. Long.	N. Lat.	
Οὔνη (Oune)	... ...	66° 20'	28° 40' (properly 28° 2' 30").
Μοδίανα or Μοδοῦνα (Modíana)	...	66° 40'	27° 45' (El-Muwayláh ?).

Thus Modíana lies twenty miles west and fifty-five miles south of Aynúnah.

Ἵππος ὄρος (Hippos Mons)	...	66° 40'	27° 20' (Jebel el-Sharr ?).
Ἵππος κώμη (Hippos vicus)	...	67° 00'	26° 40' (Sherm Zibá ?).
Φοινίκων κώμη (Phœnicum oppidum)		67° 20'	26° 20' (El Wijh ?).
Ῥαυνάθου κώμη (Khaunathi pagus)	..	67° 15'	25° 40' (Wady Aunid ?).
Χερσόνησος ἄκρα (Chersonesi extrema)		67° 00'	25° 40' (mouth of ditto ?).
Ἰαμβιά κώμη (Iambia vicus)	...	63° 00'	24° 00' (properly 24° 5' 30").

We are thus certain of two points in this valuable list, of Oune and of Iambia (Yambú-'a el-Nakhíl), the northern and the southern.

Gasab" (*Kasab*), is mentioned, together with that of El-Akrá,* by Abu Abdillah ibn Ayás in his book (A.D. 1516), *Nashh el-Azhár fi Ajáib El-Attár* (Smelling of Flowers in the Wonders of Lands), as "pilgrim-stations" (*Manázil el-Hajj*) "on the shore of the Red Sea." He continues : " In the Uyun el-Kasab there are springs of running water, around which grows the Persian reed (*Arundo donax*). It is a resting-place for the pilgrims, who pitch their tents on the bank, and bathe themselves, and wash their clothes in the springs. This is the spot of which the poet sings :—

"O my friends! forget not your vows to the nameless youth,
Whose companion is sorrow, and whose eyes are wet with tears :
He remembered his vow to you on the road to El-Héjaz,
And neither in El-'Uyún nor in Akrá did he taste of sleep."

This valley and El-Akrá are the limits assigned to the Wady Dámah between Dhobá and Istabl 'Antar, and to the possessions of the Orbán Balíy in the olden time.†

Finally, the first glance at Aynúnah told me that it was hopeless to expect, in this once civilised region, the wealth of nuggets which the old Greek describes as ranging between the size of an olive-

* El-Akrá is the first pilgrim-station south of El-Wijh. El-'Uyún, also, in the last verse quoted below, is the abbreviated form.

† Háfiz Ahmad, in his "Historical Compendium of Egypt," also gives a list of the Pilgrim-stations on the Egyptian road. Wallin refers to No. 9972 of the Brit. Mus. MSS.

stone and a walnut.* Gold, the metal which appears to have been produced last, and to have first been used by man, is easily removed from the superficial strata, and can scarcely be exhausted in sand and stone. The Land of Midian is at present, in fact, much like California, when the pick and fan men had done their work : she is still wealthy, but her stage is that when machinery must take the place of the human arm. I by no means despair of finding virgin regions where the gold grain, or granulated gold, still lingers ; but they evidently will not lie within hail of the coast.

* See chap. ix.

CHAPTER VI.

FROM WADY AYNÚNAH TO THE WADY MORÁK
IN THE JEBEL EL-ZAHD.

ON April 4th, when examining the site of Aynúnah, we came upon a flock of goats attended by women and children. The former wore the nose-bags of Egypt, and the latter screamed when we offered them small silver coins. Nevertheless, they recognised Sálih the mulatto guide, and readily bore a message from him to certain petty chiefs of the Tugaygát clan, who were encamped in the neighbouring northern valley, Wady el-Makhsab. The result was a visit from four of the head men, Shaykhs Ráfi'a, 'Ayd Alayán, Munákid, and Abd el-Nabi, who, recognising the viceregal authority, at once agreed, for a consideration, to transport the tents and baggage from the sea-shore to the palm-grove of Aynúnah. Their half-wild camels made sad havoc with the boxes and bottles.

In conversation they told me that some twenty years ago a Frank had visited them from Túr Síná

(Sinai) to collect plants. I afterwards heard from Colonel Middleton, of Cairo, that he had met an old Englishman, named Wells, in New York, who had travelled east of the Akabah Gulf on camels, and who described the country as full of ruins and minerals. Yet, curious to say, they had not the least knowledge of Dr. Beke's visit in January, 1874 — the last excursion before his lamented death.

These men belonged to the Huwaytát,* a large and growing tribe, which holds the greater part of the sea-board, including El-Akabah, to the mountain called Istabl 'Antar (Antar's Stable),† extending for seven or eight hours' journey eastward into the interior, till they are met by their hereditary enemies, the Beni Ma'ázeh. They are originally Egyptian Fellahs, natives of the Nile-Valley and subjects of the Khediv, who have become Bedawinised, abandoning their ancient homes, Túrah (Ta-Roau, the Greek Troja), Rasátín, and Hahsán (les Bains), the Cairene Sanitarium. The emigration is said to date

* In the singular, Ḥuwayṭí. Há'iṭ is a wall or an inclosure, generally round a palm-orchard; and its diminutive would be Ḥuwayṭ. Thus Ḥuwayṭi would mean a man of the small walls, and must not be used to explain classical names of tribes. My learned friend, Prof. Palmer, following Robinson, habitually calls them "Harweitat," which is, I think, a mistake for Ḥuwayṭát.

† Wellsted (ii. 183) makes their southern limit the ruined castle near Marsá Ezlam (Wady Azlam), where the Balíy tribe begins, and stretches to the Juhaynah lands.

from about 150 years ago. Thus these *partim nomades, partim agricolæ*, as the ancients described the coast-people,* are unmentioned by the Arab genealogists, and they have not a single tale nor tradition connected with the old mining cities of Midian. Their chief 'Bráhím (ibn) Shadíd, domiciled in the Husayníyyah quarter of the capital, is well known to the Viceroy. His second in command, Mohammed ibn Rufayyah of the Tugaygát clan, whose brother Alayán came to us in Sherm Yáhár, pitches his black tents near the mountains of Libu and 'Antar, some six or seven hours of dromedary-riding from our farthest southern port, Sherm Zibá.

The tribe still shows its origin by the tattooed beauty spot and by the indigo-dyed dress and veiled faces of their women; moreover, instead of horses, they have asses which are small, weak, and valueless. From the Bedawin they have borrowed the practice of plaiting their hair in the small pig-tails called Kurún (horns), and of never appearing without arms. Matchlocks are common: guns are used by the chiefs, and double-barrels are not wholly unknown. Even the boys are armed with swords, often longer than themselves; and on a good old blade I read the legend *Pro Deo et Patria*. Numbering, like the Jehaynah and the Beni Ma'ázeh, about 5000 males, they are considered a strong,

* See chap. ix.

and by no means a quiet tribe. They are quarrelsome and on bad terms with all their neighbours. *Má yahibbu' el-nás*—they do not love mankind—is the verdict of the settled Arabs concerning the Huwaytát.

Rüppell, who judges their morals harshly, mentions (p. 223) that, shortly before his visit to El-Muwayláh, the Huwaytát had driven off all the cattle belonging to the Fort-garrison, and when hotly pursued had cut the throats of the sheep and goats. They talk of Fakihs (clerks) who have been educated in Egypt; but they are extremely ignorant of their religion, and I never yet saw one of them at his devotions. Like all the nomads, they act upon the old saying, "We do not fast the Ramazán, because we are half starved all the year round; we never perform the Ghusl or the Wuzú (ceremonial ablutions), because we want the water to drink; and we never make the Hajj (pilgrimage), because Allah is everywhere."

I never saw the faces of their women unveiled; but the men are not an uncomely race, with olive-coloured skins, lamp-black hair, features tolerably straight, and lithe, supple, active figures. Some of the fisher-lads show Shúshehs (top-knots) discoloured ruddy-brown by sea water, the practice well known to the Venetian beauties of Titian's day. Of course we can hardly expect in these regions the highest charms of hair, especially of young hair, those lights and shades which shift with every angle. Their eyes are piercing and strong. Our Bedawin escort saw better with the naked organ than the Egyptian officers, natives of a valley plain, with their binocular glasses. Though healthy in body and mind, they are by no means a clean people, reserving fresh water for drinking, and bathing in the sea, like the lower animals, only in the warm weather. The hatred of cold water, combined with old rags, results in what may readily be imagined, but must not be described. The pure uncontaminated air makes them cheerful and even merry: they endure all their hardships without dreaming of "a grumble." Their principal occupations are pasturing, trading, and fighting. They buy or barter grain at the several ports for sheep and clarified butter, for matting-reeds, for grass and forage, and for charcoal and other minor matters.

The Huwaytát are divided as usual into a score of clans,* including those affiliated. I formed a high

---

* The names given to me were—
+ 1. Orban Amírát (not Umrát), who occupy the Shifah.
+ 2. ,, Masá'íd: they dwell about Maghárat Shu'ayb, and were probably a separate tribe incorporated with the Huwaytát.
+ 3. ,, Sulaymíyyín in the interior, east of Jebel 'Antar.
+ 4. ,, Jeráfín, in the Jebel el-Shárr (mountain of El-Muwayláh).
    5. ,, Ghanámiyyín, south of the Shárr.

opinion of the young Abd el-Nabi (Slave of the Prophet), whom M. Marie very naturally named Abd el-Nabíd (Slave of Strong Liquor). His attractive features, his soft voice and deferent address would be admired in any *salon* of Europe. He is illiterate; he can neither read nor write, yet he observes everything; he would pick up all points of ceremony at the first sight. Moreover, he knows

    6. Orban Mawasah, the tribe of 'Brahim ibn Shadíd; behind Sherm Zibá.
    7.   „   Tagátkah, in the Wady Dámah, south of Zibá.
+ 8.   „   Tugaygát, before mentioned: owners of Wadys Aynúnah and Makhsab: Wallin misnames them Dakíkát.
    9.   „   Arámleh (not Umrán), in Wady Abú Salám.
+ 10.   „   El-Kur'án, (in Wady Azlam and Suwayyah?) extending to El-Wijh.
+ 11.   „   El-Masháhír, in Wady Shagaf.
+ 12.   „   El-Ulayyát, who frequent the Wady Tiryam together with—
  13.   „   El-'Adasín, goat-keepers affiliated with the Huwaytát.
  14.   „   El-Jawáhirah, also in Wady Tiryam.
  15.   „   El-Zamáhrah, in Jebel el-Kharís, near the Jebel el-Abyaz, which we shall visit.
  16.   „   El-Buraysát, in Wady Abú Salám.
  17.   „   Ziyábin, in the Wady Tiryam.
  18.   „   El-Rakábiyyeh, near Wady Sharmá.
+ 19.   „   El-Salálimah (not Musalimeh), about the Jebel el-Jimm: this clan has two minor divisions—
          a. Hayáyineh.
          b. Surhaylát.

The names marked with a cross are given with more or less correctness by Wallin: he adds 20. 'Ureinát (Uraynát), 21. Sughayin, and 22. Sharmán, "who frequent the districts south of Muweilah, and towards Iṣṭabl 'Antar."

what he wants to know ; he rides and shoots well, and is a judge of dromedaries and camels, sheep and goats. He can tell you the name and nature of every plant that blooms on his native hills, especially the simples useful for man and beast, holding the while to the Bedawi axiom, *Akhar el-Dawá el-Kay* —" The end of medicine is (the actual) cautery." Lastly, he is ever ready to risk his life for his tribe : and no Hidalgo of the bluest blood was ever more ticklish on the " Pun d'onor."

The Bedawi, who becomes fawning and abject when corrupted by contact with the town-Arab, is still a gentleman in his native wilds. Easy and quiet, courteous and mild-mannered, he expects you to respect him, and upon that condition he respects you—still without a shade of obsequiousness or servility. Hence the difficulties found by the official class, Egyptian as well as Turkish. Disdaining to observe any of the little punctilios of the race, these begin with the loud authoritative address, *Ya Shaykh el-Orbán!* ending, perhaps, with some rough order. The Bedawi turns his back, and simply replies, " We are not Shaykhs of the Orbán ! " The man of the wilds has a dignity of his own, a perfect contrast with the unfortunate Fellah who, a slave for the last 2000 years, cannot be treated well without waxing fierce and kicking—in his own phrase, " becoming a Pharaoh." Moreover, the Bedawi never tells a lie, and, when told one, never forgets it. His confidence is gone for ever, and all the suspiciousness of his nature is aroused.

Should we find it necessary to raise regiments of these men, nothing would be easier. Pay them regularly, arm them well, work them hard, and treat them with even-handed justice—there is nothing else to do. I presume that this was the Roman system of garrisoning the forts and outposts to the east and the south of Syria.

The wild men will also work well, as was proved when digging the Suez Canal. But the Bedawi is ever on the alert, like the cold northern sea, to use the smallest flaw in the artificial dyke of civilisation. Hence the ruin of the strong places further north, of the basalt burghs of Bashan and the 'Ulah (Hamath), of the limestone strongholds of Moab, and probably of the mining cities of Midian.

Professor Vidal seems to think that the latter may have been destroyed by the incursions of the nomads under the reign of Valens, Emperor of the East (A.D. 364-378), when the power of Rome began to decline; or during the life of his successor, Theodosius, when the riots took place at Antioch. The date is hardly likely to be so early. In the days of Mohammed, Akabat-Ayla was still ruled by a Christian prince, John, who accepted El Islam (Robinson, i. 243).

Abd el-Nabi is young and ambitious, and, despite his gentle manners, I suspect that he can deal a smashing blow. Like a man of honour he is ever ready to fight, as we saw on an occasion which will be noticed. He is honest too: I engaged camels from him when suspecting that our party was being delayed at El-Muwayláh, and advanced him $15. When it came up, he returned the 'Arbún (earnest-money), although I should have hesitated to demand it after the trouble he had taken to collect the beasts. When prompted by his tribesmen to make an exorbitant demand, he exchanges a smile of warning. The lithe agile figure climbs up the trotting dromedary, and glides from saddle to ground like an acrobat.

One of our officers, who had been in the Súdán, attempted to give him the go-by in a camel race, and was passed as if he was standing still by the little "Nágah" (dromedary), which at once entered into the spirit of the sport. Like all Bedawi, he is a keen sportsman, perfect at stalking his game. He accompanied us to the last, till he saw us safe on board the corvette at Makná. Briefly, Abd el-Nabi and I became friends—in the Desert man meets man as an equal,—and on parting I gave him my bowie-knife, with many hopes that it will serve him well.

I agree with Professor Palmer that the Bedawi,

the "father," not the "son, of the Desert," is, like the noble savage generally, a nuisance to be abated by civilisation. Yet the race has high and noble qualities which, as the old phrase is, the world would not willingly see die ; and perhaps the pure blood of the wilderness may be infused to good purpose into burgher-men, as into their horses.

Guided by Abd el-Nabi we minutely inspected the Wady Aynúnah. Like Sinaitic Wady Gharandal, it is a typical valley, *palmetis consita, fontibus irrigua*, even as its settlement is a typical mining town. M. Marie, to whom I explained the difference between the popular idea of emerald islands in the sand-sea and the true oasis, a perennial spring bordered with tall palms, so common throughout Maritime Arabia, called it *un oasis* sérieux*. This Nullah is said to come from a distance of three days' march, and, as we afterwards learned, it absorbs a multitude of minor streams extending south to the water-shed of Wady Sharmá. The spring which feeds the basin wells from the ground close within the gate. It is distinctly Arabian—that is, warm and medicinal with

* The hellenised form of the Egyptian " Wáhe:" hence the Arabic "Wáh," still used by the Copts, meaning an inhabited station or place in the Desert; almost always a Wady. The ancients of the Nile valley expressed Oasis by Otou, a place of embalming before burial. Strabo, xvii. 1, says, "The Egyptians give the name of Auases (Oases) to certain inhabited tracts, which are surrounded by extensive deserts, and appear like islands in the sea."

the pleasant taste of alum, and the picturesque hue of sulphur. It reminded me strongly of the "mawkish" and mephitic Palmyra-pits. Like these, it tarnishes silver, and deposits a coating of carbonate of lime upon the fetid mud which lines the channels.* The Bedawin declare that, after the Nile, it is the best in the world—a favourite popular boast.† The soldiers said of Aynúnah, "Her air is the air of Paradise : her water is the water of Jehannum!" They were right about the climate. The atmosphere was delightfully sweet and cool, even when the mercury was showing a hundred degrees (F.) in the houses of Cairo.‡

The water of Aynúnah, I have said, is called the Ayn el-Kasab,§ or Fount of the Canes, from the

* A bottle was filled for analysis and emptied by some thirsty soul.

† So in the Tíh Wilderness, the Wells of Ma'yin are said to yield "water sweet as the waters of the Nile." Wellsted (ii. 162) notes that the valley of "'Aïnúnah" is celebrated among the "Bedowins" for fine and abundant water.

‡ In the Aynúnah gorge, on April 5th, the observations were—

	At 6 a.m.	At 10 a.m.
Therm. (F.)	69°	83°
Hyg. (Sauss.)	30°	29°
Aner.	29·98°	29·90°

§ The word is pronounced "Gasab," with the peculiar Bedawi perversion of the Káf; and hence, I presume, our word "Gossypium" properly applied to the Mawaceæ. Sprenger (*loc. cit.* 22) says, "Später hiessen die Pilger die Station in oder bei 'Aynûnâ ''Oyûn alquçab.'"

FROM WADY AYNÚNAH TO WADY MORÁK. 159

quantity of sedge (*Cyperus* and *Scirpus*); rushes (*Juncus Spinosus*, Fersk.), the Arabian Simár, which are cut and sent in bundles to Suez for making *hasír* (mats), and *Arundo donax*, which form a dense thicket, preventing all access to the spring or springs. A little way above the fountain, water is found by digging the usual Themail (pits) some eighteen inches deep. Below the gate it sinks and flows irregularly, depending, the people say, upon the tides. After heavy rains the whole line must roll a furious torrent; but in the hot season, though never dry, it cannot reach the Wady-mouth, distant some three miles.

Hence Aynúnah is a station for the Hajj, which from El-Muwayláh marches along shore, crossing the mouths of the Wadies, but not visiting their Nakhíl,* or date-orchards. The larger vegetation

* Between El-Muwayláh and El-Akabah, the stations described to me by the Bedawin were as follows; Rüppell's marches (pp. 216–19) are also subjoined in the list :—
1. El-Muwayláh to Aynúnah, 12 to 13 hours (=12½ hours *viâ* Wady Tiryam and 12 direct, Rüppell) = 28 direct miles.
2. Aynúnah to Maghárat Shu'ayb, 14 hours (=13 hours, R.) =28 direct miles. Half-way there is a Mahattah, or halting-place, called Umm Rujaym, where water flows only after rain from the Jebel el-Muk.
3. Maghárat Shu'ayb to El-Sheraf, 12 hours, a desert station without water: beyond it the people speak of the Mahattah Sharafah.
4. El-Sheraf to Hagul (Hakl, Agh'ale of Ptolemy), 14 hours: on the Gulf of Akabah with palm-groves and water.
5. Hagul to El-Akabah, with fort and garrison, palms and water.

is the palm, which thrives best where its feet are in water, and its head in the fire of heaven : it is of the two species, the date and the dorn, or Theban palm (*Hyphene Thebaica?*), peculiar on account of its numerous branches. The former is barbarously neglected, being never pruned nor masculated, although here and there a reed fence is run round some choicer specimen.

The grounds, which might be made a Garden of Irem, are strewed with the mummied corpses of trunks and fronds; whilst, worse still, many of the stumps still standing are mere " black-jacks." The swamps are peopled with tadpoles and froglets, with snakes, and with little fresh-water land shells, the *Melanopsis acicularis* of Férussac, common in Arabia. In the cool shade, and during the dark hours, flies and gnats are so troublesome that travellers always camp in the sunny open below the trees. Moreover, here, as in the drier parts of the country, there is a small black beetle like a coccinella, by the Arabs called " Ba'úzah," * which amuses itself by a sharp bite, apparently without object, and running away.

We explored the upper valley of Aynúnah above the furnaces, which are easily reached in twenty minutes. There we found various metals, especially

* In classical Arabic meaning a gnat, a mosquito: *mukh ba'úzah* (gnats' brains or marrow) is equivalent to our "mare's nest."

argentiferous galena in the quartz. The banks in many places are seamed and striped by eruptive dykes, veins and filons of dark-green porphyry cutting and altering the lower and earlier plutonic formation of a red syenitic granite. We also pushed across the broken plain on the right bank of the Wady, a succession of yawning gorges and rough divides, which Sálih, the guide, called "El-Jebel" (the mountain),* and which explained why the ancients had cut a rock-road to strike smoother ground.

In the hollows we found the Kabah (*Aristida*, or *Wüsten-gras*) with feathery top, equally prized by horse and camel, and collected near the sea-shore in bundles for exportation. The Bedawin greedily ate the small green warty pod of a milky plant which they called Jurá, and which the soldiers named Khíyár el-Barr—desert-cucumber. Wild sorrel (*Rumex Vesicarius* ?), of surprising size and surpassing acid flavour, springs from the fissures of the rocks, and more than once supplied us with an anti-scorbutic dish.

The surface of the smoother lands was granite gravel, overlying minute dust of the same formation; and the stone-scatters were composed of petrosilex, porphyry, diorite, peridot, and felspathic matter

---

* As opposed to the seats and road-lines of civilisation which affect the plain.

generally. We saw nothing of the basalts and chlorites which were conspicuous further north. Quartz appeared in various shapes: the hyaline yielded nothing; the common and the waxy varieties showed at the fractures small dots of pyrites, with a suspicion of gold ranged in lines. We had only time to break the pebbles as we met them, not to trace the veins to their source; but the discovery explained to us the use of the mortars sunk in the rock at Aynúnah.

Our walk ended at a range of remarkable buttresses on the right bank, about a quarter of the distance between the water and the nearest mountain. The material is of argillaceous marl like the *falaises* of the true coast, capped, on a regular and horizontal base-line, by brown grit, the sand of the Desert, a modern formation, still growing as the grains are gradually compacted by dew and rain. These buttresses, rising sharply from the hollow plain, measure the extent of denudation which has taken place around them. We also followed the Hajj-road to the north, where, winding seawards of the *falaise*, it bends round inland to north-east between the mountain Zahd (Aynúnah) and the "Tayyibat Ism" block.

On April 7th the caravan, preceded by the Sayyid Abd el-Rahím, straggled in, under Shaykh Hasan ibn Sálim of the Beni Ukbah. Mr. Clarke had met with a "cropper," his beast having started off at an unexpected gallop: a mule would have broken his neck, whereas his hand and arm were only barked—another instance of the Arab saying.* The old Haji, as he waddled to the tents, exclaimed, *Bid'dak taktul-ni!*—"Thou art resolved to be the death of me!" and he was not restored to life without an abundance of beer. They had engaged fifty camels, for which they were to pay twelve piastres per diem, at the rate of only eighteen to twenty piastres to the dollar. Finding that the Huwaytát would not travel in the company of the Beni 'Ukbah, I dismissed the latter with bakhshish ($5), and a present of cavendish, giving them at the same time a letter of satisfaction to the Commandant of Fort El-Muwayláh. The over-zealous official at once placed several of them under arrest, and dismissed them only when a dromedary-messenger carried to him a peremptory order to do so. I had no wish, in view of future contingencies, to give these men a grievance; they are the only tribe which, having no blood-feuds with their neighbours, can carry travellers into the far interior.

Shaykh Abd el-Nabi at once set out to collect the required carriage, forty-one camels and ten Hijn, or dromedaries, the latter costing, in this region, a maximum of fifteen Napoleons. We spent April

* "Sind Revisited," chap. vi.

8th in resting our weary travellers, who had been two days on the march; in pounding the stones and washing the sands, and in taking counsel concerning the line of country. I at first thought of marching straight upon the next caravan station, Maghárat Shu'ayb, where, in all probability, Haji Wali first found the auriferous sand. M. Marie, however, offered cogent arguments in favour of following up the Wady, at least as far as the Zahd Mountain; and of ascertaining the site whence the quartz comes. I therefore determined to divide the caravan, and leave at Aynúnah my old friend, whose presence was not now wanted; ten soldiers under charge of Lieutenant Abd el-Karím; and Marius the cook, a willing lad, but quite unbroken to desert travel.

On April 9th we set out with the normal difficulties of a first march. It was 6 a.m. before I could take in hand the Mash'ab, or hook-stick, the sceptre of the Egyptian and Assyrian kings, of the hieroglyphs and the cuneiforms, a type which has survived the lapse of years numbered by the thousand, and which in Midian still keeps its old station, distinguishing from the many-headed, the despotic Básh-Kafilah, or *tête de caravane*. The weather had changed, and a Khamsín wind (scirocco) which lasted through the week had set in. We were, however, approaching the mountains; and we had no suffering from heat. The sun was strong between 10 a.m. and 4 p.m.,* but the mornings, the evenings, and the nights were glorious.

The largest of the dromedaries, a good stepper, but a rough old beast, was set apart for me. It appeared to be of Syrian blood, quite different from the lean and light breed ridden by the rest of the party, and on the third day I learnt that it had been "lifted" from the Beni Ma'ázeh. We ascended the left bank of the Wady Aynúnah, whose gate, choked by vegetation, and cut by streamlets, allows only a footman to pass. After a short divide, the path fell into one of its influents, the Wady Umm el Nírán (Mother of Fires), thus leading us round the obstacle.

The upper part of Aynúnah shows, by scattered vegetation, that water is near the surface. Many of the larger trees had been hewn and burnt for charcoal; and the survivors were chiefly dorn palms, capparideæ and samur (*Inga unguis*), whose thorns, disposed in pairs, like the African *Acacia fistula*, pierce all but the strongest boots or the leathery sole of a veteran Bedawi. The sandy tract grew the *Cucumis prophetarum* (Jonah's gourd), with the warty yellow apple, and the smooth balls of the true colocynth (*C. Coloquintida*). The Bedawin

---

* At the end of the march, about noon, the aneroid showed 29° 2', and the mercury 120° (F.) in the sun, and 90° under the thin shade of a gum-tree.

hollow out this bitter apple and fill it overnight with laban, or soured milk, which they drink in the morning. I have never tried the draught, but can easily imagine it potent as the croton-nut of the Gold Coast.*

A large fungus, which thrusts up the sands of the Wadys, was also found in many places; but nowhere could we hear of the white truffle, which, after wet winters, grows so abundantly in the Desert of Palmyra and in the great Syrian wilderness. We were not a little surprised to see, as we advanced, the quartz diminishing in quantity till it completely disappeared, and we did not find out the reason till the next day.

Our direction was northerly towards a great gash in the Zahd or Aynúnah † Mountain; and, after a slow march of four hours, covering fourteen miles, we reached the camping-ground at the mouth of the Wady el-Morák, so called from its fine spring. The ground was level, except where a huge jorf (gravel-bank), a broken segment of unstratified sand, possibly artificial, and built up by the washings

---

* Considered a most powerful remedy: the green nut is split into four, and a slice, duly seasoned with spices, is administered to the patient: unfortunately, I lost the prescription.

† Keith Johnston calls it Jebel el-Ayoon (Mountain of Springs), a name certainly unknown to the Arabs. Müller (Map vi. "Geog. Gr. Minores") has Dj Ain-oune, a nearer approach to correctness, but too classical.

of ores, projected from the right jaw of the gorge. The Bedawin declared that on the other side of the mountain-block, and distant twelve hours' march, they had seen "Afrán" (furnaces) and a large masonry-well. These men exaggerate, but do not invent. I showed one of them a bit of quartz, when he at once told me that whole hills of that "white stone" are to be found on the south-eastern line. Having thorough confidence in the Bedawi's *coup d'œil* for collecting minerals as well as plants, I sent him off with a promise of reward. He started on a violent little "Nágah" which, during the march, used to "curse and swear" at the slowness of the pace whenever the halter was drawn tight. He returned within seven hours, bringing specimens, he said, from every part of the hill. This determined our direction for the next day.

In the evening we explored the gorge, whose right bank showed vestiges of a causeway and steps. Fortunately, the geologist, unlike the botanist, finds all he wants in the valley, without requiring to scale the mountain. The lower part of the Jebel el-Zahd is composed of granites and syenites; the upper of homologous red porphyry—hence its remarkable rounded sky-lines. The same rock forms the backbone of Edom, clothed with the new red sandstone—a fact eminently suggestive. Every pebble that we broke contained more or less metal; we added antimony * to our list, and we found dark-coloured tourmalines. I remembered that the " Kimberley Diamond-mine" in South Africa is surrounded by a non-diamantiferous porphyry or greenstone; but we had neither stores nor time for anything except what came in our way. The Pentateuch mentions the diamond (Exod. xxviii. 18, and xxxix. 11),† alluding to its being engraved, and the Talmud preserves a tradition that Jethro's rod was of the Queen of Stones. Sir John Maundeville, speaking of the Land of Job (chap. xiv.), tells us that the "diamonds of Arabia are not so good (as those of India) : they are browner and more tender."

One of the party at once acquired the *sobriquet*

---

* The mineral used for the eyes by the ancient Egyptians was called " Mas Mut," and was brought by the Shasu (Bedawin) of Madi (Midian) and of Pitshu (Arabia Petræa). Brugsch, p. 100, *Hist. d'Egypte*, etc. Leipzig, 1875. The Arabs are also called 'Amu and Hirusha, or "they who (are) on the land."

† יהלם in the first as well as in the second quotation is translated ἴασπις by the LXX., *jaspis* by the Vulg., "demant" by the Germ., and "diamond" by the A.V. Professor Maskelyne, of the British Museum, asserted to me that the cutting of diamonds was unknown to the classics. The Adamas of Pliny was certainly a diamond, for it cuts and polishes all gems (xxxvii. 76); it was found in India and Arabia (*ibid.*, 15); it was prized by kings (*ibid.*), and it was tested on the anvil (*ibid.*). He calls it "a nodosity of gold;" and, in the Brazil, I have seen a speck of gold inside the crystal. Moreover, it was sought by lapidaries, who set it in iron handles. The vulgar idea is that Louis Berquen of Bruges, in 1456, invented diamond-cutting; but how long before his day was the art known to the Hindús? Maundeville (*loc. cit.*) alludes to their being polished in A.D. 1322.

"Abú Nátrún" (Father of Nitre).* He had heard the Bedawin speak of saltpetre, and, after his evening ramble, he brought back some fragments of a brown and crusted clay which, when duly smelt and tasted by him, had suggested a mixture of salt and ammonia. Unfortunately, we insisted on seeing the spot; and loud were the shouts of laughter when it was discovered to be a halting-place for camels. I presume that the desert air caused our unusual exuberance of spirits: it was the merriest journey I ever made. The minutest bit of "wut" sufficed; and "Abú Nátrún" supplied us with guffaws for many a day.

This wild gorge is a fine study of "il bello orrido," the savage picturesque, a gloomy and rugged rent in the mountain flank, red and ruddy with black dykes and dark veins above, and striped with a ghastly white below. This water-mark shows the violent rush of a boiling, roaring sayl (torrent), which, after heavy rains, must roll fathoms deep, and must whirl and wash down the hugest boulders as though they were pebbles. The bed, here sharply sloping, there falling perpendicularly, is covered with

* The word is probably Egyptian. "Nuter" has the primary signification of purifying: hence the "nitre" used by the ancients to clean the interiors of their temples and houses. It is found in the dust of ruined villages, and is scraped off the walls as well as off the interior of caves. For a description of making sal ammoniac in Egypt out of the *fiente de Chameau, la plus forte et la meilleure*, see "Shaw's Travels," ii. Append. xxix.

gigantic blocks and "hard-heads," torn and weathered, from the towering walls. Now and then we crossed the crystal-clear streamlet, rippling from under cover; and in the lowest level it bares its virgin charms upon a bed of the purest golden sand. The merest sketch of a sheep-path zigzags up the right side to the source, where three palms are said to grow. We found the water better flavoured, or rather less evil-flavoured, than that of Aynúnah, whilst its effects were still more dolorous. A bath in a rocky basin, cleared of water plants, frogs, and tadpoles, consoled us for the loss of the " Hammám " which we had dug for ourselves at the last station.

During this first march we saw no game, the only exception being a small hare with ears as long as the "jackass-hare" of the Western United States. There were, however, earths of the hyæna (*Zabá*), of the porcupine (*Nís*), and of the hedgehog (*Kunfud*); whilst the jackals (*Sa'alab*) and the foxes (*Abu'l husayn*) had made for themselves frequent hole-homes. Every day afterwards we saw troops of gazelles; usually three to five, animals with large startled eyes and asinine ears, evidently the growth of racial watchfulness—life in a perpetual state of guard. One pretty thing followed a lad into camp, and sat like a dog at his feet.* In an evil hour it

---

* The same has been remarked of the wild goat of Sinai, presently noticed.

was bought by one of the officers; it travelled in a cage on camel-back, and when it was dying its throat was cut for venison. How can men be such cannibals as to eat pets? Three other young ones were embarked from Sherm Zibá: one died, and the rest were landed safely at Suez. I asked after the Beden (*Capra Sinaitica*) of the neighbouring Peninsula, in Syria called El-Wa'al, whose noble ringed and recurved horns are sold for knife-handles, and form favourite "trophies of the chase." Apparently it does not extend to these mountains, although the Bedawin spoke vaguely of a stag with large branches.

Birds were so rare near the shore that we started whenever the silence was broken by a stray note. The people told us that they had all followed the tents into the interior (*fauk*), where rain-water still abounds. A few were found about the pools, especially the yellow and the white and black wagtails (*Motacilla flava* and *alba*), called by the Arabs 'Usfur barríyyeh, and sundry varieties of tits. All were too tame and trusting to be shot; moreover, this was the nesting time—*yassawwú bayt*,— "they are building their houses," as the people said. Flights of sand-grouse (*Pterocles Alchata*) winged their way towards water before sundown. I never shoot the beautiful Katá after he saved my life in Somaliland. The pin-tailed species so common in

Egypt is seemingly rare here. We flushed quail, but no partridge; we saw hawks, but no vultures and crows; martins appeared, but never a sparrow. On the stony tracts were hoopoos (*hudhud*), the crested lark and bright-coloured jays (*coracias garrula*); and the blue rock-dove (*Columba livia*) dwelt in the holes of the Aynúnah cliffs. Our dark hours were enlivened by the cuckoo-like cry of a night-jar, but we never heard the owl, which so unpleasantly affected a fair friend at Corfu. The green merops (*Ægyptius*) hunted flies over the valleys. The swallows were already on the wing, and, in early May, when steaming north from Alexandria we were accompanied by weary flights that nestled for the night wherever they could find a shelf. The shore abounded in white gulls that skimmed the waves; whilst cormorants, which plunged like plummets of lead, confined themselves to particular localities. The swampy Wady-mouths housed the snow-white paddy-bird, called in Egypt "Abú Kirdán:"* the "father of a (long) neck" is never killed, because it accompanies the Fellah and destroys insects.

We found the "waran," or true chameleon (*C. vulgaris*, also called Lucerta Nilotica by Hasselquist and Fuskâl); and the large Lybian lizard, known by the generic name of Zabb (*Lacerta Egyptia?*), besides many smaller species. Two snakes were killed by

* "Kirdán" possibly derives from the Persian "Gardan."

Haji Wali at the waters of Aynúnah, but the cerastes (*Hasselquistii*), so common in the desert, was not seen. In the morning the ground was covered with yellow locusts, and many species of brown grasshoppers, especially the large, dark leathery species Jemal el-Yáhúd (Jew's Camel*), enjoyed the sun. I bottled a fine spider (*Lycosa*), called by the Arabs Abu Shabah (Father of a Web), and the subject of as many tales as the Tarantula, or the yellow and black Ananu of the Gold Coast. The butterflies, with the exception of a chocolate-coloured species, seen near El-Muwayláh, were all white. Large hornets (*Zabur*) were seen in the wilderness; and the flies (*Tabarus?*) at Shamá were compared by the officers with those of the Shillúk and Dinka countries (*Tsetse?*), which kill horses and cattle. Specimens of the beetles, grasshoppers, ants, ticks, camel-ticks, and other creeping things which abound, were sent to the British Museum.

* Some Bedawin apply "Jew's Camel" to the chameleon, and call the grasshopper *Himár El-Banát* (Ass of the Girls) or *El-Shaytan* (of Satan).

CHAPTER VII.

MIDIAN AND THE MIDIANITES.

THE Land of Midian is still known to its inhabitants as "Arz Madyan," the latter form being equivalent to the Madian of the A.V. (Apocrypha and Acts vii. 29.) North it is bounded (N. lat. 29° 29') by El-Akubat el-Misríyyah, or the Egyptian steep, as opposed to the El-Akubat el-Shámíyyah, the Syrian, traversed by the Damascus Caravan, a similar pass one day's march to the east. The former gives its name to a fort-village frequented mostly during the Pilgrimage season : it was the birthplace of Lukmán the Wise (prophet), who has absurdly been named Esop. All my informants agreed that El-Muwayláh (N. lat. 27° 39') is the southernmost point of Madyan Proper ; and this is an argument in their favour who would identify the "little Salt" with the Ptolemeian* Modíana or Modo'úna. Thus the length represents

---

* Lib. vi. 11. (See chap. v.) In chap. xii. we will notice the Alexandrian's Mákna or Máina.

1° 49' (=109 dir. geog. miles); * a figure which rises to 160, if we measure along the coast line, neglecting the minor sinuosities, but including the great eastern staple of the Akabah Gate; the classical *Flexio Sinus Ælanitici*, now called Ras Fartah. Further north of Midian Proper begins the vast Wady el-Arabah, connecting, after a fashion, the Elanitic branch with the Red Sea trunk. Southwards, the lands of the Balíy, the Juhaynah, and other Bedawin separate it from El-Hejaz, the Moslem's Holy Land, whose frontier in N. lat. 25° is formed by Jebel Hassání, on the parallel of an island similarly named. The eastern frontier is still un-

* In the wild book written by the Abbé Guénée to confute the errors of the noble Frenchman who created religious liberty in France, we find (part iii. let. 1, § 6) that Voltaire believed Midian to be a " Canton of Idumæa in Arabia Petræa, beginning north with the Arnon torrent, and ending south with the torrent Zared, lying amid the rocks, and on the eastern shore of Lake Asphaltitis, and thus about eight leagues long by a little less of breadth: it is held by a small horde of Arabs." Elsewhere he owns that "the sandy region of Midian may have contained some villages." But, as the Abbé, or rather his Hebrew friends, pertinently ask, "Who shows that the southern boundary was the Zared?" The "brook Zered," which parted Mo'ab from Edom, and which limited the thirty-eight years' wanderings (Deut. ii. 14), is a Wady falling into the south-eastern corner of the Dead Sea. Robinson (ii. 555) identifies it with El-Ahry (El-Ahsa?), still separating the districts of El-Jibál and El-Kerak. Professor Palmer says (p. 524), " The brook (Wady) Zared may either be Seil Garahi, or Wády 'Ain Feranji, South of Kerak : *Zared* signifies ' willow,' and corresponds to the Arabic *Sufsáfeh*, the name given to a small Wády which unites with the last of the two valleys mentioned."

explored, and we heard of ruins far in the interior. The business of the next winter will be to trace the auriferous and argentiferous deposits to their sources in the north and east. Westward it abuts upon the Elanitic recess of the Red Sea; but in modern parlance it does not extend to the opposite coast, the Sinaitic Peninsula, where the old Midianites undoubtedly dwelt. As Bedawin, they would wander far and wide. The name of their habitat would be vague, and its area would extend or shrink according to their numbers, and to the resisting power of their neighbours.

Hence the general remark of modern geographers is true, namely, that it is difficult to lay down the precise frontiers of Midian.* Hence, too, as Rabbi Joseph Schwarz remarks (p. 173), we find Midianite hordes about Gaza (Judg. vi. 4); in Moab (Numb. xxv. 6); in the Amorite land (Josh. xiii. 21), and in Edom, especially about Rekun (Petra).† But there is no reason for the various emendations introduced by the translators and mappers of Josephus, who are determined to have two Midians. He declares (Antiq. ii. 11) that "Moses, when

---

* Munk (p. 111, *Palestina*, Ital. transl.; Venice, 1853) opines that the Biblical writers do not determine the Midianite country, but that the mediæval Arab geographers are more satisfactory.

† The same may be said of the kinsmen of the Keni, or Kenites (Judg. iv. 11; 1 Chron. ii. 55; 2 Kings, x. 9), the descendants of Jethro, also called Bene Rechob and Shalmaii (Onkelos and Jonathan in Numb. xxiv. 12).

flying, came to Madian City on the shores of the Red Sea, taking its name from Mídan, son of Abraham." But he does not make the people distinct from the Madianite who occupied the country east of the Sinus Asphaltites, and south-east of the tribe of Reuben.*

Midian country and city thus had, and still have, the same name, a common practice in this part of the East; witness " El-Shám," Syria and Damascus, and " El-Misr" (*Masr*), Egypt and Cairo. It is palpably derived from its own tongue, meaning in Hebrew, strife, contention, a litigious people, or a race struggling for the possession of a country equally coveted by Asiatics and Africans (Egypt).†

" Midian" and " Madyan" are represented by " Mádi," a word occurring in many hieroglyphic texts; the plural would be Mádí-án or Mádí-ná, and the term is barbarous and unmeaning. Thus the land would adjoin *Pitshu*, not Pit-shu (Petræa), of the *Shasu* (Hyksos; Brugsch, *Geschichte*), and Aduma, Edom, Idumæa (Brugsch, *Hist. d'Egypte*, p. 146). The primitive Troglodytes, whose memory is preserved in Josephus (*loc. cit.*), were probably ousted by the Rubu or Arab races typified by the descendants of Esau; and the new-comers did not change the old names.

* On this subject, see chap. xii.
† This is the interpretation of the learned Hebraist, Professor Vita Zelman, of Trieste.

Hence an inscription of Rameses III. says, "I made destruction of the Sa'ar of the tribes of the Shasu;" where Sa'ar would be correspondent with the Hebrew Mount (Seir), and the *Shasu* with the Bedawin inhabiting Aduma. It is not to be confounded with *Pun* or *Ta-heter*,* the region of the Gods, the "Holy Land" which sent forth Osiris and Isis; the country bordering upon the mouth of the Red Sea, both in Asia and Africa, which older students referred to the Sinaitic Peninsula, and which, according to Professor Leo Reinisch, "belonged to Egypt as early as the sixth dynasty, and supplied her with the noble metals."

"Midian" is quite ignored by the classical authors of Greece and Rome; although it frequently occurs in the sacred books of the Hebrews, and in the Talmud and Rabbinical writings, and finally reappears under the form "Madyan" in the mediæval Arab geographers, and in the language of the present possessors.

Although the classical writers never adopted the

* "Ta-heter," however, is a disputed term. Some apply it to Phœnicia; and others (Chwolson, p. 186, and De Rougé) to Babylonia. The same is the case with "Pun." Brugsch contends that it means (Southern) Arabia. Mariette has lately made wild work with the old definition of "Pun or Pouno, bordering upon Tohoutes or the Holy Land." According to him, it is not Yemen but Somali-land, fronted by Socotra, the "divine ground," because Osiris was there born. From Pun he would derive Punici, Pæni, Phœnicians, who had nothing to do but to cross the Red Sea and, as Herodotus tells us, to march northwards into Syria.

word Midian, they have left ample notices of the Midianite region, or, as they called it, Nabathæa and Nabatæa. The first, and not the least satisfactory, is Agatharkides of Cnidos* (B.C. 130), whose description of the Erythrean Sea has been preserved by the Sicilian of whom Pliny said, *Primus apud græcos desiit nugare Diodorus*, and by Photius, the literary patriarch.

Cap. 87. "Touching this place," says the guardian of the young Ptolemy, "is a place which men called Nessa,† or of seals, from the abundance of those animals; and this Nessa lies near a promontory (Ras Mohammed ?) eminently well wooded.‡ Thence a straight line extends (northwards ?) to the (city) called Petra, and to Palaisténa; whither the Gerrhaioi and the Minaioi,§ and all the Arabs

* Pp. 177–181, "Geog. Gr. Minores." Müller, Paris, 1855.

† Rüppell (*Reise*, p. 187) says that the Halicore, often caught in the waters of the gulf, is called by the people *Nákat el-bahr*, or "She-Camel of the Sea." As Νῆσσα means Anas, a duck, the words "or of seals," may be an interpretation.

‡ Possibly in those days the bluff called by the Arabs Ras Mohammed may have been an islet. It is now bare as a bone, but I have suggested (chap. x.) that the comparatively luxuriant vegetation about Beersheba, with its Malvaceæ, Chrysanthemums, Amaryllids, and Lotus Arabicus, and its rich thick carpet of various grasses, Fistula, Stipa and Ægilops, may once have extended as far south as the now arid and thorny regions around El-Akabah.

§ The Gerrhæi owned " El-Jara'á " (pronounced Gera'á), meaning "a bald place where earth grows nothing." Their chief town was in or near the Persian Gulf (Erythrean Sea) commanding the region now called Hasá, El-Hasá or Lahsá, and well known to

dwelling in the neighbourhood, bring from the upper country frankincense, it is said, and bundles of fragrant things."

Cap. 88. "After the Gulf Laianítes (El-Akabah), around which dwell the (Nabathæan ?) Arabs, is the land of the Buthemánes,* which is spacious and level, well-watered, and deep : nothing, however, is there cultivated but *medica* (lucerne, clover, Pliny xvi. 43), and herb-*lotus* (melilotus, Plin. xxi. 63), which attain the stature of a man. By reason of these growths there are many wild camels (?) ; many troops of stags and antelopes (*A. dorcas ?*) ; also many flocks of sheep, and infinite herds of cattle and mules. Upon these gifts of fortune attends the nuisance that the earth breeds numbers of lions,

---

modern travel. The Minæi were the *gens magna* of the classics, the great trading-race, settled to the south-west of the Gerrhæi ; and their capital, Karn el-Manázil, lay east-north-east of Meccah, which also belonged to them. For an exhaustive description of the "Minæan Confederation," under the Kindá dynasty, see Sprenger (*loc. cit.* pp. 212–220), and his excellent note appended to the little map of my Pilgrimage-route (Tauchnitz Edit., vol. iii. 169).

* The "Thimanei" of Pliny (vi. 32), who follow the Nabatæi : they are possibly the Bene Teman of Scripture. Müller ("G. G. Min." p. 179) appears to accept Ritter's opinion that the modern Hutaymi preserve the name. Sprenger (p. 9) makes Teman ("that which is on the right hand or south") synonymous with El-Yemen, and "Benú Temán" to mean Southerns, because dwelling in Southern Idumæa. These sons of Eliphaz (Gen. xxxi. 11–15) are opposed in Ezekiel (xxv. 13) to "Dedan" on the Persian Gulf; and Baruch (iii. 22) notices them as merchants.

wolves, and pards; and, thus, that which makes the happiness of the land, causes unhappiness to its inhabitants."*

Cap. 89. "From the nearest shores there is a gulf which runs inland to a depth of at least 500 stadia.† Those who live about it are called the Batmizomaneís; and they are hunters of wild beasts."

Cap. 90. "Beyond this region are three islands forming many ports. The first is sacred to Isis, whilst the second and third are called Soukabuá (Sucabya) and Saludó (Salydo). All are uninhabited, and are shaded by the olive-trees which grow in these parts, and which do not resemble ours." ‡

Cap. 91. "These islands being passed, stretches a long and stony shore, the land of the Thamondéni § Arabs. For 1000 stadia (*i.e.*, from El-Muwayláh to El-Wjih) the coast is here most troublesome to navigators, for there is no safe port, nor

* He is one of your moralizing travellers, rich in truisms; and his Italian translation and annotator emulates him with the old saw—*Nihil est ab omni parte beatum.*

† In Ptolemy 500 stadia = 1° of latitude : here the degree is probably 600. Measured from the eastern jamb of the Akabah Gate, the bottom of Aynúnah Bay may be recessed forty miles, but not more. The Batmizomeneís are the Banizomenes of Diodorus. (See chap. v.)

‡ All the islets, except Umm Maksúr, are now quite bare. For a synopsis of their names, see chap. xii.

§ Evidently the Tamúd of Arab genealogists (see chap. x.) The eastern shore to the south is very foul with shoals and reefs.

anchorage-station, nor bay of refuge, nor artificial mole which may shelter the mariner in his need."

The author, who has now passed southwards of Midian, describes the gold sands of the Débai (Debæ) * region; and the nuggets of the country held by the Alilaíoi (Abilæi), and the Kasandreís (or Gasandenses, the Beni Ghassán). Finally, he reaches the Kárbai (Carbæ of Upper Khaulán) and the Sabaío (Sabæi) of El-Yemen.

Diodorus (iii. 42–44) preserves other details from Agatharkides; such as the massacre of the Maraníta by the Garindaneís (Garindanenses) whilst the former were offering their septennial Camel-hecatomb to the Gods of the Grove. He also mentions that the devotees carried some healing water from the fount, exactly as pilgrims now preserve the waters of Jordan, Zem-Zem and Lourdes. He warns navigators that there are few ports upon this shore of North-Western Arabia, on account of the impinging of high mountains, which, adorned with a variety of colours, afford a splendid spectacle to the voyager.† "Passing onwards, you enter the Laianítes (Læanatic) Gulf, bordered by many villages of the Arabs, whom they call Nabataíoi. These men not only occupy a great part of the

* This tribal name is generally derived from the Arabic "Dahab," gold. For other particulars concerning the metal-working tribes, see chap. ix.

† How true this is may be judged from my chap. v.

littoral, they also stretch far into the interior, for the region is populous and very pecorous. Formerly they lived according to the rules of justice, satisfying themselves with their flocks and herds ; but when the Alexandrian kings had made the Gulf navigable for traders, they maltreated shipwrecked sailors, and, moreover, equipping light piratical vessels,* they pillaged navigators, emulating the ferocious and nefarious customs of the tribes dwelling in Pontic Taurus. At last, they were attacked on the high seas by the Quadriremes ; and they received well-deserved punishment." After describing the rich plains of medica and lotus, the abundance of game (including wild camels), and the savage beasts, Diodorus passes on to the " bay of paradoxical nature,"—the harmless and respectable Aynúnah—to which he adds peculiar horrors.† Lastly, after the tract of wild coast, he lands us among the Debæ, the Alilai, and the Gasandeis, where the pure gold (χρυσὸς ἄπυρος) does not require fusing.

Strabo (xvi. 4, § 18), who evidently borrows from

---

* Λῃστρικὰ σκάφη, probably of the species of the Sanbúk. The latter is thus mentioned by Ibn Batutah (see p. 35), who ended his wanderings in A.D. 1353. "I then went on board a Sanbúk, which is a small *boat*" (read "craft"). Hence, possibly, the harp called Σαμβύλη by the Greeks, and the *Sambuca*, a kind of trumpet used by the Roman armies : Bochart, Vossius and others, however, find the "Sambýke" in סבכא (Sabeca, a harp) of the Book of Daniel (iii. 5, 7, 9).

† I have translated his account in chap. v.

the same sources, notices the Ælanitic Gulf and Nabatæa,* a thickly inhabited country ; he tells us the tale of the pirates, making them use rafts,† and, further south, opposite the well-wooded plain, he places the island Dia (Tírán ?) It is followed by three desert islands, a stony beach, a rugged coast, and the "paradoxical bay," none of whose fancied horrors have been spared.

Every reader of the Torah, and of Josephus's " Targum," knows that Abraham, after Sarah's death (*cir.* B.C. 1860), had by Keturah the " bound one "‡ (Gen. xxv. 1) several sons, the fourth being Midián (מִדְיָן) or Medán (מְדָן).§ The latter, again, became the sire of five : Ephah, Hefer ('Efer) Hanoch (Hanúkh), Abidah, and Eldaah,‖ who in Hebrew tradition represent the progenitors of the Midianites and their Pentarchy.

* Strabo's interesting details concerning the Nabathæan kings will be found in chap. viii.

† Probably meaning the *Kelete*, or inflated skins, which are supposed to have named the Arabian "Askitai" (Ascitæ), and which are still used upon the Euphrates.

‡ Sprenger (p. 295) has "Söhne der Qetûra, d. h. des Räucherwerkes" (of frankincense-working).

§ The LXX. prefers Μαδὰλ, Μαδάν, and Μαδιὰμ, the latter resembling the Μαδιάμα town of Ptolemy (vi. 7, § 27) ; whilst the Hebrew "monument" suggests that the latter "a" was pronounced long = Midián. In the Palestine Targum (Jonathan), the word is written Midyan.

‖ The variants are Eipher, Epher, Hanok, Abida and Aldaah (Pal. Targum) and Eipha, Ephir, Hanok, Abidah and Eldaah (Onkelos).

The country must have been occupied much as it is now in B.C. 1491, when Moses, the meekest of men, having slain an Egyptian—a " rash act," says a modern traveller—fled to the Eastern Desert, probably because all the civilised roads were closed to him. Approaching Midian city about noon, he sat down near a well where the seven virgin daughters (the Moslems say two) of the local Rabba, or priest, Raguel,* whose cognomen was Yetro (Jethro), being in charge of the flocks, as was the custom of the Arab Troglodytes, came to give them drink.† They were driven away by the shepherds, who wanted the water, and they were defended from insult by the future Lawgiver. The girls told the tale to their father; the Priest-prince sent them to bring the stranger, adopted him as a son, and, on condition of his doing service for eight to ten years, gave him to wife Zipporah, whom the Arabs call Saffúrah, and believe to have been the eldest. This connection subsequently gave offence to Moses' kinsfolk (Numb. xii. 1) because she was a " Kúshiyat." ‡ By her he

* "Raguel," or rather Rhagouel ('Ραγουηλ) in LXX.; Ruel in A.V. (Exod. ii. 18); Hobab (in Judg. iv. 11, and perhaps in Numb. x. 29) had, according to Josephus, " Iothor for a surname." The Moslems are also as abundant in nomenclature.

† The tradition of the "well of Jethro's daughters," from which " Moses watered the flocks of Shu'ayb," was preserved by the mediæval Arab geographers, but apparently it has died out amongst the Maknáwi, or modern Midianites.

‡ A Cushite (Kushite), not "an Ethiopian." The old fashion was to translate " Kush " by *Æthiopia super Egyptum*, the Nubia

had two sons, Gersham, "a stranger there," and Eliezer, or "El (God) is my help." Moses was placed in charge of the flocks, one of the sources of patriarchal wealth; and the Vision of the Burning Bush (Exod. iii.) happened when he led them "to the backside of the Desert,* and came to Horeb." Here, then, we see that the Hebrews extended Midian over the Sinaitic Peninsula, a tradition preserved during many years. In the Antonine Itinerary, finished *circa* A.D. 180, the town of Pharan is part of Midian. Antoninus Martyr † (Itin. cap. xl.) says of the same place *ipsa terra est Midianitarum, et habitantes in ipsâ civitate : dicitur quia ex familia*

and the Abyssinia of the present day. In Habbakuk (iii. 7) "Cushan," the country, is evidently an equivalent of Midian in the same verse, possibly a more general term.

* The Heb. words are אחר המדבר (Akhar ha-Midbar) which Dr. Beke (Orig. Bib. i. 193) would render "West of the Desert;" Calmet (*s.v.* East). "The Hebrews express east, west, north, and south, by before, behind, right and left, according to the situation of a man whose face is turned to the rising sun:" this undoubtedly favours his theory that Yamm Suph (the Sea of the Sedge) invariably applies to the Akabah, not to the Suez Gulf. The LXX. has ὑπὸ τὴν ἔρημον; and the Vulg. *ad interiora deserti.* The Targ. Pal. says, "He (Mosheh) led his flock to a pleasant place of pasturage, which is behind the desert; and came to the mountain on which was revealed the glory of the Lord, even Horeb." The Targ. Onk. : "He led his flock to a place of the best pastures of the wilderness," etc.

† See Tuch, *Antonius Martyr, Seine Zeit und Seine Pilgerfahrt nach dem Morgenlande* (Leipzig, 1864, 4° p. 37); also *De locis Sanctis quæ perambulavit Antoninus Martyr, mit Bemerkungen; herausgegeben Von T. T. Tobler*, 1863; quoted in App. to Professor Palmer's "Desert of the Exodus."

Jethro soceri Moysis descendant (*i.e.*, the eighty serfs and their households). Eusebius (*ob. circ.* A.D. 340) assigns "Rephidim," where the Amalekites were defeated (Exod. xvii. 1), and Horeb to Pharan, and the "Har ha-Elohim," (Mount of God, *ibid.* xviii. 5) to the Land of Midian.* But, as Dr. Richard Lepsius remarks,† "although Moses lived with Jethro in Midian, this fact offers no ground to place the Mount of the Law in Midian, for that is nowhere said." Finally, Burchard or Brocardus, the Dominican, in A.D. 1232,‡ speaks of the *Gens Midianitarum, qui nunc Beduini et Turonioni* (*i.e.*, from Tor) *dicuntur*.

The Talmud of Babylon, I am informed by the Vicar Rabbi Moïse Tedschi, of Trieste, hints as follows at the existence of a Midianite army in

* S.vv. Ῥαφιδίμ and χωρήβ. His words are Τόπος τῆς ἐρήμου παρὰ τὸ χωρήβ ὄρος, ἐν ᾧ ἐκ τῆς πέτρας ἐῤῥύησε τὰ ὕδατα, καὶ ἐκλήθη ὁ τόπος Πειρασμός (Heb. Massah = temptation) ἔνθ καὶ πολεμεῖ Ἰησοῦς τὸν Ἀμαλὴκ ἐγγὺς φαράν—" Pharan " the φαρὰ of Ptolemy (v. 17, § 3), an inland settlement, possibly took its name from the "Wilderness of Paran" (Numb. x. 12); and the same was the case with the Episcopal City of Fírán, where the famous bishop, Theodorus, smote the Monothelites; with the Oratorium and the Monastery Dayr Fárán, *alias* Segilla. Professor Palmer (p. 510) would extend the name "Wilderness of Paran" to the whole northern desert, El-Tíh, of which Mount Paran is the southernmost plateau.

† "Letters from Egypt," appendix, p. 546; Bohn's trans. London, 1853. Professor Palmer (p. 5) holds that "Exodus iii. 12, seems to leave no doubt that the Mountain of the Law and the Mountain of the Burning Bush are the same."

‡ Locorr. Ter. S. descriptio fol. p. 324.

Egypt: *—" Three of them were called (by Pharaoh to) Council. Balaam advised the drowning (of the new-born males); and paid for it with his life (Numb. xxxi. 5). Ayyub (Job)† was neither for nor against, and was covered with sores from head to foot. Yetro (Jethro) opposed it, and, when his advice was rejected, gave up his post and fled; for which reason his posterity became members of the Sanhedrim."

In the so-called Middle Ages, a curious Rabbinical and philological dispute ‡ arose concerning the flight of Moses. Maimonides, the Jew who taught Christians to read revelation by the light of reason, determined that Midian was distant from Egypt. He thus understood from the words וישב, (Va-

---

* Treatises Sofà fol. 11 a., and Sanhedrim 106 a.

† Sig. Tedeschi has lately published a short work, arguing that the Book of Job (meaning the "persecuted one") was written by an Arab, not, as the vulgar opinion was, by Moses. In the Satan of this work he finds an idea quite distinct from the same personage in Numb. xxii. 22, and in Zach. iii. 1–2, and, he believes, in direct derivaticn from Persian Dualism, during the Babylonian captivity, and the early days of the Second Temple. He observes that the prosaic part imitates the Pentateuch, and the poetic is formed upon the Psalms, the Proverbs, Jeremiah, etc.

‡ This controversy was brought to my notice by Dr. Gabrielle Pereyra, Archiviste of the Institut. Égyptien. That diligent student finds "Va-yesheb" rendered ῴκησεν in the LXX.; *moratus est* by the Vulg.; *andò a stare* by Martini; *si fermò* by Diodati; *andò ad abitare* by Professor Luzzato; *wohnete* in the German version; *s'arrêta* in Professor Cahen's French version; and *dwelt* in the Authorized Version.

Yesheb), which he proposes to translate "and he rested himself" (*i.e.*, after a long journey). Ben Esdra, on the other hand, maintains that Midian lay near Egypt.

We are now able to lay down with some exactitude the limits of the Greater Midian in the widest sense of the word. It was bounded west by the Suez-Gulf; east by the Bedawi tribes, called the Ishmaelites, the Keturites, and many other names; and south by the mountain-block forming modern El-Hejaz. But I must wholly object to Professor Palmer's theory (p. 527), which would "identify Midian with the extensive ruins of El Midáyen,* a Station on the Darb el-Hajj, between Damascus and Mecca, three days' distance from the latter town," and then extending deep into modern El-Hejaz. For reasons before given, the northern frontier was ever vague and uncertain. It extended far when the Shaykh or King of Edom, Hadad ben Bedad, "smote Midian in the field of Moab" (Gen. xxxvi. 35). Moreover, after the Exodus we find the upper limit "on this side Jordan by Jericho (Numb. xxii. 1–4). Thus the boundary then stretched to and even north of the River Arnon (Wady Mojib), the great chasm which, still splitting Moab

---

* The verbal resemblance is merely superficial, Madáin being the plural of Madináh, a city, and thus applied to Mandain or Ctesiphon.

in two, falls into the mid-eastern shore of the Dead Sea.*

The country is described by Jewish writers as hot, sandy, and in places desert: despite which it abounded in sheep, goats, deer (gazelles?), and especially in the camels, which were needed by caravans—for instance, that which passed through Sichem (Gen. xxxviii. 28), carrying merchandise between Gilead and Egypt. M. J. Salvador † declares that "The many sons of Abraham by Keturah and his other wives became *Letoukhim* (metal-workers), *Assourim* (merchants), and *Leoumim* (heads of tribes and people): among the latter was reckoned Midian, the nation occupying the eastern shores of the Red Sea." ‡ As was proved by the Khedivial Expedition, Midian contained a large settled and industrial population, as well as a nomad race.

During the wanderings of the children of Israel, when Moses was training a family of slaves to become a nation of warriors and conquerors, and especially throughout the "Encampment by the Red Sea," the Midianites, probably through fear of the

---

* Josephus, Philo and Calmet, *s.v.* ; also Reland, iii. p. 98. This northern extension of Midian probably gave rise to the separation of the Land of the Keturites, "The East Country," and the Land of Midian ; the former being a part of the whole.

† *Hist. des Institutions de Moïse*, Bruxelles, Hanman, iii. chap. 3.

‡ Cf. St. Jerome, " Questions on Genesis."

multitudes occupying their pastures, became hostile to the distant kinsmen. The tribe was then apparently a Pentarchy under five kings, or Shaykhs,* and according to Josephus (Antiq. iv. 7, § 1), the second, Recem, or Rekem, gave a name to the "most conspicuous city among the Arabs, called to our day under every King, Arecema (Arekema = El-Rekem), and by the Greeks, Petra."† Professor Vita Zelman, of Trieste, holds that the tribe was ruled by ancients, meaning that it was a kind of republic with chiefs, after the fashion of the Arabs. The Midianites joined the Moabites, their relations and northern neighbours, in opposing the "people come out of Egypt" (Numb. xxii. 5); and their elders, "with the rewards of divination in their hands" (*ibid.* 7), went to Balaam, in order that he might "curse Jacob and defy Israel." According to the Talmud, many of the seniors refused to join in this proceeding, pleading impotence after the wondrous works of Jethro's son-in-law. The Prophet advised the Midianites to send their daughters splendidly dressed, to offer the Hebrew camp the seducing

* See Numb. xxxi. 8, quoted below.
† This "chief city and capital of all Arabia" is called in Hebrew (2 Kings xiv. 7, and xvi. 1) "Ha-Sela' *the* Cliff, from Sela' or Selah, in Arabic Sila', a mountain cleft. Its importance and celebrity justifies the suspicion that "*Petræa*" may originally have meant not the Stony, but belonging to Petra. The Arabia Sterilis of Pliny (v. 13) *non nisi Monte Casio nobilis*, is the Long Desert of modern travel, between Egypt and Syria.

worship of Baal-peor (Belphegor). This agrees with Strabo, who makes the Nabathæans adore the sun.* Josephus (Wars iv. 6) gives a long and detailed account of the manner in which the work of perversion was carried out. The peculiar "honours of hospitality," alluded to by the fair women, are still not unknown to certain of the Arab tribes;† and in Central Africa this guest-rite was, if it is not now, the general rule. When the wanderers halted at Shittim (*ibid.* xxv. 1.) a plague fell upon them, because they had bowed down to strange gods, and had taken to themselves stranger-wives. It was stayed by the simple expedient of a massacre. The death of Zimri, the Simeonite Chief, is especially mentioned, possibly because he openly called Moses a tyrant, who had deprived men of the "Sweetness of Life—Liberty." He was found cohabiting with a "Midianitish woman," Kozbi, the daughter of the Shaykh Súr (Zúr); and both transgressors were slain by the youthful Phinehas, son of Eleazar, the priest.

---

* See chap. viii.

† Sprenger (pp. 40 and 97), following Burckhardt, remarks this absence of natural jealousy amongst the clans living inland of Dahabán in Southern Arabia. The Arabs of "Tzafâr" (Dofar or Zafar in Hadramaut), who are of old descent, probably preserved the custom from their pagan forefathers. The Merákash, Himyari Bedawin, east of Aden, are also notorious for the loose morality of their women; the sale of wives is not unknown, and men often take the matronymic, as "Abdullah bin Fátimeh." See Zehme (p. 50) of the Murakkid (tribe) *d. h. der schlafen lässt.*

Thereupon the fatal commands to Moses went forth, "Avenge the Lord on Midian : vex the Midianites and smite them!" and thus began the first Midianite War (B.C. 1452), whose horrors cannot better be told than in the dreadful language of the original (Num. xxxi.) :—

And Yahveh (Jehovah) commanded Mosheh (Moses), saying,

Avenge with vengeance the Bene-Israél upon the Midianyím (Midianites) ; afterwards shalt thou be gathered unto thy people.

And Moses commanded the people, saying, Ho! Arm some of your men unto the war, and let them go against Midian, and avenge Yahveh upon Midian.

A thousand from this tribe, a thousand from that, throughout all the tribes of Israél, shall ye send to the war.

So there were gathered out of the thousands of Israél, a thousand from every tribe, twelve thousand armed for war.

And Moses sent them to the war, a thousand of every tribe,* them and Fíniha̋s (Phínehas) ben Ele'azar the Kohen (priest), to the war, with the holy instruments and the trumpets to blow (he gave) into his hand.

And they warred against Midian, as Yahveh commanded Moses; and they slew all the males.

And the Kings of Midian they slew, over and above the rest that were slain ; namely, Evi, and Rekem, and Súr (Zúr), and Húr, and Reba', five kings of Midian : also Bala'am ben Be'or they slew with the sword.

And the Bene-Israél took as spoil all the women of Midian captives, and their little ones, and all their cattle, and all their flocks and all their goods.

And all their cities wherein they dwelt, and all their goodly castles, they burnt with fire.

---

* So small a force as 12,000 men would suggest that only a part of the Midianitic region near the Dead Sea was attacked; possibly a race not subject to Jethro, the Theist (Exod. xviii.), and certainly worshippers of Baal-peor, or Belphegor, like their neighbours of Moab.

And they seized all the spoil and all the prey, both of men and of beasts.

And they brought the spoil, the captives, and the prey unto Moses and Ele'azar the priest, and unto the congregation of the Bene-Israel, unto the camp at the Araboth (plains) of Moab, which are by Yardan (Jordan) near Yeriko (Jericho).

And went forth Moses and Ele'azar the priest, and all the princes of the congregation, to meet them without the camp.

And wroth was Moses with the officers of the host, with the captains over thousands, and captains over hundreds, which came from the battle.

And Moses commanded unto them, Why have ye saved all the women alive?

Behold, these caused the Bene-Israel, through the counsel of Bala'am, to commit trespass against Yahveh in the matter of Pe'ur (Peor), and there was a plague among the congregation of Yahveh.

Now therefore slay every male among the little ones, and every woman that hath known man slay ye!

But all the women children, that have not known a man, keep alive for yourselves.

And abide ye without the camp seven days : whosoever hath killed any person, and whosoever hath touched any slain, purify on the third day, and on the seventh day, both yourselves and your captives.

And all your raiment, and all vessels made of skins, and all work of goat's hair, and all vessels made of wood, purify ye!

And Ele'azar the priest commanded unto the men of war which went to the battle, This is the ordinance of the Torah (law) which Yahveh enjoined Moses;

Only the gold, and the silver, the copper, the iron, the tin, and the lead,

Everything that may endure the fire, ye shall pass through the fire, and it shall be clean : nevertheless with the water of separation it shall be purified : and all that endureth not the fire ye shall pass through the water.

And your clothes on the seventh day ye shall wash, and ye shall be clean, and afterwards ye shall come into the camp.

And Yahveh commanded to Moses this command,

Take the capital-sum of the prey that was taken, both of man and of beast, thou, and Elea'zar the priest, and the head fathers of the congregation :

And divide the prey into two parts : between them that took the war upon them, who went out to battle, and between all the congregation.

And levy a tribute unto Yahveh of the men of war which went out to battle : one soul of five hundreds, both of the persons, and of the beeves, and of the asses and of the sheep :

Of their half take it, and give it unto Ele'azar the priest, for an heave-offering of Yahveh.

And of the Bene-Isráel's half, thou shalt take one portion of fifty, of the persons, of the beeves, of the asses, and of the sheep, of all manner of beasts, and give them unto the Leviyyím (Levites), which keep the charge of the tabernacle of Yahveh.

And Moses and Ele'azar the priest, did as Yahveh had enjoined Moses.

And the booty, being the rest of the prey which the men of war had caught, was of sheep six hundred thousand and seventy thousand and five thousand,*

And of beeves three score and twelve thousand,

And of asses three score and one thousand,†

And of persons thirty and two thousand in all, of women that had not known man.

And the half, which was the portion of them that went out to war, was in number of sheep three hundred thousand and seven and thirty thousand and five hundred;

And Yahveh's tribute of the sheep was six hundred and three score and fifteen.

---

* Horses and mules, found in the classical authors, are not mentioned here : the sheep are, as now, the more numerous; the goats do not appear, and the ass was used then as at present. The pastures must have been far better in ancient days; the modern land would never carry 72,000 head of flock cattle.

† As has been shown, Voltaire (Polit. and Legist. vol. xxx.), found the number excessive; but he had unduly contracted the limits of Midian. As regards the tribe, 32,000 × 2 (males of the same age) = 64,000 × 2 (the adults and old) = 128,000; a total not too large to be defeated by 12,000 men.

And the beeves were thirty and six thousand; of which Yahveh's tribute was three score and twelve.

And the asses were thirty thousand and five hundred; of which Yahveh's tribute was three score and one.

And the persons were sixteen thousand; of which Yahveh's tribute was thirty and two persons.

And Moses gave the tribute, which was Yahveh's heave-offering, unto Ele'azar the priest, as Yahveh had enjoined Moses.

And of the Bene-Isráel's half, which Moses divided from the men that warred

(Now the half that pertained unto the congregation was of sheep three hundred thousand and thirty thousand and seven thousand and five hundred,

And of beeves thirty and six thousand,

And of asses thirty thousand and five hundred,

And of persons sixteen thousand),

Even Moses took of the Bene-Isráel's half, one portion of fifty, both of man and of beast, and gave them unto the Levíyyím (Levites), which kept the charge of the tabernacle of Yahveh; as Yahveh had enjoined Moses.

And came near unto Moses the officers which were over thousands of the host, the captains of thousands, and captains of hundreds:

And they said unto Moses, Thy slaves have taken the capital-sum of the men of war which are under our charge, and there lacketh not one man of us.

We have therefore brought a Kurbán (oblation) for Yahveh, what every man hath gotten, vessels of gold, chains and bracelets, rings, ear-rings, and tablets, to make an atonement for ourselves before the face of Yahveh.

And Moses and Ele'azar the priest took the gold of them, even all wrought vessels.

And all the gold of the offering that they offered up to Yahveh was sixteen thousand seven hundred and fifty shekels,* of the captains of thousands, and of the captains of hundreds.

---

* The gold shekel is here evidently a weight. These passages suggest that the Midianites had metal-smiths amongst them, and, if so, they would have all other known handicrafts. The silver shekel which Luther translates "Silberling" was worth about 1s. 6d.

(For the men of war had taken spoil, every man for himself.)
And Moses and Ele'azar the priest took the gold from the captains of thousands and of hundreds, and brought it into the tabernacle of the congregation as a memorial for the Bene-Isráel before the face of Yahveh.

It is long before an Arab tribe can recover from such a blow. We may fairly believe, however, that when all the males were slain on the northern frontier, the nomad families in Sinai and elsewhere escaped. After a lapse of two centuries the Midianites again grew powerful ; and their oppression of the Israelites, or rather their revenge upon their terrible kinsmen, ended in the second Midianitic war (B. C. 1249). I propose to borrow, from the picturesque pages of Dean Stanley,* a description of this tragedy, which, in Hebrew Writ, ranks with the drowning of the Egyptians and the destruction of Sennacherib's host.†

"The next battle was of a very different kind, and one of which the present aspect of the plain (Esdraëlon) can give a clearer image. No one in present days has passed this plain without seeing or hearing of the assaults of the Bedouin Arabs, as they stream in from the adjacent Desert. Here and there by the well-side, or amongst the bushes of the mountains, their tents or their wild figures may always be seen, the terror alike of the peaceful villager and the defenceless traveller. What we now see on a small scale constantly is but a miniature representation of the one great visitation which lived for ages afterwards in the memory of the Jewish people ; the invasion, not of the

---

* Chap. ix. pp. 340-43, "Sinai and Palestine." London : Murray, 1873. The author's notes are marked S. ; mine are unsigned.
† Judges, vi.-viii.

civilised nations of Assyria or Egypt, or of the Canaanite cities, but of the wild population of the Desert itself, 'the Midianites, the Amalekites, and the Children of the East.'* They came up with all the accompaniments of Bedouin life, 'with their cattle, their tents, and their camels;' they came up and 'encamped' against the Israelites after 'Israel had sown,' and 'destroyed the increase of the earth,' and all the cattle [in the maritime plain] 'till they came unto Gaza; as locusts for multitude, both they and their camels without number' (Judg. vi. 3, 4, 5). The very aspect and bearing of their Shaykhs is preserved to us. The two lesser chiefs (Sári, or 'princes,' as they are called in our version), in their names of Oreb † and Zeeb, 'the Raven' and 'the Wolf,' present curious counterparts of the title of the 'Leopard,' now given to their modern successor, Abd-el-Aziz, chief of the Bedouins beyond the Jordan. The two higher Shaykhs, or 'Kings,' (Melekai) Zebah and Zalmunna, are mounted on dromedaries, themselves gay with scarlet mantles, and crescent-ornaments and golden ear-rings (Judg. viii. 21–26); their dromedaries with ornaments and chains like themselves, and, as in outward appearance, so in the high spirit and lofty bearing which they showed at their last

---

* Judges vi. 3. Of another nomadic incursion at a later time few traces are left—that of the Scythians or Nomads of the North, in the reign of King Josiah, known only through the brief notice in Herodotus, and the allusions in the writings of Zephaniah and Jeremiah. One of these few traces, however, shows that they settled like their predecessors and successors in the plain of Esdraëlon. From thence, Bethshan, at the foot of Mount Gilboa, probably derived its Greek name of Scythopolis (Pliny, v. 18).—S.

The children of the East were the Benë-Kedem. Pliny's words are "Scythopolis, formerly called Nysa, from the nurse of Dionysius having been buried there, its present name being derived from the Scythian colony which was established there.

† Smith's Dictionary of the Bible (*s.v.* Midian) translates "Oreb" the "raven," or, more correctly, "crow." The word is etymologically the same as the Arabic Ghuráb, which, applied to a Bedawi chief, would certainly mean a raven. The word has passed into the Aryan languages, *e.g.*, the Latin *corvus*.

hour, they truly represented the Arabs who scour the same regions at the present day."

"Such an incursion produced on the Israelites amongst their ordinary wars, a similar impression to that of the invasion of the Huns amongst the comparatively civilised invasions of the Teutonic tribes. They fled into their mountain fastnesses and caves as the only refuge; the wheat even of the upland valleys of Manasseh had to be concealed from the rapacious plunderers (Judg. vi. 11). The whole country was thus for the first time in the hands of the Arabs. But it was in the plain of Esdraëlon that then, as now, the Children of the Desert fixed their head-quarters. In the valley of Jezreel (Judg. vi. 33), that is, in the central eastern branch of the plain, commanding the long descent of the Jordan, and thus to their own eastern deserts, 'they lay along all the valley like locusts for multitude,' and their 'camels'—unwonted sight in the pastures of Palestine—'were without number as sands by the seaside' on the wide margin of the Bay of Acre 'for multitude.' As in the invasion of Sisera, so now, the nearest tribes were those which were first moved by a sense of their common danger. To the noblest of the tribe of Manasseh—to one whose appearance was "as the son of a King,' and whose brothers, already ruthlessly slain by the wild invaders on the adjacent heights of Tabor, were 'each one like the Children of Kings'—was entrusted the charge of gathering together the forces of his countrymen.* All Manasseh was with him, and on the other side of the plain there came Zebulun and Naphtali, and even the reluctant Asher to join him (Judg. vi. 31). On the slope of Mount Gilboa the Israelites were encamped by a spring, possibly the same as that elsewhere (1 Sam. xxix. 1)† called 'the Spring of Jezreel,' but here, from the well-known trial by which Gideon tested the courage of the Army, called the 'Spring of Trembling.' " ‡

---

* The Dean of Westminster omits all mention of the Miracles of the Meat (Judg. vi. 19-21), and the sign of the Fleece (*ibid*, vi. 37-40).

† In the A.V. incorrectly a "fountain."—S.

‡ Judg. vii. 1. "The Spring" (mistranslated "well") "of Harod," that is of "trembling" in evident allusion to the repetition of the same word in verse 3, "Whoever is fearful and trembling." The

"On the northern side of the Valley, but apparently deeper down in the descent towards the Jordan,* by one of those slight eminences† which are characteristic of the whole plain, was spread the host of the Midianites. It was night, when from the mountain side, Gideon and his servant (Phurah) descended to the vast encampment.‡ All along the valley, within and around the

---

modern name of the spring is Ain Jalud, the 'Spring of Goliah.' This may perhaps originate, as Ritter observes, in a confused recollection of the Philistine battle in the time of David, but more probably arose from the false tradition current in the Sixth Century, that this was the scene of David's combat with Goliah (Ritter, "Jordan," p. 416). Schwartz (164) ingeniously conjectures that it is a reminiscence of an older name attaching to the whole mountain; and this explains the cry of Gideon (vii. 3), "Whoever is fearful and afraid, let him return and depart early from Mount Gilead." But we may suppose either that Gilead is there a corruption of (what in Hebrew strongly resembles it) "Gilboa;" or that it was the war-cry of Manasseh—eastern as well as western,—and that hence "Mount Gilead" was employed as a general phrase for the whole tribe (Ewald, *Geschichte*, 2nd edit. 11–500).—S.

Josephus (Ant. v. 6) explains the trial that those who bent down on their knees, and so drank, were men of courage, but all those that drank tumultuously did it out of fear of the enemy.

* Hence the expression "the host of Midian was beneath him in the valley" (Judg. vii. 8).—S.

† *Gibeah*, rightly translated "hill," as distinct from mountain (Judg. vii. 1).—S.

‡ It is evident from the sequel, and from the conversation with Zebah and Zalmunna (viii. 18), that Gideon understood the dialect of the Midianites, which, like Hebrew, was a rude northern branch of the great and polished Arabic family. Josephus, however (*ibid.*), speaks of the diversity of the language which caused many Midianites to fall by the swords of one another. The grammarian Yákútin El-Mu'ajam asserts that a Southern Arabian dialect is of Midian. Prof. Vita Zelman, judging from the names of the chiefs, holds the tongue to have been, like the Hebrew of the period, Assuric. During my flying visit I had hardly time to inquire whether the Maknáwi had preserved any expressions

tents, the thousands of Arabs lay* wrapped in sleep† or resting from their day's plunder, and their innumerable camels couched for the night in deep repose round about them. One of the sleepers, startled from his slumbers, was telling his dream to his fellows,—a characteristic and expressive dream for a Bedouin, even without its terrible interpretation, that a cake of barley bread‡ from those rich corn-fields, those numerous threshing-floors of the peaceful inhabitants whom they had conquered, rolled into the Camp of Midian, and struck a tent and overturned it, so that it lay along on the ground (Judg. vii. 13). Reassured by this good omen, Gideon returned for his three hundred trusty followers, the trumpets were blown, the torches blazed forth,§ the shout of Israel, always terrible, always like 'the shout of a King' (Num. xxiii. 21), broke through the stillness of the midnight air; and the sleepers sprang from their rest, and ran hither and thither with the dissonant 'cries' (Judg. vii. 21) so peculiar to the Arab race. 'And the Lord set every man's sword against his fellow, even through all the host;' and the host fled headlong down the

---

unfamiliar to the tribes around: they appeared to speak the half-Fellah and half-Bedawi tongue of their neighbours.

* Such is the force of the Hebrew word translated "lay" (Judg. vii. 12).—S.

† Gesenius has "encamped."

‡ "Such a barley cake as could hardly be eaten by man, it was so vile," explains Josephus (Ant. v. § 4): barley being held the vilest of grain, and the Israelites the "vilest of all the people of Asia."

§ Here we find no allusion to the most characteristic part of the attack, Gideon's night-surprise of the enemy by breaking the "empty pitchers and lamps within the pitchers," which were held in the warriors' left hands, the right grasping the ram's-horn trumpets. In Cairo, before the days of paper-lanterns, the police, when going their rounds, had for dark lanterns and bull's-eyes lighted torches in earthenware pots (Lane, vol. i. chap. 4). Josephus says (*ibid.*), "The enemy's camp took up a great space of ground; for they happened to have many camels: and as they (the Midianites) were divided into different nations, so they were all contained in one circle."

descent to the Jordan, to the spots known as the 'house of Acacia' (Beth-shittah) and the 'Margin' of the 'Meadow of the dance' (Abel-meholah, Judg. vii. 22). These spots were in the Jordan-valley, as their names indicate, under the mountains of Ephraim.* To the Ephraimites, therefore, messengers were sent to intercept the northern fords of the Jordan at Bethbarah.† There the second conflict took place, and Oreb and Zeeb were seized and put to the sword, the one on a rock, the other at a wine-press, on the spot where they were taken. The two higher Shaykhs, Zebah and Zalmunna, had already passed before the Ephraimites appeared; Gideon, therefore, who had now reached the fords from the scene of his former victory, pursued them into the eastern territory of his own tribe, Manasseh. The first village which he reached in the Jordan-valley was that which, from the 'booths' of Jacob's ancient encampment, bore the name of Succoth (Gen. xxxiii. 17) :‡ the next, higher up in the hills, with its lofty watch-tower, was that which, from the vision of the same patriarch, bore the name of Peniel, the 'Face of God.' Far up in the eastern Desert—among their own Bedouin countrymen 'dwelling in tents'—the host of Zebah and Zalmunna 'was secure,'§ when

---

* The "Acacia" (Shittah) is never found on the mountains; the "Meadow" (Abel) is peculiar to the streams of the Jordan. Abel-Meholah must have been close to the river, being named with Zartan or Zererath (1 Kings, vii. 46) and Bethshean. Abel primarily means to be wet like harvest grass, never applied to tree-grown lands and water-meadows, as is Abel-maim (of waters), Abel-Ceramum (of vineyard), etc., etc.—S.

† The LXX. reads Βαιθήρε. In chap. vii. p. 310, Beth-abara is rendered the "house of passage," from Abara (plur. Abaroth), a ford. The LXX. translates the latter Διάβασις as if it were a moving raft, and Josephus (Ant. VII. xi. 2) Γέφυρα as if it were a bridge, whilst the Authorized Version has "the ferry-boat."

‡ Soc, or Succah, (plur. Succoth), a booth or covert, from Sakek, to cover as with boughs, always the habitation of man or beast made of leafy boughs. The English Bible has "tabernacles," the Vulg. Tabernaculum, tentorium, umbraculum.—S.

These booths are the Mod. Arabic "Ushash" (chap. v.).

§ They had fallen back upon Karkor (Judg. viii. 10) with their 15,000 swordsmen who survived. Kark, according to Sprenger

Gideon burst upon them. Here a third victory completed the conquest. The two chiefs were caught and slain;* the tower of Peniel was razed; and the princes of Succoth were scourged with the thorny branches of the acacia-groves of their own valley (Judg. viii. 16).

"This success was, perhaps, the most signal ever obtained by the arms of Israel; at least, the one that lived most in the memory of the people. The 'spring' of Gideon's encampment, the rock and the winepress which witnessed the death of the two Midianite chiefs, were called after the names then received; and the Psalmist and the Prophets long afterwards referred with exultation to the fall of 'Oreb and Zeeb, of Zebah and Zalmunna, who said, Let us take to ourselves the pastures † of God in possession,—the breaking of 'the rod of the oppressor as in the day of Midian' (Isa. ix. 4). Gideon himself was by it raised to almost royal state, and the establishment of hereditary monarchy all but anticipated in him and his family."

We may add that the battle-cry, "The Sword of the Lord, and of Gideon," has been perpetuated by long generations, and has even added a horror of its own to the civil wars of Puritan England. After the ruthless destruction of "an hundred and twenty thousand men that drew sword," and

(p. 150), is the Kerake of Ptolemy, in N. lat. 30° 5': Karkar meaning a large smooth plain (plur. Karakir, often changed to Korakir, whence the Biblical Karkor); and Karkarah, a smaller feature. He distinguishes from the Idumæan Karak, the Karkeria of Eusebius.

* How proudly and heroically they died we are not told in "Sinai and Palestine;" we are in Judges (viii. 21), "Then (when Gideon's son, being a youth, feared to slay them) Zebah and Zalmunna said, Rise thou and fall upon us: for as the man, so his strength. And Gideon arose and slew Zebah and Zalmunna, and took away the ornaments that were on their camels' necks."

† Such is the more accurate translation, as well as the more vivid in the mouths of the nomad chiefs (Ps. lxxxiii. 12).—S.

fifteen thousand more,* the Midianites lifted up their heads no more. In fact, they fade out of Hebrew history, and serve only as references to the poets and the prophets.† To the explorers of the Mining Cities of Midian the most interesting part of the story is the quantity and variety of metals produced by the land—gold, silver, copper, tin, and lead‡ (Numb. xxxi. 22). Part of the booty taken by Moses and Gideon ("jewels of gold, chains and bracelets, rings, ear-rings and tablets" (*ibid.* 50); and golden ear-rings, weighing 1,700 shekels; together with ornaments, collars, purple raiment, and chains for the camels' necks) was doubtless made by trade. "Midianites merchantmen" (about B.C. 1729) drew Joseph out of the pit, and sold him for twenty pieces of silver to the " Ishmaelites " (Gen. xxxvii. 28), their kinsmen.§ But the discovery of the later

* Yet the squeamish sentimentalism of the present day shudders when it hears of 20,000 Russians or Turks being put *hors de combat*, whilst it can read unmoved the massacre and the concomitant atrocities which destroyed 135,000 Midianites. Truly what Voltaire said of distance in space, applies equally well to distance in time.

† Psa. lxxxiii. 9–12. Isa. ix. 4 ; x. 26, and lx. 6. Hab. iii. 7. See Joseph. Ant. v. 6. Even the Talmud notices them only in connection with Moses and Gideon.

‡ All these were found by the Expedition of 1877; besides zinc, tungsten, antimony, and various forms of iron, especially titaniferous and hæmatite.

§ " For they " (the Midianites) " had golden ear-rings, because they were Ishmaelites " (Judg. viii. 24). Thus the Midianites and the Ishmaelites both belonged to the Bene-Kedem or " people of the East "—Bedawin, and tent-dwellers.

mining-establishments and of the precious metals still unextracted, shows another and an indigenous source of wealth.

Under Trajan (A.D. 98–117) the Land of Midian probably shared the destinies of Edom, or Idumæa, which, after its conquest by A. Cornelius Palma, was raised to an especial province, with the title of *Palestina Tertia seu Salutaris*. To that epoch I would refer the establishment of Aynúnah which was probably destroyed by the troubles and dissensions following the earliest political revolt of El-Islam. The other remains at Makná, Sharmá, and Wady Tiryam show, by an inferior style, a barbarous occupation, possibly of the Nabat, Christian Arabs, who held the soil till the Mohammedan conquest. Lastly came the Bedawi,* who have reduced the land to what it now is; the abomination of desolation taking the place of the "fatness of the earth."

* For the probable date of the Bedawi incursions, see chap. vi.

CHAPTER VIII.

FROM AYN EL-MORÁK TO THE WHITE MOUNTAIN:
THE INSCRIPTION AND THE NABATHÆANS.

THE caravan began on the second day to assume shape and order. Between three and four a.m. I called up Antonin, the *marmiton*, to make ready tea and coffee for six, besides the Bedawi Shaykhs and the Chiefs of the native party: the latter also had their own brew, which I need hardly say was far better than ours.* We, the Europeans, setting off on foot, carefully examined the country whilst the confusion of packing and loading reigned in camp. After an hour or two the dromedaries came up, and we rode to the next station. Breakfast, prepared overnight, was spread upon a cloth under some thorn-tree, about 11 a.m. We had generally a long draught of laban (soured camel's milk), and we

* The Gishr (Kishr), or coffee husk, is here unknown: it is universally used about Aden in Western Yemen and at Sana'á, and a modern traveller compares it with the mixture of tea and coffee formerly drunk under the name of "twist" in England.

eked out our civilised supplies with the mutton of the Huwaytát, which, fed upon the fragrant Shíh (*absinthium*), the balm-like Za'atar (Thyme, *Th. Serpyllum*), and other perfumed herbs of the desert, has a surpassing flavour, far superior to the grass-fed venison at home.

We then rested during the heat of the day. Sleep, both at night and by day, is remarkably light in these highly electrical regions, despite the purity and cleanliness of the " Nufiez," or soft sand, which the Arab so much enjoys. In the afternoon we resumed our work, climbing, exploring, and collecting specimens, which the soldiers carried in bags and baskets, whilst the Egyptian officers made their sketches and plans. We dined at sundown, and passed the evening and part of the night in chat with the Bedawin, gathering the very scanty information they could afford. I am not certain that my companions did not look forward to a little more sleep and a little less work when the excursion ended.

Setting out at 5 a.m. (April 10th) in the mountain-wind, cool and high, we took a line towards the White Mountain, on the south-east, and skirted the seaward base of the Jebel el-Zahd, whose tall eastern heights now justified the 6090 feet of the chart. Hence, also, we could distinguish the Wady between the two *Massifs*, Jebel Arawah to the north, and Síg to the south. From the sea they had appeared a single wall.

Presently we came upon a newer formation, sandstone-grit; in this strange land every Wady shows a change. Reaching, after an hour's walk, the valley El-Khim (for Khiyam, tents), we found its sole striped with what seemed to be black sand. The bundle carried off for testing was remarkably heavy. I suspected emery; M. Marie said oxide of tin; and it proved to be chloride of lead almost pure. The supply of quartz, much of it white, a little of it pink; with a fair proportion of hyaline, which was as usual barren, increased as granite, taking the place of porphyry, became more abundant. In many parts, huge weathered and rounded blocks, like crumbs that had fallen from the tables of the Titans, cumbered the bed.

We crossed the upper part of the Wady Aynúnah, and ascended the broad and winding Wady Intaysh, which was marked by a large fragment of angular quartz. Here and there lay tombs that resembled those of the Bedawin on a large scale: the people, however, declared them to be Christian, and about half-way Mr. Clarke detected a "written stone," a block of red porphyry, the same material which bore the Himyaritic inscriptions, copied by Sutzen in Yemen.

It shows two crosses; and in this point, as well

as in the letter ⊏⊐, it much resembles the three inscriptions in ill-formed characters copied by Dr. Wallin (*loc. cit.* p. 313).* The latter were engraved upon immense stones, which had been detached

No. I.

THE INTAYSH (MIDIAN) STONE.

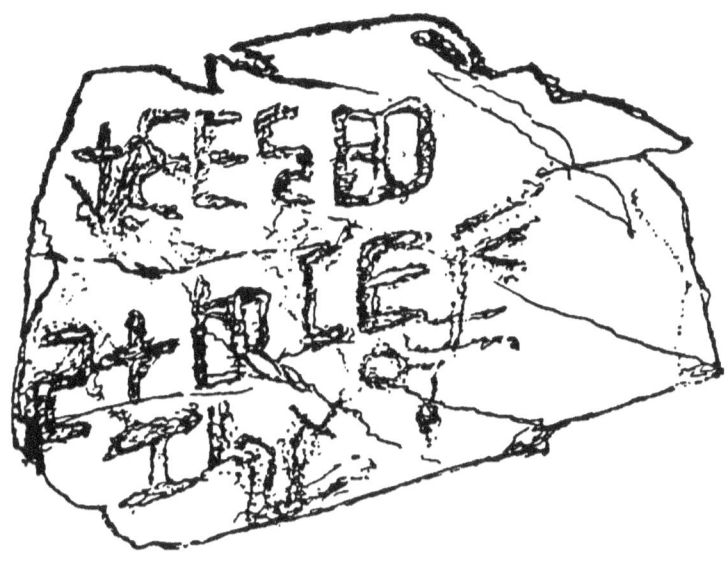

from the mountains overhanging a ravine where it entered the Hismáh; and he found them near a cemetery of the Beni Ma'azeh tribe, where, from

* The learned Orientalist, Rev. G. C. Renouard, who annotated Dr. Wallin's paper, remarks that the characters do not resemble those of the Sinaitic Jebel el-Mukattab, or the Himyaritic alphabet, anciently used in Yemen and Hazramaut. They "correspond, in some degree, with the ancient Phœnician character, but no satisfactory conclusion can be formed from such short inscriptions, copied, probably, in great haste."

P

No. II.

DR. WALLIN'S INSCRIPTIONS.

Found on large stones where the Wady Unayyid debouches upon the country called El-Nisma.

1.

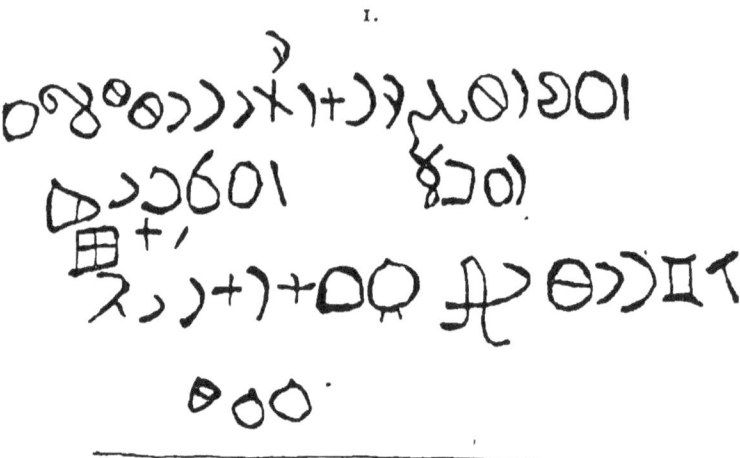

2.

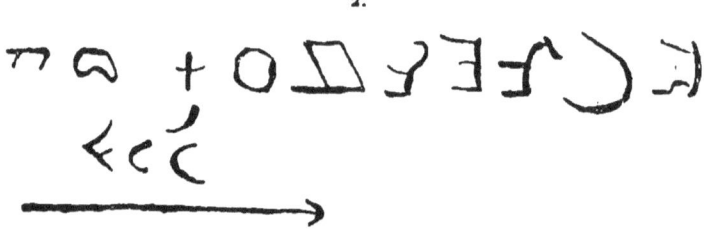

ΑΥΝ EL-MORÁK TO THE WHITE MOUNTAIN. 211

No. III.
Dr. WETZSTEIN'S INSCRIPTIONS.

Older Inscriptions.

1. Found on a Rijm or stone-heap about ten minutes southeast of Ka'akúl : the slab is surrounded with a circle.

2. Found about a quarter of an hour south of Odesíyyah.

Later Inscriptions.

3. On the way from Shbikket el-Nemárá to the Hanián.

4. At Shbikket el-Nemárá.

5. At the Rijm Ka'akúl.

6. Shbikket el-Nemárá.   7. From a Rijm near Odesíyyah.

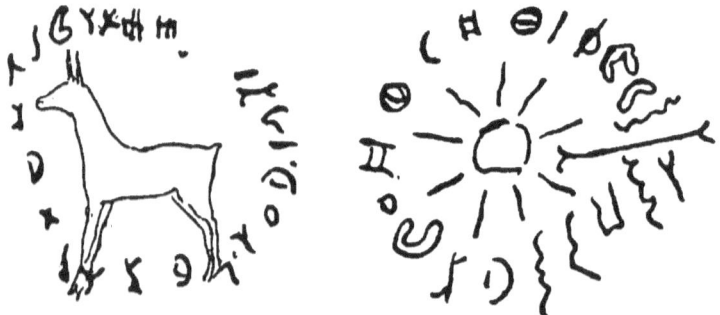

8. Copied from Rijm Ka'akúl.

ancient times, their Shaykhs and other persons of consideration were buried. "Upon other stones were graven clumsy representations of various animals, such as camels, sheep, and dogs, probably the work of Bedawi shepherds." *

No. IV.

INSCRIPTION FROM THE WADY EL-MOYAH, NEAR EL-WIJH (Wellsted, ii. 189.)

* Similar tracings were found and figured by Dr. J. G. Wetzstein, whose interesting book (*Reisebericht über Hauran und die Trachonen*. Berlin : Reimer, 1860) I have translated and annotated. M.M. Socin and Gildemeister agree in disconnecting our find with the inscriptions of the Harra and the Haurán (Wetzstein's). Upon this subject I have still doubts, and the tracings are therefore offered to the reader, together with those of Wellsted from near El-Wijh. It will not be difficult in a few years to obtain a "corpus inscriptionum," Nabathæan, Himyar, Hebrew, and Arabic from maritime and inner Arabia.

No. V.

From Dr. R. Dozy's "Die Israeliten zu Mekka,"
Leipzig, Haarlem, 1864.

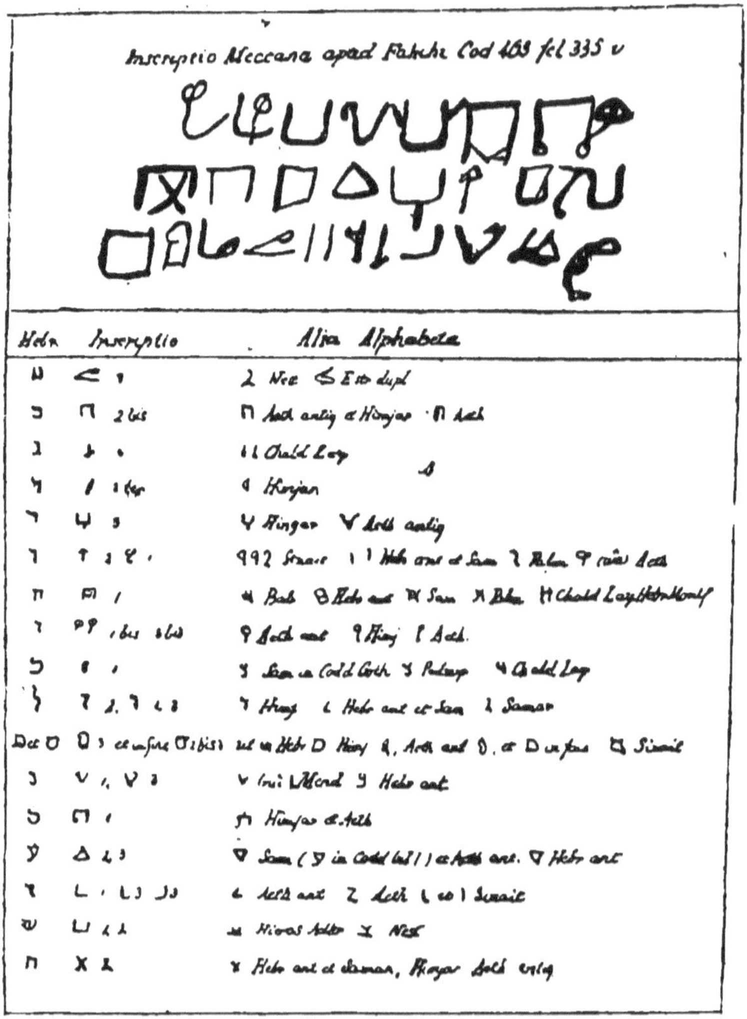

This inscription is peculiarly interesting, as it shows what may have been the character in which the Koran was written.

The written stone was triumphantly carried off and deposited with H.H. the Viceroy, after it had been duly photographed; and copies were sent to Professor Sprenger, of Bern, who forwarded it to Doctor O. Loth, of Leipzig; to Mr. C. Knight Watson, of Burlington House, and to Professor Socin, of Bâle. The latter kindly took the trouble of sending it to MM. Euting * (famous Semitic Alphabetist), Nöldeke (Arabic scholar), and Geldemeister, of Bonn (Orientalist); and all four agreed that more matter is required before it can be deciphered. Professor Socin was of opinion that the inverted E (Ǝ) is rather Greek than Nabathæan, and that the ligature ⌶ (OƎ) might be an Ǝ, with the Nabathæan form of Míno (m), whilst the frequent occurrence of the Cupid's bow, or inverted Σ (ᶎ), arouses a suspicion that it cannot be a Káf (K). Might it not be an M?

Mr. Clarke presently remembered that, when riding out from El-Muwáyláh to Aynúnah, he had observed something of the kind, whilst crossing the Wady Shermá; but not being prepared for inscriptions, he had neglected to secure it. This little business was duly confided to the care of Sayyid

* "Outlines of Hebrew Grammar," by Gustavus Bickell, D.D., Prof. of Theology at Innsbruck (1869–70). Revised by the author, and annotated by the translator, Samuel Ives Curtiss, Ph.D., Leipzig, with a lithographic table of Semitic characters by D. T. Euting. Leipzig: F. A. Brockhaus, 1877.

Abd el-Rahím. The Bedawin also spoke of a "writing" similar to ours in the Shifah (mountains), east of the line of march, and as big as a house—for which I would suggest a tombstone. After my return, Professor Sprenger sent me the following extract from the Jehan-Numá. "Near Midian are Alwáh (tablets? or rock-faces?) covered with inscriptions, containing the names of ancient kings;" and he is unable to say whether Makná or the settlement El-Bad'a* (the Madyama of Ptolemy, now Maghàrat Shu'ayh?), about seven leagues to the east, is meant. Also between Madyan and El-Akabah he has had notices of a narrow valley, in whose precipitous stone-walls is a "Kawwat" (niche in the rock) which may contain interesting remains.

The left bank of the Wady Intaysh showed reefs of dazzling white quartz, some of it recently broken. This could hardly have been done by our messenger of yesterday. Presently, on the right, appeared a small rounded mamelon of the same substance, rising abruptly from the dwarf flat, and stained yellow by wind and weather. Lastly, we sighted the Jebel el-Abyaz (White Mountain), also called Jebel Maro; and, winding along the southern foot, we encamped on the plain, or rather the valley-head, El-Maka'adeh—the place

* Rüppell calls the place "Beden" (an ibex?).

of sitting.* Here all was dry, and we vainly sank a pit some six feet deep. The Bedawin, however, declared that water is to be found amongst the hills at the distance of an hour's march. I lay under a siyál (acacia) enjoying the breath of the Desert, and wondering what had become of my companions, till 11 a.m., when, hearing that their guide was a "ghashím" (Johnny Raw), a party was started with water and provisions to lead them into camp. They had lost their way, and had done the wisest thing they could in sitting down till their absence was remarked, carefully finishing their bottle of wine in the meanwhile.

During the afternoon we ascended the White Mountain, which rises about 600 feet above the adjacent plain. The base is composed chiefly of porphyry, metalled with iron in sandstone grit: this is overlaid by gray granite, seamed and stratified with thick veins of quartz, and the latter outcrops from the summit, forming a regular cap. Whilst M. Marie remained below, I climbed the head, and took note of the prospect. Some half a dozen similar *pitons* of quartz dotted the lower lands

* Our march began at 5 a.m., and ended at 9.45 (=4 h. 45'). Of this total 1 h. 30' (4½ statute miles) were employed in walking, and 3 h. 15' (=13 miles) in slow riding. The time would give about 17½ miles; whilst the caravan, which came in at 11.30 a.m., had occupied 6 h. (=18 miles). The Aneroid (Casella, Compensated) showed an altitude of 29·98 = 1050 feet.

between our Mamelon and the Jebel el-Arawah to the east; and looking seawards, it was easy to lay down the position by means of the several islands.* After building what in Syria is known as a "Kákúr" † (stone-man), I was descending when M. Marie cried out that he had made a discovery. Striking from east to west, measuring from a yard and a half to two yards in breadth, and standing well out of the quartz-mass, was a vein which we at once named *Le Grand Filon*. It passes clear through the hillock, and, forking in the bowels, reappears double on the eastern side : the depth and the width shot up from the earth can, of course, be ascertained only by working. It resembled from a distance porphyry, while much of it had a pavonine lustre, like the argentiferous galena of the Silver States in North America. The great weight suggested one mass of metal, and part of it had evidently been worked.

On our return to Cairo, specimens of the *Grand Filon* were at once submitted to examination by Gastinel-Bey, who worked by the *voie humide*, whilst M. Marie preferred the dry way. The latter melted

---

* The compass-sights which fix the site of the White Mountain and of its pale-faced neighbours, are—
1. South end of Yubú'a 215°–218°.
2. The Small Shúshú' island 240°.

† This kind of landmark is called in the Koran "Áyah" ('Áyah, a sign); in Yemámah "Batíl" (plur. Butul), and in North-Western Arabia "Iram" (plur. Aram), a word sometimes confounded by the inexperienced with (the garden of) "Irem."

and cupelled his fragment in the usual manner.* It proved to be a highly composite formation containing some ten metals, the base being titaniferous iron, with a certain amount of wolfram or tungsten; the oxide of iron amounting to about 86·50 per cent.; copper 3·40, and a trace of silver ($\frac{1}{1000}$ by *voie sèche*), the latter, according to M. Gastinel, not easily separated, except in the laboratory. On the other hand, Colonel Middleton, who has had great experience in these matters, declares that the process is simple—spalling the ore, roasting, pulverising, and precipitating with sal ammoniac or with common salt.

After my return to Cairo, I proposed to the Viceroy an immediate start, with a party of engineers and a load of gun-cotton or dynamite, to blow up the vein in masses weighing tons, to carry it bodily off to the Capital, and to show the world a specimen of Midianitic metal. But on April 24th the Russo-Turkish war broke out, with the usual exorbitant requisitions of men and money from unhappy Egypt. I felt that my proper place was at my post, and the hot weather was rapidly coming on. The project, therefore, remained in abeyance until November, when we supposed that

* To 25 grammes of ore he used as flux—Litharge (100 grammes); Carbonate of Soda and Borax (each 40 gr.); and Nitrate of Potash (2 gr.). The stuff was readily melted, but the cupellation was imperfect.

the Campaign would cease to engross public attention. Meanwhile, my facetious friend, Colonel Lockett, of Cairo, suggested a tin dollar; and a pert young Levantine-Frenchman informed the public, not confidentially, *c'est de la blague.*

Returning to camp by another direction, where we found signs of a made-road, we enjoyed a pleasant evening talking over the prospects of the *Grand Filon,* and admiring the exquisite beauties of the sky, whose deep blue crystalline vault gained double distance by its purity and serenity. Never did the after-glow, the zodiacal light, though clearly visible every evening, appear so brilliant; changing from purple and indigo to gold and pink, and finally to a pale sea-green. It was so distinctly defined that the apex of the pyramid seemed to touch the zenith.

A height of upwards a thousand feet had placed us above the grosser vapours of the shore. Seawards, the stars—glowing red sparks like distant ship-lamps or lighthouses—showed themselves upon the very line where air and water meet. Inland, the misty giants in panoply of polished steel towered above the huge curtain of the bulwark, enchanted sentinels guarding the mysterious regions of the East; till presently the shades thickened, and we saw nothing but an army of grey phantoms behind us ranged in grisly array.

Before nightfall we noticed an unusual disposition

in the camp : the camels were all collected, tethered and pegged down, whilst the number of fires had greatly diminished. Presently Shaykh Abd el-Nabi quietly disappeared, heading many of his merry men, and without saying a word of scare, for the purpose of holding the passes of the White Mountain, whence his hereditary foes, the Beni Ma'ázeh, generally issue in force upon the plain. This was communicated to us by the Governor of El-Muwayláh, who had joined the caravan last night. We at once made our preparations. Rifles and revolvers were placed upon the table ; and my carbine-pistol appeared at last to have a chance of distinguishing itself. My two companions kept guard till midnight, exhorting the patrol when it failed, to cry out, " One, two, three, four ;" and I undertook the morning watch. The alarm came to nothing ; nor could this be regretted. The loss of a man or two would have made me for ever repent having divided a weak party into two. But not a syllable had been whispered to us about the possibility of such an adventure ; and it seemed at the first aspect impossible that a tribe which trades with Egyptian ports should attack a party of Government troops.

Sayyíd Abd el-Rahím explained the difficulty by remarking that the Bedawin have no sense, and will assault anything and anybody, at every possible opportunity. Moreover, they are mischievous as children or monkeys, and, like the knight-errants and Raubritters of old, they are ever spoiling for a fight. The onset would, of course, have been upon the Huwaytát, not upon us; on such occasions, however, the Wild Man expects those whom he protects to protect him—it is a question of " Pun d'onor." This turbulent tribe,* also half-Fellahín and of Egyptian origin, may muster some 5000 males. Its habitat lies east of the Hawaytát, extending north to El-Arísh and inland some four or five days of dromedary riding, at least 2° (= 120 geog. miles) into the Hismá, or Region of Red Soil.† They are

---

* They have been mentioned in chap. iii. Wallin (*loc. cit.* p. 310) gives the following names of the principal clans—
1. Orbán Sabt or Beni Sabút, which he finds mentioned in El-Kalkashendi, and supposes to be of Jewish extraction, deriving the word from Sabt, the Sabbath, Saturday. I also heard of their custom of ringing at sunset a large bell hung to the middle pole of the Shaykh's tent. 2. El-Atíyyeh composed of the family and relations of the Chief Shaykh. 3. Rubaylát. 4. Duyufíyyeh. 5. Tujárá. 6. Sulaymát. 7. Alíyyín. 8. Khazará. 9. Amríyyín; and 10. Sa'adániyyín.

† In Keith Johnston, and other maps, the Hismá Region is, I suspect, made to extend too far North. Wallin places the Beni Ma'ázeh and the Beni Atíyyeh over all the land from the Birket-el-Mu'azzam, the second pilgrim station south of Jabúk, to the Wady Musa of Petra, where they sometimes descend from the mountains and mingle with their kinsmen the Tiyáheh, or people of the Tíh (desert), north of Sinai. They levy the Ukhuwweh, or protection-tax, from the people of Ma'án, a town south-east of Petra. Their other districts are El-Akhzar and Zát-el-Hajj, the first pilgrim station north of Tabúk, where a ruinous walled town, with buildings, caverns, and treasures guarded by a black dog is spoken of. Their " Madrak," or district of escorting pilgrims,

divided into as many Kabáil (clans) as their western neighbours; and they are subject to two great Shaykhs, Mohammed bin Atíyyeh in the Hismá, and Sálim bin Khazar near the Magharát Shu'ayb. Their wealth consists in camels and asses, sheep and goats; with about a dozen horses kept for the Ma'íreh, or raid—want of pasture prevents breeding the animal. Mules, mentioned by the Classics, are now quite unknown to Midian. There should be no difficulty in managing this people, as they trade with El-Arísh (Rhinocolura) and with Suez *viâ* Akabah; and they will not cease to trouble travellers until their chiefs are induced to settle at Cairo. We did not see any of the tribesmen; but their enemies told us that they were pure Bedawin who never tattoo their faces.

I will conclude this chapter with a few notices of the Nabathæans, who have, as has been seen, left their mark on the land of Midian, a mere point in their wide possessions, and whose remains justify the tradition of the people that the old cities are the "ruins of the Nazarene." The frequent mention of this most important race by the Classics, both in verse and prose, has, despite distance of space and

lies between Ma'án and Birket-el-Mu'azzam. We find them spread over Egypt, and extending into Northern Africa. From their features and character Wallin judges them to be of Syrian origin, although this is not noticed by the Arabian genealogists; and he does not give them a bad name.

date, preserved its memory even in the vulgar modern literature of Europe. Camoëns (Lusiad, i. 84) by Nabathæan—

"Já o raio Apollineo visitava
Os Montes Nabatheos accendido "*—

simply means " Eastern : " in this he follows Ovid (Met. i. 61)—

" Eurus ad Auroram Nabathæaque regna recessit,
Persidaque et radiis juga subdita matutinis."

And in Eastern Arabia, especially about El-Hasá, the people still sing " Nabati verses."

I may here remark that as " Midian " and the " Midianites " are unknown to the so-called Profane, so are "Nabathæa" (Nabatæa) and its "Nabathæans" almost ignored by the Sacred or Canonical books.† The word has been derived by St. Jerome and the Commentators from the *"primogenitus Ismaelis, Nabajoth,"* or Nebajoth, their " symbol " (נְבָיֹת Ναβαιώθ, Gen. xxv. 13, and 1 Chron. i. 29, " Nebaioth ").

* " Already lit Apollo's morning ray
The Nabatean hills with burning light."
† We can hardly call Isaiah (lx. 7) an exception : " All the flocks of Kedar shall be gathered together unto thee, the rams of Nebaioth shall minister unto thee." Evidently, however, the " Nabathites " or Nabatheans (Vulgate) of 1 Macc. v. 24–25, and ix. 35, to whom Jonathan sent his brother John, and who are made " inhabitants of Eastern Jordan," refer to these people. As is remarked by Rabbi Joseph Schwarz (p. 171, *Das heilige Land*. Frankfurth am Main : Kaufmann, 1852), we cannot lay down precise limits to the possessions of nomads.

Thus a so-called Scriptural name has evidently been given, after the fashion of the Jews, to a race much older than Abraham, Noah, and the Hebrew "Adam" * himself. The late M. de Quatremère, of whom more presently, found the ancient nation not in the Nábit (Nebajoth) of the Arabs, but in Nabat, Nabít (plur. Anbát) or Nabatu (Heb.), the expression corresponding with what we popularly understand by "Semitic."

The Nabathæans are mentioned by Diodorus, who wrote in the days of the first Emperors, as living on the Ælanitic Gulf; † whilst Agatharkides (*De Mari Erythræo*) describes the country at the Gulf-head, and yet does not name the Nabataioi. Strabo says, categorically (xvi. 2, § 34), "The Idumæans are Nabathæans;" and in the same book (4, § 21), he gives the following detail: "The Nabathæans and the Sabæans situated above Syria are the first people who occupy Arabia Felix.‡ They

---

* This is not the place to enlarge upon the pre-Adamite Kings of orthodox Islam; but any reader of Chwolson will understand me. See his p. 174.

† Lib. iii. 12. 48. See chap. vii.

‡ This passage, amongst many others, warns us not to confound the Ptolemeian and classical "Arabia Felix," as has often been done, with the comparatively small province El-Yemen in Southern Arabia. The Greeks and Romans knew only the country between Egypt and the Persian Gulf, including Syria and the line of the Euphrates, whilst they applied the term "Arab" as vaguely as we do. 1. Arabia Petræa was the province about Petra, which is not more stony than either of its neighbours.

were in the frequent habit of overrunning this country before the Romans became its masters, but at present both they and the Syrians are subject to the Romans." After describing Petra the Capital, in the words of his philosophic friend, Athenodorus, an eye-witness, he gives an account of the unfortunate expedition sent under poor Gallus "to subdue the Arabians."* The Nabathæans had promised their co-operation, and supplied one thousand men under Syllæus. This treacherous minister of King Obodas of Petra having caused a complete failure, with corresponding loss of life, was beheaded at Rome.

According to Strabo, "Petra, which has excellent laws, is always governed by a King of the royal race; his minister being one of the Companions is therefore called Brother.† The Nabathæans are prudently fond of accumulating property: the community fines a citizen who has wasted, and rewards him who has increased, his substance. They have

2. Deserta was the Great Syrian Desert, the north-western prolongation of the central waste, but still peopled according to Ptolemy. 3. Eudæmon or Felix (Yemen or Teman), the land extending south of El-Akabah, was thus a vague term containing the remainder of the Peninsula.

* It is an old remark that this march, which promised so much information, geographical and ethnological, has only tended to confuse our knowledge of Arabia.

† The good Ibn Batútah (see chap. xi.) found a similar confraternity among the Turkomans; the members were styled "The Youths," their president "The Brother."

few slaves, and are served for the most part by their relations, or by one another, or each person is his own servant. This custom extends to their monarchs, who court popular favour so much that they sometimes minister to their subjects. These *reguli* * must render frequent accounts of the administration to the people, and moreover they are subject to inquiries into their private life.

"The citizens eat their meals in private companies *consisting of thirteen persons;* but the king gives many public entertainments in great buildings. Each dinner-party is attended by two musicians; and no guest drinks more than eleven cupfuls from separate cups, each of gold. Ignoring tunics, they wear girdles † around the loins, and walk about in sandals : the royal dress is the same, but its colour is purple.

"The houses are sumptuous and of stone; and the cities require no walls. A great part of the country is fertile ; lacking, however, olives, whose

---

* The Periplus, chap. xix., makes the Μαλίχα (Malik) of the Nabatæi inhabit Petra : the latter was connected by a highway with the southernmost port, Leuke Kome, where, in the days of subjection to the Romans, a centurion was stationed (Sprenger, 28). Thus the Nabathæan possessions would include Thamuditis as well as Midian. Ma'an afterwards succeeded to the honours of Petra.

† Evidently the waist-cloth, primitive form of the kilt; the Pilgrim garb and the Shukkeh of the modern Arabs, a word which has extended into the heart of Africa.

place in the mill is supplied by the grain Sesamum. The sheep have white fleeces, the oxen are large, but the country produces no horses.* For the latter, camels are the substitutes, performing the same kind of labour.

"Some merchandise is altogether imported into the country : other articles are not so, being *native products*, as *gold and silver*, and many of the aromatics. But brass (copper) and iron,† purple garments, styrax, saffron and costus (or white cinnamon), pieces of sculpture, paintings, and statues are not found in the country.

" The Nabathæans look upon the bodies of the dead as no better than manure, according to the words of Heracleitus, ' dead bodies are more fit to be cast out than dung :' whereupon they bury even their kings beside midden-heaps. They worship the Sun—the Sabæan ' Sonnencultus,'—and they build his altar on a housetop, pouring out libations and burning incense upon it every day." * * *

Pliny contents himself with naming the peoples adjoining the Nabatæi (v. 12, and vi. 32) : he also

* This is the case still both in Nabathæa and in Midian. The horse, essentially an animal of the plains, which thrives upon the high and healthy rolling uplands of Nejd, is not fitted for hot and mountainous regions like the Tehámeh el-Hejaz, Hazramaut, and the *massifs* of El-Yemen.

† As has been seen, iron is very common, and copper is also found abundantly in the rocks of Midian. Both metals are mentioned in Num. xxxi. 22.

reports the most esteemed kind of Teuchites (an *Andropogon*), a sweet-scented rush, and prized as a stomachic and a curative of many affections, as growing in the country. Pomponius Mela has nothing to say about Nabathæa and the Nabathæans. Josephus (Ant. 1, 12, § 4) declares that the country extending from the Euphrates to the Red Sea was occupied by the twelve sons of Ishmael, who gave it the name of Nabatena. It would thus border upon Egypt and Petræa, and contain the Deserts and the Highlands extending eastward to the Persian Gulf. Moreover, he calls the inhabitants of the land Nebajoth " Arabs."

The old classical dictionaries and guide-books * content themselves with telling us that the Nabathæans were roving pastoral Ishmaelites, a mixed race of Arabs and Edomites, originally bounded west and north-west by the Moabites and the Edomites ;. that they subsequently extended westward into Sinai ; and that their habitat at last became synonymous with the whole of Arabia

* Amongst which we must include the last edition of "Murray's Handbook for Syria and Palestine." That very naïve person, the author, assures us that "the Mahommedans were the instruments by which the fearful predictions of Scripture (quoting the 'theocratic cursings' of Ezekiel xxv.) were fulfilled." He has evidently never thought of the Bedawin who destroyed his Giant Cities of Bashan—Christian towns which lasted till the sixth century of our era. And thus history is written—in Handbooks !

Petræa on both sides of the Ælanitic Gulf, and with the mountain-region of "rugged" Seir, where they established their capital, Petra, about the third century B.C; that these shepherds developed to a nation of traders, whose head-quarters, between Egypt and Syria, upon the highway to "Babylon," a centre of trade with the Sabæans of Southern Arabia, and with the Gerrhæans on the Persian Gulf (Strabo, xvi. 3, § 4–5) secured to them absolute pre-eminence in the commerce of the East before it was diverted to the Nile-Valley,* and enabled them to establish an overland route for the Indian traffic; that this most ancient line extended from Leuke Kome (El-Hawara, in N. lat. 25°), their southernmost port in the Red Sea, to Mediterranean Rhinocolura; that Nabathæa thus became a powerful monarchy; allied itself with the Jews after the Captivity, and was able to resist the attacks of the Græco-Syrian Kings; that under Caligula (A.D. 37–41), though nominally subject to Rome, an Ethnarch at Damascus was called Aretas the King, *i.e.*, of the

* The first of the many overlands was from India up the Euphrates, with a branch from India to Hazramaut, and thence by caravan. The second was by way of Leuke Kome, and Ghazzeh (Gaza), and the third lay through Egypt. The valuable Indo-European trade, ever striving for the shortest line of route, will eventually take the direct diagonal across the Western Asiatic Continent; and, possibly, in the far future, Erzerum shall become the half-way station between the Persian Gulf and the Black Sea.

Nabathæans;* that under Augustus they sent auxiliaries with Ælius Gallus; that in the reign of Trajan their head-quarters, Arabia Petræa, were raised to the rank of a Roman province (A.D. 105–107); and, finally, that from the fourth century until the Moslem Conquest, the province became part of Palestine, and the diocese of a Metropolitan, whose See was at the "Rock city of Edom" (Petra). Thus the Nabathæans were made originally a Bedawi or Ishmaelitic tribe of Arabia Petræa; then a settled and commercial people; and, lastly, civilised Christian Arabs.

The researches of the lamented Etienne Marc de Quatremère† consigned to oblivion the descent

* He died on September 18, 1857, and a *notice historique* of his life and labours was printed by *M. le Secrétaire perpétuel*, in pp. 243–49, tome 1, *Nouvelle Série; Bulletin de Juillet et Août*, 1865; *Académie des Inscriptions et Belles Lettres, Comptes rendus des Séances de l'Année*, 1865.

† These Ethnarchs were Beni Ghassán, which, however, the new school would naturally include under the Nabati family. "Aretas" (El-Haris, King of the Minæi), and "Obodas" (El-Ubayd, King of Petra), with the favourite Greek termination in "as," for barbarous words, were possibly dynastic names like "Abimelech" amongst the Philistines; the "Atábeks" of Persia, the "Fazli," the "Anlaki," the "Rezáz" near Aden, and other ruling houses on a small scale. See d'Herbelot *s.v.* Gassaniah; and Sale's Koran (Prelim. Discourses, sec. 1). The flood of Aram, so important an event in Arab story (*temp.* Alexander the Great?) caused the rise of two Kingdoms: 1. Ghassán, so called from a water near Damascus, a realm founded by the Beni Azd; and, 2. Hira in Mesopotamia, established by the descendants of Kahtán. Both these monarchies, and notably the Gassamides, became Christian.

of the Nabathæans from Nebajoth, which was accepted long before the days of St. Jerome (Comm. in Gen. xx. 13, and xxv. 13); whilst they opened to the modern world a vast and wholly novel perspective of the origin, the racial affinities, the languages, the religion and the history of the NABAT, as we shall now call them. He had been struck by the fact that El-Mas'údi (Katab el-Tanbih), and other writers of repute, instead of including the fancied descendants of Nebajoth among their own people, and calling them "Arabs," like the Greeks and Romans, formally attached them to the Aramean,* or Palæo-Syrian family; and even made them the primitive and indigenous possessors of the vast tract extending to, and even beyond, the Great River (Euphrates); and including Syria and Assyria, Bayn el-Nahrayn (Mesopotamia), El-Irák (Chaldæa) and Babylonia. Presently the French savant found a fragmentary Arabic MS. in the Bibliothèque Impériale of Paris, which confirmed his previous impressions.

The fragment proved to be an Arabic version of the *Faláhat el-Nabatíyyah*, a treatise on Nabati

---

* "Aram," which the Greeks rendered Syria, Suria, and Soria, means the "Highlands," as opposed to Canaan (Kan'án), the lowlands, the latter extending to Babylonia. A modern traveller has been pleased to call the word Syria, "the invention of a Greek Geographer," when we find SVRVS (a Syrian) even in early Roman inscriptions.

Agriculture. Forming two books out of a total of nine, it contained about 600 pages of Arabic writing. The subjects were an Astronomical Calendar, as exact as it was extensive, and a learned and precise nomenclature of the flora, especially of cultivated plants which never flourished in the arid waters of Arabia Petræa. The translator was the well-known Abubekr bin Ahmed of Kassín, surnamed "Ibn-Wahshíyyah," whose genealogy shows his Chaldean (Rasdání) descent; a Moslem *Albertus Magnus* of the third century (Hegira=circa A.D. 904); and he dictated his work to a favourite scholar, Abu Tálib el-Zayyát (the oilman).

De Quatremère* admitted the assertion of Ibn-Wahshíyyah, who identified the "Nabat" with the Assyrians in the general sense of the word. He found in them the elder race of the great Aramean family, the inhabitants of Babylon, before the Chaldeans, and the originators of geoponics and georgics, of magic, natural and artificial; of astronomy, of angelology, of medicine, and generally of the sciences which the world has attributed to the latter.† According to him they were established

---

* The *Mémoire sur les Nabateens*, communicated to the Académie des Inscriptions in 1823–26, was published by the author in Jan.–March, 1835, in the *Nouveau Jour. de la Société Asiatique de Paris*, instituted in 1822: and was printed in a separate form ; Paris, 1835.

† This dispossession of the Chaldeans, whose learning has for

from all antiquity in Mesapotamia, submitting to the successive dynasties of Nineveh and Babylon. There they throve and waxed wealthy, assiduously cultivating, not only the ground, but the world of mind, and producing a literature, impressed in a high degree with the spirit of the race, especially philosophical and astrological, pantheistic and superstitious—in fact, Chaldean.

Under these circumstances a part of the population would inevitably addict itself to Art and Commerce ; and, for reasons now unknown, it would throw out distant establishments connected with the mother-country. One of these was Petrà, whose ruins, as every traveller has remarked, contrast strongly with the architecture of the Semitic race in all its other developments. Hither the Nabat transported their arts and sciences, their literature and their works, which their Arab successors deemed worthy of translation.

The fragment on "Nabati Agriculture" is a singularly original remnant of a literature, bearing upon it the impress of Mighty Babylon. Internal

---

long ages been one of the commonplaces of literature, may be compared with the fall of the Incas, who, according to my old friend and colleague, Mr. Thomas T. Hutchinson, late H.M.'s Consul, Callão ("Two years in Peru." London : Sampson Low, 1873), only borrowed from the Chimmoo and other races which preceded them, and who, being essentially destructive, and non-constructive, only injured what they borrowed.

reasons suggested to De Quatremère that it belongs to the most glorious epoch of the Chaldæan Empire, the reign of Nebuchadnezzar (circa B.C. 600) who, however, is not mentioned. The French savant believed that it would be possible to recover the whole manuscript;* and his broad outlines of the religion and the language are now generally accepted. The coins of the Nabati Kings were first described by that polite and munificent scholar, the late Duc de Luynes, who, in his valuable paper,† adduced facts to prove the name of "Nabat," ‡ and to confirm the theory that the mysterious race was of Chaldæo-Aramean origin. Already El-Mas'údi had stated that "the Nabít differs (from the Syrian) only in a small number of letters, but the basis of the language is the same." Caussin de Perceval § believes the original tongue to have been Chaldæan, and the modern a corrupt Arabic.

This sketch was amplified by the learned MM.

---

* I have heard of a copy, and my excellent friend, M. Yacoub Artin Bey of Cairo, is kindly looking after it. Whether the manuscript be complete or not cannot yet be determined.

† *Revue Numismatique*, Nouvelle Serie, iii. 1858.

‡ Mr. Reginald S. Poole (see chap. xi.) tells me that in the Duc de Luynes' paper the coins are published, but the Nabati alphabet has been converted into square Hebrew. For the older form he refers me to Langlois, *Numismatique des Arabes avant l'Islamisme* (1 vol. 4º, 1859 : Rollin et Feuardent, Paris and London).

§ *Essai sur l'Hist Arabes*, etc.

Chwolson,* Professor of Oriental languages at St. Petersburg, who supports the claims of the Nabat to rank with the most interesting races of antiquity. According to him (page 10) the remains of its literature consist of four works, one fragmentary; 1. The Book of Nabati Agriculture † (before mentioned); 2. The Book of Poisons; 3. The Genethlialogs of Teukelúnha of Babylon, and 4. The Book of Decomposition, *alias* the Secrets of the Sun and Moon. Ibn Wahshíyyah,‡ the Arabic translator, informs us that No. 1 was begun by El-Zaghrít (Daghríth), was continued by El-Yanbúshád, and was completed by El-Kusámí (Kuthámi.)

M. Chwolson (*Übersetze*, p. 68, etc.), disregarding the internal dates, makes the earliest live about

---

* *Über die Überreste der alt Babylonischen Literatur in Arabische Übersetzung*, St. Petersburg, 1849. He found his materials not only in the "Book of Agriculture," but also in the Dictionaries, as in the Siháh and Kámús; and in the mediæval Arab geographers, as El-Mas'údi ("Meadows of Gold"), etc. The latter expressly states that the Nabat founded the City of Babylon.

† This may sound like "Chinese metaphysics," but it is not so. The Bedawin treated the Nabat like Helots; while the settled Arabs, even to the present day, alluding to the superiority of the old "Nabat" in georgics, call works on farming generally, *Faláhat el-Nabatíyyeh*, Agriculture of the Nabat, and this is a fair testimony to the fact that such treatises did exist. The Jews of El-Medinah, in the days of the Apostle of Allah, were also, according to Arab tradition, Nabat.

‡ He is noticed by D'Herbelot (*s.v.* Falahat) as Ebn Vahaschiah; another author on georgics, Ebn Aovâm al Cothai, is quoted by the French Orientalist.

2500 years B.C., the second some three or four centuries later; and the last, whom he holds to be the chief of the trio, while Ibn Wahshíyyah considers him little more than the Editor, he would consign to the thirteenth century B.C. This date is obtained in the book by the mention of a Canaanite dynasty, which he and Bunsen ("Egypt," iii. 432) find corresponding with the Fifth or Arabian line of Berosus; nine Kings reigning 245 years B.C. 1521-1276. Moreover, he suspects that the latter were the mysterious Hyksos. Later commentators have remarked, "formidable intrinsic difficulties;"* such as the mention in Nabati literature of names closely resembling those of Adam (Adami), Seth (Ishitá), Enoch (Anuhá), Noah, Shem, Nimrod (Namroda), and Abraham; and the occurrence of corrupted Hellenic words like Armísa (Hermes); Agathadím'un (Agathodæmon) and Yúnán (Ionians, Greeks).† Even M. Chwolson himself confesses that the circumstances related of the patriarchs seem to have been borrowed from the Hebrew writings; or even from the later Jews, with the important reservation, however, that much may

* See Smith's Dict. of the Bible, s.v. Nebaioth. The objectors were Ewald (*Goettingische Gelehrte Anzeigen*, 1857-1859); Renan (*Journ. de l'Institut*, April-May, 1860); and M. de Gutschmid (*Zeitschrift d. Deutsch, Morgenländ, Gesells.* xv. pp. 1-100).

† I do not include amongst the suspected "Tammuz" (Adonis), a word which may be of any antiquity.

be due to the translator's hand. I may observe, moreover, that both sacred and profane writers may have taken their information from the same sources: and this, indeed, is rendered more than probable by the flood-legends of the so-called Izdubar or Nimrod (B. C. 2000?), and by the creation-myth, in six periods, each of a thousand years or a day, which seems to have been common to Egypt and to the whole of Western Asia.* Of the other apparent evidences of modern thought which have been detected—such as the subjects of Nabati literature, scientific and industrial, being by no means those usually chosen by the Aryan and the Semitic world, and suggesting the inquiry whether the work should not be dated several centuries after the beginning of our era—I would further remark that not only Arab translators are in the habit of taking considerable liberties with their authors, the Semitic versions of the holy books of the Hindus supplying any number of instances of paraphrase and of insertion, but also that the Nabat treatment of many subjects, notably of history, utterly un-Arab, suggests the literature of a wholly different race.

If the startling results of MM. de Quatremère and Chwolson are to be accepted, the four Nabati

* In pp. 91–92 of "Etruscan Bologna" (London: Smith, Elder & Co., 1876) I have offered some notice of this Creation and Fall of Man myth, drawn from the labours of the late lamented Mr. George Smith.

books introduce us to a great unknown nation of the remotest antiquity, whose civilisation was to that of the Greeks as the latter is to ours, and prove that the elaborate treatment of Science is at least as old as the oldest monuments of Egypt.* Scholars naturally object to accept such radical innovations ; and they will suspend judgment at least until some of the cuneiform texts are submitted to the world. The first step has been taken. Already we hear that Nineveh has yielded the "Observations of Bel," a treatise in sixty books, dating from the seventeenth century B.C., and describing the stars as they stood 2540 years before our era, when Alpha Draconis was Polaris. But for the present we content ourselves with accepting the theory that the Nabat of Chaldæa are the same race as the Nabathæans of Arabia Petræa.

It has been suggested that Nebajoth, one of the "sons of the concubines,"† whose early history has

* See Professor Chwolson's conclusions in pp. 170–176. I have already quoted the Nabati views on cruelty to animals, which are advanced as those of any Humane Society of the nineteenth century, including the anti-vivisectors. There are other thoughts, which startle us ; for instance, the opinions of the Canaanite and the Chaldean sages that "everything mundane is governed by eternal immutable laws, without any connection with the deeds, good or evil, of mankind."

† This term of reproach is rather Christian ignorance than Jewish *outrecuidance*. The Hebrew "Faljas" means a "second wife," of course inferior, as amongst all polygamic peoples, to the first.

been left in darkness, might have travelled to the East, whence his grandsire Abraham came, have intermarried with the Chaldeans, and become the forefather of a mixed race—the Nabat. But this is a genuine retrogression to the mediæval theories which made Hebrew the "venerable sire of Greek and Latin;" the ancestors of the Jews the progenitors of mankind; and the Pentateuch the foundation of all literature, the *origines* of all authentic history, the shrine of the primæval revelation, and so forth.* "Alláhu a'alam!" as the Moslems say.

The following eight specimens of Nabatí Alphabets were supplied to me by the kindness of an old friend, W. S. W. Vaux, Secretary to the Royal Asiatic Society: they are copied from M. François Lenormant (*Essai sur la Propagation de l'Alphabet Phénicien dans l'Ancien Monde.* Paris, 1872, planche xv). Of this valuable work one volume, in two parts, has been published at intervals of three years.

* Nor are these days yet passed. See preface, p. viii., to "The Targums of Onkelos and Jonathan ben Uzziel," etc., by J. W. Etheridge, M.A. London : Longmans, 1862.

AYN EL-MORÁK TO THE WHITE MOUNTAIN. 241

No. VI.
NABATÍ ALPHABETS.

No. 1. B.C. 60, Inscriptions.
— 2. B.C. 95-50, Coins.
— 3. A.D. 1st Cent., Coins.
— 4. ,, ,, Inscriptions.
— 5. A.D. 47, Inscriptions.

No. 6. A.D. 75-105, Coins.
— 7. A.D. 100, Inscriptions.
— 8. A.D. 2-5 Century, Inscriptions from Sinai.

CHAPTER IX.

HOW THE GOLD WAS FOUND IN MIDIAN: THE GOLD MINES OF ARABIA.

THE readers of my "Pilgrimage"* may, perhaps, remember certain pleasant reminiscences of a bluff and genial old friend, one Haji Wali Alioghlú Arslánoghlú, my neighbour in the Wakálah (Caravanserai) Siláhdár, and the companion of my leisure hours whilst preparing for travel to El-Hejaz. A genuine Tartar of the Kipchak tribe of Kirghiz, which pitches its tents near Ákmasjia, east of the Caspian, and which lives on mutton, milk, Kurút† and Kimmiz—the Koumiss, now a fashionable remedy in Europe,—he has wandered far and wide

* Vol. i. chaps. iii. and iv.
† Kurút, in Arabia "Afík," a favourite article of diet with wandering pastoral tribes, is made as follows: A quantity of "laban" (artificially soured milk) is placed in the sun for two or three days; the serum which remains after evaporation is strained off, and the remainder is made into balls and dried. I should hardly recommend this rude conserve of milk to the epicures of Europe, but in the Desert, when dissolved in water, Afík makes a cooling and thirst-quenching drink.

over Táshkand, the "Stone Town," * Bukhárá, Khiva, and Samarkand.

When I parted with him in 1854, he was a Persian subject trading in Cairo. He then became a Russian Simsár (broker) at Zagázig ; and here he was living with his wives and children, as comfortably as a man numbering eighty-two summers can expect to do, when I swooped down upon him, and carried him bodily into the Arabian wilderness.

It so happened that during the cold season of 1849, as Haji Wali, an item in the Cairo caravan, was returning from his second pilgrimage, he was led by the will of Allah to hit upon the gold. On the second or third of March—for his memory, though admirable, cannot retain every trifle—he and his companion, Ákil Effendi of Alexandria, exchanged their camels for asses, and preceded the Kafilah. By way of rest he dismounted, and going off to the right of the road, where a single tree grew, he sat down under it.

He describes the place as showing to the left (west) a rounded mountain or hill drained by two Wadies to the sea (Gulf of El-Akabah); whilst on the right was a "báb" (gate), somewhat like that of Wady Aynúnah, a dry watercourse running between two tall bluff cliffs. In the rude

---

* Sprenger (p. 4) translates Táshkand "turris lapidea," *i.e.*, Lithino-pyrgo : Haji Wali explains it by Bilad-hajar (Stone-town).

sketch which he drew from memory, he places to the north "Ishmah," meaning a spot where water is easily dug; but there is no such word in Arabic, and it is an evident confusion with the Jebel Tayyibat Ism of the maps. Seeing the torrent-bed sparkle—doubtless with the mica, which has proved fatal to so many fortunes in Brazil, in California, and in Australia,—he scooped up a double handful of the sand, probably the granitic gravel which strews these fiumaras, tied it in his kerchief, stowed it away in his Sahhárah, or pilgrim's chest, and, rejoining his companions, went his ways in the name of Allah to El-Akabah.

Arrived at Alexandria, Haji Wali, who does not belong to the futile tribes of the South, showed his *trouvaille* to a Shíshnáji (essayer), one Zayni Effendi. The latter pounded the sand in a mortar, mixed it with water, and, by means of quicksilver, produced in his presence a bit of gold about half the size of a grain of wheat, and weighing a Kamh, or the fourth of a Dirham.

The Haji, now persuaded that his fortune was made, represented the matter to a friend, Háfiz Bey, who acted as the head of the Alexandrian Customhouse; and this old navy-captain reported the fact to Hasan Pasha Monastirli, the Kahiya, or Steward, of Abbas Pasha, then reigning. This high officer sent for the Shíshnáji, and inspected the crumb of precious metal. After minute inquiries he curtly remarked, " This is not what Egypt wants ; her gold is her own ground : her crops are her gold." He was, in fact, quoting an old Law amongst the Turks, that agriculture is the " red sulphur " and the "philosopher's stone" of the world. The remark, slow and sensible, was repeated by the Gumrukji (Custom-house official) to Haji Wali, who declares that he ceased to think about the discovery. Not so the Shíshnáji ; the unfortunate at once set out in search of the place and, after a time, his family heard of his death—probably his murder by the Bedawin.

This was told to Haji Wali by his old companion 'Akil Effendi, who died at Alexandria about two years ago. On the other hand, the Haji once confessed that there was an understanding between the Shíshnáji and himself ; and it is my profound conviction that he has tried in all directions, and ever since 1849, to make money out of his find.

I have reason to think that gold-washing has never been forgotten at El-Muwayláh ; that it has been done in secret, and that it has brought large fortunes to men who ostensibly dealt in charcoal. Some of the old folks at Suez still declare that the works were abandoned years ago because the produce did not cover expenses—exactly what would be bruited abroad of a rich placer. Moreover,

Shaykh El-Nabi of the Huwaytát openly told me, when I was asking about copper and other metals, that we must apply to the Elders, the greybeards of the tribe, adding that they were "tammá'ín" (men of greed), who were not likely to part with the secret gratis. There were other indications; but the suspicions are vague, and it would be unfair to mention names.

In 1853, when Haji Wali and I became fast friends at the Wakálah, he strolled one day into my room, and with much show of mystery showed me a little of the sand, probably that underlying the gravel. True to Oriental practice he had prudently withheld a part, even from his friend and confidant the greedy Shishnáji. I examined it with a Stanley lens, and distinctly saw minute dots of gold, whilst my complete confidence in the honour and honesty of the man forbade the suspicion that he had "peppered" the stuff by mixing up gold filings with it.

He also showed his confidence in the discovery by proposing that we should both dress in rags like pauper pilgrims, travel on foot to the spot, and wash the metal—the show of poverty being necessary to baffle the Bedawin, who go wild when they hear the word "Dahab" (gold). I remember asking him why we could not go as Effendis, he as a merchant and his companion as a doctor, and his answering me that we could not without a regiment of foot. Finally, I observed that his project was no good : that we might collect two or three pounds of metal, but that the affair would probably end in our throats being cut by the Wild Man.

The idea, however, had taken root firmly in his mind. I called upon the English Consul at Cairo— his name is not worth mentioning,—and asked him to represent the matter to H.H. Abbas Pasha. The "obstructive," a model of his unkindly class, contented himself with declaring that in his sapient opinion "gold was becoming too common." In this he was not singular. Marvellous to relate, the same answer was made to me by a Secretary of State when I offered to open up some most valuable diggings on the West Coast of Africa, if he would appoint me Governor, assist me with half a West India regiment, and not inquire too curiously into local matters. It is impossible to understand such men : they go back to the childhood of our race, when even the wise could utter intolerable bosh like *aurum irrepertum et sic melius situm.** It would

---

* Pliny (vi. 31), speaking of Babytace city on the Tigris, says, "Here, for the only place in the world, is gold held in abhorrence; the people collect it together and bury it in the earth that it may be of use to no one"—a silly *witzkopf* commentator adding, "the buryer excepted, perhaps." I can produce another and a modern instance of misochrysy. Throughout the Eastern Coast of Guinea the precious metal was "put in Fetish" (excommunicated) by the medicine-man (1860–65); and in 1865, if you offered a

be quite as logical to deprecate the plucking of cotton, or the cutting of sugar-cane.

Haji Wali, disgusted with this second failure, used, he told me, the sand to powder a letter; and I set out for Arabia: hence my wanderings extended to East Africa, to the Crimea, to East Africa again, to Central Africa, to South America, to West Africa, to Brazil, and to Syria. For nearly a quarter of a century my secret was kept to myself. During the reign of Abbas Pasha, and under the administration of the retrograde Doctor-Consul, nothing was to be done. The successor, Said Pasha, was wholly occupied with the grand idea of the *Canal des deux mers*, and was too often the prey of a dominant will: I had also learned the full meaning of the phrase, *trabalhar para os outros* —" to work for others."

At length, in 1863, H.H. Ismail Pasha became Viceroy of Egypt, and the long-wished-for opportunity presented itself. My old friend, Hugh Thurburn, whose lamented death took place on February 17, 1877, by diligently inquiring at the Khàn Khalíl, and at the other bazaars of Cairo, at length traced Haji Wali, and wrote to me that a very old man of that name, weighing some sixteen stone, and now a Russian subject, was living in New Bubastis.

sovereign to a negro near the Volta, he spat upon it, and threw it on the ground.

Presently England, despite herself, or rather despite the governments which are supposed to represent her, began to play the foremost part in the reform and the development of Egypt and the Egyptians. This was evidently the moment to act, and being no despiser of "opportunism," so ungrateful to the Gallic mind, I acted accordingly. Returning with my wife from a winter in Western India (1875–76), I passed through Zagázig, where, after a few minutes' conversation with Mr. J. C. J. Clarke, Telegraphic Engineer and Directeur des Télégraphes, I placed him upon the scent which he cleverly and patiently followed. A long correspondence ensued.

The Haji, despite his years and alleged infirmities, showed himself more anxious about the affair than was to be expected: he has four young children and a fifth coming. With peculiar tenacity he had probably done his best for many years to sell his discovery, and failure had only sharpened his appetite. He told my Wakíl (agent), Mr. Clarke, that he would fetch from Alexandria a plan of the place, with the tree marked upon it; but he delayed so long that his sharp-witted companion suspected him of concerting with two strange Turks, who were about to set out with the Hajj Caravan in November 1876.

As regards the local government our secret was

safe. He feared, as an Eastern always does, that pressure would be put upon, him and that his personal attendance at the place would be required; and here he was right. He was terribly "bullied" and badgered after his return for having trusted his secret to Franks; he was universally called an old fool, and his friends laughed aloud at his reverend beard—had he been an Egyptian he would not perhaps have escaped so easily.

But to return to preliminaries. After five months of *pourparlers*, it appeared at last that no plan existed, but that a letter written in Turkish contained certain jottings of the road. After committing himself by showing this document, Haji Wali became very fidgety; he had probably intended to sell his discovery to me upon the old principle of a bird in the hand. At last, on March 20th, I passed, as has been seen, through Zagázig, and carried off my old friend nothing loath. His subsequent adventures will be found in the following pages.

Midian is not included by Hebrew Holy Writ in auriferous Arabia : * yet it has evidently supplied

---

* The chief gold countries are Sheba (Sabá? El-Yemen?) and Ophir. Those of minor importance are Hazeroth (Deut. i. 1), Uphaz (Jer. x. 9, and Dan. x. 5), and Parvaim (2 Chron. iii. 6). Gesenius believes "Uphaz" to be a corruption of Ophir, the two words being the same with and without the masoretic points. Parvaim, we shall see, is easily identified ; we need not go to

the precious metal in abundance, and it still deserves a place amongst the mining-regions which in olden time made the Peninsula " Eudæmon." The following note contains the scholarly and exhaustive notice by Sprenger (pp. 52-59) of the places and diggings mentioned in Arab literature. Its length will hardly be objected to when we find in popular works (*e.g.*, Smith's Dict. of the Bible, *s.v.* Ophír), " the supposition that, notwithstanding all the ancient authorities on the subject, gold really never existed either in Arabia, or in any island along its coasts."*

I have included amongst the auriferous sites the disputed passage in Deuteronomy (i. 1.) " These be the words which Moses spake unto all Israel, on this side Jordan in the Wilderness, in the plain over

S. America with Arius Montanus (Bochart, *Geog. Sacra, sen Phaleg et Canaan*, cape. ix.) who made the dual word to signify the "two Perus," *i.e.*, Peru Proper and New Spain.

* The same excellent work tells us (*s.v.* Ophir)—" As to gold, far too great stress seems to have been laid on the negative fact that no gold, *nor trace of gold-mines*, has been discovered in Arabia. Negative evidence of this kind, on which Ritter has placed so much reliance, is by no means conclusive. Sir R. J. Murchison and Sir C. Lyell concur in stating that, *although no rock is known to exist in Arabia, from which gold is obtained at the present day*, yet the peninsula has not undergone a sufficient geological examination to warrant the conclusion that gold did not exist there formerly, or that it may not yet be discovered there." The classical authors who minutely describe the gold produce of Arabia, are Agatharkides (before quoted), Artemidorus (adopted, like the former, by Strabo, Diodorus, Siculus, and Pliny), Eupolemus, who lived before the Christian Era (*Fragments*, etc. C. G. A. Kulmey, Berlin, 1840).

against the Yamm Suph (Sea of Weeds, Red Sea? or Sirbonitis Lake?), between Paran and Tophel, and Laban and Hazeroth, and Dizahab." The latter word in the LXX. is rendered χαταχρύσεα; by the Vulg. *ubi auri est plurimum;* and *Hazeroth, dove si trova moltissimo oro,* with the gloss *paese ricco per miniere d'oro* in the Abbate A. Martini's translation (Venice : D. Fracasso, 1835). The A.V., in translating "Hazeroth and Dizahab," instead of "Hazeroth where there is gold" (or which owns gold), thus turning an epithet into a proper name, has taken an unwarrantable liberty with the text. Hazeroth, the "fenced enclosures" of a pastoral people, is identified with "Ayn Hadhirah," the old monkish colony, north-west of the Jebel el-Samghi, near the eastern shore of the Sinaitic Peninsula, and Professor Palmer ("Desert of the Exodus," i. 261) gives an illustration of its charming scenery.

NOTE.

Sprenger's "Alte Geographie," §§ 53–56.*

Par. 53. Are we to believe all these reports, the mere fancies of poets, especially those treating of the haven Dzahubân (Dahabán, the place of gold)†, distant only 500 miles from Berenike,

* I retain the spelling of my learned friend, at times explaining it by the "Jonesian," more familiar to Englishmen.
† The *Thebæ oppidum*, or *Tabis*, so called from the Arab tribe Debai; both words evidently connected with Dahab, gold. The port lies in N. lat. 21°, and about 1° south of Meccah, and nearly 3° (= 180 m.) south of Berenike on the opposite African shore. It was held the best for shipping the produce of the 'Aqyq, the Bysch, and the Hogayra workings.

where merchants bartered for the precious metal? Hamdâny (*Jezîrat el Arab*, pp. 260-67) heads one of his chapters, " Mines of Yamâma and Diyâr-Kuby'a, where at present the Oqayl (*Ukayl*) bin Ka'b dwell." Among these diggings he includes one of silver, and another of copper, both near Schamâm (Hd.* p. 260), together with the following five of gold. 1. Al-Hasan, a rich placer, apparently the same as Ahsan, also called from its industry Ma'din-al-Ahsan (Mine of El-Ahsan): it is a village on the north-westerly road of the Yemûma, between this place and Himà-Dharayya (the "State-domains of Dharyya"); and it is held by the Abû-Bakr, a tribe deriving from the Beni Kilâb. 2. Al-Hofayr (the little digging) in the 'Amâya region. 3. Thanyya (Byna?) of the Bâhilitic Ibn 'Içam (Hd. 260). 4. The gold-mine of Tiyâs ; and, 5, that of 'Aqyq ('*Akîk*) in the 'Oqayl country, not far from Byscha-Yaqtzán.† The latter (according to Ym. ii. 826) is the best yielder in all Arabia, and the Apostle of Allah said of it, " The land of the 'Oqayl raineth gold."

Besides these five sites Hamdâny notices, without specifying what ores they yield, six others, viz.—1. Al-Dhobayb. 2. Al-'Ausaga. 3. The mine on the Baghdâd-Mekka (Meccah) road, which, however, may be the same as No. 6 ; lying between 'Omaq and Ofay'ya. 4. Byscha‡ in Yamâma, the mid-length of the great Baitius Valley. 5. Al-Hogayra (Hujayra) ; and 6, That of the Banu Solaym, from long marches north-east of Medina.§

* The abbreviations are "Hd." (Hamdánî) ; "Ym." (Yákût's well-known work, the " Mu'jan el-Buldan," or " What is known of Countries "—*Jacut's Geogr. Wörterbuch, herausgegeben Von. F. Wüstenfeld ;* 6, Sände, Leipzig, 1866-73. Yákût, in full, Abu Abdillahi Yákút ibn Abdillahi El-Hamawi, sur-named Shiháb el-Dín or " Shooting-star of the Faith," was born in the Bilád el-Rúm, or Asia Minor, A.D. 1178-80; lived at Baghdád, and died there, A.D. 1228-29) ; " Yd." the Marásid el-Ittilá'a, often alluded to in these pages.

† As Sprenger remarks (p. 50), this second Pilgrim-station north of the Benát-Harb is the only Arabic word which preserves the memory of " Joctan : " in p. 264 he identifies Byscha with the Biblical Mesha (Gen. x. 30).

‡ This valley, famed for its lions, must not be confounded with the Wady Bíshah in El-Yemen, which heads near the town of Kaukabán, and which ends in a considerable stream, the Sardúd (p. 8, " Notes of a Journey in Yemen," by Charles Millingen, M.D. in the Turkish Army, read before the R.G.S. Feb. 23, 1874, and reprinted by Clowes, 1875).

§ The Professor writes to me: " I have taken great pains to ascertain the exact sites of the Central Arabian mines, but without much success : this much, however, is clear to me that, with the exception of the Ma'din Baní Solaym, they are in Wahhâbi territory."

Some maintain that the latter yields silver, others say iron; but the rest of the five were certainly gold. The placers of Al-Hasan, Al-'Ausaga and others (in their neighbourhood) lie on or near the highway connecting the Persian Gulf with Syria, and thus in the trade-zone of the Ramah (Ræmitæ) * merchants who, according to Ezekiel (xxvi. 22), occupied the fairs of Tyre "with chief of all spices, and with precious stones (pearls?) and gold." We may believe that they bartered goods for the noble metal while marching through Nagd (El-Nejd).

54. Hamdâny confines himself to mentioning a few mining-sites in Nagd, and even in these his amounts are incomplete. At Thachb (*Sakhb*) in the Kilâb country, gold and white 'Aqyq (agates) † are found (Ym. i. 920). There was also a gold-mine at Himà-Dharyya (Ym. ii. 324), and another at Chazba (*Khazbá*), possibly the same as the 'Aqyq digging (Ym. ii. 436). A doubtful placer appears to have been at al-'Yçân (Ym. iii. 753) and a fifth at Nâçi'a (*Nási'*) between Yamâma and Makka (Yd. iii. 190). Moqaddasy (El-Mukaddasi) expressly says (i. 101) ‡ that there is a gold-mine between Yanb'o (*Yanbú'a*) and Marwa; § and Ya'quby (*El-Ya'kúbi*, p. 103) mentions another at Qaschm (*Kashm*), near Tathlyth (Taslís). These lists could be greatly extended.

My object, however, is to prove from Arab writers that gold has been dug, not in Arabia generally, but especially in the Litus Hammæum,|| and in Chaulân (Khaulán).¶ Unfortunately Ham-

* Bochart, on the authority of the LXX., has identified the Biblical Raamah (Re'amah) with the Rhegmapolis of Ptolemy (vi. 7, § 14), in N. lat. 23° 10'. The city lay near Ras el-Khaymah, a place made known to India by the expedition against the Jawásimah (Kawásim) pirates.

† For the onyx and the carnelian, see chap. x. of this volume.

‡ The MS. of the geographer was brought to light by Professor Sprenger, and has lately been published by Professor Goëje, of Leyden, who is now translating it.

§ More generally called Zu'l Marwah, the classical Mochura, a tract still occupied by the Juhaynah tribe, in N. lat. 24° 10'; four marches north-east of Yambú'a, and about the same distance north-west of El-Medinah.

|| Pliny, vi. 32. "*We there find the Clari* (var. Glari), *the shore of Hammæum* (var. Mammæum and Mamæum, now the coast of Hamidha or El-Hamidah), *in which there are gold-mines; the region of Canauna* (a Wady Kanúnah enters the sea in N. lat. 19° 8', near the modern " Goonfoodah "); *the nations of the Apitami* (the Alitæi of Agatharkides?), *and the Cassani* (var. Gasani; the Gassanitæ, the celebrated Beni Ghassán). It has been suggested that these mines may have been the objective of Ælius Gallus.

¶ Khaulán (Wallin's "Alkhawlá ") is generally assumed to be the Havilah

dány gives no chapter on the gold-mines of Yaman (el-Yemen), though the whole object of his book is to describe that region: perhaps Iklyl (Iklíl) supplies the details. He says (p. 211), however, "in Dhankân (Zankán) is a well-yielding mine; and its Tibr (unmelted gold) is not bad"—meaning uncommonly good. The site, well-known to Arabian geographers, lies some two hours' march south of Port Dzahabân and three north of Hamidha. Thus it is certainly upon the Hammæan shore; and must not be confounded with the "Sancan" of Niebuhr. At Dhankân may have been the gold-bearing stream mentioned by Agatharkides.* Ya'kuby (*El-Ya'akubi*, p. 103) includes six places under the provinces dependent upon the Makka government, ending with "this is the sea-coast." The first may be read 'Asuf, which is qualified as "gold-mine"; the second is Baysch, and the one before the last is 'Athr.†

We have now travelled southwards to the borders of the Chaulân district, where, however, we have not yet found gold diggings. "Wady Baysch‡ (according to Ym. i. 720) is one of

of the Book of Genesis; and the country of the Χαυλοταῖοι; the later Greeks knew it as Εὐιλα. The common opinion of the Arabs is that Khaulán was a descendant of Kahtán (Joctan?); other genealogists say of Kahlán brother to Himyar; and he named a district in North-Western Yemen between San'aá and El-Hejaz. Sprenger places it in N. lat. 17°, amongst the Arabanitæ (Arhab); and west with a little southing from Marib of the Dyke.

* Geog. Gr. Min., cap. xcv. p. 184: *Debæ, partim nomades, partim agricolæ* (as the Midianite tribes are now); *quorum per mediam regionem amnis labitur, naturâ tripartitus; qui et ramenta* (spangles) *auri defert tam conspicuâ ubertate, ut limus ad ostia conservatus procul inde rutilet* (mica, or mica-schist?).

† Or Aththar (*Asr, Assar*), the name of a district about Wady Baysh; containing a town of the same name (Athr, etc., or Baysh), the latter a favourite trading place. According to Hamdâny (211), "Aththar is a glorious stretch of coast; it contains the capital city Baysh; the fertile and cultivated lands of Abrâq (*Abrák* or *Abrán?*), and the Wadies known as Al-Amân, Baysh, Itwad (in the Adm. Chart "Ewid," N. lat. 17° 34'), Bayd^h, Raym, 'Aramram, Onayf (or *Zonayf*), and 'Amud (Sprenger, § 48). For "Wâdi Bischa," see Zehme (*Arabien*, etc., pp. 45-47).

‡ "Bayshun"=Pishon. It is the *Baitii Osiâ* (Ptol. vi. 7, § 6) in N. lat. 20° 40', and 25 miles south of it (20° 15') lay the "Badeo Basileion" (Bayshtown or El-Asr). Baitius, the celebrated *flumen auriferum*, and represented to be 400 long, was certainly made by the ancients to "encompass the whole land of Havilah," as far as the latter is synonymous with the Khaulán district. It is, however, an imaginary stream, composed of at least three several Wadies, the latter separated by great deserts and high-water partings. It divided the

the countships (Mikhláf) of Yaman, and contains a number of mines." The truth is that it is a Wady, the Pison, or Pishon, of Scripture, and its chief settlement is called, from the frequent storms which afflict it, Abû Torâb, "father of dust" (dust-hole). Gold is here not named, but it is generally understood by Arabs under the generic word "Ma'din" (mine) used without qualification. And even if the geographer allude to abandoned works, we may hold that borings and shafts had been sunk there for the precious metal. In order to place this region correctly, we must seek Niebuhr's Attuiê in N. lat. 17° 36'; it corresponds with the Wady 'Itwad before mentioned.

Mahall Aby Torâb, properly called al-Râha, or the resting-place, lies some four hours' march to the north of 'Itwad, and consequently where Niebuhr (map of the Red Sea) shows the Dsjâbbel Nakâb (*Jebel el-Nukkáb*), the Knappenberg, or Miners' Hill. An allusion to such works may also be contained in the name "Al-Qayn"* (metal-workers), which (in Ym. iv. 219) is a town situated north of, and belonging to, Aththar (or Bayeh) City; it lies at the entrance to Yaman. Although this indication does not precisely fix its position, Al-Qayn must be close to Abû Torâb. Strictly speaking, these diggings hardly belong to Chaulân. Yet the division is not so marked as to prevent Hamdâny himself (p. 202) including the coast in that province. The Tihámat (lowlands) of the Chaulânites penetrate into the sea-board of Abrân near Baysch (Hd. 125), and into the shore of Umm-Gahdam.

In Chaulân proper is the place where Chron. (ii. 3. 6), speaking of Solomon's Temple, says, "the gold was the gold of Parvaim." The Arabs call it Farwa, and we find (Ym. iv. 147) a mine, one hour's march from it, thus noticed, " Al-Qofâ'a " is in the Ça'da Region,† or, more exactly speaking, in the Chaulân Province of Yaman: it is inhabited by the Banû Ma'mar b.

---

land of the Khaulataioi (Khaulán, Havilah) from Gaubitis, which Aristocreon, in Agatharkides, calls " Chabinus ;" and now it forms the demarking-line between El-Hejaz and El-Yemen.

* Hence the Beni El-Kayn (Qayn), the " sons of the metal-workers," are the mixed race of autochthons and Kudá'a (Qodhâ'ites), who exploited the mine of the Beny Solaym (Salma) lying nearly due north of Makka (Sprenger, p. 287).

† Sa'adah is the capital of Mara, north of Sana'á, capital of El-Yemen.

HOW THE GOLD WAS FOUND. 257

Zorara b. Chaulân, *and on that spot is a gold mine."* Hamdâny's text is corrupt where it says (201) *Al-Foqâ'a (sic!) is a market town* (there is) *the mine of Lahra;* or, as the sentence may also read, *Al-Foqâ'a is a market town, and a mine of the Horra.*

The site of these Farwa diggings can apparently be laid down with sufficient correctness. Hamdâny (82) remarks that Al-Chaçuf and Ca'da lie upon the same parallel (N. lat. 16° 35′, or rather 16° 30′); and the former, being upon the Golb (Jolb) River, was therefore named by Niebuhr after the Gholöb. We now ascend from the valley, and hard upon the highest part of the water-shed we find Al-Qofâ'a and Al-Bâr, the latter a heathen sanctuary at which the people of Yaman worshipped. Another fork of the Golb comes from the Ras Golb, near Al-Kadd in Al-Qarfâ'* or the Highlands of Chaulân (Hd. 130). Crossing the water-shed, and descending the eastern slope, we fall into the hydrographic basin of the Wady Nagran† *Nejrân*. This feature (according to Hd. 148–49) "receives the Fiumara that drains the country lying west of Ça'da, namely, the waters of 'Alâf, Al-Boqâ'a, Schi'b-Yr (Shi'ib-Ir), Al-Hadâyiq, Farwa, No'man, Afqyn, and Al-Aslâf. Thence trending to Al-Faydh, to Al-Çahn (*El-Sahn*), to . . . . and to Ça'da, the valley takes from the latter point the direction of Nagrân. No'mân, Al-Manfir and Farwa (Hd. 200) form a region with a winter-torrent and fountains, but without flowing water, except at Al-'Oschscha (*El-Ushshah*, the hut?) and Al-Batu, where there are rivulets.

Farwa and Al-Qofâ'a thus occupy the straight line, about eighty (geog.) miles, connecting Al-Chaçuf with Çad'a. Of these two places the first lies high above the eastern slope, and the second occupies the crest of the western declivity, whilst the distance between them perhaps does not exceed one hour's march. It is to be noted that Hamdâny's wadies (river-beds) begin with the water-shed, whether their springs are there or not. Even if no gold-mines exist in Farwa, the ores of Al-Qofâ'a may have borrowed its name.

I must also mention the gold-washings in Çirwâh (Sirwáh), which, according to Malvéy, the modern traveller in Yaman, are

* Thus the Karbai of Agatharkides and the Carphati of Pliny (vi. 32) are the Highlanders of Khaulán.
† The far-famed region east of the Asír Mountains, whose western faces shed to the Red Sea.

S

still worked. Part of this burgh existed in the days of Hamdâny, who remarked that it could not rival in greatness the other old settlements. It lies in Chaulân, or rather in Upper Chaulân; yet it is brought into connection after a remarkable manner (Iklyl, p. 37, and Ym. ii. 383) with the Qodhâ'itic* Chaulânites. Sa'd† (in the Iklyl As'ad) here dwelt, and hence, it would appear, the tribe in question removed to the Michlaf Ça'da. This notice goes so far back that its value must be based, not upon the verse of a comparatively modern poet, but upon some inscription in Çirwâh, containing the name of this Sa'd; and such a find is possible. We may then consider Çirwâh as a stage of the people of Chavila (Havilah) on the way to their later settlements in Michlâf-Ça'da; moreover, we may hold that the same race gave its name to Upper Chaulân, a name accepted by their successors, although belonging to another family.

Par. 56. Agatharkides ‡ notices that the nuggets (*gold klumpen*) found in the Debai region consist of the purest metal called ἄπυρον, because not requiring purification by fire. This epithet agrees with the Arabic "Tibr," unfused gold or nugget-gold, purer than stream-ore (washed from the sands); Tibrá being a nugget, whilst Dzahab (Dahab) is the generic name of the precious metal. The greater part of the gold known to the ancients was derived from their *pépites*,§ and some of them were of immense size.

---

* The Kudá'a, a great and powerful tribe, the Catabani or Cottabani of the classics, originally settled behind the modern Ras el-Hadd. About the time of the origin of El-Islam they extended inland, occupied larger tracts in North-Western Arabia, and gave their name to the cinnamon-like Laurus *Cassia*, probably through the Heb. "Kadí'a."

† His descendants took possession of the El-Jará'a, the land of the old Girrhæi, and stretched far to the east. See chap. vii.

‡ He gives (cap. xcvi.) a highly interesting account of gold amongst the Alilæi (? people of Hali, in N. lat. 18° 15′) and the Kasandreis (Gassandenses, Beni Ghassán). "In the crusty substrata of those lands they find a quantity of gold, not dust melted and treated with technological skill, but produced by nature, and called by the Greeks *Apyron*. The smallest pieces are not less than an olive-stone, the medium-sized equal a medlar, and the biggest a walnut. They wear these nuggets round their wrists and necks, threaded alternately with transparent stones, and sell them cheaply to their neighbours: brass (copper? zinc?) is worth thrice, iron double, and silver ten times its weight of gold." These harder metals, as I have shown, also exist in the mines of Midian and further south; possibly they were beyond the power of the savage smelter.

§ The nugget-formation is superficial, and, as I have warned the reader

Idrsy relates (i. 2) that the King of Ghâna preserved, as a rarity, a lump weighing thirty Ratl (each = 12 oz.) ; it was, however, of African, not of Arabian origin.*

As the Greeks probably had their own term for "Tibr" (nugget-gold), I am disposed to consider the *apyron* of Agatharkides a bastard-Grecian of a Semitic word. Hamdâny and Abûlfidâ (p. 157) distinguish the finest metal as "red gold" (*Dahab Ahmar*) ; and the Persians call the coins made of it Dynár-i-surch (*Surkh*). The Iklyl (viii. 77) relates that in Dhahr was found a woman's corpse, whose anklets weighed 100 Mithgâl (each 1½ drachmas), of "red gold," and this treasure-trove was so common as to give the popular name "grave-gold" (*Duhab Kubúri*) to the finer sort. The same work (p. 52) also notices that many such buried hoards were unearthed from the ruins between Gauf (*El-Jauf*) and Mârib.

In Pliny (xxi. 2, § 66) "Apyron" bears the sense of "red gold" : " Helichryos florem habit auro similem. . . . Hoc coronare Se Magi, si et unguenta sumantur ex auro, quod *apyron* vocant, ad gratiam quoque vitæ gloriamque pertinere arbitrantur." If in this passage "Magi" be the nominative of "vocant," the epithet *apyron* would appear to be an expression familiar to the Persians,† and, at any rate, it can hardly be distinct from the Ophir-gold, which is synonymous with "fine gold" (Is. xiii. 12).

A notice of gold in Arabia would not be complete without a few words touching the site of Ophir, which is so strongly fixed in the English brain, that my discoveries in Midian were at once reported to have brought to light Ophir. This famous mart has been found in almost every auriferous spot of the old and new hemispheres. Setting aside palpable absurdities such as Java and Sumatra, Malacca and the Moluccas, Armenia, Ceylon, and Peru, the principal claimants are now four : the two Sapphars, Soúpara, and the "Sofala, thought Ophir," of Milton.

In Southern Arabia there are two cities of similiar name. One, in Northern Hadramaut, is Dofar or Dafar, Zafar, Zafari, or

---

(chap. v.), we could not expect to find it in the well-worked lands of maritime Midian.

* I may add that the throne-stool of the King of Asiante (Ashantee) is composed of a single nugget in quartz.

† May it not be the translation of some such term as Zar-i-phushk, "dry gold"?

Tzafar (Sprenger), apparently the *Oraculum Dianæ* of the classics. The other, supposed to be the Sephar of Genesis (x. 30), and the capital of the Sabæans, is the Supphar of Pliny (vi. 26); the Saphàr of the Periplus (cap. xxiii.); the Supphàr of Ptolemy (vi. 7); the Tápharos of Philostorgius (Hist. Eccles. iii. 4, p. 478); the Tárphra of Ammianus Marcellinus (lib. xxiii. 6, § 47); the Tárphara of Stephanus; the Dophar of El-Idrísí; the Sifár or Difár of the Turk Haji Khalfeh (*Jehán-numá*); the Dsoffar or Zafar of Seetzen (*Monatlich. Correspond.* xxxviii. p. 228), and the Tzafar der Himyar of Sprenger. Niebuhr (*Beschreibung Arabiens*, pp. 236-290), who visited the site, placed it fifteen leagues from the sea, and, with El-Hamdání, about three marches south of Sana'á and nearly upon the same meridian.*

The next claimant is the Soúppara (Suppara), which Arrian (Perip. cap. 52) places between Burygaza (Baroch, Broach) and Kallíenapólis, the well-known Kalyan ("the prosperous") behind Bombay. It is called Soúpara by Ptolemy (vii. 1, § 6) and by El-Idrisi Soupara (i. 171), which Benfey (i. 28) would render "pulcrum litus" (*Su-para*). This famous old mart is usually identified with Surat, the capital of Surashtra, the "good land," the "land of the Saura worshippers." Much has been written upon the Suppara-Ophir connection, but my volume is not the place to enter into that fraction of the subject.

Lastly, "Sófala" in the Mozambique Channel (S. lat. 20° 15') should be Safálah, feminine of Safal, "the low-lying"; whilst "Safál" is still applied in Arabia to coast-plains. It would *not*, however, correspond with the Hebrew Shephâlah, in sense at least, as Smith's Dictionary of the Bible appears to think.† In the LXX. Ophir becomes Soúfir, Soufeír, Sōfír, Sōfeír, Sōphērá and Sófará; and from the latter Sefala or Safalah would easily be corrupted by the great South-African family of language, which habitually confounds the two liquids.

A fifth and modern claimant to the ancient honours of Ophir

* Of course this inland mart would have a port; possibly Muza or Mouza on the same parallel.

† *S.v.* Ophir. As regards Mr. Crawfurd's assertion (*ibid.*) that sandal-wood is unfit for such articles as pillars and stairs, the boxes made at Bombay should have shown him that it is well fitted for veneering. Similarly, the three columns inside the Ka'abah, or *Maison Carrée*, of Meccah ("Pilgrimage," iii. 289), are covered with carved "aloes-wood" (*Aquilaria Ovata* or *Agallochum*, agila or eagle-wood).

was brought home by the late Dr. Carl Manch, in the shape of the South African ruins of Zimbabye (S. lat. 20° 15'). Dr. Beke, after examining facsimiles of the drawings made by the ill-starred traveller who perished so miserably, distinctly denies that the remains are Tyro-Israelitish, and suggests that the founders were those Southern Arabians who, as the representatives of the Biblical nations Sheba and Ophir, traded in the remotest times with, and still hold settlements upon, the East African coast. He thus concludes, " the buildings at Zimbabye are, not improbably, of the same age as the cities of Bashan; which were, without a single exception, erected during the six centuries which elapsed from the time of Christ till the age of Mahomet." Sprenger, highly scandalised by the pompous title, "Ancient Ophir Rediscovered," which, applied to Zimbabye, went the round of the German press, wrote (p. 58) in ridicule of Herr Petermann, the Wise Man of Gotha, the following tirade. "Upon the identity of the two there is no doubt in the mind of the enterprising traveller, as he found the ruins of a temple like that of Jerusalem, and traces of Israelitic worship. Probably the Psalms were also sent thither, to be chaunted as soon as they were composed; and perhaps Dr. Manch was only just too late to catch their latest echoes."

Sprenger, who evidently thinks the three-years' voyage to be a mere exaggeration, would place Ophir, the country, in Southern Arabia, and perhaps identify it with Havilah or Khaulán. Dr. Krapf found Ophir in the Áfer or Danákil tribe, settled in Africa opposite El-Yemen; unfortunately the land contains no gold. Dr. Beke would put Ophir close to Sheba; and he has been true to his theory since 1834, when he published his *Origines Biblicæ* (p. 511). Then he placed Ophir near Opis to the west of where the Erythræan Sea, or old Persian Gulf, heads, in the immediate neighbourhood of Havilah (west of Baghdád), and Sheba (south of Havilah). In a subsequent publication ("The Sources of the Nile." London: Madden, 1860), he derived the "gold of Ophir" from Eastern Africa. His strong position is the natural influence that " the mention of Ophir in connection with (and between) the two Arabian countries of Sheba and Havilah (Gen. x. 28–29) ought to be conclusive that Ophir itself was in Arabia." * I

---

* See Dr. Beke's letter of March, 1872; quoted by Mrs. Beke (note to chap. xii.).

cannot, however, agree with him when he says, "during the brief interval* (of the 250 years enjoyed by the Red Sea commerce), it is not likely that the Tyro-Israelitish fleets continued their voyages to the East Coast of Africa, even if the Arabians had allowed them to interfere with their monopoly; and still less that they should have penetrated as far inland as Zimbabye." Both these objections are weak. The Jews might have traded with the Africano-Arabs; and the inland travel in those days would have been no great feat.

I prefer the opinion that "Ophir," instead of being a single mart, applies to several countries: that it means the "Red Land," an epithet equally fitted to Eastern Africa and to Western India; and that when the "Ships of Tarshish and Ophir," are mentioned, the reference is to large vessels built for buffeting the stormy seas of the farthest West and the farthest East.† "Ofir" which in Central Arabia would be pronounced "Áfir" (Sprenger, p. 57), means "red" in Southern Arabia; and the Mahrah tribe of Hadramaut still call Mare Rubrum "Buhr Ofir." The late Baron von Wrede's little Himyaritic vocabulary (*Journ. R.G.S.*, xiv. 110), is *not* the "authority of a single traveller." Maltzan (xxvii. 230), whose attention was devoted to philology, gives the word Ôfir, Ohfar, and so forth, confirming the *Journ. As. Soc., Bengal*, (iv. 165), in which the people of Socotra are made to assign the same signification to the word. Thus Maltzan rejects the 'Ayn ‡ which Dr. Carter, writing "'Aofer," evidently would retain; and in classical Arabic 'Ufr (عفر) = red, certainly cannot be written with an "Alif." But we find signs of the same anomaly in Hebrew. The few passages in the Books of Kings and Chronicles all give ארפיר ('Ofîr), whilst in Job (xxviii. 6) we find עפרות זהב ('Ofirúth Dahab); in the A.V. "dust of gold," or gold ore, written in the plural with the Oin.

By assuming that "Ophir," the Red Land, is generic, and not applied to a single emporium, firstly, we get over the difficulty of

* That is between Circa B.C. 1014, when Solomon and Hiram equipped the Ophir-fleet, and B.C. 740, when Elath was taken from the Jews by Rezin, King of Syria. See chap. xii.

† I shall attempt to prove that "Tarshísh," the city, was situated in the Bay of Gibraltar.

‡ The assertion (Smith's Dict. *s.v.* Ophir), that the Alif and the Ayn are interchangeable is most objectionable: the latter in all the Semitic tongues is one of the most tenacious of letters.

the three-years' voyage, if this period be not "writ large" in the three versions of the episode. Secondly, although an emporium in Yemen, or even an island in the Red Sea, as Eupolemus believed, may have collected gold and silver, ivory and peacocks; yet the word Tukkíyyím, in Kings (i. 10. 22), and Túkíyyím, in Chronicles (ii. 9. 21), is evidently borrowed from the Tamil-Malayalam.* With them "Tokei," or "Tókei," with the first vowel now short then long, denotes the "bird with the (resplendent) tail." In order to turn the obstacle, certain theorists have proposed to metamorphose the turkey into a parrot, thus sweeping away with a stroke of the pen, the tradition of nearly three thousand years. Why will Biblical students forget that there are such things as Talmuds and Targums?

The "peacock," which does not exist either in Arabia or in Africa, may fairly suggest that the Ophir-voyage extended to the Western Coast of India. But if to India, what more probable than that one of the three years should have been spent upon the Mozambique Coast? The Phœnician sailor, who explored the stormy Baltic and the wild seas of the West Libyan shore, would hardly be deterred by the dangers of Zanzibar and the Koukan.

In a private letter addressed to me from Wabern (May 18th), the author of the *Alte Geographie* says, "The credit of having made a discovery, whose results cannot be overrated, is due to you. I think, however, that you have, as yet, taken only the first step; and that much greater and more profitable results are awaiting you in Southern Arabia. Do not forget the old mines in Dhankân; in Dsjäbbel al-Nuḳḳâb; in the Wady Baysch, and in Kufâ'ah or Fukâ'ah. Do not neglect Mogaddasy's gold-digging of Marwa, only four days from Al-Higr, on the western road to Madyna: further west of Marwa, on the way to Haurâ, the harbour, you may, perhaps, find coal; and, though I am not sanguine as to its quantity, still it would be worth while to make a trial. Nor do I think it impossible that the mines of Nagd (*Nejd*) may prove even richer than those of Southern Arabia; the latter, however, are all near the coast, and none of them extend inland beyond forty (English) miles. It is the interest of the world to assist you in making further researches; and I hope that

---

* P. 91. 2nd edit. "Comparative Grammar of the Dravidian Languages," by the Rev. Robert Caldwell. London: Trübner, 1875.

in a couple of years you will be able to throw full light upon the subject."

In contrast to these sober and sensible views, I cannot help quoting the following curious letter addressed by a Mr. William Gosling to the Editor of the *Jewish Chronicle and Hebrew Observer* (No. 9, March 25, 1855), and headed "Gold and Silver in Palestine":—

"It is now more than three years since I had the honour of addressing the Earl of Shaftesbury on the subject of the gold and silver mines in Palestine; and although I have not had an opportunity of making any practical geological researches, yet by dint of close study I have been led to conclude that gold and silver are more abundant in the land of Israel than in those of Australia and California. For I find it written that 'The land is also full of silver and gold, neither is there any end of their treasures' (Is. ii. 7. Comp. Deut. viii. 9, describing the Promised Land, 'Whose stones are iron, and out of whose hills thou mayest dig brass'). . . . What then will be the great source of attraction to the Jews to return to the Land of Palestine? I answer, *The discovery of Gold and Silver in the hills of their own country, particularly that of Sidon and Sarepta*, where I believe it will be found in such abundance that it will eclipse the discoveries made in Australia and California. I am glad, therefore, to find that the *inhabitants of Sidon are bestirring themselves in the matter* (?). To my mind it is like the little cloud, which the Prophet Elijah's servant saw, about the size of a man's hand, which was the precursor of abundant rain. So it will lead to great discoveries."

CHAPTER X.

THE RETURN FROM THE WHITE MOUNTAIN TO EL-MU-
WAYLÁH, *viâ* WADY SHARMÁ AND WADY TIRYAM.
NOTES ON BOTANY.

WITH a last fond look at the *Grand Filon*, we set out next morning (April 11th), westing towards the Erythræan Sea. Nothing could be more refreshing than the sense of complete freedom, of breathing boundless air, of feeling that the world lay open before one. The sunrise was of splendid wildness, the rays of light being divided by the peaked and pinnacled sky-line of the mountain-wall into distinct and several shafts which, sharply defined on the east, melted away before they reached the zenith.

The gorgeously-tinted gala-robes worn by the giants of earth; seawards the *ora variis ornata coloribus*, which even the ancients, who cared little for landscape, described as a *Mirificum præternavigantibus Spectaculum;* and the infinite shades and shiftings of colour, which made the features of the ground mobile as the face of the waves—were the especial charms of the morning hours. Nor could we help admiring the perfumed vegetation of the Desert; small, tender and *mignonne* as that of Iceland, and filling the liberal air with its lavish fragrance.

After many a halt to "prospect," we entered the smooth line of the Wady el-Maka'adah, which begins at the station. A carriage* and four could be driven along it, avoiding only the normal outcrops and islets of grey granite, here and there weathered to whiteness. Presently this rock entirely disappeared, and we saw nothing but *débris* of porphyry, which had slipped from the lofty red walls of the cañon.

The dromedaries came up with us after a walk of fifty minutes; and now we determined to try their speed. After travelling about nine miles, we were shown on the left the head of Wady Sharmá, the objective of our march: we presently learned why the guides did not take the direct road down the great southern fork, whose "báb" (gate) is rendered impassable to camels by a marsh. The Bedawin pointed out to us the valley-banks of ruddy-pink, and told us that the same material formed the surface of the Hismá.

* I lately heard of a dignitary making the Pilgrimage from Cairo in a carriage. Presently there will be Wenham Lake ice on the Hajj road, and the days of Hárún el-Rashíd will be revived.

Presently we reached the seaward gap of Wady el-Maka'adah, and once more felt the delicious gulf-breezes full in our faces. This breach in the *falaise*, as usual about 200 mètres broad, is distinguished from its inhabited neighbours by being waterless; consequently there are no ruins, and thorns usurp the place of palms. Here we stood nearly opposite the southern end of the long strip of wooded island "Umm Maksúr." The shore was close at hand; and we were shown the place where the Arabs collect, when the waters are dried up, a coarse and sandy salt. The lower bed of the Fiumara, after issuing from the gate, hence changes its name to Wady Melláhah of Salinas.

We then wound along the seaward face of the ancient cliff, and passed, on the left, a second gap, or rather crack, tortuous and rock-strewn, which splits the wall from top to bottom. This gorge also has evidently never had tenants. On the right was a small cemetery of Bedawin graves, over which no man recited a Fátihah; and after a sharp trot of nearly three hours,[*] we sighted with pleasure the long and broad "Nakhil" (*palmetum*) that announces Wady Sharmá, with its dates and dorns, reeds,

[*] We set out at 5.10 a.m., and arrived at 8.45 (=3 h. 35'): of this we walked 50' (= 2 miles) and rode 2 h. 45' (=14 miles), or a total of 16 miles. At Camp Wady Sharmá, the aneroid showed 29·30 and the therm. (F.) at 2 p.m., when the Khamsín was blowing; 93° in the shade.

sedges, and rushes. Water, treacherously clear and crystalline, but highly sulphureous, flowed over the sands in a prattling stream, and below camp formed a long pool, where all the birds of the neighbourhood assembled to chat and drink. A bath was immediately hollowed out; and the tents were pitched upon the raised right bank, beyond the reach of the *mali culices*, the gnats, the mosquitoes, and especially the flies, which here, I have said, are considered poisonous.

When the air had somewhat cooled, Mr. Clarke and Shaykh Abd el-Nabi set out on their dromedaries to bring up the remainder of our camp from Wady Aynúnah. I had resolved to rendezvous at the next station, and to march in one body upon El-Muwayláh. We then proceeded to inspect the "houses of the Nazarenes," which had been described to us as larger and more important than in the other cities of Midian; whilst the local supply of iron-ore is famous amongst the Bedawin.

The shelf upon which the tent stood was a mass of *débris*, pottery-sherds, scoriæ, and ashes—in fact, animal and vegetable matter, capped with that saline efflorescence which the people connect with ancient ruins. A couple of men, set to dig, found nothing save a scorpion. We then walked to the place where the Wady splits and forms a long flat holm, uniting somewhat below it. This was the site of a strong fortress, with angles adapted to the ground, and with the usual complicated entrance, apparently a long *couloir*. It was several kilomètres in circuit, and the plan-tracing occupied Lieutenants Árif and Hasan until noon the next day. They also hunted out the furnaces, whose scoriæ strewed the maritime plain; while I collected pottery, but failed to find any glass-fragments. The only other remarkable work of the old town was a deep cut in the soft rock, apparently artificial, and possibly used for metal-washing : it extended from the ruins to the northern bank of the stream's southern branch, where the waters slept in a dark, deep, and sullen pool, which did not invite a header.

Thence we walked up the Wady Sharmá, a generic name made proper;* and found the fine palm-grove in the same neglected condition as that of Wady Aynúnah, while traces of Bedawi fires appeared in the shape of scorched trunks, standing as well as felled. A swamp defends the upper part of the islet, while the right bank, choked with marsh and vegetation, hardly affords a footpath. The tall and stiff *falaise*, now based as usual upon granite, is composed of the normal stalactite-like corallines and meandrinæ. The material shows frequent moulds of Venus, oyster, and other modern

* Sharm being a bight or creek : the principal port in Hadramaut is also called Sharmá.

shells, with impressions of pectens and crystallised carbonate of lime in patches, which make good cabinet specimens. Throughout the lower part appeared poor carbonate of iron in masses. This somewhat puzzled us; the signs of working were extensive; the white stone had been laid bare; and yet, of what value could such metal have been? The next march, however, explained away all our difficulties.

Nothing would be easier than to dam the valley, like that of Aynúnah, and to secure a good head of water for stamping the less valuable yields. The stone in which gold or argentiferous galena occurs would repay the expense of sending to Suez. The form of dykes will demand the study of an experienced engineer. At times the momentum of the torrent must be enormous; but as the ancients evidently succeeded in such works, there is no reason why we moderns should fail. The upper heights of the old sea-cliff were strewed with ferruginous grit and fragments of porphyry, giving a red and white colouring, both equally vivid. I asked Sálih, the guide, whether any settlement was to be found above. He replied by a categorical "No," and presently excused himself, protesting his ignorance.

We swarmed up, by a rain-gash, the highly-inclined flank of the *falaise;* and at once, on reaching the top, came upon the workmen's quarters. The site is curious, a buttress or snout projecting from the right cliff-wall far into the Wady, running east to west, with a hollow semicircle facing south, and defended by an almost perpendicular fall northwards. The houses, made of rough stone laid in mortar, occupied the base and the tip of the tongue. As at Aynúnah, the tenements were huddled together, and did not exceed the size of Hindú huts. It was night before we reached camp, and want of time prevented our visiting the sea-board to ascertain whether Sharmá, like Aynúnah and Tiryam, had its settlement of *richards* near the sea. The hot walk and climb were bad preparations for the damp raw air of the well-watered valley, where we dined *à la belle étoile*.

The next march, Sharmá to Wady Tiryam, began with a walk of two hours and a half, over the Tihamat-Madyan—the nature-reclaimed maritime flat with the normal bulging stripes or waves of dark stone, alternating with parallel lines of deep, loose, and light-coloured sand. The direction was southerly, with a little westing. We crossed, after about six miles, the large Wady Nakhbár, and we saw, at a considerable distance inland, the great gap of the Wady Kuhlah: it is the upper course of the Wady Tiryam, whose broad and broken bed debouches into the sea a little north of the Ras or promontory, the latter marked by the high sand-heaps which we had seen from the Sambúk.

After four hours of slow work, covering thirteen to fourteen miles,* we came upon an irregular enceinte of rough stone, protecting a broad shelf on the right bank of the Fiumara. It also defended a large cistern much resembling those of the Wady Aynúnah, but of inferior construction; the mortar contained very little brick, and the cement was of coarser texture. Remembering how the Hajj-road had been supplied with tanks by the piety of Zubaydah Khátún † and others in the olden day, I suggested to the Bedawin that this "hauz," or rather Kárif (= reservoir), might be one of the number. They all declared that it was the work of the Nasárá; and the Egyptian officers, when making their plans, discovered it to be the head of an aqueduct intended to feed the maritime settlement.

Wady Tiryam, evidently one of the most important positions, with the broadest and deepest torrent-bed, has no rivulet. The Bedawin assert that apparently causeless changes have taken place during the last few years; and none of them remembered any shocks of earthquakes.‡ Rüppell (p. 217) on

* We set out at 4.20 a.m., and arrived at 9.20 (= 4 h.): of this we walked 2 h. 30' (= 7 miles) and rode 1 h. 30' (= 7 miles), or a total of 14 miles. The caravan came in at 10.30 p.m.
† See my "Pilgrimage," iii. 2.
‡ The disappearance of springs is common in Arabia: Wallin heard of the phenomenon at El-Karayá, near Tabúk, and at the ancient site, El-Feríri in the Ketayfi mountain.

July 8th, 1626, here found a flowing *bach* seven feet broad and four inches deep. Above the camping-place, on a kind of terrace, surrounded by palms, and showing by its large mounds and its salt earth that it was once inhabited, there are a few shallow pits in the Wady-sand which supply turbid water. The "mud-doctor," as he is irreverently called, has long ago untaught me the old-Adam prejudice against drinking clean dirt. *En revanche*, the air is exceptionally light (*i.e.*, heavy) and elastic after the heavy (*i.e.*, light) dampness of Wady Sharmá.

Shortly after we had breakfasted, the remainder of the caravan came in from Aynúnah,* and Haji Wali rode up with all the air and spirit of a middle-aged man. He "nakh'd"† his dromedary, which he had preferred to the weak-kneed Huwayti donkeys; and he carried his baggy galligaskins with a *jarret tendu*. The old man was in excellent spirits, having heard of our good fortune: he no longer feared to return home with a "black-face." He had drunk beer during the whole of his halt, declaring that the water disagreed with him; and a couple of bottles a day had evidently suited his constitution—he even

* The caravan set out at 5.30 a.m., and arrived at 12.45; a total of 7 h. 15′ = 15 miles, or three hours of moderate dromedary travelling. Mr. Clarke rode the distance in 5 h. 45′, and Haji Wali in 6h. 15.

† To "nakh" is to make the camel kneel by ejaculating "Ikh! Ikh!" and by touching the neck with the staff. See my "Pilgrimage," chap. viii. and xiii., vol. i.

T

talked of marrying a fourth wife. But, having returned to respectability and Zagázig, he touched very lightly, I am told, upon the matter of the Giaour beverage.

During the afternoon we examined the right bank, which gave a view of the island-town's site; although nothing of it remained but the earthwork fronting northwards. The high and hilly ground bounding the Wady had evidently been guarded with unusual care; and, though the fortifications had become mere piles of large rounded pebbles, it was easy to trace their form and extent.

Above the rough enceinte of dry wall through which we had approached the valley, and occupying a small platform strewed with red porphyries, petrosilex, and ferruginous grits, were the ruins of a number of detached towers. A little higher rose a square work (Masna'a), with three round bastions facing the north. Still higher upon the eastern heights appeared two more "burj" (*pyrgoi*), and outlying heaps crowned the summits which commanded the upper course of the stream. The right bank explained the mystery of the Sharmá settlement. Evidently the blood-red earth of the Hismá had here been washed. It lay in patches upon the hills, and formed part of the Fiumara-cliffs, where oxygen had converted it, like the Taná of the Brazil, into marbled masses of pink and mauve.

Our evening "Samrah" (Chat) was enlivened by a certain Háj Akil bin Muhaysin, who called himself, what he was not, Shaykh of the Masá'id clan, tenants of Maghárat Shu'ayb.* I did not much like the man, a *parlous* youth that boasted too much of his position. He was grasping as an Icelander and overgreedy of bakhshísh, even applying for a companion whom he had brought with him. Some day, however, he may be useful in escorting travellers inland, where the other Huwaytát cannot accompany them. He also described Tabúk and El-Hijr, both of them stations on the Caravan-road from Damascus, and both full of interest to me.

Tabúk † is a village and a pilgrim-station for the Syrian caravan in the Hismá-land, belonging to the Beni Ma'ázeh, and built on the eastern *versant* of the second or inland parallel chain. It is known to

* See chap. vi. Rüppell (p. 214) makes his "Musaiti" occupy the land between Beder (Bada' or Magharat-Shu'ayb) and El-Akabah : he suspects that they were Jews early converted to El-Islam, reports their want of hospitality, and ignores their numbers.

† Written Tabuc by Sale (Koran, p. 143, n.), who describes it "as a town situate halfway between Medina and Damascus." Belonging to the Greeks under the Emperor Heraklius, it was attacked by Mohammed with 30,000 men in A.H. 9 ; and it is the northernmost point of the Apostle's campaigns from El-Medinah. Wallin's map places it in N. lat. 28°, and in E. long. 37° 10' ; while Sprenger prefers N. lat. 29°, a little south of, and some 30° 30' (=210 dir. geog. miles) east of El-Akabah. The Kánún has E. long. 58° 50', and N. lat. 27° ; and the Atwál the same longitude, but with N. lat. 30°—an error on the other side.

geographers by the detailed account of Wallin,* who travelled under the name of Haji Wali. He places it in the centre of a large plain, the Hemádat Tabúk, amongst the red *buttes*, an oasis in a dry and thirsty land, plentifully supplied with sweet water, and growing garden-stuff and a little grain, dates, pomegranates, almonds, and even vines.

Abulfeda,† who died in A.D. 1331, notices that it is in the third climate, near the great Bádiyat el-Shám, the desert south and east of the Holy Land (not *les campagnes de Syrie*),‡ and lying between

* Wallin, *loc., cit.* 312-320. The Swede was an excellent traveller, hardy, and temperate as a Bedawi; but he lacked the fine ear that distinguished Burckhardt. His descriptions of desert-life are charmingly simple and natural.

† *Géographie d'Abulfeda* (Isma'íl ibn Ali bin El-Sultan el-Muzaffar, etc.), *traduction française par M. Reinaud: Imprimerie nationale.* 2 vols. in fol. Paris, 1848. The reigning Prince of Hamáh (Hamath) wrote two great works: 1. Takwím El-Buldán (Table of Countries), disposed by Tables according to the order of the Climates, with longitudes and latitudes after the Ptolemeian pattern; and 2. El-Mukhtasar fí Akhbári 'l Bashar (an Epitome of the Universal History of Mankind). From the latter Pococke (edit. 1806) drew his "Specimens." The mediæval Arab writers who preceded, or are associated with, this kinsman of the great Saladin, were Ibn Khordábeh, El-Mas'údi, Abu Zayd, El-Istakhri, Ibn Haukal, El-Bayrúni, El-Idrísí, Yakút, Ibn Sayd, El-Kazwíni, Ibn Batútah, Sidi Ali Chelebi, and Haji Khulfah.

‡ Golius (4°, 1669 Amsterdam, *Notec in Alfragano, i.e.*, El-Ferghání, who flourished A.D. 800) more correctly says, "Regionem hanc (*i.e.*, El-Hejaz) quoque terminat ad boream Arabia deserta, quam illi (*Bádietu-l-Shám*) *desertum* sive *campos Syriæ* vocant." This vast wilderness extends, with a few scattered oases, to the valley of the Euphrates.

Syria and El-Héjaz. It has a spring and palm-trees, and it was occupied by the men of El-Ayká,* to whom Allah commissioned Shu'ayb † (Koran, surat vii., Sale, p. 116, and s. xi., Sale, p. 170); the latter, however, belonged not to them, but to the tribe of Madyan ("Ahl Madyan"). As a rule Arabian geographers connect the names of Tabúk and Madyan, the city, placing the former to the east and the latter to the west. Tabúk may be so honoured in consequence of the tradition which makes Mohammed ascend a hill in the neighbourhood, and turning northwards exclaim, "All this is Shám" (Syria), and turning southwards, "All this is Yemen."

Even more interesting is El-Hijr,‡ head-quarters of the Troglodytic Tamúd, the rocky place or Petra, the townlet also called Madyan Sálih, which Sprenger (p. 146) identifies with the Egra of Ptolemy, and places in N. lat. 26°, or 3° (180 miles)

* El Ayká (others write, after Egyptian and Syrian fashion, Al Eiké) is supposed to be a wood in the land of Midian, where Shu'ayb or Jethro prophesied to the Midianites. See Ayrton's note to Dr. Wallin's Route, p. 318.

† In both places the Koran says, "And unto Madyan we sent their brother Shu'ayb."

‡ Wallin (p. 237) believes the Wady el-Kora to head at El-Hijr (the ring-wall), and to debouch at El-Wijh, the latter being Strabo's Egra, meaning the port-town of El-Hijr. According to Sprenger, El-Hijr had three havens: 1. El-Amid to the north; 2. El-Wijh the central; and 3. El-Haurá the southern, where most geographers find the Leuke-Kome, the Nabathæan port.

south of Tabúk, also upon the Damascus-Medinah line. Here a mountain still bearing the name of Jebel el-Nákeh (of the she-camel), attests the Judæo-Arabs' miracle of Nabí Sálih and the men of Támúd.* It is related that when the Apostle of Allah passed through the demon-haunted defiles, he veiled his head, muffled his face, and hurried his pace on account of the Jinns and Ghúls which infest them, forbidding his followers to halt there either for food or drink. We rationalistic moderns have determined that El-Hijr must contain, besides inscriptions, statues or reliefs of the pagan day; but as yet no traveller has visited it.

* The Tamúd (Thamoudeni of Agatharkides) are the same as the Themuditæ of Pliny on the south coast of El-Muwayláh; north-western Arabia being known generally as Thamuditis. These names derive from the posterity of Tamúd, the grandson of Aram, and consequently of the Arab el-Aribah, the pure or genuine Arabs. Sprenger (§ 329), quoting Uranius, says that their city was near the Nabathæans, and derives the name of the Horite-Idumæan race from Thamad; scarcity of water. They fell into idolatry, when the Prophet Sálih (Bochart identifies him with Selah and D'Herbelot with Phaleg, both probably being misled by Biblical prepossessions), who lived during the interval between Húd and Abraham, was sent to bring them back to the worship of Allah. I need hardly waste time upon the tales of the pregnant she-camel issuing from the rock; the impious slaughter of the beast, and the "visitation of Providence," an earthquake and a terrible noise, the voice of the Archangel Gabriel crying, "Die, all of you!" Sálih and his few converts retired to Palestine, and died at Meccah (Sale, Prel. Disc. p. 5). The more general idea is that Sálih fled to Palestine, and is buried in a cave under the "White Mosque" of Ramleh. There must have been later Tamúd like the later Ád, for their horsemen served in the Roman army.

Years ago Hofrath Alfred von Kremer, the learned author of the *Cultursgeschichte des Orients unter den Chalifen,* now Austrian Commissioner in Egypt, visited Damascus by the advice of Baron von Hammer-Purgstall, with the intention of exploring El-Hijr. He failed from the difficulty of finding a guide, and owing to the exorbitant sum demanded for camels and escort. I also had made arrangements with Findi El-Fá'iz, Shaykh of the Beni-Sakr who convey to El-Medinah the Tayyárah or plying caravan, to transport me, when that "unspeakable Turk," the late Aali Pasha of infamous memory, caused my recall from Syria.

On Friday, April 13th, we returned to El-Muwayláh. There was some trouble in leaving Wady Tiryam : the Huwaytát declared that they could not detach their camels for fear of the Beni-Ma'ázeh, who infest this border-station ; and the Egyptian officers wished to measure the ruins, to survey the site, and to follow us at their leisure. We, the Europeans, set out down the Wady at 5 a.m., to inspect the maritime settlement, with a Bedawi guide and six soldiers, leaving the rest in case of a possible Kaum (raid). The walking in loose sand and over crumbling Sabkheh (salt earth) was not a pleasure. After an hour and a quarter we reached the "houses of the Nasárá," which, like the other settlements, have been rased to the ground. It was a scatter of large tenements, a Leuke-Kome, a white village or castle, built of snowy coral (madrepore); and apparently it had been walled round. We picked up many fragments of green-blue glass, more or less iridised; and were shown the aqueduct, whose terminal tank * is now buried under the sands. The Tiryam establishment was one of the largest, and it lies a few yards south of the Wady, and directly north of the sand-heaps and the projecting yellow point known as Ras Wady Tiryam. Somewhere hereabouts must have been the old pilgrim-station El-Silah.

This Tiryam is the third large establishment which we have found between El-Muwayláh and Aynúnah, a distance of only twenty-seven direct geographical miles. In fact, I may say that every Hydreuma, as Strabo calls the Wadies supplying water, was provided with its several settlements of metal-workers. How far these men extended eastward into the interior we could gather only from hearsay; but the distance may safely be laid down at fifteen hours' march. It must be evident that what enabled such towns to live and thrive, can hardly fail to enrich the industrials of our modern day. And here we see, well displayed, the life of old Midian; the "cities" and "goodly castles" near

---

* Rüppell (p. 217) describes it as a rhomb-shaped hydræum or piscina, with sides about forty feet long, ten feet deep, and revetted with stucco.

the sea, and the hordes of tent-dwellers of the interior who meet the Bene-Kedem, the eastern Bedawin. The only difference is that now the nomad has prevailed over the citizen; but the turn of the latter will come again.

Our riding-camels found us without delay; and we fell at once into the Hajj road, at a place where the wretched Maghribís or North-Western Africans encamp. From El-Muwayláh to Wady Aynúnah the line skirts the shore; hence the pilgrims, who know the ready shooting of the Bedawin too well to straggle from the beaten path, see from a distance, but never visit, the "palmeta" of Wadies Tiryam and Sharmá. The march to El-Muwayláh was monotonous enough, with the flat sand-banks seawards, and inland the peaky sandstone hillocks, one detached and tall; but we were consoled by the sight of the corvette lying at anchor off the Fort.

The country was a succession of divides and valleys; the latter, as usual, all honoured with names. At last we debouched upon the reefy shore; and, passing the tombs of Shaykh Abdullah, we entered the Fort. We were received with the effusion which our success deserved. As we drank coffee under the cool main-entrance,* speci-

* We set out walking at 5 a.m., and reached the debouchure of the valley at 6.15 (= 1 h. 15' = 4 miles). We rode alternately fast and slow between 6.30 a.m. and 10.20 (= 3 h. 50' = 16 miles), or a total of 20. On the chart the direct distance between the

mens of the promised seed-pearls were asked for, but they had not been procured. The only "antikás" were a Portuguese silver coin with the castles, and a copper piece bearing the "seal of Solomon," with the legend "Zuriba fí Mishk" (struck at Damascus). We carried away, however, a fine specimen of free gold in a water-rolled fragment of porphyritic greenstone. According to local accounts, it had long been lying about the Fort, and had lately been picked up there by the little daughter of the official who presented it to me. Finally it was taken by the Princesses in Cairo, who framed it and placed it in their museum.

I was careful to collect botanical specimens throughout the region which we visited, the septentrional Africano-Arabian zone connecting Morocco with the Persian Gulf, and including Sinai and the Libanus. But the work was a *hors d'œuvre;* and, as the Persians say, time was "narrow." The Bedawin lent willing aid, and gave me the names and the peculiarities of every plant, rarely saying, "I don't

Ras Wady Tiryam and the Muwayláh Fort is 11 miles. Our marches and stations were thus :—

	Miles.
1. (April 9) from Aynúnah to Wady Morák ...	14
2. (April 10) to the Jebel el-Abyaz	17·50
3. (April 11) to Wady Sharmá	16
4. (April 12) to Wady Tiryam	14
5. (April 13) to El-Muwayláh	20
	81·50

know it." Their excellent memories enabled them to remember every item that we gathered; and they took the kindly interest of the Eastern man in adding to my store. This unaffected and childlike display of benevolence in small things, be it genuine or affected, is, perhaps, the great charm of Oriental life and travel; and it explains the fact that many an ancient maiden has regarded with peculiar complacency her berry-brown dragoman and his very big bags.

Convinced that every botanical specimen from unknown Midian would be useful to connect it with the adjacent flora, and suspecting that the Highlands—which we ascended to about 1,500 feet, until many plants were stunted to an inch or two—might possibly afford novelties, I gave as much time as could be spared to collection. The *hortus siccus* was, of course, very imperfect. We were wholly unprepared; we wanted press and even brown paper, the place of which was taken by bits of newspaper; and many of the specimens brought by the Bedawin lacked flower or fruit, or both. Such as it is, however, the harvest was forwarded to Professor Balfour, of Edinburgh, after being tidied by my friend and fellow traveller, Dr. Carlo de Marchesetti, of Trieste, who favoured me with a few manuscript observations.

The flora of the region which we traversed

remarkably resembles that of Sinai and the Desert between it and the "Holy Land," extending down the Arabian coast as far as its southern apex. Geographically speaking, the Nile forms a distinct frontier between the two *facies;* Syro-Arab to the east and Lybio-African on the west; but the vegetation does not submit to this law. Dr. Anderson * tells us that the growth of Aden closely resembles that of Arabia Petræa, of which it is evidently the extension. The botanical characteristic of this Desert is the small proportion of species to the inordinate number of genera and natural orders; indeed, he declares that this holds true even when the flora is compared with those of places having similar areas and similar relations to the mainland.† While

* "*Florula Adenensis.* A Systematic Account, with Descriptions, of the Flowering Plants hitherto found at Aden." By Thomas Anderson, Esq., M.D., F.L.S., H.M.'s Bengal Medical Service. *Journ. Proceed. Linnean Soc.* Supplement to vol. v. "Botany." London: Longmans, 1860.

† At Aden Dr. Anderson found the total number of natural orders 41; of genera, 79; of species, 94. The following table shows the actual paucity of species at the "Coal-Hole," proving that the great relative preponderance of natural orders and genera does not necessarily distinguish the vegetation of similar localities, since it is entirely due to climatic causes, instead of being the result of situation or of isolation:—

	Natural Orders.	Genera.	Species.
Aden affords	41	79	94
Hongkong	122	560	965
Ischia (Bay of Naples) ...	86	372	794
Gibraltar	68	243	456

Professor Ascherson, who accompanied M. Gerhard Rohlfs in

the species are limited, only a few of the more arid forms preponderate. Here the sun plays the part of the Campos-fires in the Brazil, and in both places the vegetation has to contend against excessive heat and dryness, conditions tending to the extinction of life.

Foliage is reduced to a minimum, and the superfluous moisture, given off by leaves in less arid climates, is stored up in fleshy stems against seasons of long-continued drought. The dryness of the atmosphere, while reducing the amount of cellular tissue, favours the production of spines; and though, in many cases, the development has not attained actual spinosity, still the modifying influence of climate appears in rigid or distorted members, and asperities of stem and foliage. In some the leaves end with sharp recurved hooks; in others the stipules are spinous; in a few the bracts are prickly: in an Euphorbia (*Cuneata*) the short stiff branches are terminated by dwarf thorns; and a grass (the *Aëluropus Arabicus*) bears leaves so sharply armed that specimens of it are not readily gathered.

Several species exude gums or resinous matter, that encrusts their stems, probably resulting from the bark cracking under exposure to great heat at

1869 to the Libyan Sahará, found 91 species growing spontaneously at Faráfreh, and 183 in the oasis of Dakhel.

Aden, alternating, in Arabia Petræa, with dry cold. Many of the plants have glaucous stems or leaves, or are completely covered with a hoary pubescence. Not a few are viscous, adhering to the hand like glue; and a large proportion is distinguished by more or less pungency or aromatic odour—qualities always possessed by the growth of the Desert.

With Dr. Anderson, we may lay down as follows the limits of this growth, which, especially in Continental Europe, is known by the general name of "Flora of the Sahará." Starting from its headquarters, the rainless regions of Arabia, it extends over the whole Peninsula, except only the mountainous buttress of El-Yemen to the south and the south-west. It follows the shores of "The Gulf," whence it penetrates into Southern Persia; it overspreads Beluchistán, Sind, Southern Afghanistán, and the Western Panjab, its southern limit being N. lat. 23° (Sind) and 30°-31° (Afghanistan and Panjab): southwards it forks to the Nerbaddá; disappears and reappears in the form of an oasis at the southern point of the Dakhan (Deccan) in the Madura territory. Westward of Arabia Petræa this "Bedawi vegetation" passes into Egypt, Nubia, and partially into Abyssinia; and it stretches over the African Sahará, where, in about E. long. 5°, it attains the greatest breadth. Here it covers the wilderness between N. lat. 10° and 37°; whereas in Asia the upper or northern fork shrinks to a zone of 7° to 8° in depth. It passes to Senegal, and finally it reaches its western limit in the Cape de Verd Islands, retaining to the last its Desert type.

The exception, as has been said, is El-Yemen; and here we even now depend for information upon Peter Forskâl,* the energetic student of Natural History, who accompanied Carsten Niebuhr in 1761, and who died at Jerim on July 11, 1763. During his hurried visit to Sana'á and to the Coffee districts, he found thirty new genera and he described some 800 species, a number which he might greatly have increased, had it not been for his conscientious determination to admit nothing but what had been carefully examined. Seetzen † is still the first au-

* The works edited by Niebuhr form the three well-known *Flora Ægyptico-Arabica* and *Descriptiones Animalium*, 1775: and the *Icones Rerum Naturalium*, 1766.

† Born at Sophiengroden (Jan. 30, 1767): studied medicine at Göttingen (1785), where he published his inaugural dissertation, *Systematum de morbis plantarum brevis dijudicatio* (1789); travelled about Europe and wrote many short studies till August, 1802, when he descended the Danube to Constantinople; reached Smyrna and travelled through Asia Minor to Aleppo (Nov. 23, 1803), and made Damascus his head-quarters. From this time to the end of his life he wandered far and wide about Syria (1805–6), including the neighbourhood of Jerusalem (1806–7), and he travelled to Sinai, Suez, and Cairo (1807–9), where he halted to rest and to prepare for more extended journeys. On Oct. 10, 1809, he reached Meccah from Jeddah; performed his pilgrimage, and became Haji Músá el Hakím (the doctor);

thority for the Tíh Desert, which he crossed from north to south in 1807. Of all the scientific travellers of the present century, he is perhaps the least known in England. Though inspired by Niebuhr, his style is clumsy and heavy. His numerous and careful studies were published in a detached form, and the collected edition did not appear till 1854.*

made the visitation to El-Medinah, and halted at Mocha, whence his last letters to Herr von Zach, of Gotha, were dated Nov. 14 and 17, 1810. In Sept., 1811 (æt. 44), he resolved to cross Arabia, and to march upon Maskat and Basra (Bussorah) viâ Sana'á. He lived between June 2nd and 27th (1811) at the capital of Yemen, whose modern name, dating only from the Abyssinian invasion, derives, according to Sprenger (181), from *Sinu'*, strong. The older term "Uzál," he identified, after El-Hamdáni, with the Uzal of Genesis (x. 27). On Sept. 11 he set out with thirteen camel loads (the Life prefixed to the four-volume edition says seventeen). Two days after leaving Mocha, he was found dead at Taas, supposed to have been poisoned by the Imám. The reports of his death were collected by Dr. Aykin and Mr. Forbes, agent of the H.E.I. Company at Mocha. Mr. J. Bird, recounting his coasting-journey along Southern Arabia in 1833 (R. G. Soc. iv. of 1834), heard that Seetzen had been murdered by order of the father of the then reigning Imám. The worthy successor of Niebuhr could never persuade Moslems that he was one of themselves, and Buckingham blamed him for travelling with so large a number of camels.

* Ulrich Jasper Seetzen's *Reisen durch Syrien, Palästina, Phöniceen, die Transjordan-Länder, Arabia Petræa und unter-Egyptïen.* Herausgeben und commentirt von Professor Dr. Fr. Kruse in verbindung mit Prof. Dr. Heinrichs, Dr. G. Fr. Hermann Müller, etc. 4 vols. 4to. Berlin, 1854: G. Reimer. The copy in the K. K. Universität Bibliothek (Vienna) was kindly forwarded to me at Trieste, at the instance of my friend Prof. Leo

Hence we are not astonished to find a popular work on Arabia asserting that the hopes of the scientific world were disappointed by his premature death at Akaba (supposed by poison).

But North-Western Arabia is more accessible to travellers than El-Hejaz or Yemen; and modern botanists have been able to add something to Seetzen's store. Of especial value to those who would study the flora of Arabia Petræa are two papers, which appeared in the *Journal of the Proceedings of the Linnean Society*.* One is on the "Vegetation of the Western and Southern Shores of the Dead Sea," by B. T. Lowrie, M.R.C.S. Eng., read April 6th, 1865: it treats of the Ghor or Jordan Valley, botanically the least-known section of Palestine before the author's visit in January, 1864. The other, which comes even nearer, is the " Notes on the Flora of the Desert of Sinai," by Richard Milne Redhead, Esq., F.L.S. and R.G.S.

As we have seen, all the older classical authors, who have described the Nabathæan country round the head of the Akabah Gulf, concur in making

Reinisch, the Egyptologist. A short correspondence between Seetzen and his old patron M. de Zach, of Saxe-Gotha, was translated and printed in 1810 by the Palestine Association. Mr. Keith Johnston obliged me by copying from Ritter's *Erdkunde* (West Asien, p. 74, dritte Buch, zwölfte Theil) the pages containing Seetzen's " Reise durch Yemen in J. 1810, von 28 May bis mitte August."

it a land of exuberant gramineous vegetation. It is difficult to believe that here imagination did not play a great part, when we stand in presence of the bare peaks of small-grained gray granite; of ruddy syenite and mica-schist; of the rounded heads of hard and homogeneous red porphyry, apparently fire-baked argile; of greenstone and greenstone-slates, often a misnomer, for much of it is coal-black; of quartz hills, dingy outside, but of brilliant and dazzling white where fractured; of chloritic slates and sands; and of the sterile and ghastly sub-ranges, chalk, gypsum, and selenite, which cannot bear a blade of grass.

But about Bir-el-Seba (Beersheba) the fertility of the country rapidly increases, and with it the variety of the flora, whilst one march north of it opens a vast undulating plain of rich thick pastures, brilliant with the scarlet Ranunculus and Adonis (Redhead). Possibly this luxuriant tract may, two thousand years ago, have been prolonged to the southwards. That great changes for the worse have taken place in the Sinaitic Peninsula, and in the Négeb, or South Country, we know from the expeditions of Messrs. Tyrwhitt-Drake and Palmer, who found undoubted traces of rich pasturages of watered ground and of human habitation, where all is now a howling waste.* Moreover, the

* The "Desert of the Exodus" (p. 25); also "The Literary

custom of supplying Egypt with charcoal,* as the Land of Midian has done for many generations, favours the growth of Desert: in many places we found only stumps and torn branches where the largest trees had been.

The affinities of the Midianite vegetation generally are with those of the Sahará and of Northern Africa, especially the Desert-growths of Upper Egypt and Nubia. Dr. Lowne also remarked the same of the flora of the delta-like flat extending from the mouths of the Wadies Zuwayrah and Maháwat to the shore of the Dead Sea. He found it, "by comparison with the collection from Sinai deposited by Major McDonald (Macdonald) in the Kew Herbarium, precisely similar to that of Arabia Petræa." Dr. de Marchesetti observes that the "Sahará flora" in my little collection is not pure; the mixed type reveals the influences of the Desert-steppes on one side, and on the other of the neighbouring Mediterranean, whose immigrants would easily find their way down the Wady el-Arabah from the Dead Sea to the Gulf of El-Akabah.

Remains of the late Charles F. Tyrwhitt-Drake, F.R.G.S.," by Walter Besant, M.A. London: Bentley, 1877 (p. 239).

* When the mines are to be worked, the first step will be positively to forbid this injurious form of industry. The Sinaitic diggings and the immense smelting operations under the Pharaohs, whilst proving that the Peninsula had a plentiful vegetation, and, consequently, a more copious rainfall, must have been permanently destructive to the country.

The peculiarity of the part of Midian visited by the Khedivial Expedition is the importance of the Wadies, true Oases which are supplied with perennial springs. Three of these, not including the dried-up Wady Tiryam, were found within a space of thirty-five direct geographical miles; and they would exert an important effect upon the barren lands lying between them.

As in the adjoining Sinai, the notable growth of the valleys is the date, which, being completely neglected, gives a poor fruit.* The groves (*Nawákhilah*) have a most picturesque appearance; the untrimmed fronds form a regular circle around the head, quite unlike the trimmed broom-like deformity of civilisation. The Daum-trees showed neither flower nor fruit to determine whether they belonged to the *Hyphæne Thebaica* or to the *H. Cristata*, the latter, according to Von Wrede, found in Hadramaut. Sprenger (60–61 and 20), notices the Bdellium placed by Dioscorides about Madyan: the Daum is also called in parts of Arabia " Nakhl el-Mukl," *Persicè* Darakht-i-Mukl, or palm-tree of the gum-mukl; and the latter he identifies with the Bdellium of Genesis.†

* I have read in books of (but I never saw them) date-kernels soaked in water till they became soft, and given to cattle instead of barley.

† See chap. ii. 11–12: "And the name of the first is Pison (Wady Baysh?): that is it which encompasseth the whole land of Havilah (El-Khaulán?) where there is gold. And the gold

These palms shelter luxuriant and impenetrable thickets of reeds (*Arundo donax*) and rushes (*Scirpus holoschœnus*), with Salvolas, Senecio, Sinapis, Resede, Veronica, and a bitter Nasturtium * (*Officinale*), growing near the water upon grounds encrusted with a white efflorescence, apparently salt and sulphur. The curious and grotesque Asclepias (*Calotropis procera*),† a large shrub with oval dark-green leaves, woolly underneath, was found only in the Wady Makná, springing from the sands beyond reach of the rill. The same was the case with the Zizyphus, whose dried and shrunken flesh contains a single round hard ston≥. Mr. Redhead compares it

of that land is good : there is bdellium (bdolach), and the onyx-stone (Eben ha-Shoham)." This resin is called by the Greeks Bolchon and Madelion (Dioscorides) ; by the Latins, Brochon, Maldachon, and Malachum (Pliny) ; and Sprenger explains the latter word by a transposition of the two last consonants, "M k l" corrupted to "M l k." For the various kinds of gum, Arabian and Indian, Bactrian, Scythian (Indo-Scythian from Sind ?), and Jewish, the reader is referred to Sprenger's learned work. Marvellous to relate, Dr. Beke (*Origines Biblicæ*, p. 53) approves of Diodati's version, which renders Bdolach "pearls." The onyx was supposed by the ancients to be the peculiar produce of Arabia (Pliny xxxvi. 12) ; and the Greeks probably translated the word from the Arabic Zofr (Plur Azfar), which also means a nail or claw. Onyxes, used for knife-handles, etc., are still found in many parts of Arabia, including Khaulán (Havilah ?). A specimen of a worked carnelian was brought to me at Wady Tiryam ; the upper edge has been pierced, and it has evidently served as a talisman.

* The Arabs call it El-Narrah, " the hot (plant)."

† Like the Salvadora Persica, it is supposed to be an Indian plant, yet both are equally common in Upper Egypt and Nubia.

with a Siberian crab, and he found the "reddish orange fruit very pleasant to the taste." From the rocks near all the Wadies we collected a fine Runex (*Vesicarius ?*) " with large membranous, shiny seeds, and foliage in appearance and flavour like the Oxyria, excellent as a salad " (Redhead).

The chief arboreal vegetation of the dry Wadies and of the adjacent plains are the acacias, some of them dwarfed to small shrubs. The common species are the Sunt or Sont (*Acacia Nilotica*), Athl and Talh (*A. Fortilis* or *Gummifera*), which Burckhardt calls the "gum-Arabic tree," and which produces, says Wellsted, the "gumma Terræ;" the Samgh or Samur (*Inga unguis*), and especially the Siyal (*A. Seyal*), whose trunk affords the best charcoal, while its bark yields the best tannin. The latter is supposed to be the chittim-wood of the Torah (Exod. xxv.) and the traditional " Burning Bush." * The bole is reddish, the tender shoots are used as forage, and the long grey spines are disposed in twos.

Upon our line of march we nowhere saw the

* The Koran (chap. vii.) has not improved upon the Biblical accounts of this Thauma. As Moses was returning with his pregnant wife and his family to Egypt, he saw a bush on fire, and going to fetch a brand for domestic purposes, he found it green; while a voice cried unto him, "Blessed be he who is in the fire, and whoever is about it," etc. The Greeks always depict the Virgin and Child in the centre of the flame, their theory being that the mystery typified by the marvel was the maidenhood of the mother.

Butm, or terebinth (*Pistacia terebinthus*), nor the prickly oak (*Quercus pseudoconifera*) * so common further north, nor the fruit-trees and the Difu (oleander) with their beautiful rosy bloom. The Athil and Tarfá (*Tamarix Orientalis*), the hardy growths which extend from the tropics to Dovercourt in Essex, were mostly single, rarely forming thickets. As a rule, they are cut down when young, and the hard wood is used for boat-knees, camel-saddles, and similar small articles.

We remarked the straggling and spiny Balanitis Ægyptiaca, the Arab Yakkúm, or "Tree of Jehannum." It bears a "fruit in size, form, and colour resembling a large unripe plum ; and it yields the straight yellow wands and walking-sticks of

* The Elah (terebinth) and Allón (oak) of the Jews, both generically derived from El (Allah). The latter is one of the difficult roots in the Hebrew tongue : applied to trees, it seems to have arisen from their strength or their overshadowing and protecting power. The plurals Elim (masculine) and Eloth or Elath (fem.) signify palms, dates etc.; and the learned Vice-Rabbi Tedeschi, of Trieste, remarks that both the Scriptures and the Talmud seem to have noticed the difference of sexes in vegetation. He gives the derivations as follows : El-force, power; Elohim = the *ensemble* of forces : Ela', oak, terebinth, or other large tree ; with plur. Elim, Eloth and Elath (masc. and fem.), Elon and Allón, an oak grove ; plur. Allonim : Alla (plur. Alloth), the reduplication denoting increment, formerly translated an oak, now a terebinth, and supposed to be derived from some kindred dialect.

Brugsch Bey denies that *Elim* (masc. plur.) means "palms." He would place the Mosaitic station *Elim*, or *Aa-lim*, at Heröopolis, near Suez, and translate the word " Fisch-stadt."

'balsam wood,' upon which the wood-turners of Jerusalem cut the word Jordan in Hebrew" (Redhead). The Retem, or broom (*Ratama*, or *Spartium mono-spermum*), the supposed "Juniper" of the English version, was also common. Caper-bushes (*Capparis spinosa*), the Arab's Asaf or Lasaf, with fleshy leaves in bright green tufts, hang from the rock-clefts; the Arák, another Capparisdea, shows bunches of fruit like currants; and the Salvadora (*Persica*) is common as in Sind.

Amongst the families principally represented in the collection, appear the *Compositæ* and the *Cruciferæ*; several species of *Crepis*, *Erigerum*, *Picridium*, *Senecio*, and *Pulicariæ*, with *Brassica* and *Malcolmiæ* both greedily devoured by camels. The *Gramineæ* are represented by the *Aristida* (*plumosa*) and the *Pennisetum* (Cenchroïdes), which extend from the Canaries to the Panjab; and in the less arid places are found the grassy tufts of Andropogon and paneck-grass (*Panicum*). Then follow the *Leguminosæ*, the *Labiates*, the *Antirichinæ* and the *Borragineæ*, the latter flourishing high up the mountains. The Egyptian plants which have extended eastward are the thistle-like Centauria (*Ægyptiana*); the edible Salsola (*Echinus*); the Malcolmia (*Arenaria*); the Trigonella (*hamosa*); the Parietaria (*Alsinæfolia*); the Medicago (*helix*) with its curious snail-like legume, the Picris (*pilosa*), the Croton (*oblongifolium*), and others of lesser import.

The following are the growths belonging to the flora Mediterranea and to the plains of Palestine, which have pushed their way south and southwest as far as the Nile-Valley: the blue-berried Solanum nigrum; the Solanum coagulans with purple flowers like the potato, and yellow fruit by some identified with the "Apple of Sodom;" Picridium (*tingitænum*); Heliotropium (*luteum*); Antirrhinum (*Orontium*); Lycium (*Europæum*); Trifolium (*Stellatum*); Salvia (*Claudistina*); Asphodelus (*fistulosus*) and the Geranium, the Storchschnabel of the Germans.

The lower grounds with saline bottoms support the plants which are found upon the littoral dunes of Suez and Palusium, and which form a vast band around the shores of Egypt and Cyreniaca: Suæda * (*fruticosa*); Salsola (*Sodæ*); Saliconica (*fruticosa*), a drooping shrub, olive-green and reddish; Zygophyllum (*desertorum*), Scripus (*holoschænus*). Dr. de Marchesetti was much pleased to recognise old friends which he had collected at Aden and on the mountains at the mouth of Bab el-Mandeb: Statice primrosa (rough and coarse); Reseda Amblyocarpa (here very common as in the Ghor and the Aden

* Forskâl made the Suæda a distinct genus: several species of this plant supply an alkaline salt, which serves as soap.

Crater); *Zygophyllum simplex*, *Fagonia Cretica* (*Sinaica*, Boiss.); Cleome (*droserifolia* and *trinervia*) Aëluropus Arabicus; the Arua (*javanica*), also frequent in Aden and India; the *Cucumis prophetarum*, and others. Senna (*Cassia Senna*) was common as in most parts of Arabia, and some of the best is said to grow in the neighbourhood of El-Arish: another favourite medicinal plant is the Euphorbia. We missed the oleanders (*Nerium odorum*), the laurel rose, the nosegay of St. Joseph, whose lovely pink blossoms are the pride of the Syrian Valley; we did not remark the Sabr ("patience-plant)," or Aloe, so common in the South; and apparently the Balisan, or Balm of Meccah, does not now extend so far north.*

* "Pilgrimage," iii. 138. This "balm of Gilead" is said to have been grown in the Jordan Valley, "where kings warred for what is now a weed."

CHAPTER XI.

THE CRUISE DOWN SOUTH; SULPHUR AND TURQUOISES:
NOTES ON FISHES AND SHELLS.

AT El-Muwayláh we re-embarked on board the *Sinnár*, whose good Captain received us with a hearty welcome, and on the same day we proceeded south, to inspect a "mountain of Sulphur," and a turquoise mine of which we had heard from the Bedawin and from the "wall-jumpers."* After an hour-and-a-half's steaming, we cast anchor in the Sharm Jibbah,† about eight miles beyond the Sharm Yáhár. Running from west due east, with a clear channel of seventeen to fifteen fathoms, it is a close bight, hammer-headed as usual, the entrance being the handle; and it is distinguished by a remarkable

* Nuttát El-Hayt, jumpers or climbers of walls, is the offensive term applied to villagers generally, and especially to the Hutaym, the Huwaytát and other tribes not Bedawi *pur sang*.

† So the people pronounce it. Captain Ali Bey Shukri writes the word Júbáh; and the Hydrographic Chart, which gives a plan, calls it "Sherm Joobbah."

cavern in the cliffs of crumbling sandstone which form the southern sea-wall.

The knob known to the people as "Tuwayyil el-Kibrít" appears, when seen from the sea, a tolerably regular pyramid, with a dwarf yellow cliff, like a notch or cornice, near the western apex: its site is the northern flank of the Wady Madsús, the sister formation to the south being Wady Jibbah. The Egyptian officers landed, and after a quarter-of-an-hour's walk, reached the foot of the hillock, whence they brought back specimens from the several altitudes. They found the prevalent formation to be carbonate of lime. The sulphur was made evident by the colour and odour when washed, but we had neither rods to bore with nor retorts to ascertain its proportions.

The Wild Men have not learned to extract it; and they import their gunpowder from Egypt. As may be imagined, this well-adulterated stuff has, like the home-made, little strength; and no present is more welcome to a Bedawi than a pound or two of good English "bárút." Experience of brimstone in Iceland has taught me to suspend opinion of the "Long-little Sulphur (Hill)" till drills are sunk from twenty to forty feet deep.

Our return on board was fêted by a sailors' "Fantasia," a genuine survival of the old Canopic fun, which formed a farcical contrast with the grave dry humour displayed on the deck of an English ship of war. All the *dramatis personæ* were men from Lower Egypt. One of them made a tolerably pretty girl, who walked with the true Trieste wriggle, and who danced mincingly Almeh-fashion : she was waited upon by the chief-buffoon, Kara-gyuz,* a short, squat fellow in an impossible costume, including the tail. Ali, who thus represented the clown, had served in that capacity at Alexandria, and his low bow with the wave of the two arms that followed each tumbling-feat smacked of high civilisation. He had fallen out and fought with his brethren of the circus, the punishment being condign enlisting. It is related that the Captain once hung him by the heels for an hour without the least prejudice to his health or his good humour.

Next came the Kázi, in a tremendous white beard, a huge turban, and a broom-stick by way of staff. Of course, he thrashed everybody, and he kissed the pretty girl with his mumbling jaws in every corner. The Arnaut (Albanian), with a peaked and horizontal mustachio, big as a Bologna sausage ; a weapon-stuffed waist-shawl that dwarfed the divine's head-gear ; perpetually using his stick upon his servant after shouting " Yá Velet ! "† and

* See my "Pilgrimage," 1–118 ; and Lane, 11–19.
† The Yá Walad! (O boy !). Walad is the origin of our "valet ;" and certain French travellers in the East have coined *un yavalet*, by which we are to understand a little foot-page.

calling all his Moslem brethren by most opprobrious names, such as " Karátá " and " Mu'arras," was carried in by two men, mounted upon one of our camel-saddles. He was married by the Kázi with due ceremony to the pretty girl; both were publicly placed upon the nuptial couch, and the mode of awaking the bridegroom next morning was, to say the least of it, peculiarly striking.

Perhaps the spectator who most enjoyed the sport was the Mullah Effendi, the *Aumônier* or Chaplain of the corvette, a good-humoured, portly Cairene, who enjoys a cigar, sleeps upon the quarter-deck sofa, delivers the Azán or prayer-call from the bridge, and acts Imám (fugleman) to the rare-pious amongst the Faithful. The next was the venerable Haji Wali, who has acquired the habit of saying, when told it is the hour for devotions, " Kamán Shuwayy "—" Wait a bit ! " I confess that the play was very "shocking;" and that my sides ached with laughter.

On the following day we proceeded in the corvette to examine a turquoise-mine, concerning which we had heard many details from Shaykh Ayd Alayán of the Tugaygát clan. I had also seen a bright-blue " Fayrúz " from these diggings set in the stock of a Bedawi matchlock, and notched across to resemble a screw. Though exposed to wear and weather for some fifty years, it had lost nothing of its colour. In fact, it was pure silicate of copper, which is not affected by oxygen and other acids; whereas the carbonates of copper speedily change to sub-carbonatis, and break out in green spots. This is almost always the case, although there are some notable exceptions, with the yield of the Sinaitic mines, first worked by the Egyptians * and last by the unfortunate Major Macdonald.

Once the handsomest man in the British Army, the hospitable "King of Sinai" utterly ruined himself, and died in poverty at Suez. His Egyptian servants, whom he trusted, plundered him to the last; and, despite long inquiries, I could never discover what became of his great find, a perfect stone about the size of a hen's egg. There are beliefs connected with turquoises; and I know a lady who would have spent a small fortune in securing this prize.

Steaming under the shadow of the tremendous Jebel el-Shárr,† which hardly altered its shape as

* One of the hieroglyphic inscriptions in Sinai mentions the "Goddess Hathor (or Athor), Mistress of the Land of the Turquoises;" and another in the Wady Mukattab names the "Goddess of Copper." The Arabs still fumble in the old mines, and of late some good bargains have been made at Cairo.

† I have explained the word, which is an active participle from Shárr, exposing (*e.g.*, to dry), and which Wallin is wrong to write Gabal (Jebel) Shâr (Shár),. Berghaus gives, after his fashion, Djebel-Schaar, as if it were the "hair-mountain."

the corvette changed angle, we passed the two points known as Rás Maharrash and Abu Sharírah;* and, after covering 14·30 sea miles from Jibbah, and 22·30 from El-Muwayláh, we cast anchor at 9.10 a.m. off the Burj Zibá, the Deba of Niebuhr, which our charts write Zibber, probably upon the principle which converts "you" into "yer."† The coast is here bluff with coralline cliffs, and from their base a narrow strip of sand extends to the pointed reefs and sharp-edged ledges, upon which the sea breaks even in calm weather: this wall rises abruptly from great depths, and hence the surf so much feared by the natives. All assured us that landing was impossible.

We moored the corvette fore and aft. The shallow bight is an "Acathartus," or Foul Bay, and the least wind from the south-west makes it dangerous. Indeed the description of Wellsted (ii. 183) is almost as frightful as those of Agatharkides and his copyists, Diodorus Siculus and Photius. There is an inner harbour, with a fortified well used by pilgrims; but the water is too shallow for any

---

* In the chart called Ras Maharash and Ras Abusharirah; these naval surveyors always misspell when they can.

† And (proh pudor!) an anchorage to the south, is written Mersa Zebaider (Zubaydeh); whilst that of El-Ghaláfikah becomes "Gulafugger." And the worst part of these errors is that they become stumbling-blocks to students, being copied into serious works. See, for instance, Müller (Geog. Gr. Min.). p. 181, note.

but the smallest native craft. This place, possibly the Hippos Vicus of Ptolemy,* is now a dependency of El-Muwayláh, occupied by the garrison some three or four years ago. The settlers have built a fair tower which flew its flag on our approach ; and the houses, though of the same homely kind, are better than those of the mother-town, which decidedly has seen better days.

Outside the settlement, numbering some 300 souls, rise the black tents of the nomads, who do a considerable trade with the citizens, selling sheep and clarified butter, charcoal and mat-rushes. The sea is rich, as we saw by the troops of gulls and cormorants; and the lads, paddling and occasionally upsetting their crank monoxyles, brought us excellent rock-cod and another fish, succulent eating, which somewhat resembled tunny. The baskets showed the quaintest shapes, and coats bright-coloured as the Coralline "Gardens of the Sea." Some were monsters all head, with tremendous gapes; others showed mere lines like worms, and others again all body; these appeared flat

---

* I would place it here because there is no other fitting site. Sprenger (p. 24), confused by the calography of the maps, seems inclined to find "Hippos" in Dábbat (Lasttheir, Pford). Zibá would be the plural of Zaby, Capra Gazella (Forsk.) ; in the feminine Zabych = Tabitha = Dorcas : it is rarely used in comparison with the words "'Ard," the male, and "Ghezáleh," the female Gazelle. Wellsted (p. 11-81) writes Sherm Dhobá.

x

(*Balistes* and *Chætodons*), and those owned bird-shapes rather than fish-forms. Unicorns abounded: there were Scorpœnas and Acanthi, weaponed with dreadful spines; and the Diodons (*hystrix*, etc.) and Jetrodons (*Sceleratus*, etc.) represented giant bladders clad in thorny coats of mail.

All the hues of the peacock and the rainbow were there: purple and orange; lake-green, emerald-green, and blue variegated green; dark blue and cerulean blue; blood-red and green and coral red; citron and pink; crimson with yellow fins; silver-white and lamp-black, regularly marginated, banded, zebraed, ocellated, lined, cinctured or pointed with the purest gold. We seemed to be in the region of the Arabian Nights. We should not have been surprised to hear that the fish were the transformed citizens of the Horse's village; the white being Moslems; the red, Magians; the blue, Christians; and the yellow, Jews.

It appeared quite natural to read, "And lo! there came forth a damsel of tall stature, smooth-cheeked, of perfect form, with eyes adorned with kohl, beautiful in countenance, and with heavy swelling lips; wearing on her head a Kúfiyeh-kerchief interwoven with blue silk; with rings in her ears, and bracelets on her wrists, and rings set with precious jewels on her fingers, and in her hand was a rod of Indian cane: and she dipped the end of the rod in the frying-pan and said ' O, fish, are ye faithful to your covenant?'"*

Despite the Khamsín, which was blowing heat and glare, the energetic Egyptian officers landed, and walked over the rough plain to the north, till they reached the Jebel Shekayk,† which is seven or eight hours' march from El-Muwayláh. But unfortunately the guides failed them; the range, which looked from afar small and low, proved long and broad; and nothing was brought from it but specimens of chloritic sandstone. Meanwhile we landed to inspect the place and to enjoy a bath in the creek, defended from sharks, and abounding in large jellyfish, Medusæ (*octostyla*), etc., which swam nimbly before us in all directions, while the crabs dipped and dived into their holes. Wady Zibá is the usual "gate," apparently waterless, growing dorn-palms and thorn-trees instead of dates; and the coast-line is composed of the normal coralline, based on hard conglomerate, and revetted with scatters of porphyry. Outside the "Báb" stands a walled building surrounding a well sunk by Sultan Selim for the benefit of pilgrims: this is probably the birket or reservoir mentioned in Burckhardt's Itinerary.

We drank coffee with Haji Mohammed, the principal merchant, who supplied us with sheep;

* Lane, vol. i. pp. 100 and 110.
† Apparently the diminutive of Shukak, the Merops Apiaster.

and we bought some curiosities found in the neighbourhood, and more likely to be the work of a civilised *vicus* than of the Wild Man. One was a truncated cone, pierced and polished, of granite resembling that of the Channel Islands, white and black, somewhat like a plover's egg; the other was one of those curious objects, a coin-weight of green glass,* similar to what is still made at Hebron, but bearing a Kufic inscription. Mr. R. S. Poole finds it = 61 grains (= 1 dinár), these glass weights being generally light; he assures me that it differs from all in the large collection of the British Museum, and he reads it thus:

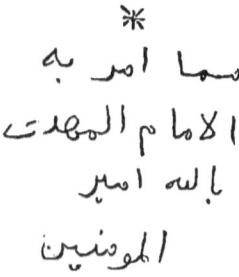

that is, "By command of the Imám (*præses*) El-Mahdi B'illah, Amír El-Múminín." My corre-

* The vitrine discs stamped on one side were formerly held to be tokens or equivalents of coins: they have been accepted as weights since 1873, when my learned colleague, Mr. Edward T. Rogers, published his study in the *Numismatic Chronicle*. He holds that they were not made at Hebron or in Syria, where very few have been found; that the head-quarters of the manufacture would be Egypt, and that they were the usual Arab imitations of the Byzantine system. The earliest dates, it is believed, from A.H. 96 = A.D. 711.

spondent has no doubt that this El-Mahdi is of the Fatimah Caliphs. The style suits his time better than the Abbásahs; moreover, the latter is styled El-Mahdi Mohammed.

After we had left Zibá, and when, as often happens, it was too late, we heard of some ruins four hours to the south. The people call them Umm Ámil; and they are said to show houses, furnaces, and other appurtenances of an industrial establishment. The Governor of El-Muwayláh had spoken to us about them; but he was vague upon the subject, and we could hardly learn from him whether the site, distant thirty miles, lay inland from the Fort, or along the sea-board. Umm Ámil was the most southerly of the mining-cities of Midian concerning which we could collect any notices, but that is no reason why others should not exist.

Rüppell (p. 222) was told by a chief of the Huwaytát at El-Muwayláh that two long marches to the east led to the Jebel-Maktúb (written mountain), where ruins with inscriptions and figures (statues?) abound. He was unable to visit the place, but he recommends the trip to his successors.* Wellsted (ii. 187) explored a ruined town about four hours in the interior from El-Wijh; copied an in-

* I did not see his excellent volume till after returning to Trieste. The eleven pages of this able naturalist (213–233) contain an immense amount of matter, but he apparently had no idea that he was visiting large mining establishments.

scription in the Wady el-Moyah (p. 189); and, after walking some ten miles from the Fort, found the "Buyút el-Nasará." These remains were partly built of hewn stone, the house-walls measuring full six feet thick. The length was estimated at two miles, and they lay scattered at intervals in a rocky valley with a general north-eastern direction. Two hills projected across the hollow, leaving a narrow central defile; and on either brow were traces of small forts, probably like those which we saw at Makná and Sharmá.

Again, about seventy-five miles further south, in N. lat. 25°, near El-Hawará (Leuke-Kome?), also called Daya El-Ishrín, because it is the twentieth station on the Hajj-road, he heard (ii. 195) of buildings and columns which his short stay did not permit him to examine. Thus, we have notices of former civilisation between Jebel Tayyibat Ism (N. lat. 28° 30) and Hawará, fronting Hassáni Island, in N. Lat. 25° = 210 direct geographical miles.

As an Italian writer remarks, the squalid sterility that reigns on the rough borders of the Red Sea contrasts strangely with the life abounding in its waters; the latter being, unlike the land, the very image of fecundity. The sun, which parches and scorches the shores, bespreads its bottoms with luxuriant and many-coloured algæ; favours the marvellous stony vegetation of the polypes; and breeds an infinite variety of being—endless shoals of fish; crustaceæ of a thousand shapes; strange annelids, elegant echinoderms, and molluscs whose beautiful shells form the delight of collectors.

For the ichthyology of the Red Sea we are, as usual, driven to Forskål, who described 114 species with more care than he applied to his molluscs; named 56 which were observed at Smyrna, in Constantinople, and the Arabian waters; and published a catalogue of the fish of Malta, communicated to him by a learned physician. His most numerous genera are the Sciænæ or Maigre family (25 species); the Chætodons (15); the Icarus or parrot-fish, *novum genus* (10); the Scomber (10); the Labrus (9), and the Perca (8). It is needless to say that many of these have been otherwise distributed by his successors. The most useful part to travellers is the addition of the Arabic names: unfortunately, the illustrations are few; the Chætodon Teira (Platax Teira, Klunz) in Tab. xxii. and the Chætodon Unicornis (Tab. xxiii).

A valuable *Synopsis der Fische des rothen Meeres**

* *Verhandlungen des K. K. Zoologisch-botanischen Gesellschaft in Wien.* I. Theil: Percoïden-Mugiloiden (xx. Band, iv. Haft, pp. 669–834, Jahrgang 1870); II. Theil: Schluss (xxi. Band, i. und ii. Haft, pp. 441–688, Jahrgang 1871); und III. Theil: *Systematische Uebersicht der Fische des rothen Meeres* (xxi. Band, iii. und iv. Heft, pp. 1352–1368, Jahrgang 1871). Dr. Klemsinger is, I hear, employed in sketching the natural history and geology of Upper Egypt for Messrs. Blackie & Co.

has been published by the Austrian doctor, C. B. Klemsinger, M.D., a sanitary officer, stationed four years at El-Kusayr (Cosseir), where I believe he is still serving.* His especial object was not to describe new species (*arten*), of which, before November, 1870, he had observed some fifty; but to determine by sharper lines the specific differences which, in the extensive labours of his predecessors,† had not satisfied him. For this purpose he had observed live, or at least fresh, specimens numbering 400 species, or three-quarters of the total number known in these seas; and on returning to Europe he was assisted in his task by studying various collections at Stuttgart, Frankfort-on-the-Main, and Berlin.

In his preliminary observations (part i. p. 671) he carefully lays down what he considers to be the characteristic of species. The system which he adopts is that of Joh. Müller, with modifications by Günther and Bleeker; ‡ and he accepts the nomen-

* In the Austrian *Meteorological Journal*, June 15th, 1877, Dr. Klemsinger gave a summary of one year's observations on the climate of the Red Sea.

† The faunists whom he quotes are Forskâl, Bloch, Russell, Lacépède, Quoy and Gaimard, Cuvier and Valenciennes, Ehrenberg, Rüppell and Leuchkart (*Symbolæ Physicæ*, 1828), Cantor, Bennet, Richardson, Schlegel, Bleeker, Peters, Günther, Kner, and Playfair.

‡ (Theil III.) The divisions are Sub-class 1, Teleostei (Joh. Müller); Order I. Acanthopteri (Müller); II. Anacanthini (do.); Order III. Physostomi (do.); Order IV. Plectognathi (Cuv.); and Order V. Lophobranchii (Cuv.); Sub-class 2, Chondropterygii (Günther); and Order I. Plagiostomi.

clature* proposed by the Report of the Committee (British Association, Von Strickland, *Silliman's Journal*, July, 1869), ending family names with *videi*, and sub-families with *ini*. He supplies in the Latin alphabet the Arabic names of fishes current at El-Kusayr; and as he gives no illustrations, it is to be hoped that when his valuable labours are brought to a close, he will reprint the papers in a detached form, with all the honours which they deserve.

The Malacology of the Red Sea, and especially of the Suez Gulf,† has been treated by Signor Arturo Issel (*Malacologia del Mar Rosso*, etc. Pisa: Biblioteca Malacologica, 1869), who visited the Isthmus of Suez in 1865, and whose interesting volume describes 100 species as new. From the Gulf of El-Akabah we have 120 species, and from Suez 21, or a total of 141 species, described by the Marquis G. M. Arconati; ‡ and the compari-

* The terminology is truly distressing. For instance, the Percalineata of Forskål is the Perca Arabica of Linnæus, and the Centropomus Arabicus of Lacépède. The Cheilodipterus Arabicus of Cuvier is the Cheilolineatus of Rüppell, Günther, Playfair, and Klunz. This is only a specimen taken at random, and not chosen. It is to be regretted that the popular European names, like "rockcod," are not added to Klemsinger's fine work.

† It is curious to note with Vaillant (*Recherches*, etc., *Journ. de Conch.*, 1865, p. 97) that the shells of the Suez Gulf, instead of showing the vivid and beautiful colours which distinguish the same species in other places, rather remind one of the "chlorotic representations of a tropical fauna."

‡ A list of the shells found on the shores of the Gulf of El-Akabah (March 11–13, 1864) is given by Mr. R. M. Redhead,

son is interesting, because, of these 120, as many as 15 genera were not found in the Suez Gulf, though existing in the Southern Seas, while only 39 species are common to both. It has also caused surprise that whilst there was no solution of continuity between the Mediterraneo-Adriatic * and the Red Sea in pleiocenic and meiocenic or post-pleiocenic days, the fauna of the two was entirely distinct, with the exception of the few species which crossed the strait. Herr Fischer, one of the two Directors of the *Conchological Journal*, in opposition to the opinions of Cazalis de Fondouce, of Professor de Philippi, and of Woodward (Manuel), wrote *il n'existe aucune coquille commune à la Mer Rouge et à la Mediterande*. But a more careful examination enabled Signor Issel to detect seven living species common to both, namely, Cypræa (*Annulus* and *Moneta*); Nassa (*Costulata*); Critheum (*scabrum*); Solecurtus (*Strigilatus*); Donax (*trunculus*); and Arca (*lactea*). At the same time he notes certain differences in the typical forms, possibly the result of many ages of separation, which pro-

(*loc. cit.*), "with great diffidence as to the complete accuracy of the species named." P. Forskâl (1775) also offers (*Descr. Animal.* pp. xxx.–xxxiv.) a catalogue of land, river, and (Red) sea-shells, including eighteen of the latter.

* According to Signor Issel, the Mediterranean was zoologically dependent upon the Erythræan Sea, and, consequently, upon the Indian Ocean; in later geological periods it became, what it is now, tributary to the Atlantic.

duced at first equivalent varieties and, subsequently, equivalent species.*

According to him, a mollusc living at Port Sa'id, and its equivalent at Suez, are the two forms derived from a single stips, alive or extinct; and from a type existing in a given place can proceed equivalent species and varieties, if the locality has undergone changes more or less radical; whilst geographical species and varieties result only from the diffusion of the same type to great distances, where the new media gradually evolve new characteristics.

The lovely coral-fields of the northern Red Sea are described and figured in colour and perspective by Eugen Baron Ransonnet.† One of his drawings represents an aquarium-like coral-group in the harbour of Tor. It is an oasis containing some twenty-one objects, especially the large dome-shaped Careophyllina; the rounded Meandrinæ; the Polypi (*Alcyonia* and *nephthya*); the rosy-red Seriatopora; a Scutella (*Raghîf el-Bahr*), prickly like the urchin; the representative Madrepora (*porites*), ochre-yellow

---

* Of these equivalents in the Mediterranean and the Red Sea, our author gives (pp. 39–40) thirty instances. All were collected at Suez.

† *Reise von Kairo nach Tor, zu den Korallenbänken des rothen Meeres.* Verhandlung des K. K. Zoologisch-botanischen Gesellschaft in Wien (pp. 163–188, Jahrbuch 1863, xiii. Band. Braumüller).

and carmine, or round and rosy; the leathery Spongia (*retifera*); the fan-shaped Padina (*pavonia*); the conus-shell which furrows the sand; the regular globes of the Favosites, one of the cacti of the sea; the sponge-like Madrepora (*conglomerata*); the purple-red "organ-coral" (*Tubipora musica*); the fan-shaped Millepora (*complanata*) which burns the skin; and the leaf-like Monticularia.

The higher life is represented by the hermit-crab (*Pagurus bernardus*), the small Blennius, the coffee-fish, and the shark. The Baron's other illustration shows the section of a big coral-bank near the entrance of Tor, containing a large and rare Monticulari; two Heteroporas growing like a stalk of erica; a mushroom-shaped Alcyonium; and the branchy Sertularia, haunted by the bird-like Platax, and by the violet-ringed Medusa (*aurita*), the latter also belonging to the seas of Europe.

CHAPTER XII.

THE CRUISE NORTHWARDS TO MAKNÁ, CAPITAL OF MADYAN.

ON April 15th the *Sinnár* steamed out of Sherm Zibá and, passing El-Muwayláh, anchored for the night in a snug Khor (natural port), a kind of Sandy Hook, on the western flank of the circular Sináfir or Senáfir Island.* The lumpy, low-lying, water-lacking rock, about 150 feet high, and utterly bare

---

* The following is a synopsis of the identifications, by various writers, of the six islets which, beginning from the south, outlie the Midian shore:—
1. Silah, a mere coral-reef, is Sprenger's Salydó (Agatharkides) and Müller's Sela I.
2. Yubú'a (not Ye'úbáh) is Sprenger's Soukabuá (Agath.), and Müller's Isura (Plin.).
3. Baráhkan (not Burrahghan), identified both by Sprenger and Müller with the "Isidis Insula" (Agath.).
4. Shu'shu'a (not Abou Choucha); Müller's Soukabuá.
5. Sináfir, Müller's Salydó.
6. Jazírat, or Jebel Tírán (not Tehran); the Iotábe of Procopius and Malchus; Müller's Dia (Agath. and Strabo); and Mannert's "Isle of Seals" (Agath.).
All were visited in 1833 by Lieut. Wellsted (ii. 173–179), but he does not name Umm Maksúr (p. 173), the peninsula-island.

of the trees with which the classics forested it, is the only feature which bears an Egyptian name; possibly from "Senofern, Pharaoh the Ameliorator ('who makes good'), the twenty-fifth (?) and last King of the Third Dynasty; the 'Conqueror of Stranger Peoples' who overran Mafkat-land (Sinai of the turquoises), and whose memorials may still be found in Wady Magharah;" and this suggests that it may be the Isis Isle of Agatharkides.

A party landed in search of ruins, snakes, and guano, but found neither this, that, nor the other: Tírán, also, shows none of the huge and venomous reptiles with which the Arabs stock Sinafir. They brought back specimens of madrepores and corallines based upon decomposed granite, the general intrusive formation; and especially the brilliant red-purple Tubipora (*Musica*), called by the Arabs Dam El-Akhwán, or "Brother's Blood."* Burckhardt has remarked that the coral of El-Akabah is mostly red, while the white prevails in the Suez Gulf. They found fragments of petrosilex and ruddy rock-salt in bits of agglutinated sandstone similarly coloured: this material is also supplied by Sinaitic Sherm el-Shaykh, and, as we shall presently see, by Wady Makná.

* "Brother's Blood" is also the popular Arab name of the mediæval drug, known to Europe as "Dragon's Blood." Forskâl (Descrip. Anim. xxix.) writes, by a clerical error, "Damm el-Akharayn."

Long-spined echini and hermit-crabs (*paguri*) were observed in numbers : every "flower of the sea" seemed to lodge a tenant, and the latter had ample choice of quarters in the heaps that strewed the shore. Mr. J. Gwyn Jeffreys, to whom my few specimens were submitted, declared the shells to be interesting, although common, on account of the inhabitants. The plants proved to be those of the mainland. The fishermen were unusually successful, and we all enjoyed the excellent Tawín (*Perca Tauvina*, Forsk. p. xi., and *Serranus Tauvina*, Klemsinger, i. 683).

Next morning we set out, at 5.30 a.m., in a northerly wind which frequently fell calm, with a *mar vecchio*, the heave and wash of gales which had broken to the south. After steaming for an hour and a half we doubled the tall and grim Bird Isle (Tírán), conical above and queerly triangular below. We could hear nothing of the naphtha, which Wellsted declares (ii. 160) is produced abundantly enough to serve for "paying" Arab-boats. Then we found ourselves in the dangerous *socte* of El-Akabah.

This *Sinus intimus*, the eastern fork of the Erythræan, has been cursorily treated by the earlier classical geographers. Dr. Beke declares (Orig. Bib. p. 185) that in the days of Herodotus, the Akabah Gulf was "unknown to the Egyptians and, *à fortiori*, to the Jews resident in Egypt." But, granting the ignorance of the "Father of History," how could the subjects of the Pharaohs have ignored the feature, when there were large military establishments and gangs of slaves working the mines of Sinai within sight of its waters? Agatharkides and Diodorus, we have seen,* mention the Laianitic Gulf and its settlements; but they do not allude to the perils of its navigation, whilst dwelling upon those of tranquil Aynúnah Bay. The same is the case with Strabo and Pliny; and for realistic descriptions we must wait till the days of the later Greek historians.

Strabo (xvi. 2, § 30) places Ailána† or Œlana (now Akabat-Aylá) "on the innermost *mychos* (recess) of the Arabian Gulf. The latter feature has two forks: one, trending towards Arabia and Gaza (*hod.* Ghazzah), is called after its city Ailanites;‡ the other lies in the direction of Egypt, towards Heroöpolis (the old town near Suez), to which Pelusium is the shortest road (between the two seas). Travelling is performed on camels through a desert and sandy country, where snakes

* See chap. vii.
† The translators Hamilton and Faulconer (Bohn, 1857) explain "Ailah" by *Hale* (for Haila), or by *Acaba-Ila*.
‡ He repeats (chap. iv. § 4), "Ailána is a city on the other recess of the Arabian Gulf, which is called Ailanites, opposite to Gaza, as we have described it."

are found in great numbers." He further observes (xvii. 1, § 35) that Lower Egypt, and the lands as far as the Lake Sirbonis, were once sea; and confluent, perhaps, with the Erythræan at Heroöpolis, and with the Ailanitic recess of the (Arabian) Gulf." This remark is right worthy of the nineteenth century. We now hold that the Suez Isthmus was under water during the inferior and the middle Tertiary periods; that it rose wholly or in part, during the succeeding Pleiocene, when it produced large arboreous monocotyledons, many of them now petrified; that it sank again in the post-Pleiocene; and, finally, that it became what it is during the comparatively recent age, when the emersion of the great African Sahará determined, according to Desor, the end of the Glacial Epoch.*

Pliny (v. 12) merely mentions the Heroöpolitic and the Œlanitic Gulfs. He speaks (vi. 32) of the "inner recess (*Sinus intimus*), where dwell the Læanitæ, who named it; also Agra,† their royal city, and, upon the Gulf, that of Læana or, as others say, Œlena; for which reason some writers have called it the Ælanitic, and others Ælenitic: Artemidorus (in Strabo) has Alenitic, and Juba Læanitic." Ptolemy (v. 17, § 1) places the Elána Kome, here

* Possibly it may be proved that the Wady El-Arabah has seen the same vicissitudes.

† Sprenger (p. 139) derives the word from Hajar (pronounced by the Bedawin *Hagar*), a town or village.

Y

meaning *castellum* as well as *oppidum*, in E. long. 65° 40', and in N. lat. 29° 15'. St. Jerome (*ob.* A.D. 420) adds that the ancients called it Ailath, and the moderns Aila. The LXX. has 'Αἴλαδ, (in which the δ = th) and Αἴλων; Procopius Aïlàs, and Eusebius Êlat and Êlas. The Hebrew would be Ailath (Elath) or Ailoth (Eloth), meaning the " palms " or the " terebinths," and hence their name for the fork '' Yamen Ailath " (ים איל‎).*

In the later Greek historians we find excellent sketches of the Gulf. Procopius (*nat. circ.* A.D. 500) when describing Palestine in his Persian Wars (i. 19, § 2), thus notices the land " on the east of the Red Sea, which extends from the Indus to the frontier of the Roman Empire.† On its eastern shore rises the city called ' Ailàs,' where the sea coming to an end, as has been related to me, contracts itself to a very narrow strait. To one thence sailing forth,‡ the mountains of the Egyptians are (visible) on his right, trending towards the south wind; whilst on

---

* Robinson (i. 253) gives full historical details concerning El-Akabah, the town, a subject which does not belong to these pages.

† Here again we see the Erythræan or Red Sea including, after ancient fashion, the Persian Gulf. The mythical King Erythras was buried at Ogyris, which Sprenger (pp. 100, 101, and 120) identifies with the larger island of " Mâçyra " (Mâsírah), on our maps Mosera, between Ras Madrak and Ras El Hadd.

‡ Ἐνθένδε ἐσπλέοντι, here and below, must be an error for ἐκπλέοντι, as the mariner is going southwards or out of the Gulf.

the other hand a country, mostly uninhabited, stretches towards the Boreas. Nor does the navigator ever lose sight of this land on either side as far as the island called Iotábe, distant from Ailàs not less than 1000 stadia. There the Hebrews lived independently* from a remote period; but during the reign of the present Emperor (Justinian), they have become Roman subjects. From this point the sea expands greatly, and the land on the right hand of those approaching the island cannot be seen.† Mariners always anchor on the left side when night falls :‡ it is impossible to navigate this sea in the dark, for those who would so do, mostly chance upon the shoals. There are many harbours, not made by man's hand, but by the nature of the country; and so sailors, who want refuge, find it without diffi-

---

* This statement lends authority to the opinion of Dr. Wilson and others, that the turbulent Bedawi tribes about Petra, especially the Liyásinah (from Lais, the lion of Judah?), are Simeonites, or other Bene-Israél, converted or perverted to El-Islam. According to Professor Palmer (p. 433), these unmitigated scoundrels "retain not only the distinctive physiognomy, but many of the customs of the Jews, such as wearing the Pharisaic lovelocks." Dr. Wolff's identification of the Khaybarís with the Rechabites (Jer. xxxv.) is, of course, trivial; but there is evidently much Hebrew blood in the land. Rüppell (*Reise*, pp. 214–15) surmised that both the Masá'id and the Emradi tribes were Jews.

† Incorrect. The Sinaitic highlands are always conspicuous on the west; even from Aynúnah Bay, distant forty to fifty miles further off than the Akabah mouth. Equally visible are the eastern ranges.

‡ As will be seen, the anchorage places are now on both sides.

culty."* In the next paragraph (§ 3) Procopius, after leaving Palestine, mentions the Sarakenoi,† whose king was Abocaralus, and (§ 4) the "Saracens called Maddeni," *i.e.*, Ma'adani, the miners. Malchus, ‡ (Frag. Hist. iv. 113) speaking of the seventeenth year of Leo the emperor (A.D. 474), says, "Amorkísus, of the Nokalian race, was among the Persians, but whether he did not happen to find honour there, or that for some other reason he better liked the regions under the dominion of Rome, he leaves Persia and fares to the neighbouring land of Arabia.

---

* These "Sherms," which will be described, were possibly less obstructed by the coral insect fourteen centuries ago.

† Here the word may be derived from the Arabic "Shuraká," or confederates, because they served as mercenaries in the Roman army. Hence the *Desertum Saracenorum* of St. Jerome, southeast of Akabat-Aylá. Their customs are well described in A.D. 363 by that "excellent Gentile," Ammianus Marcellinus (of A.D. 390), the friend of Julian called the Apostate: he speaks of the *Scenitas Aubjs, quos Saracenos posteritas adpellavit*. They are called Skenitæ (Scenitæ, or tent-dwellers) also by Malchus: the word would be equivalent to the Hebrew Sukkiyín, men who dwell in the Sokh σκηνή, or tent (plural Sukkah, hence "Succoth"). See Sprenger (p. 200), whose map places "Sarakene" in Nabatæa, north of El-Akabah; and he suggests that the Skenitæ or Sakunitai of Ptolemy may be the Beni Sakún of Daumat el-Jandal (Domatha). The king's name in Procopius, purely Semitic, is probably Abú Karb.

‡ Malcus or Malchus (Μαλιχός), a Christian rhetorician or sophist, born at Philadelphia (Ammán) in Syria, wrote seven books of "Byzantiaca," covering the years A.D. 474–480: of these fragments are preserved by Photius. I have been able to find only the *Antichi Storici Greci Minori* (vol. iii. 295–300), translated by Giuseppe Rossi.

Making this his point of operations, he set out on forays, and he waged wars, not with any of the Romans, but with the Sarakenoi, who are always at hand. After a little while, having gained an increase of strength, he took forcible possession of an island belonging to the Romans and called Iotábe. Turning out the Roman tithe-collectors, he held it; and, receiving its taxes, became possessed of no small wealth there."

El-Akabah sounds terrible in Arab ears. The entrance is foul and narrow. The sea-river, about a hundred miles long by only fifteen to sixteen wide,* is girt by high bald mountains rising abrupt from hot and sandy plains, and making it a windbag. The appearance is that of a vast lone lake, which native craft do not care to plough; it does not show even a wreck. The water is deep, and without bottom at eighty and even two hundred fathoms; there are many reef-lined bights, but few ports to shelter a ship. The two storm-winds are equally redoubtable.

The "'Illi," which the Doric-speaking Bedawin call El-Ali, is a high north-north-wester, that drives vessels upon the eastern shore; whilst the Azyab, or south-easter, with its subtle sand, urges them

* When Ibn Sa'íd makes the Gulf-breadth about 100,000 paces (= 1 Mijrá = 1 day's sail), M. de la Roque (p. 305, *Voyage dans la Palestine*) understands this measure to represent the distance between Madyan city and the sea-shore.

to the west. During the furious gales the Gulf becomes a sea of breakers; the waves rising in long parallel ridges, so deep and hollow as to imperil the stoutest native craft. Wellsted, in January, 1833, pronounced it to be one of the most dangerous places he had ever seen. Finally, it is full of sharks, which have been worried by steamers out of the Suez Gulf : * we saw their dark triangular fins in all directions—a sinister sight.

The Bugház, or throat of El-Akabah, is formed by Ras Fartah † and by the shoals and rocks outlying conical and triangular Tírán Island. Including these, only five miles of water, which shrinks to one of clear way, with sixty fathoms' depth, separate it from Ras Nasráni, the western jaw upon the Sinai shore. Consequently it is much narrower than its sister formation "Jobal;" and it will require the engineer's art to prevent it being choked, and

* A quarter of a century ago the Suez roads were full of sharks, which, however, were mostly too well fed to attack man : of late years they have greatly diminished there and increased at Trieste—the effect, it is popularly believed, of the canal. The latter is also accused, by some Marseilles engineers, of having lowered the level of the Mediterranean to the extent of three and a quarter inches.

† Or Ras el-Fartah, which Zehme (p. 172) calls also Ras Sankira. There is an Eastern Ras Fartah, the classical Syagros Akra, or "Point of Wild Swine," on the Hadramaut coast, which the ancients held to be the "greatest promontory in the Oikoumene," and which Carter describes as "the most striking on the southeast coast of Arabia." The word "Fartah" means to powder, to reduce to atoms.

adding to our list a third *Mare Mortuum*. According to Ehrenberg, the coral-insect of the Erythræan, which is unable to build cliffs, like those that work in calmer seas, can perfectly repair the reefs already built.

As we steamed along the western edge of Bird Island, whose calcareous head rises 1500 feet high, and whose flanks are ribbed with regular parallel lines, like steps or terraces, trending north to south, and varying in number from four to six, the air felt still, and we all noticed the unusual heat.* There was no sea breeze till 10.30 a.m.; and this want of atmospheric pressure must tend, as at West African Lagos, to develop billows and breakers. Westward is a rear view of the Sinaitic group, rising almost from the coast, and based upon the low arenaceous shore. Unlike the aspect from the Suez Gulf, it is anything but picturesque. It wants the broad sandy plain El-Ká'a to give the contrast of horizontal with perpendicular. The eastern continent, flat and gravelly, behind Ras Fartah, has two "Sherms:" El-Mujawwa' to the south, and El-Dabbah, which

* Mr. Redhead registered 112° (F.) in the shade at El-Akabah at about one p.m., with a north wind blowing. He is in error when he speaks generally of the "almost tideless waters of the Gulf." Off Makná, the movement may be compared with that of Suez: rise of tide at the equinoxes, $6\frac{1}{4}$ feet; springs, $5\frac{3}{4}$; neaps, $2\frac{1}{2}$; depression under northern $1\frac{1}{3}$, and rise under southern winds, $1\frac{1}{2}$ feet.

is here translated the "high place," * nine miles beyond it, ten from Makná, and fifty-two from Sináfir Island. Both have foul entrances, a few yards wide, and both are fit only for small native craft.

As we advanced, the eastern coast became bolder and the formation completely changed. High lumpy buttresses and "horse-backs"—as they are called in the northern seas—ghastly white and grisly bare, capped with cliffs of gypsum, here impure, there crystallised, and often becoming pure selenite, denote a secondary formation violently upthrust by the primaries upon which it is directly based. In places a faint and sickly greenish-yellow, dear to the eye of the mineralogist, denotes the chloritic sands and slates. The same gypseous deposit, overlying red granite with dark porphyritic dykes, may be seen on the western Sinai shore, about Ras Jehn or Jehan ; north of Tor and south of the Melláhah (salterns).

Presently the large blocks of mountain to starboard again showed the incorrectness of the

* The dictionaries give only "Dabah," a sandy plain. In the Admiralty chart we find "Sherm Dhaba, good anchorage ;" and to the north of it a Kadd (shoal or sandspit) Dhabá. The similarity of such words as Dabbah, Júbáh, and Zibá, when rapidly pronounced by the Arabs, has evidently confused the inexperienced nautical ear. In Wellsted (ii. 130) El-Mujawwa' becomes "Sherm Majowwík."

CRUISE NORTHWARDS TO MAKNÁ. 329

Admiralty charts.* "Jebel Makná" is not a single cone, but a group of hills over whose sky-line tower five distinct heads, the summits of the Jebel el-Namrá, which we shall visit. Again, the Jebel Tayyibat Ism ("Of the good name"), which some mappers wrongly call "Jebel Taurán,"† really abuts clean upon the Gulf; whilst the chart has conferred the name upon a detached *massif*, some twenty-five miles in the eastern interior. And yet it is a notable group, rounded and lumpy as that of El-Zahd; not pinnacled like Sinai, nor castled like the giants behind and north of El-Muwayláh.

* Moresby (chart) wrongly writes Maḳn'a, which ends in an Alif. Rüppell borrows the Bedawi fashion (changing the dotted Káf into a hard "g"), "Magna;" and this explains the "Mugnah" of the Hydrographical map, 1871–72. Wallin, who did not visit it, correctly gives Maḳnâ. The survey of the several features is also inexact. The Wady is not made to debouch, as it should, directly upon the shore; the tents or huts are transferred from the immediate seaboard somewhat inland; there is a non-existing permanent village to the north of the Fiumara; and the "ruined fort" is too far from the left bank.

† Keith Johnston (sen.) probably borrowed it from Ritter, who took it from Robinson. In the "Biblical Researches" (i. 222), we find that "a high mountain was seen (from Sinai) across the Eastern Gulf, called Jebel Taurân." This would suggest the Ταυρηνῶν ὄρος, where was a celebrated pilgrimage of the Sarakenoi Arabs, *Ein Vorbild der Wallfahrten nach Mekka und den Wanderbrunnen Zemzem* (Ritter, xiii. 774). The name also appears in Nonnos, who wrote the history of his embassy, under Justinian, to Ethiopia and other parts. The compendium found in Photius (Frag. Hist. iv. p. 179) is alluded to by Fabricius (Bibl. Græca, vii. p. 543) : see also Geog. Gr. Minores, Müller, note p. 178.

Shortly after noon, when the fresh sea breeze had somewhat restored us, the corvette anchored off Makná, an inlet receiving the embouchure of the Wady in which the old city was built. Ptolemy (vi. 7, § 27) shows that navigators in his day were chary of affronting the Elanitic Gulf; hence we cannot recognise the three first names of his cities in Arabia Felix, which, like the fourth, were probably not "Mediterranean" at all.* Moreover, between Elána (Akabat-Aylá) in his N. lat. 29° 15', and 'Oune (Aynúnah) in his N. lat. 28° 50', the distance recorded is only twenty-five direct geographical miles, the true being eighty-three.

Much unnecessary discussion has arisen upon

* The following is his list of "Mediterranean Cities," nearly all maritime:—

	E. Long.	N. Lat.	
Ἀραμαύα	67° 30'	29° 18'	(Aram, or Iram, the stone-heaps.)
Ὀστάμα	69° 30'	29° 00'	(?)
Θαπαύα	71° 40'	29° 00'	(?)
Μάκνα } Μαίνα } Μαήνα }	67° 00'	28° 45'	(True, 28° 24'.)
Ἀγκάλη	68° 15'	28° 45'	(El-Hakl or Hagul on the coast.)
Μαδιάμα	68° 00'	28° 15'	(Maghárat Shu'ayb?)

Here the latitude of Makná agrees tolerably with the modern ruins of the same name: this is also the case with Μαδιάμα, lying further east. "Madyan" is placed:—

	E. Long.	N. Lat.
By the Atwál	55° 45'	29° 00'
„ Kánún	56° 20'	29° 00'
„ Ibn Sa'id	61° 00'	27° 52'
„ Rasm	61° 20'	29° 00'

Thus in latitude we find a divergence of sixty-eight miles.

the site of Midian, the capital. Josephus (Ant. ii. 12), in a passage before quoted, tells us that "to the present day there is a village south of Akabah, on the Red Sea coast, called Midian;" and that this was the place to which Moses fled. Eusebius (*sub voc.*) and St. Jerome transfer it north to the river Arnon (Wady Mojib), south of Areopolis or Ar-Moab, the city of Moab, and affirm that the ruins were visible in their time.*

The mediæval Arab geographers have absolutely settled the question; and we cannot suspect that in this case, as is the custom, they transferred the name of the capital to its chief port. Abulfeda (Table iv.) has these words, "Madyan is in the beginning of the Third Climate,† and belongs to El-Hejaz. It is a ruined town on the shore of the Red Sea, and it contains the well where Moses watered the flocks of Shu'ayb.‡ Madyan primarily

---

* Hence the "Encyclopædia Britannica" (*s.v.* Madian) makes it a town of Arabia Petræa, near the Arnon, and remarks that St. Jerome speaks of another Midian or Madian, whose people were called Madianæi and Madianitæi, whilst the land was known as the Madianæa Regio.

† The First Climate (nearest the Equator) would be distinguished by Aden, the Second by Meccah, and the Third by Damascus. (See Muhammedi's *Alfragani Chron. et Astronom. Elementa.* M. Jacobus Christmannus, Frankfurti, 1590.)

‡ "Shu'ayb," corrupted by the Bedawin and the citizens of Madyan to Sha'íb, is synonymous with Jethro (Yetro, *Arabicè* Gáthar or Gháthar). The Rev. Mr. Badger boldly suggests that as Yahab' Altáhá is pronounced in Syria "Yau Aláhá;" so "Yetro"

designated the tribe to which Shu'ayb belonged, and the word was presently extended to its habitat. We find the following reference in the Koran (surats vii. 83,

might originally have been Yathrib (Jatrippa), the old name of El-Medínah. Jethro's Moslem title is "Khatíb el-Anbiyá," or Preacher to the Prophets, on account of the words of wisdom which he bestowed upon his son-in-law (Exod. ii. 18), and which would be useful to many an unwise head of department in this our day. Some writers have made him the son of Mikhail, ibn Yashjar, ibn Madyan ; but they are charged with ignorance by Ahmed ibn Abd el-Halím. El-Kesái states that his original name was Boyun; that he was comely of person, but spare and lean ; very thoughtful, and of few words (Sale's Koran, p. 117). Other commentators add that he was old and blind. In the "Berakhoth," Jetro and Rahab are Gentiles, or strangers, affiliated to Israel on account of their good deeds (p. 48, M. Schwab's version. Paris: Imprimerie Nationale, 1871).

As regards the wonder-working rod, Josephus (Ant. ii. 12) makes it a shepherd's staff, which, thrown upon the ground, became a serpent, with head raised high as if in wrath: when taken up it recovered its original form. According to the Talmud (*Pirké Rabbi Eliezer Agadol?*), it was a wand set with jewels, which lay in the gardens of Jethro : the latter had often vainly attempted to uproot it with all his oxen; but Moses, pronouncing the sacred name, raised it at once. To my friend James Pincherle, of Trieste, I owe this quaint legend, which finds so many a parallel in Christian and Moslem thaumaturgy. The commentator Rushi (Exod. xvii. 6) makes the substance adamas or diamond (*Sampirin* or *Sampirinon*) : his argument is that when the Lord ordered Moses to smite the rock in Horeb (Exod. xvii. 6), the words are not "on the rock," but "in the rock" (ba-tsúr); thus showing that the rod was hard enough to break stones. Sampir may be the sappir or sapphire of which the Médrash says the Tables of the Law were made. Moslems declare the "Asá" (rod) to have been the branch of a Paradisial myrtle-tree, bequeathed by Adam to Shu'ayb, and used by the latter to defend his cattle from wild beasts.

CRUISE NORTHWARDS TO MAKNÁ. 333

and xi. 85), "And he sent unto Madyan their brother Shu'ayb." The commentators add that Shu'ayb, though blind, was divinely commissioned to convert his fellows by preaching the True Faith revealed to Abraham. The Midianites, however, mocked him, and were destroyed by fire from heaven, whilst the land was wasted by an earthquake. Jethro alone escaped, fled to Palestine, and was buried near Safet.*

Abulfeda (chap. i.) again mentions Madyan town, and places it before Yambú'a, as the first passed by the traveller going south along the sea. His Solinus, or ape, El-Sipáhí † (*ob.* A.D. 1572), adds: "El-Kanún says Tabúk is in the Barr (interior) opposite Madyan: I say that Tabúk is in the east and Madyan to the west." He also states, "Madyan is a ruined town on the Hejazi shore of the Red Sea, where the Gulf of Akabah has the breadth of only one mijra (= day's run); opposite Tabúk, and distant about six days' marching. It contains, in addition to a spring of water, that same well from which, in

---

* His tomb is one of the objects of the grand tour in Syria. There is a Wady called after Shu'ayb in Mount Sinai; and a "Sikkat Shu'ayb" (Jethro's road) near the mouth of the Wady El-Dayr.

† In full *El-'Abd el-Fakír, Mohammed el-Shahír bi Ibn el-Sipáhí* (the slave, the pauper Mohammed, known as the "Son of the soldier"). His geographical compendium, which is Abulfeda alphabetically ordered with a few additions and corrections, is named *Anzáh el-Mesálik ilá Ma'arifat el-Buldáni w' el-Mamálik* (Light for the road to a knowledge of cities and countries).

former days, our Lord Musá gave drink to the flocks of Shu'ayb." Ibn Sa'íd remarks that "Fronting the sea near Madyan, with a little northing, lies the town El-Kusayr (Cosseir) on the western (or African) shore."

In the *Marásid el-Ittilá'a* we find (*sub voc.*)— "The city of Madyan, say the Arabs, is the city of Shu'ayb; and it lies opposite Tabúk, on the coast of the Bahr El-Kulzum (here, the Akabah Gulf); between them is a six days' journey. It is larger than Tabúk, and in it is the well from which Moses watered the flocks of Shu'ayb." All the Arabs of the present day, the settled as well as the nomad tribes, call the ruins indifferently Madyan and Makná. Rüppell (p. 221) supposes that the monks, for whom he finds a "kloster," taught the people that Makná was the old site of Midian city; a tradition which he found still in vogue.

Many modern geographers have grossly erred by confounding the Μαδιάμα of Ptolemy,* in N. lat. 28° 15', with his Μοδίανα in N. lat. 27° 45'. D'Anville ("Compendium," etc. London, 1810) says, "The position of Madian, called by Ptolemy (iv. 5) Modiána, not far from the sea, is known to the Arabs as Mígar-el-Shuaib, or the grotto of Shuaib." My late friend, F. Ayrton, caused further confusion

* Chap. v. gives the Ptolemeian "sites in Arabia Felix," along shore from 'Oune (Aynúnah) to Iambia (Yambu'a el-Nakhil).

by writing and translating "Mugheir-al-Sho'aeib, the Garden of Sho'aeib."* Lastly, Mr. Forster, of the One Primeval Language, in an incorrect and uncalled-for book on the Geography of Arabia, declares (ii. 116) that "the Modíana of Ptolemy identifies itself with the Madian of Abú-l-Feda', and the Midian of Scripture, at the mid-coast (read southern fourth) of the Gulf of 'Akaba'."

The Maghárat-Sha'íb (Shu'ayb) is, I have said,† the second return pilgrim-station on the section between El-Muwayláh and El-Akabah. From Aynúnah the caravan-road winds a few miles along shore, and then, bending abruptly to the north-northeast, skirts the southern flanks of the great buttress called in the chart Jebel Tayyibat Ism. Travelling up the Wady Makná, the distance is seven hours by dromedary or ten by camel, about = twenty-five miles.‡ Deriving its name from a small cave,

* " Maghárah " is the Arab form of the Heb. "Me'arah," a cave or grot. I cannot see, when we denote the letter "Ayn" by a comma, why the hapless "Oin" should be perverted à *discretion* into an "h," an "r," and an "ng".

† Chap. vi. gives a tabular list of the stations and their distances.

‡ Wallin estimates the walk of a "fast camel" at five miles an hour, and he covered 260 miles in fifty-two hours; this, however, is a pace that kills. Robinson (i. 545) gives $2\frac{1}{2}$ stat. miles per hour for short distances, and for long $2\frac{1}{3}$ (= 2 geog. miles). Sprenger makes the caravan march in three days, or thirty-three to thirty-six hours, twenty (direct?) geograph. leagues (= 1°): he sensibly cautions travellers (p. 142) not to confound the *Zeitstunde*,

originally a catacomb, where the Prophet, like the Apostle of Allah on Jebel el-Núr, used to retire for prayer and meditation, it is still visited by the pious; and I have suggested (chap. v.) that its honours may derive from an older date.

Rüppell, who gives an illustration (No. 8) of what he calls Magháyir Shu'ayb (Caverns of Jethro),* visited it on July 11th, and found, to his surprise, water in places one foot deep by fifty paces broad. He calls the site *Thal von Beden* (of the ibex), possibly a corruption of the Bedawi name El-Bada'; while Wellsted (ii. 123) places Beden two and a half hours' march from his "Mahárehi Sho'aïb." On the southern side of the valley the German traveller remarked ruin-heaps and a few column-shafts: the Catacombs, locally called "Bíbán" (doors) from their pylores and façades of smoothed rock, lay to the westward of these remnants, and consisted of square mortuary chambers cut in the sandstone. The resemblance to the Petra style of building suggests an old Nabatí miningtown: what remained of it in Mohammed's time was probably demolished during the succeeding wars.†

Our nomad informants, who dwelt lovingly upon

or hour of time, with the *Wegstunde*, or hour of road (the Schænus, Farsakh or Parasang, numbering thirty-two to forty stadia or furlongs); the latter being about double the former. See chap. v.

* The plural is an error. For the Magháyir Shu'ayb, another place, see Sprenger, p. 147.

† Golius in Alfrag. p. 143.

the manifold beauties of the site, the palm-groves, and the purling spring, spoke of a mosque, and of ten to thirteen "houses of the Nasárá," ruined but still standing. Here, then, we have, evidently, the Μαδιάμα of Ptolemy, probably a summer retreat for the wealthy citizens. It is hardly likely that a nation of traders, like the settled Midianites, would have placed their capital in an inland valley, when they had such a fine naval position as Makná.

We landed (12.45 p.m.) at the old port of Midian, where the water was deep enough to carry a frigate within biscuit-throw of shore. The corvette, not liking the look of the place, stood over to the west of the Gulf, where, fifteen miles away from us, she obtained partial protection and unsafe quarters at the Sherm el-Dahab.* The "Creek of Gold," whence, by-the-by, fine specimens of pure hæmatite were brought, derives its name, according to local legend, from the gold of Ophir being there landed. Sulaymán bin Daúd was evidently a better botanist than a mineralogist, or he would not have sent ships on a three years' voyage for a metal which lay at his threshold: but—

"They didn't know everything down in Judee."

---

* Such was our captain's report, and he found fault with the chart for stating "good anchorage, safe from all winds," when the cove is open to the dangerous Azyab, or south-easter. According to him, Abú Zatát, the creek to the south, is slightly better, and El-Nebiki, the southernmost on the western shore, is a little worse.

Sherm el-Dahab * is a hook at the mouth of the great Sinaitic valley, where Wady Táhmeh from the north anastomoses with Wady Nasb from the opposite direction. Thus it is easily connected with "Hazeroth, whose gold is abundant." † Wellsted (ii. 153), who lay at anchor here for several days, describes this "only well-sheltered harbour in the (Akabat) Sea," as "nearly surrounded by a semi-circular belt of coal, on which the lapse of ages has deposited a thin layer of sand." The rock-ridge, which, rising but a few inches above the *wasserspiegel*, is covered by high water, shows at ebb-tide a broken line of vertebræ, "which gave the name of Esiongeber or (giant's) backbone." ‡

Hence he suspects the ledge of having broken the joint fleet, ten sail, of Jehoshaphat and Ahaziah, about B.C. 896 (2 Chron. xx. 37). But Asiún-geber (מעינ גבר) Numb. 33–35), or "the giant's shoulder-

* The *Sacra Bibbia di Venee* calls the place *Minat el-Dahab*, or harbour of gold (vol. ii. p. 477, 5th edit., by Sig. Drach, illustrated and annotated by Prof. Bartolomeo Catena, Milano, Stella, 1831). The "Gold-creek" was visited by Dr. Laborde and Linant in 1828. Beoche assures us that the epithet "golden" does not take its origin from a tradition that gold was formerly brought there, but from the mica glittering in its sand. Mica, however, appears everywhere in these regions. Wellsted also noted that "the teeth of two Ibices received on board were covered with a substance resembling gold;" and remembered that the same is the case with sheep in the Libanus (?).

† See chap. ix.

‡ There is still work to do at Sherm el-Dahab, where mounds stud the western side of the Scorpion's tail-point.

blade," the old ship-building port, must be sought to the north,* "beside Eloth (El-Akabah) on the shore of the Red Sea, in the land of Edom." Schubert would place it on the islet Kurayyah, a rock some 300 yards long. Dean Stanley ("Sinai," etc., p. 85), who identifies "Elath" with El-Akabah, opines that we have no means of fixing the position of Ezion-geber. The latter may be Robinson's *Ayn el-Ghadyán*, lying some ten miles up the Wady el-Arabah, where possibly the Gulf-head once extended.

And now to describe the actualities of the ancient Midianitish capital, which once ruled the seaboard between El-Akabah and the frontier of El-Hejaz. Makná baylet opens westward; and is provided by nature with two coralline reefs, a northern and a southern, converging and forming rude moles. These breakwaters are covered by the

* Hence we find in the Peutinger Tables:—
1. From Haila (Ela, El-Akabah) to Diana (Ghadyán, Eziongeber, the letters in Arabic and Hebrew being the same), sixteen Roman miles (=14⅓ English).
2. From thence to Rasa (? to the north), sixteen Roman miles.
3. From thence to Gypsaria (Kontellet Garaiyeh, Palmer), sixteen Roman miles.

Dr. Laborde and Linant (*Voyages de l'Arabie Petrée*, etc. Paris, 1830; and *Commentaire Géog. sur l'Éxode*, etc.) place "Elath" on the north-west of the Gulf-head, near the mouth of the Wady El-Arabah; and Ezion-Geber facing it, while they assign to "Madian" its present traditional site.

high tides, which here rise about six feet; and at low water they show signs of a brilliant leek-green vegetation. Both bear signs of work; and we agreed that nothing would be easier than to build upon these foundations a secure dock.

Beyond the two piers are the "gardens of the sea," reefs of the strangest appearance. In misty weather such as the Azyab brings, they look like sheets of verdigrised copper, and long lines of the loveliest emerald-green alternate with stripes and patches of the deepest blue. The "sands" are mostly gravel-fragments of ruddy syenite, washed down by the Wady whose mouth is waterless at this season. Here stand two groups of Ushshash or date-frond huts, which may number 150, some uncovered, many of them roofed, and supplied with the usual verandahs of the same material. All are now empty and ragged because the tribes are in the interior; but, as the hot season advances, each will be "tidied" and occupied by its own family of Ichthyophagi.

The "tabernacles" of "cadjan," mat, sometimes divided by screens in a poor attempt at a harem, contain only old hand-mills, grinding stones, rude hearths, the carapaces of fine turtle,* heaps of

* Hereabouts, in A.D. 1615, Pietro della Valle saw "tortoises as large as the body of a carriage." During two centuries and a half they have had time, like other things, to assume reasonable dimensions.

cockle-shells, and the remnants of lobsters which are said to be excellent.

The clump to the north of the Fiumara belongs to the Beni Ukbeh; southwards are the Maknáwí,* some forty or fifty families, the pauper descendants of the wealthy Midianites who hung their camel's neck with gold-chains, and who strewed their line of flight from the Three Hundred with earrings, collars, and purple raiment. We saw from the corvette the few then occupying the huts, and all ran away when we landed. Presently one family returned and, after a long *pourparler*, supplied us with a kid, the only one in the village—our bibulous *marmiton* had left all the mutton on board.

Nothing could be more wretched than their booths; and these "Midianitish women" would not even unveil. Along the beach lie rude towers of dry untrimmed stone, evidently the modern repre-

---

* Wallin (p. 303) calls them " El-Fawáideh ;" and says they are nomadic Fellahs who, like the Jabalíyyeh in Sinai, associate themselves with the Bedawi owners of plantations, and receive by way of payment for cultivation a certain proportion of the date crops. When the fruit is ripe, the proprietors assemble to gather it, and hold a kind of fair : the prospect of trading and bargaining attracts from remote districts many Arabs who have no interest in the palm-groves. The Rev. G. Percy Badger proposes to explain Makná and Maknáwí by Maknat or Maknuwat (plur. Makání), a space upon which the sun does not shine ; and he quotes Freytag, who considers the term as opposed to Madh'hat, the outside or suburbs of a settlement. This would readily explain the Μάκνα of Ptolemy ; for the gorge is the deepest we have yet seen.

sentatives of the old maritime settlement; and on the borders of the Wady-mouth clumps of dates extend almost to the shore, where the spray breaks over them, and where the percolating tide forms a pool and a fine bath.

The Báb, or Gate, opening a few hundred yards from the sea, has jambs of grey granite, capped and overspread, as by a table-cloth, with the hardest breccias and conglomerates; the latter here and there revet sandstones of new formation and chloritic aspect. The *falaise* is composed of the normal stalactite-like calcareous carbonates passing, here and there, into crystallised lime like arragonite; and the lower corallines blackened, like the granites, by the action of the sea-salts, are mixed with oxides of iron agglutinated by the dews and rains. The scatters of slag and scoriæ are rare, as might be expected, in a place still inhabited; and none could tell us where the furnaces had been. The Maknáwí are the meanest tribe we have yet seen; they preserve no traditions of the Bene Ganbá-Ganbá Jews, who here numbered some 600 in the days of Mohammed, and who lived chiefly by fishing.

The sea-cliff ends to the north with a huge, bald white buttress, which Icelanders would call a "horse." From its pale shoulders rise, beautifully blue, the heights of Tayyibat Ism; and southward lies El-Muzayndi—a range of red syenitoid granite, whose rapidly decomposing slopes are pimply and warty, like the earth-pillars and stone-capped pyramids of Tyrolese Botzen. The whole breadth of the Wady is traversed and streaked by broad bands of green porphyry, which play hide-and-seek in the most fantastic way. The gate leads to a dense " Nakhil " of neglected dates which must number more than one thousand ; in fact, it is a long thick grove, tree rising above tree, and, viewed from the sea, giving the idea of a torrent of verdure. The dead and the dying mingle with the live trees. As usual, all are untrimmed, and the modern Midianites ignore even palm-wine.

After pitching the tents and establishing the kitchen-buttery, as usual, under the palms, we engaged Sa'ad, an old Maknáwí, to show us the ruins. Professing complete ignorance concerning Moses' Well, he led us up the left side of the deep and shady Wady, south of the gate, by a road whose regular zigzags marked the maker's hand, to a saddleback about 250 feet high. Capped with the usual conglomerate, whose face had been washed and weathered into broad and overhanging eaves, the commanding height was corniced and bluff inland or facing towards the valley that lay at its feet.

This place is called by the Bedawin the Burj or Citadel. The high town was built in the normal style, rough stones bedded in mortar; but the fine Roman cement had made way, in this region of pure gypsum, for a barbarous material more than half mud. In fact, the general appearance was modern, making Rüppell suspect that it was a convent of early Christians. Possibly the strong site had been preserved and restored when the remainder of the settlement was destroyed, and probably its survival had extended deep into Islamitic days. It seemed, in fact, to belong to the class of ruins which Wellsted and Miles found at Husn Ghuráb or Ravens fort.*

"Cernimus antiquas nullo custode ruinas."

From the crest we could distinctly trace the foundations, though half-buried by the hand of Time, of the *basseville* which occupied a waterless sandy slope gently falling, like a Wady, towards the main valley. We dug into a grave in the fort, and found bones but no skulls; and we carried off a fragmentary hand-mill of the hardest basalt, a stone which now began to puzzle me.

Descending to the Wady Makná by an abrupt path, round the corniced front, we crossed its breadth from south to north. It is by far the finest we have seen. The sands are grown with the apple of

* See Captain Miles's valuable paper, "Account of an Excursion into the interior of Southern Arabia, with M. Werner Munzinger" (Pasha), C.B., Hon. Corr. Mem. R.G.S.

Sodom, the gigantic 'Ushr (*Calotropis procera*) : but the medicinal uses of " the silk-tree " are here unknown. Much less has the silk-plant been utilised for its strong white fibre, one of the best known,* and now become such a favourite in Europe. On both banks of the water, enclosures, like gardens, hedged with reeds, protect the small fragrant green limes prized throughout Arabia ; the thorny Jujube (*Zizyphos vulgaris*),† a few figs, almonds, pomegranate, and, they say, grapes, the "*Weinreben*" having been seen by Rüppell in fruit (July 12th). Here and there was a patch of Durrah (*Serghum vulgare*), which grew lush and luxuriant.

The place might be converted, by damming the stream and retaining the water, into a " paradeisos." Upon the high-raised right bank, a second and parallel feature, bubbling up from under the driest of sands, forms a small rivulet and a series of cascades, in one place actually four feet high. Its tinkling song really startled us—who ever expected such music in arid Arabia ? This Ayn el-Tabbákhah (Spring of the She-Cork), which is lost in

* See my " Pilgrimage," iii. 122.
† Wallin, who evidently had not the slightest tincture of natural history, describes (p. 339) the rhamnaceous "lote-bush" as "small acacias, called in Arabic Sidr." The berries, distinguished by the name of Nabk, have, when dry, a sickly sweet flavour, which is much relished by the Bedawin, and the reason is probably the usual crave for saccharine matter where sugar is unknown.

the palm-thicket, must have been the principal charm of ancient Midian, the northern half of whose *basseville* lay immediately above and beyond the palm-grove.

Here again we found stone basements, glass and fictile fragments. Further up the valley the people show the Masjid or praying-place of Sayyidná Músá, over which, they say, a mosque formerly stood. The stones, of fine white marmorine texture, bear signs of tooling, somewhat remarkable in these regions; others are of red and weathered syenite. They form several inform heaps, but the plan might, perhaps, be discovered by removing the sand.*

In Midian-land, I have said, the rock-formations are ever changing. Here the characteristics are carbonate of lime, so fine that it becomes at times white marble; and the abundance of chlorite, which stains the sands, and covers the stones with a coating, like enamel, of pale green-yellow. We were

* In Note (p. 358) will be found the only two letters addressed by Dr. Beke to the *Times*, and reprinted here with the express permission of Mrs. Emily Beke. I am told that some sketches appeared in the *Illustrated London News* of April 18, 1874. Mr. John Milne, F.G.S., who accompanied the explorer, published his notes in the *Quarterly Journal of the Geological Society* for February, 1875. I have not yet seen them, but I am assured that never a word about metals occurs in them. Finally, a paper with two views of Midian, and headed "Land of Midian," appeared in the *Illustrated London News* of June 9, 1877. Still never a word about the mineralogical wealth of the land.

shown a coarse and impure rock-salt, which is said to be produced by the cliffs bordering the upper valley. Hearing of a Jebel el-Abyaz, or sulphur-mountain, rising to the south-east, about four hours' march from the sea, we sent two Huwayti lads to fetch specimens : they failed to find the hill, and none of our Bedawin, including Haji Agib of the Mesa'id, knew the way. There is a comparative deficiency of quartz, and a remarkable abundance of lava and basalt occurring in scattered blocks. These plutonic formations, so common in El-Hejaz, are said here to be washed down from the heights about Maghárat Shu'ayb. We heard, further, of a Jebel el-Harrah, in the eastern interior beyond the Shifah ; and wherever this name meets the ear, an experienced Arabian traveller, I have said, expects to find Vulcanism.*

* Wallin (p. 327) quotes a statement by Ahmed ibn Yahyá El-Shá'ir (the poet), author of the *Kitáb el-Buldán* ("Book of Countries"), that the lands known by the name of El-Harrah in Arabia are eight. There must be hundreds of the minor outbreaks, so old that, like the traps about Bombay, they show no signs of crater or place of issue : upwards of a score were found by my late friend, Charles F. Tyrwhitt Drake, scattered amongst the nummulites, hippurites, and calcareous formations of Palestine. Wallin (p. 321) often mentions *black* fragments ; *black* porous stones of peculiar lightness (*ibid.*) ; layers of *black* fragments, by which the natural red colour of the sandstone is hid in parts of the Harrah-Mountain (p. 329); and finally (p. 327) *black*-looking peaks of *volcanic appearance*. These words in italics are omitted by his annotator, Mr. F. Ayrton, who wrong-headedly remarks (p. 321),

During the night of April 16th, the wind blew great guns, threatening to level the tent. The next morning showed an "Azyab" day, cool and calm till the hot ozone-laden wind of noon arose, murky, like an English November, and promising rain, which never came. According to the Bedawin, this state of the atmosphere accompanies the heliacal setting of the Surayyá (Pleiades). At the same time a violent Khamsín, more westerly than the Azyab, did much damage at Cairo and Suez, raising the mercury to (F.) 100°, in the cool hall of Shepheard's Hotel.

The most curious action of the Khamsín is the active part which it plays in the deposition of nitre, but it is readily explained by the Kinetic theory of gases. The intensely dry and electrical wind, a non-conductor, causes violent molecular agitation in the upper atmosphere, with a proportional development of ozone; the latter is pre-

---

" It is possible that the rock of these hills is ferruginous sandstone; the red colour being due to the presence of oxide of iron, which becomes a black peroxide after having imbibed more oxygen from the atmosphere; and thus small fragments become externally quite black, and from the action upon their surfaces, have very much the appearance of cinders. The same thing may be observed in the Valley of Koseir, about twelve miles west of the town of Koseir, on the route to Keuné, in Egypt." Nothing of the kind! the light-weighing stones were simply lava and black basalt. For a notice of the " Harrahs " near El-Medinah, see my " Pilgrimage," ii. 230, 235.

cipitated by the cold, still night, and it finds affinities on the ground.

Next morning, whilst Lieutenants 'Amir and Hasan were making their plans of the harbour, fort, and ruins, we set out to examine the Jebel el-Hamrá, the Red Mountain, which closes the horizon to the east. Its jagged crest of ruddy peaks, cut by dark dykes of porphyry, and fronted by two pale, leprous patches, had excited our curiosity last evening. We could not understand the white, and the red was so vivid that, despite the syenitic gravel on the shore and in the Wady, we suspected ferruginous grit, or the New Red of Petra. One line lay up the "Water of Makná" proper, or the southern rivulet called the Ayn el-Hafáyir (Spring of Pits). Like its fellow of the She-Cork, it wells from the sands; the taste and hue are sulphureous and medicinal; and, as usual, it tarnishes silver.

The growth of sorrel was remarkable in the fertile nooks; but the Wady was mostly choked with loose boulders and with projecting spines of bare and worn granite, into which the waters had cut and bored deep channels. One projection showed a number of shallow "cup-marks," forming holes, like those with which Egyptians play their favourite game, El-Mankalah.* Beyond the springs

---

* Lane (Mod. Egypt, ii. chap. xvii.) gives an illustration of the board, and describes the game at full length. Some years

the valley is nude and bare of vegetation, except a thorn-tree or two in the re-entering angles, which have been most watered. We collected the plants, which gradually became more stunted as the land rose, and we added a variety of beetles, especially the "Umm Ámir," to our bottles. The birds were Katâs, and a small black species, with a snow-white tail, in shape not unlike the wheat-ear. The hornet was unusually large and lively.

Here and there little mounds of stone denoted, according to the people, the deeply-sunk Bayt, or home of the Su'ubán (*Coluber Guttatus*, Forsk.), the large male serpent, cockatrice or dragon, so famous in the history of Nabi Músá.* Skinks, or sand-lizards (Sikankín), abounded; and after a sharp chase, we captured the young of a Zabb,† a lizard,

ago it was introduced into England by some ardent Anglo-Egyptians, but it lived the short life of an exotic.

* Surat vii. sab. 118 : " Wherefore he cast down his rod and behold it became a visible serpent (*fa'-iza hiya Su'ubánun*). Al Bayzáwi and the commentators say that this dragon was hairy : when it opened its mouth, the jaws were eighty cubits asunder, and when its lower mandible was on the ground, the upper reached the palace top. Pharaoh and the whole assembly were so terrified, that 25,000 men lost their lives in the press of the flying crowd. Moses took the serpent by the mouth, at the command of Allah (Surat xxx. Sale, 236), although it was swallowing stones and trees, and this earthly kin of the Great Sea Serpent once more became a rod. The word Su'ubán is also applied to the Constellation Draco ; especially to the Draconis, which was the Polaris *circa* B.C. 2790.

† The Lacerta El-Dsobb of Seetzen, who gives the measurements (p. 437, iii. Reisen, etc. Berlin, 1855).

some four feet long, which burrows far into the ground: it changes colour, but not so remarkably as the "Waran," or true chameleon.

The Makná fiumara drains, according to the Bedawin, the waters of Maghárat Shu'ayb, which Rüppell places further south.* Here it has a lovely rose-pink hue, the effect of sunlight playing upon syenitic sand and gravel. Its principal branches, the Wady El-Kharag and El-Mab'ug, are on the left bank: the latter contains, they say, bitter water near the head. We quitted the Makná where it winds between the dark Jebel el-Ábidín to the north and the ruddy Jebel el-Hamrá southwards; and, with the conviction that my old friend had hit upon the gold in its upper course, we reformed its name to "WADY HAJI WALI."

After two good hours, ascending some 1500 feet, we stood at mid-height on the chain, which is broken, and everywhere threaded, not by the usual chasms, but by sandy water-courses, easy even to a camel.

The syenite, containing very little silvery mica, was traversed, as usual, by broad dykes of bottle-

* P. 221. On his return from Magná (Mákná) to Mohila (El-Muwayláh), after five hours and a half in a south-easterly direction, he noted a valley which carries off the surplus supply of "Wadi Beden." Thence four hours to the south-south-east placed him at the sandy plain and spring "El-Gear," where stood the huts of the Musaiti (Masá'id) Arabs. The site is four hours from Aynúnah.

green porphyry; and the discovery of the day—for almost each day had its own—was the chloritic slate, the matrix of the Brazilian gold mines, especially that of São João del-Rei. To this we did due honour in an evening bowl of punch, which sent the weak heads reeling to bed.

April 18th—our last day in Arabia—broke with a fine 'Illi, or north-wester, which tossed the water about like a mid-wintry easter in our Channel. Luckily for us the corvette did not like the weather. She had promised to pick us up in the morning; and she gave us nearly the whole day. We sketched the booths which have supplanted the tents of Shem, and we wandered about the sea-shore attempting, but failing, to catch the sea-snakes. M. Marie considerably scandalised the half-starving Maknáwi by eating raw sea-eggs, owning the while that he would have preferred his *oursins* cooked in the shell, or made into omelets.

There are two kinds of these Echinidæ, which the Arabs call Gunfud el-Bahr (sea-hedgehog); one small, the other with stony spines three inches and a quarter long,* and not unlike the imitation cigars made of chocolate: the latter is also

---

* I find the *Grand Hérisson de Mer* figured by Shaw (ii. 74), and described (ii. 89) as having points larger than a swan's quill. (See the fine French translation, two vols. quarto. La Haye, Jean Neaulure, 1743.)

found on Bourbon Island. The beach was rich in the large scalopped shells which the French term Bénitiers (*Concha imbricata*, Shaw); and another production of Makná is the whorled operculum of a large species of Turbo,* known as the *Hajar el-Akrab*, or scorpion's stone: I collected some hundreds for making buttons.

Tired of the shore, we "took," as the Bedawin say, "the pole-star between our eyebrows," and walked, studying the accidents of ground, to the great white horse-buttress north of camp. Composed of pure gypsum and salenite, it is based upon granite decomposed almost to schist. Some of these formations assume the quaintest shapes; one in particular was an enlarged copy of an Indian "Shola topi;" and the harder veins of rock, quaintly weathered, stood up like smoke-stacks. Diorite and porphyry were scattered over the plain, and there was the usual medley of metals. We picked up a fragment containing *lapis calaminaris* (oxide of zinc), and almost every stone we broke contained spots or lines of mineral, even the hard black and porous basalt showing silvery streaks, which, upon analysis, proved to be free

---

* The operculum much resembles that of the *T. Argyrostomus* of Java, but never reaches the size of *T. Aleurius*.

2 A

gold.* We only regretted not being able, on account of the dangerous wind, to visit the Land of Ád, and the mining-ruins reported in Jebel Tayyibat Ism.

Sprenger (pp. 199-200) places to the north-east of Madyan City and north of the Sarakeni the "Oaditæ" of Agatharkides; and he identifies them with the Beni Ád (Ádites), holding, like certain Arab geographers,† that this race dwelt between Syria and Yemen. Their first king, Sheddád bin Ád, fourth in descent from Núh (Noah), built the garden of Irem, so useful to Eastern poets. The fate of the Ádites was similar to that of the Beni Tamúd: the Himyarite prophet, Húd, was sent to convert them from idolatry; and, when they refused to hear the words of wisdom, a Simúm entered into their nostrils, and, passing through their bodies, mummified them. The Koran (xlvi. 20) transferred them to the Ahkáf, or the Sandheaps near Hazramaut—the Home of Death—where their paradise is now buried; perhaps a confusion with the Nufúd or arenaceous tracts of the Hismá. Also the Oaditæ,

---

* The report of the official analysers confirms this statement. What I call "porous basalt," however, appears to M. Marie to be "porphyres-pyritique," or "porphyre basaltique" (chap. xiii.). The free gold thus appeared in two formations; the other being the lump of porphyritic greenstone before referred to.

† He quotes Beladzori's *Ansáb* (Genealogies), fol. 3. "Adite," in Arabic, means anything very old: the term, for instance, would be applied to Cyclopean walls.

east of Madyan, might have been the later or junior Ad, afterwards changed into monkeys, and this seems to be denoted by their connection with the prophet Lukman, the Wise, a native of Akabat-Aylá.

At 4 p.m. the corvette ran in from the "Creek of Gold," and we lost no time in embarking. Indeed the agility of our escort, when homeward-bound, formed a truly remarkable comparison with their slow and measured movements the other way. Besides fancy specimens intended for H.H. the Viceroy, we carried away for analysis eight boxes full of metalliferous quartz, greenstone, porphyry, basalt, syenite and chloritic slate; fourteen water-bags of granite, and other gravels; and twelve baskets of sand for laboratory work.

We were accompanied on board by the Sayyid Abd el-Rahím and the Shaykh Abd el-Nabi, who faithfully promised to forward to the Governor of Suez, within a reasonable time, specimens of the turquoises from Jebel Shekayk, red earth from the Hismá, the "written stone" in Wady Sharmá, and sulphur from the Jebel el-Abyaz of Makná. Our companions had their dromedaries all ready for the long march homewards, and, after the usual acknowledgment of their services, we bade them adieu and saw them overboard.

Decidedly the most enjoyable part of a delightful

and eventful visit to old Midian was the short stay at Makná, and the glimpse of the Dahi,* or true Desert, which it offered us. What a contrast with the horrors of the civilised city—"the clouds of dust by day, and glare of gas by night, and the noise of the streets roaring like an angry beast!" How easy to understand the full force of the Bedawi expression, " Praise be to Allah that once more we see the Nufúd!" the soft clean sand of the wilderness, with its sweet fresh breezes and its perfumed flora, "the Desert's spicy stores;" its glorious colouring and its grand simplicity that engender male and noble breeds of man and beast! Its atmosphere is the reverse of that Hesperidian air, concerning which Homer sang—

> "There the human kind
> Enjoy the easiest life: no snow is there,
> No biting winter and no drenching shower,
> But Zephyr always gently from the sea
> Breathes on them, to refresh the happy race." (Od. iv. 563).

---

* " *Dahi*," says Ayrton, "is applied to the Desert in the sense of its being a place open and exposed to the sun and, κατ' ἐξοχήν, to its wide central expanse. *Gháyit* is a land without water; *Bádiyeh* is a barren steppe; *Himádih* is gravelly, flinty ground; and *Ká'a* is a sandy plain: *Nufúd* seems to be used with reference to the comparative fertility of the part so called." *Dahuá* is the Desert (*faláh*) in general; but it is especially applied, like *Bat'há*, to a gravelly, sand surface, somewhat depressed. Lastly, *Makhraj* is the issue from the waste upon fertile, watered ground.

The climate of Midian, and perhaps I may say, of the Desert generally, is harsh—hot by day as it is cold by night. Yet no one, who has ever enjoyed its charms, fails to look back upon his journey with the fondest of memories. The Desert, with its sudden and startling changes from utter desolation to exuberant vegetation, is pre-eminently the Land of Fancy, of Reverie; never ending, ever renewing itself in presence of the Indefinite and the Solitude, which are the characteristics of this open world. The least accident, the smallest shift of scenery, gives rise to be longest trains of thought, in which the past, the present, and the future seem to blend.

In the forested land of the tropics Nature masters man; his brain is confused with the multiplicity of objects; he feels himself as prisoner in a gorgeous jail. Moreover some of us suffer from lasting sadness in the regions of evergreens, such as Central Africa, Brazil, and Western India. Much as I enjoyed my last visit to Bombay when able to leave it by the first steamer, hardly a week had passed before the old melancholy made itself felt. But in the Desert man masters Nature. It is the type of Liberty, which is Life, whilst the idea of Immensity, of Sublimity, of Infinity, is always present, always the first thought. Whilst prosaic and prosy Robinson asked, " How can a

Desert be beautiful ?" right well sang the French poet *—

"A l'aspect du désert, l'infini se révèle,
Et l'esprit exalté devant tant de grandeur,
Comme l'aigle fixant la lumière nouvelle,
De l'infini sonde la profondeur."

Adieu, Midian!

NOTE.

Mrs. Beke, the widow of my old and regretted friend, has kindly allowed me to republish the two letters addressed by her late husband to the *Times* (Feb. 27, and March 5, 1874). These are, as far as I can ascertain, the only printed records of the adventurous excursion to the Gulf of Akabah which ended an active and energetic life. It is evident from them that no idea either of mineral wealth, or of industrial establishments, had struck the traveller when he was examining the shores of Midian in search of the "True Sinai."

LETTER I.

MOUNT SINAI.

TO THE EDITOR OF THE "TIMES."

SIR,—On the 28th of January I wrote from Akaba, announcing the discovery of "Moses' Place of Prayer" at Madian, on the East Coast of the Gulf of Akaba, which I identify with the "Encampment by the Red Sea" of Numbers xxxiii. 10. This letter was forwarded by the *Erin* on her return voyage from Akaba; but, in consequence of the severe weather she was exposed to, she had to put in at Tor, whence she may be expected to arrive here in a day or two.

I am now thankful to be able to report that the object of my expedition to discover the true Mount Sinai has happily been attained, very much sooner than I could have anticipated, although not altogether in the manner I had expected.

---

* Felicien David.

CRUISE NORTHWARDS TO MAKNÁ. 359

As stated in my former letter, we reached Akaba in the steamer *Erin* on the 27th of January.

We left Akaba under the personal escort of Sheikh Mahommed ibn Iját, the chief of the Alauwin tribe of Bedouins, to whom I was the bearer of a *firman* from His Highness the Khedive of Egypt, and proceeded north-eastward up the Wady-el-Ithem (the "Etham" of the Exodus), and encamped in the evening at the foot of Mount Bárghir, one of the principal masses of the chain of mountains bounding the valley of the Arabah on the East, which are marked on our maps as the Mountains of Shera, but of which the correct designation is the Mountains of Shafeh; those of Shera, as I have myself seen, being a chain extending from that of Shafeh in a direction from north-west to south-east.

My astonishment and gratification may be better imagined than described when I learnt that this Mount Bárghir is the same as a mysterious *Jebel-e'-Nur*, or "Mountain of Light," of which I had heard vaguely in Egypt as being that whereon the Almighty spoke with Moses, and which, from its position and other circumstances, is without doubt the Sinai of Scripture; although, from its manifest physical character, it appears that my favourite hypothesis that Mount Sinai was a volcano must be abandoned as untenable.

We encamped at the foot of "the Mountain of Light," and during the ensuing night we experienced a most tremendous storm, the thunder and lightning being truly terrific, some of the claps being directly over our heads. The rain fell in torrents during several hours, threatening to wash us away altogether. I do not remember to have ever witnessed a more violent tempest either in Abyssinia or elsewhere; and its effect on my mind was this—that if the words of Scripture that at the time of the Delivery of the Law on Sinai "the Mountain burned with fire into the midst of Heaven, with darkness, clouds, and thick darkness" (Duèt. iv. 11), with other texts which I need not here refer to, are not, as would now appear, to be understood as descriptive of a volcanic eruption, still less can they be held to describe a mere thunderstorm, however violent, as is generally, but somewhat inconsiderately imagined.

As the climbing part of my expedition necessarily devolves on my young companion, Mr. Milne, he, on the following morning, ascended the mountain on Sheikh Mahommed's horse, and accompanied by the Sheikh's son and an attendant, also mounted, and by three Bedouins on foot. On his return, shortly after four o'clock in the afternoon, he made me a most valuable and interesting report, of which I now gladly publish a few heads.

The way was at first up a narrow wady, which grows more and more narrow till it becomes a gorge. On the road they passed a stone on which some inscriptions appear to have been cut, but which are now all defaced with the exception of the words "Ya Allah" ("Oh, God"), in Cufic, or old Arabic, characters. Within the gorge itself they stopped to inspect another large stone, about four feet long and two feet square, made of granite. It originally stood upright, about two or three feet away from the side of the gorge, on another stone, which served as a pedestal; but it has now fallen over, and rests between its pedestal and the side of the gorge. Near the stone the Bedouins come to pray; and, according to the statement of Sheikh Mahommed, who had heard it from his father, and he from his father, and so on, Sidi Ali ibn 'Elim, a noted Mahommedan saint, whose tomb and mosque are between Jaffa and Haifa, came here also to perform his devotions. What led him to do so my informant could not say, unless he was commanded by Allah.

On reaching the gorge the riders had to leave their horses with two of the Arabs, and perform the rest of the ascent on foot. A short way up they came to a low wall across the gorge, which latter is filled with large boulders, and close above the wall, on the right hand, is a well about three feet in diameter and about the same to the surface of the water, which may be two feet deep. From this point the ascent was a "climb," the face of the rock being almost perpendicular.

On the ridge on the left side of the gorge, about 150 yards distant from the well, is a pile of large rounded boulders of granite, consisting of four stones of the material of the mountain, three standing up facing the north and one at the back to the south, and on all of them are cut inscriptions, which Mr. Milne copied as well as his cold fingers would allow him to do so. The stones, which are much weather-worn, are externally of a dark-brown colour, against which the inscriptions make themselves visible from their being of a somewhat lighter colour. The lines of these "Sinaitic inscriptions" are about three-quarters of an inch broad and very shallow, being not more than an eighth of an inch deep.

The figures on the stones are very rude, and can hardly be phonetic; neither is it easy to say what they are intended to represent.

On the very summit of the mountain they found numerous sheep skulls and horns, with a few bones, it being the custom of the Bedouins to come up here to pray and to sacrifice a lamb, which is eaten on the spot. But none of the remains appear to be very recent. It is here, as I was told, that the Almighty is said to have spoken with Moses.

Before reaching the summit snow was found in the crevices of the mountain, and while Mr. Milne was at the top it hailed and snowed, and was so bitterly cold that it was as much as he could do to take a few angles with the Azimuth compass, and even this he could not have done had not his attendants kindled a fire by which he might warm his fingers. The elevation of the spot is estimated at 5000 feet, but it will be known more accurately when our observations on the journey come to be calculated. Though so far distant, Akaba seemed just under his feet, but on so diminutive a scale that he failed to detect the castle among the date-palm trees the general outline of which alone was visible. In other directions the landscape was blocked out by banks of cloud, fog, and rain.

Mount Bárghir, "The Mountain of Light," is one of the loftiest peaks of the range of mountains on the east side of the Wady-el-Arabah and the west side of the Wady-el-Ithem, overhanging the latter.

Without dwelling on the geological features of the mountain, of which Mr. John Milne's report will treat very fully in my book, it will be sufficient to say here that it consists of a mass of pink or reddish granite, which, in places, where it is weathered, assumes a dark-brown hue, and that the granite is traversed by numerous dykes, generally of a dark-green colour, and apparently dioritic.

On the side of the mountain are many large boulders, several of which are so much decomposed on their under sides as to form small caverns. One of these was as much as twenty feet, or thereabouts, each way across, with a height of ten feet or twelve feet at the entrance, sloping down towards the back. As the existence of a cave or caves on Mount Sinai is essential in order to meet the requirements of the texts (Exodus xxxiii. 22, and 1 Kings xix. 9), the fact that such caves do actually exist on the "Mountain of Light" is most pertinent and important.

Not less significant is the fact that this majestic mountain is visible in all directions, and that round its base towards the east and south there is camping ground for hundreds of thousands of persons.

It would be out of place to dwell here on the importance of this discovery of the "Mountain of Light," as regards the elucidation of the Sacred History. Its identification with the mountain on which the Law was delivered is scarcely open to a doubt. I had imagined that mountain to be a volcano. I have publicly declared my conviction that such must be the fact, and the journey from which I am now returning was undertaken with the express object of establishing this assumed fact. I am now bound to admit that this discovery, though in strict accordance with the principles enunciated in my *Origines Biblicæ* forty years ago, proves me to have been egregiously mistaken with respect to the volcanic character of Mount Sinai. I make this admission without any reservation, because my desire is, as it always has been, to adduce evidence of the historical truth of the Scripture narrative of the Exodus, in contradiction to the erroneous interpretation put upon that narrative, which has caused its truth to be called in question; and I should be a traitor to the cause I have so much at heart were I to attempt to bolster up my own opinions when found to be unsupported by facts. "Great is truth, and mighty above all things."

I am, Sir, your very obedient servant,
(Signed) CHARLES BEKE.
Suez, Feb. 16, 1874.

DR. BEKE'S SINAI EXPEDITION.

TO THE EDITOR OF THE "TIMES."

SIR,—In Dr. Beke's letter from Suez of the 16th ult., which you kindly published in the *Times* of the 27th ult., by which he announced his discovery of the "true Mount Sinai," he mentioned that he had written to you on the 28th January from Akaba, describing "Moses' Place of Prayer" at Madian, on the east coast of the Gulf of Akaba, which also he has been so far fortunate as to discover. On his return to Egypt, Dr. Beke found that the little steamer *Erin* had not returned to Suez, she having been delayed by stress of weather and want of coals, so that his letter to you of the 28th of January, which he intrusted to the captain, has only now reached me, and I hasten to forward it to you for publication :—

"His Highness the Khedive having been pleased to place the Egyptian steamer *Erin* at my disposal for the conveyance of myself and party to the head of the Gulf of Akaba, we left Suez in that vessel on the morning of January 18th, and arrived here in safety in the afternoon of yesterday, the 27th, after a pleasant, and, from my point of view, most interesting and successful voyage of ten days.

"The run down the Gulf of Suez was without the occurrence of anything of moment, but on our passing Ras Mohammed—the southern extremity of the Peninsula of Tor, the traditional 'Mount Sinai'—we encountered the northerly winds almost constantly blowing down the Gulf of Akaba, which during three days and more raged with great violence. Fortunately I was desirous of visiting Aiyúnah (Aynúnah?), Burckhardt's Ayoun el Kassab, the Hadj station on the sea shore, a little way east of the entrance of the Gulf, which I imagined to be the 'Encampment by the Red Sea' of the Israelites, mentioned in Numbers xxxiii., 10, and by going thither we escaped the violence of the storm; otherwise I fear it might have fared badly with our frail bark of only sixty-four tons.

"On our return into the Gulf, as the tempest had not entirely abated, we anchored on the 24th close to the shore at Magna or Madian, in 28° 23' N. lat., behind a point of land and a reef, which, though not a fit anchorage for a large vessel, afforded shelter to the little *Erin*, though we lost here one of our anchors. A Madian we had to remain a day, which afforded us an opportunity of going on shore and inspecting the place, a camping ground of the Benu Ughba Arabs, numbering about 400 souls. The Sheikh, with the main body of the tribe, was away in the interior, a few persons only remaining here to attend to the fructification of their numerous date palms—it is no exaggeration to estimate them at 1000 or more—growing near the beach and along a valley coming from the east, in which there is a perennial stream of water. With the date trees we also saw several dōm palms, lime, nebbuk, and fig trees; and there were even a few patches of barley carefully protected by hedges of palm leaves.

"We were on the point of returning to the ship, when we

were informed of the existence in the vicinity of a holy spot, where it is said the prophet Moses prayed, and over which a 'mosque' had been erected. This was stated to be at an hour's distance from the shore; and as with these people's vague estimate of distances it might possibly be much more, and I did not feel myself competent to go so far on foot, we went on board to lunch, after which Mr. Milne returned on shore and walked inland with a servant and a native guide.

"He proceeded eastward up the valley, along the side of the palm grove, gradually ascending over a sandstone slope in places worn into hummocks by the water, which during the rainy season finds its way down to the sea, and when about half a mile from the coast he came to a small stream some three feet wide, running in a channel which it has cut in the solid rock. At the point where he struck the stream the water runs prettily over the inclined but irregular surface of the rock, with a fall, or succession of falls, of about twelve feet in all, winding and losing itself among the palm-trees. The surface of the rock, which is sandstone, in places merging into a conglomerate of granite, diorite, and quartz, in stones, some as large as cocoa-nuts, cemented by coarse sand, is here quite clear, so that one walks upon the bare rock; but at a couple of hundred yards further up the valley the rock is covered with sand, which appears to be making rapid inroads. So great, indeed, is its encroachment on the date plantations, that the Arabs have made hedges round these to protect them from the sand, which hedges, however, are being overwhelmed, and others have, consequently, to be erected further in.

"On reaching the end of the palm groves, a mound is seen half as high as the tops of the trees, with numerous blocks of white stone lying among the sand, and beyond this there is a good view further up the valley, along which date palms are seen growing in patches. There are also a few dōm palms, one noticeable one overhanging the white stones.

"These remains, which instead of being an hour's journey or more from the sea, are at the utmost one mile from the beach, were found on examination to consist of blocks of alabaster, so white and pure as at first sight to be mistaken for marble, and only proved to be sulphate of lime, by its scratching with a knife and by its non-effervescence with muriatic acid. The blocks are each about three feet long and one foot six inches square, and appear to have been worked with the tool, though the edges are now much rounded by the weather. One of them seems to form a portion of a column. Together with the blocks of alabaster are some of granite, likewise much weathered. As far as a brief and hasty inspection would allow an opinion to be formed, these stones appear to lie in two parallelograms, ranging from north to south, the one within the other, the south end of the inner one being semi-circular, and there even seem to be indications of a third range of stones further to the north. But it is difficult to speak with certainty on account of the sand which covers these stones in part and threatens soon to hide them entirely. There are several mounds of sand round about, which may probably contain other remains.

"This most interesting spot, which requires to be more closely examined, is especially important to me, because I now see that here, at Madian, and not at Ayúnah (Aynúnah), must have been the 'Encampment by the Red Sea,' of the Israelites. Its proximity (half a day's journey) to Maghara Sho'eib, or Jethro's Cave, which I identify with the Elim of the Exodus, and the fact that the stream of running water must have some of its sources at or near that spot, explain why it should not have been mentioned in Exodus, xv. 27, xvi. 1, as a separate station, much more satisfactorily than I attempted, in page 38 of my pamphlet, *Mount Sinai a Volcano*, to explain the apparent discrepancy in the two statements of Scripture. The 'Encampment by the Red Sea,' was simply a continuation of that at Elim, with its 'twelve wells of water and three score and ten palm trees,' the two together stretching down the valley, with its living water, from Maghara Sho'eib, or 'Jethro's Cave' to this 'Praying-place of Moses,' at Madian.

"As one of my main arguments against the correctness of the vulgar identification of Mount Sinai and other places con- nected with the Exodus of the Israelites is based on the insuffi- ciency of local traditions to establish the authenticity of any such identifications, it would be inconsistent on my part were I to insist on the intrinsic and absolute value of the traditions attached to 'Jethro's Cave,' 'Moses' Praying-place,' etc. Nevertheless these traditions are, at the least, as valuable as any of the others, and their existence here on the distant and almost unknown shores of the Gulf of Akaba, as well as that of 'Pharaoh's Island,' within sight from where I am now writing, and 'Wady Itum,' the entrance to the desert of Nedjd, which I identify with 'Etham in the edge of the wilderness' of Exodus xiii. 20, within a two hours' journey from this spot, all serve to show that there is sufficient reason for my hypothesis that this, the Gulf of Akaba, and not the Gulf of Suez, is the Red Sea through which the Israelites passed in the flight from Pharoah King of Mizraim. A few days more will, I trust, suffice to demonstrate the absolute truth of this hypothesis.

"I am, sir,
"Your very obedient servant,
(Signed) "CHARLES BEKE.
"Akaba, Jan. 28th, 1874."

In your impression of to-day I see a letter from Mr. F. W. Holland, and one from our friend Major Wilson. The former gentleman, although he says he is quite ready to bring forth arguments to disprove Dr. Beke's theory, very rightly and kindly adds that it would be neither fair nor wise to attempt to do so until he knows further particulars of Dr. Beke's discoveries. Major Wilson also says, "I had not intended raising a discussion on the result of Dr. Beke's journey until his return to this country, nor do I wish to do so now."

I trust I may be pardoned for remarking that the contents of the Major's letter can scarcely be said to be in accordance with the intention thus expressed.

Dr. Beke will, I trust, be home in the course of a fortnight, and in the mean time I venture to ask the public to withhold their judgment until he arrives with the proofs, which I am persuaded he will bring with him of his discovery of the true Mount Sinai. I ask this because I am, like Major Wilson, delighted to see that my husband does not intend his discovery of the true Mount Sinai to end in smoke, but in truth.

In Dr. Beke's letters to me from Akaba, he tells me he is deeply indebted to the "patriotic and obliging" spirit of the Peninsular and Oriental Company for their kindness in supplying his little steamer *Erin* with the British flag and for every assistance in his preparations for his journey from Suez.

I have the honour to be, with thanks for kindly inserting this, Sir,
Yours very faithfully,
(Signed) EMILY BEKE.
March 3rd, 1874.

OPHIR AND THE LAND OF MIDIAN.

TO THE EDITOR OF THE "DAILY NEWS."

SIR,—With reference to your leading article in the *Daily News* of yesterday, May 15th, permit me to ask you kindly to give publicity to what Dr. Beke said in 1872, by which it will be seen that my husband predicted the discoveries now made by our distinguished friend, Captain Richard Burton. I rejoice to learn that Captain Burton's explorations on the shores of the Gulf of Akaba are likely once more to reawaken public interest in, and must confirm Dr. Beke's and Mr. John Milne's important discoveries in the Gulf of Akaba in January, 1874, of Aynúnah, Magna, or Midian, and other places of interest connected with the "Encampment by the Red Sea of the Israelites," and finally of the "True Mount Sinai." Dr. Beke said in March, 1872 :—

"Through the kindness of Dr. Petermann, I have received fac-similes of the drawings made by Herr Carl Manch, of some of the ornaments on the ruins of Zimbabye, in South-Eastern Africa, discovered by him, as is mentioned in the *Athenæum* of the 10th ult.; which he identifies with Ophir, and supposes to be of the Tyro-Israelitish construction. As, however, whatever knowledge we possess of Ophir is derived from the Hebrew Scriptures alone, we are not warranted in seeking for it anywhere except where, from a comparison of the various passages in those Scriptures, we find it to be placed by them. And the mention of Ophir in conjunction with the Arabian countries of Havilah and Sheba, ought to be conclusive that Ophir itself was in Arabia likewise. Taking this for granted, it should now be shown how intelligible the whole history of the Tyro-Israelitish trade with the land of Ophir becomes. From 1 Kings, chap. ix. verse 26–28, we learn that King Solomon, having obtained a footing on the shores of the Yam-Suph (Red Sea), in the land of Edom—that is to say, the Gulf of Akaba—opened a trade by sea with Ophir, at the instigation of, and in conjunction with Hiram, King of Tyre. The practical effect of this joint maritime enterprise was similar to that of the Portuguese in the fifteenth and following centuries. As this modern nation found a way to India by sea, round the Cape of Good Hope, and so diverted the commerce of the further East from the overland route through the Levant, so did the

Tyro-Israelites open a maritime trade by way of the Straits of Bab el-Mandeb with the countries in Eastern and Southern Arabia, with which they had previously traded overland. As soon, however, as the fleet reached Ophir, the Queen of the adjoining country of Sheba, having become acquainted with the fame of Solomon (1 Kings x. 1), undertook in person an overland journey to his court, taking with her no less than 120 talents of gold—nearly equal to one-third of the total quantity (420 talents) brought home by the joint fleet—'and of spices very great store, and precious stones; there came no more such abundance of spices as those which the Queen of Sheba gave to King Solomon' (1 Kings x. 10). The avowed object of this lady's visit to the wise King of Israel was 'to prove him with hard questions' (1 Kings x. 1), but it is not impossible that, like the Chinese of modern times, when the Russians first visited them by sea, the Sovereign of Sheba and her people were averse to this opening of a new trade in that direction, preferring the continuance of the ancient overland route, which could be more easily kept under native control; and that she brought with her such an abundance of the rich produce of India and Africa by the old road, in order to show how unnecessary the new one was. Be this as it may, this maritime route to Ophir and Sheba did not last long. Passing over the allusions to it in 1 Kings xxii. 48, and 2 Kings xix. 22, which show that it must have been often interrupted, we read (2 Kings xvi. 6) that in the reign of Ahaz, King of Judah (c. 740 B.C.), 'Rezin, King of Syria, recovered Elath; and the Syrians came to Elath, and dwelt there to this day;' so that, under any circumstances, the whole duration of this Red Sea commerce did not exceed two centuries and a half. During that brief interval it is not likely that the Tyro-Israelitish fleets continued their voyages to the East Coast of Africa, even if the Arabians had allowed them to interfere with their monopoly, and still less that they should have penetrated as far inland as Zimbabye. The ruins discovered there are therefore certainly not Tyro-Israelitish. They may, however, have been constructed by the Southern Arabians, who, as the representatives of the Biblical nations of Sheba and Ophir, have traded with the East Coast of Africa, and had settlements there down to the present day. Still this does not afford any reason for attributing to these buildings a remote antiquity. The prevailing notion that all 'Cyclopean' or megalithic remains must necessarily date from the earliest ages, has sustained a severe blow from Mr. James Ferguson, who, in his recent work, 'Rude Monuments in all Countries: their Age and Uses,' contends that the monuments in England, Brittany,' and elsewhere, which during centuries have evoked the wonder of antiquaries, belong to a period far more recent than the Roman age, just as he showed in the *Athenæum* of July 30th, 1870 (No. 2231) that 'the Giant Cities of Bashan,' which Dr. Porter would have us believe were inhabited by King Og in the time of Moses, were, without a single exception, 'erected during the six centuries which elapsed from the time of Christ till the age of Mahomet.' 'The buildings at Zimbabye are not improbably of the same age.'"

Hoping this may prove of interest to your numerous readers and thanking you,

I am, Sir,
Your obedient servant,
(Signed) EMILY BEKE.

Ferndale View, Tunbridge Wells, May 17th, 1877.

CHAPTER XIII.

RETURN TO CAIRO, ETC. THE "PROCÈS-VERBAL" ADDRESSED TO HIS HIGHNESS.

THE violent "'Illi"-wind of April 18th, which made us pass the night zigzagging under easy steam, and the broken tumbling sea, fell calm and smooth shortly after we had threaded the dangerous part of El-Akabah. Sailing under a cloudless sky, with a flowing sheet and a following breeze, we spent the time on board in writing our reports, in pounding our specimens, and in treating the powder with mercury which was borrowed from our obliging Captain's artificial horizon. On Saturday, April 21st, exactly three weeks after our departure, we took leave of all our friends of the S.S. *Sinnár*, including the Mullá Effendi (chaplain), and the good old Hakímbáshi (surgeon) who had been most attentive to the small maladies of our men. I may truly say that we shall be rejoiced to see them again.

We landed at Suez in the best of health and spirits, and we were received by the port-officials with all their former courtesy, and by our friends with their natural hospitality. A telegram was at once despatched to the Viceroy announcing *succès complet*, and applying for a special train, which was supplied to us by the kindness of H.E. Barrot Bey. Nothing now remained but to pay the wages and the bakhshísh of the two Europeans, Marius Isnard, the cook, and the *marmiton*, Antonin.

We set out without delay. At Zagázig, Haji Wali, despite a drenching shower of rain, rushed off to his home, after taking the shortest of leaves. Having arrived there he was so bullied and badgered by his friends for having confided such a secret to Franks, and so laughed at for allowing us to monopolise all the profits (!), that he presently rushed up to Cairo, more mad than sane, and caused an infinity of trouble. At Zagázig he also distributed amongst his cronies, as presents of price, valueless bits of quartz.

The train was slow, and we did not reach our destination before a dozen or so of hours. The tidings, too, were none of the best. War was expected, troops were getting ready for the voyage, and there was a general confusion of excitement. Mr. F. Smart, unable to wait any longer, had left for Alexandria, *en route* for Naples. I waited, however, upon H.H. Prince Husayn Kamil Pasha, the young Minister of Finance, who asked me the most sensible and pertinent of questions; showing himself a master of detail like his father, and by no means satisfied without a corresponding reply. Through the kindness of H.E. Ibrahim Bey Taufík, I had a short audience with His Highness, despite the general turmoil and the urgency of Consuls-General.

Next morning the Khediv, after receiving my hearty acknowledgments of the princely way in which he had ordered the excursion, thanked me for the service which I had rendered to Egypt, and accepted my assurance that the Nile-Valley has ever been the land of my predilection. His Highness inspected with curiosity the charts, maps, and plans of his staff-officers; and at once understood the advantage of working, with modern appliances, the ancient Mines of Midian. He also took no little interest in the measures which I briefly outlined. The first step would be to regiment the convicts, who now do little beyond dying at the local Botany Bay, Fayzoghlú. These men could be divided into companies, officered from the Engineer-branch of the service, and form a body like that which, in the more economical and less sentimental days of English colonial history, distinguished themselves on the Gold Coast and in West Africa.

In Midian they would find a healthy climate; the sea would prevent their escape on one side, the Desert on the other; and, lastly, they might look forward to pardon and freedom, the convict's best incentive to good conduct. Indeed, hands would never be wanting; the Bedawin are always ready, as they showed themselves upon the Suez Canal, to work for regular pay. I also suggested that the richer ores should be treated at a great central *usine* established at Suez, whither transport would be cheap, and where fuel, so rare and expensive in Arabia, would cost comparatively little. My ideas were approved, but political matters delayed their development—I hope only for a time.

I also took the opportunity of presenting to His Highness the following appeal on behalf of those who had served in the "Khedivial Expedition."

MONSEIGNEUR,
  J'ai l'honneur de vous annoncer que le Jeudi, 29 Mars, 1877, je suis arrivé à Suez, accompagné de M. Charles Clarke, Directeur des Télégraphes à Zagázig, et par mon ancien ami, le Haji Wali Effendi.

  Le matin suivant, je reçus la visite de Monsieur George Marie, Ingénieur des Mines attaché à l'État-Major, qui me remit une lettre de S. A. le Prince Husayn Kamil Pasha, Ministre des Finances, et me présenta les officiers suivants de l'État-Major Egyptien :
Amir Effendi Rushdi,
Hassan Effendi Haris,
Abd el-Karím Effendi Izzat.

  Ces officiers emmenaient avec eux le Sergent Ali et vingt hommes du génie. Je fis ensuite visite au Gouverneur de Suez, S. E. Said-Bey, pour prendre avec lui les mesures nécessaires à notre embarquement.

  Le jour suivant (Samedi, 31 Mars), à six heures du soir,

nous fûmes à bord de la corvette *Sinnár*, Capitaine Ali-Bey Shukri, où nous trouvâmes le capitaine du port Ra'úf-Bey qui se met entièrement à notre disposition. À 10 heures du soir la corvette se mettait en marche, et nous etions partis.

Le Lundi (2 Avril), à 11 heures 30', nous arrivions à El-Muwayláh dans le Tihámat de Madyan, où nous reçûmes la visite de l'officier commandant la garnison, Yuzbashi Abd el-Wáhid, et de l'écrivain du fort, Sayyid Abd el-Rahím. Ces messieurs s'empressèrent de requérir les 50 chameaux nécessaires à l'excursion projetée, et en attendant, la corvette *Sinnár* se retira dans le Sherm Yáhár, ou l'ancrage offre beaucoup de securité.

Le 3 Avril, accompagné de M. Marie et des Lieutenants Hassan et Abd el-Karím, et de 10 soldats je partis pour le port appellé La Khurábeh, à la bouche du Ouadi Eynúneh. En attendant, M. Clarke, avec le Lieutenant Amir resta sur la corvette pour activer nos préparatifs.

Le 4 Avril, nous fîmes une reconnaissance du pays, où nous découvrîmes un ancien établissement metallurgique ; un aqueduc d'une lieue et demie avec deux reservoirs, en apparence de construction romaine, et enfin une ancienne ville appellée Dár el-Hamrá, ou devaient habiter les travailleurs sur la rive gauche du Ouadi. Nous fûmes nous convaincre en même temps qu'à la porte la plus étroite du Ouadi il avait existé autrefois un barrage en pierre et toutes les constructions nécessaires à une exploitation.

Le 5 Avril, conduits par le Scheik Abd el-Nebi de la tribu des Houetát, nous visitâmes les fours, où nous trouvâmes des briques vetrifiées et d'anciennes scories, toutes choses qui nous confirmèrent dans la conviction où nous étions qu'il y avait en la autrefois un établissement très important. Une route pratiquée dans le rocher menait evidemment de la ville à l'usine.

Le 6 Avril, pendant que les officiers s'occupaient de relever les environs, nous visitâmes la partie droite du Ouadi Eynúneh, où nous trouvâmes que le terrain était primitif, et traversé par d'énormes filons de porphyre, coupant des masses de granit rouge, contenant beaucoup de feldspath. Nous y trouvâmes également des quartz, qui avaient été evidemment emmenés par les eaux et en cassant quelques uns nous fûmes nous convaincre qu'ils étaient aurifères et argentifères, ce que expliquait immediatement la présence dans le pays de l'établissement metallurgique.

Le 7 Avril, nous visitâmes au nord d'Eynúneh, dans le Ouadi Makhsab, une carrière de pierre, qui avait du être exploitée par les anciens. Dans l'après midi les autres membres de l'expedition arrivèrent avec la caravane : le soir nous trouvâmes qu'à droite du Ouadi près du village on avait autrefois exploité des turquoises.

Le 8 Avril, fut passé en essais des sables aurifères, et en préparatifs de départ pour le lendemain.

Le 9 Avril, nous marchâmes sur le Djebel Sahd, autrement dit Djebel Eynúneh, et après quatre heures de marche, nous arrivâmes à la bouche d'une grande gorge appellée Ouadi El-Morák. Là nous trouvâmes des traces de travaux importants, c'est-à-dire des résidus de lavage des débris de route, etc. Un Bedouin nous assura qu'il y avait, à 12 heures de l'autre côté de la montagne, des fours nombreux.

Le gorge très escarpée et très difficile était formée de granit tournant à la syénite un torrent assez important passait à travers d'immenses blocs de rocher quio parfois barraient complètement la route. Nous recueillîmes des échantillons de sable, et trouvâmes des tourmalines et de l'antimoine.

Le 10 Avril, nous transportâmes notre camp de Morák au Djebel el-Abiad situé plus au sud-est à quatre heures de marche. En traversant le Ouadi El-Khiyam nous découvrîmes du sable noir très pesant contenant de l'oxide d'etain presque pur ; c'est là M. Clarke découvrit une pierre portant une ancienne inscription, que j'ai en l'honneur de remettre à Votre Altesse, et qui éclairera sans doute la question de savoir quelle race occupait alors le pays. Dans l'après-midi nous visitâmes la Montagne Blanche, autrement dite Maro, haute d'environs 200 m. au dessus du niveau de la plaine, et dont le sommet est presque entièrement formé de quartz ; à droite et à gauche se trouvaient plusieurs autres pitons de la même formation. Dans la masse quartzeuse et la coupant perpendiculairement, sur toute la profondeur de la montagne, M. Marie remarqua un énorme filon contenant du fer titanifère et du sulfure d'argent, et qui lui sembla avoir été exploité autrefois. L'épaisseur de ce filon était d'environ 1·50 m. à 2·00 m. Vers le soir notre guide nous prevint que nous pouvions être attaqués dans la nuit par une tribu très turbulente que se nomment les Beni Ma'ázeh, habitant de l'autre côté de la montagne, et s'étendant jusqu'au Hismá ou region de terre rouge : les Bedouins sont presque toujours en lutte avec leurs voisins. Nous prîmes les dispositions nécessaires pour repousser cette attaque qui heureusement n'eût pas lieu.

Le 11 Avril, nous portâmes notre camp du Djebel el-Abiad, à la bouche du Ouadi Scherma, situé à quatre heures de marche plus au sud. Comme à Eynúneh, nous trouvâmes qu'il y avait en là une nombreuse population d'ouvriers et de mineurs. Une immense forteresse, dont le plan fut relevé par les officiers, une ancienne ville dans un îlot formé par les aux branches du Ouadi, des carrières de sable rouge, melé de carbonate de fer, exploitées sur une longeur considérable, indiquaient suffisamment qu'autrefois cet endroit était le siège d'une industrie florissante.

Le 12 Avril, notre Camp fut transferé sur le Ouadi Tiryam à cinq heures de marche au sud. Là, comme à Eynúneh et à Scherma, nous trouvâmes les restes d'une ville sur la rive gauche du torrent, et sur la rive droite des fortifications très considérables. Aux environs et en de nombreux endroits des carrières de sable rouge qui, d'après les Bedouins, est analogue à celui du Hismá, indiquaient une exploitation très active.

Le 13 Avril, nous visitâmes à pied la bouche du Ouadi coralline. À midi nous arrivions à El-Muwaylah, et sans perdre Tiryam, où nous trouvâmes les restes d'une ancienne ville bâtie en de temps nous partîmes pour le Scherm Djibbah, où se trouvé une montagne à la bouche du Ouadi Madsús, contenant du soufre dont nous prîmes des echantillons.

Le 14 Avril, la corvette partit pour le Scherm Zibá, où on nous avait assuré qu'il existait une mine des turquoises, que nous ne pûmes pas trouver par suite du mauvais vouloir des habitants.

Le 15 Avril, accompagnés par le Said Abd el-Rahím et le Scheik Abd el-Nebi, nous partîmes avec la corvette pour visiter le Ouadi Makná, dans le golfe d'Akabah, où nous arrivâmes le lendemain (16 Avril) à 11 heures du matin. En cet endroit se trouvait autrefois une ville d'une grande importance, capitale de tous le pays de Midian, s'étendant depuis Akabah jusqu'au Djebel Hassáni. Les restes d'un port se voient encore dans la mer ; une forteresse, aujourd'hui détruite, dominait sur la rive gauche du Ouadi et commandait toute la vallée et la basse ville, que s'étendait des deux côtés du courant d'eau. Des scories indiquaient que là aussi il y avait eu autrefois une exploitation ; mais les habitants ne pûrent pas nous indiquer l'endroit où se trouvaient les fours. Dans ces régions la formation primitive, à nu en bien des endroits, est au contraire recouverte en d'autres par des masses de sables chlorites, surmontées de couches puissantes de gyps contenant également du sel gemme.

Le 17, pendant que la corvette se refugiait au Scherm Dahab, nous poussâmes à pied une reconnaissance jusqu'à la montagne appellée Djebel el-Hamrá. Nous trouvâmes toujours la mêmes formation primitive, formée de filons de porphyre encastrés dans le granit rouge, et nous decouvrîmes des quartz chlorites et des chlorites absolument analogues à celles qui au Brésil contiennent l'or.

Enfin le 18 Avril, en entendant l'arrivée de la corvette, M. Marie, M. Clarke, et moi nous eûmes l'heureuse idée de pousser une reconnaissance vers le nord, et là nous nous trouvâmes en face d'une formation aurifère complète. À la simple vue l'or apparait en petites veines et en pointes nombreuses dans des galets roulés par les eaux transportés du haut du Ouadi, et formés par du porphyre basaltique. Il est évident que cette formation doit exister dans les montagnes environnantes. Les Bedouins m'assurent d'ailleurs qu'à la tête du Ouadi dans une des stations du pèlerinage, appellée Magharat-Sha'íb, se trouvent encore des restes d'anciennes maisons, des dattiers et de l'eau : evidemment à cet endroit Haji Wali Effendi a trouvé l'or il y a 26 ans. Malheureusement le peu de temps que je pouvais accorder à mon excursion, la difficulté de nous procurer des chameaux, les dangers que pouvait craindre la corvette dans ces parages peu frequentés et difficiles, ne nous permirent pas de visiter cet endroit : d'ailleurs la découverte pour nous était assurée et nous étions pressé d'informer Votre Altesse de la réussite complète de l'expédition. En conséquence aussitôt la corvette arrivée, nous nous embarquâmes, et nous arrivâmes a Suez le 21 courant.

En finissant ce rapide aperçu de notre voyage, permettez moi, Monseigneur, de vous remercier de la façon vraiment princiére dont par vos ordres S. A. le Prince Husayn Pasha a su organiser notre expédition. Nous avons trouvé chez les employés du Gouvernment Égyptien, leurs Excellences Said Bey, Gouverneur de Suez ; Ra'úf Bey, capitaine du port ; Ali Bey Shukri, commandant la corvette ; le Gouverneur de El-Muwayláh et l'écrivain du fort, le Said Abd el-Rahím, une courtoisie parfaite, et un zèle extrême à accomplir les désirs de Votre Altesse.

Je ne crois pas trop m'avancer en déclarant ici que notre

expédition a complètement réussi ; et je me permettrai de prier Votre Altesse de vouloir bien lui donner l'importance qu'elle mérite.

En 16 jours nous avons constaté l'existence de six grands établissements miniers :—

    Nakhil Tayyibat Ism,
    Umm Ámil.
    Makná,
    Wady Eynúnah,
    Wady Scherma,
    Wady Tiryam,
    Umm Ámil.

Nous n'avons malheureusement pas pu visiter le premier et le dernier. Nous avons trouvé l'or, l'argent, le zinc, la galène argentifère, l'antimonie et le soufre dans le porphyre et le granit qui composent la plus grande partie de ces montagnes ; dans le quartz qui forme des pitons entiers ; dans les chlorites et dans la terre rouge. Personnellement nous avons constaté l'existence de métaux précieux depuis Makná jusqu'à El-Muwayláh ; nous ne doutons pas que cette formation ne s'étend au nord jusqu'a Akabah et peut-être au Syrie, et au sud jusqu'à Djebel Hassáni. Quant à la largeur de l'ouest à l'est elle reste à déterminer ; mais tous les renseignements que nous avons recueillés sur les lieux nous portent à croire que le Hismá, ou terre rouge, commence a deux degrés, c'est-à-dire 120 milles géographiques de la côte, et s'étend jusqu'au cœur de l'Arabié.

C'est donc, Monseigneur, une ancienne Californie que, grâce à votre bienveillance, nous avons fait revivre ; et en conséquence j'oserai demander a Votre Altesse de vouloir bien recompenser les membres de l'expédition que j'ai eu l'honneur de diriger.

Je demande à Votre Altesse—

1. Pour le Sergent Ali et les 20 hommes de l'escorte une gratification.

2. Pour les officiers qui ont parfaitement fait leur devoir, et spécialement pour le B.-Lt. Hasan Effendi, un grade.

3. Pour M. Charles Clarke, Ingénieur Télégraphique, depuis 13 ans au service de Votre Altesse, et qui m' á très-bien secondé, le titre de Bey.

4. Pour mon vieil ami, Haji Wali, de Zagázig, qui fût le premier à découvrir l'or en 1849, et qui, malgré ses 82 ans,

á bravement supporté les fatigues du voyage, une rente viagère, sur laquelle la generosité bien connue de Votre Altesse me dispense d'insister.

5. Quant à M. Marie, qui a déjà l'expérience de ce voyage, et qui a eu le premier l'occasion d'observer les minéraux de cet Ophir Arabe, je propose a Votre Altesse de l'envoyer en Angleterre et au France pour qu'il puisse y recruter le matériel et le personnel ; et pouvoir faire ainsi une expédition sérieuse dans la saison froide, et même un commencement d'exploitation. Je me félicite d'avoir été accompagné dans mon voyage par M. Marie, qui s'est montré à la hauteur de la mission délicate que S. A. le Prince Husayn Pasha a bien voulu lui confier, et dont le qualité de français donne, suivant mon désir, un caractère international à notre voyage.

Votre Altesse voudra bien excuser la liberté que je prends en allant au devant de ses désirs, et l'attribuer à sa véritable cause, l'intérêt que je prendrai toujours au Gouvernement progressif de l'Égypte, et au bonheur du pays dont la Providence vous a confié les destinées.

   Je suis,
    De Votre Altesse,
     Le plus devoué Serviteur,
      RICHARD F. BURTON.

À bord du *Sinnár* le 20 April, 1877.

At Cairo our friendly party presently broke up. Lieutenant Ámír was ordered to Dar-For, in the very heart of Africa, vulgarly called Darfúr. Lieutenant Hasan, greatly to my regret, joined the Egyptian auxiliary force proceeding to the seat of war. Mr. Clarke, my energetic and able *wakíl*, returned to Zagázig, whence he was careful to supply me with all the news ; and M. Marie was allowed by the Khediv leave of absence to France, in order to prepare his liver for the pains and penalties of the next autumn's campaign.

CHAPTER XIV.

DEPARTURE FROM EGYPT.

I HAD still work to do before leaving Egypt. The literary City of the Arabs, *par excellence*, appeared to me the best place for investigating the origin of that mysterious alphabet known in Syria as El-Mushajjar, the tree-shaped, the branchy, in fact, the "palm-runes" of the Icelandic Edda. Of late it has gained great interest by its evident connection with the Ogham, Ogam, or Ogmic, and with even older characters. Despite the novelty of the subject, however, I must defer publication, as the researches are not yet in a fit state to appear before the world.

After paying my last respects to His Highness, I left Cairo on April 27th, and greatly enjoyed the cool Etesian gales of Alexandria, after the khamsín of the capital, whose glare and reflected heat were rapidly converting the lively *perron* of Shepheard's Hôtel into an Arabia Deserta. On May 2nd, the Institut Égyptien was pleased to confer upon me its honorary membership; and on the same day I delivered a short lecture, which was duly reported in the *Phase d'Alexandrie* (May 4th).*

* "Mercredi dernier avait lieu à l'Institut Egyptien une séance d'un haut intérêt.

"Monsieur le Capitaine Burton, l'intrépide et savant voyageur, dont les travaux ont eu un si grand retentissement, devait y rendre compte de ses dernières découvertes.

"La séance a été ouverte par S. E. Colucci Pacha, Président de l'Institut, qui a rappelé les services éminents rendus à la science par M. le Capitaine Burton, ses voyages à la Mecque et dans l'Afrique Centrale où il a, un des premiers, fait connaître l'existence des grands lacs équatoriaux.

" M. le Capitaine Burton a ensuite pris la parole, pour exposer les résultats de son dernier voyage ; l'importante découverte des anciennes mines d'or, situées sur la côte arabique, en face de Suez, et l'exploration du pays biblique de Midian.

"M. Burton a raconté, comment un de ses amis, un brave Turc, nommé Hadj Valy, l'avait informé de l'existence de sables aurifères du côté de l'Akaba, lui offrant de le faire conduire sur les lieux, habillé en Bedouin.

" S. A. le Khédive, à qui M. Burton fit part de ces indications, mit à la disposition du Capitaine une frégate à vapeur, avec le nombre d'hommes nécessaires, et lui adjoignit trois officiers du génie, et le minéralogiste M. George Marie.

" M. Burton, ainsi accompagné, se rendit de Suez à Moïla, et parcourut les diverses localités qui lui avaient été signalées.

" Il retrouva en quatre endroits différents, les traces des mines exploitées par les anciens ; les anciennes carrières ; les ouvrages exécutés, tels qu'aqueducs et barrages, des scories et des instruments de travail.

" Les mines fournissaient des turquoises, du quartz ou des sables aurifères, et de l'argent combiné avec une forte proportion de plomb ou d'étain.

" L'expédition a rapporté plusieurs spécimens de ces matières que MM. Gastinel Bey et Marie s'occupent d'analyser.

" Les lieux où se trouvent ces anciennes mines sont Gebel-Abiad par 28 degrés de latitude, Beit-el-Nessara, et les Ouadis Einuneh, Shermá et Tiriam.

At the Anglo-Egyptian Colony of Ramleh, which will some day become a suburb of the New City, I passed a week with my friend Mr. Charles (*alias* Charley) Grace, whose familiar *petit nom* shows the full measure of his well-merited popularity. If, during that pleasant time, I attempted any evil pleasantries concerning the sand-heaps of "Rumlay," and the ice-plants, and the broken bottles, and the crushed provision-tins which seem to represent its normal growth, I take this opportunity of expressing my repentance, and of promising more reverence for the future.

H.M.'s Foreign Office had kindly granted me leave of absence till the end of May; but the Russo-Turkish war was declared on April 24th; and, "Consuls, to your posts!" was the order of the day. So, resisting the temptation to make the grand tour, *viâ* Jáffá, Bayrút and Constantinople, I em-

"Le voyage au pays de Midian, sous un autre point de vue offre également un grand intérêt.

"Le Capitaine Burton a pu retrouver les vestiges de la capitale de Midianites, Makná, que les Arabes appellent encore aujourd'hui Madian. Il a rapporté une inscription Midianite dont il offre une photographie à l'Institut.

"Nous ne pouvons suivre M. le Capitaine Burton dans les détails géographiques et géologiques où il est entré, mais nous annoncerons qu'il se propose de reprendre bientôt ses études dont les fruits ont déjà été si heureux et qu'il s'appliquera à résoudre les importantes questions soulevées par son voyage sur l'archéologie et la topographie biblique et à étudier tout ce qui concerne l'exploitation des mines découvertes par lui."

barked (May 6th) on board the Austrian Lloyd's S.S. *Flora*, Captain Pietro Radaglia.

The ship was not A1. She was small and slow, her engines not having been cleaned; her first-class passengers numbered thirty bodies to twenty-four berths; and her second, and even her third class, were allowed to encumber her quarter-deck, which was always washed too late; and furtively to kiss unclean hands to the ladies. It is incredible how little good is done to the public by large postal subventions. The last steamer, despatched at a comparatively dead season, was large and roomy enough to accommodate sixty passengers : the *Flora*, and the S.S. *Vesta*, which followed her, were uncomfortably crowded, besides having to refuse about a dozen passengers. Indeed, but for the extreme civility and courtesy of the Austrian Lloyd's captains, officers, and men, complaints would be as many as travellers would be few.

Among the little knot going north was H.E. Sefér Pasha (Count Kossielsky), returning for the summer to his Château of Bertholdsstein, near Styrian Graz; and he brought with him a little fright who had been captured by the Deuka tribe, and released by the soldiers under Colonel Gordon (Pasha), lately made Governor-General of the Provinces of the Equator—Súdan and its dependencies. About the nationality of this specimen there are many doubts. M. Gessi declares that the individual is a dwarf, belonging to the Shilluk tribe, on the Sobut River; that he has known him, together with his father and family, for two years; and that he passed into the hands of an Austrian sea-captain, who forthwith declared him to be an "Áká." The first "Pygmies" brought to Europe were, it will be remembered, the two lads from the Country of Munzá, King of the Monbuttoo (Monbótú), who reached Khartúm in the boats belonging to the late M. Miani. It was the only success that ever befell the poor old Venetian traveller; and he did not live to enjoy its fruits. He died, like Dr. Livingstone, of hardship and fatigue, attended by his two dwarf negroes, and by a negroid sergeant, who afterwards escorted the dwarfs to Italy.

I could not repress a laugh when the Pygmy, Monsieur Rustam, so called after the giant-hero of Persia, came on board the *Flora*. His huge little head was clad in a new and long tasselled Tarbúsh, whilst a small great-coat, a European paletôt made in Alexandria, invested his squat, square fat body, falling like a sack upon his heels. A pair of bag-breeches, whose tail almost touched the ground, and Parisian *bottines* with elastic bands, completed the couthless, fitless attire. He sat the image of pompous dignity a yard and a bittock high, monopolising the place of honour before the cockswain, in the Port-Captain's own barge; and his tiny legs, like a duck's, far too short for the trunk, failed to reach the ground. It was, in fact, Cowper's picture—

> "The slippery seat betray'd the sliding part
> That prest it, and the feet hung dangling down."

Coming alongside, he climbed the companion-ladder with the assistance of a tasselled and silver-mounted cane; strutted straight to the quarter-deck; deliberately chose the most comfortable travelling-arm-chair, utterly reckless of its owner; settled down with an air, and looked around him as though he had been the monarch of all he surveyed. And yet this thing had been captured in the wilds of Africa only seven months before we had the honour of meeting it. A superficial glance at M. Rustam suggested that he was a dwarf eunuch-mute, attached to some powerful Harím, and much prized, as are Skyes and Dachshunds, for extreme ugliness. We had on board the Baronne de Z——, a glorious blonde, an angel in an "idiot-fringe," a

> "Daughter of the gods,
> Divinely tall, and most divinely fair."

She was talking to me when she caught sight of the creature, and it so charmed her that she exclaimed, "*Mais je l'embrasserais volontiers !*"

Presently, Sefer Pasha told me that this citizen of Lilliput-land was being sent to Vienna for the inspection of H.I.M. the Empress of Austria. I then began my study of Monsieur Rustam, or, as he called himself in his own tongue, " Borch."* He had learnt sufficient Arabic to make himself understood ; and, in little more than half a year, he had picked up some Italian and a few words of German. Unfortunately he was as stiff and proud as he was quick, observant, and intelligent ; and he absolutely declined to be measured, or even to show his teeth. Yet he condescended to play with the monkeys on board ; and the first thing he deigned to do at Trieste was to walk out and inspect the town.

The photograph given to me by his temporary owner is good, showing a certain resemblance to " Khayrullah," the younger of the Miani Pygmies. Unfortunately it presents the full face instead of the very remarkable profile. The Lilliputian measures in height forty inches and two lines, very little more than the famous Polish dwarf, Count Borowlacki, † who is described as having " perfect symmetry of form, great accomplishments, and elegant manners." M. Rustam's age appears (1877) to be about twelve or thirteen. There is little trace of deformity about the manikin, although his stunted legs, large head, and burly trunk suggest the idea of a man cut down,

---

* M. Gessi pronounces and writes the word " Botch."

† He was thirty-nine inches high, and died at ninety-eight on September 5, 1837.

and his great breadth of beam reminds us of the term "pocket-Hercules." The skin is a dark and shiny chocolate, or coffee thoroughly roasted, very unlike the dirty yellow of Du Chaillu's Obongos, who dwell in the virgin forest: it seems to belong to the people of sunny plains. His head, rather rounded at the parietes, is backed by an unusually projecting occiput—apparently a racial characteristic;* and its high *bombé* brow gives him a peculiarly thoughtful look. The hair, short and curling stiff, rises like pepper-corns from the scalp; and its colour is reddish-brown as if sun-stained. There are as yet no signs of beard or mustachio: this, again, apparently distinguishes the Áká race. The nose has literally no bridge; the root is flush with the cheeks; and the tip, with petalous nostrils, rises suddenly from a dead flat: the feature irresistibly suggests a broken-nosed pug-dog. The lower face is oval, and the malar bones, though somewhat prominent, are not so highly developed as in the African race generally. The eyes are partially closed by the fat eyelids, and the "whites" are, as usual, a dull brown. The glance is acute and intelligent, wholly lacking the "untamable wildness" of the Obongo. The ears have very little lobule, and the latter has not been pierced for rings. The oral region forms a

* I have remarked this occipital projection in all the Ákás yet seen by me.

muzzle; the lips are somewhat everted, the upper being notably short. The jaw is orthognathic, without the elevations and depressions noticed by Schweinfürth; and the chin does not retreat as much as is usual with negroes and negroids. The profile, with its overhanging forehead, its trilobate nose all tip, and its oral region projecting, despite the short upper lip, like a cynocephalus, is also characteristic of the Aká. The body is evidently steatopygous; at the same time there is no letter S form, no undue prominence of stomach. The hands are "pudgy;" the fingers resemble a small bunch of bananas; the upper skin is scaly, like that of a black fowl, and the palms are notably yellow. The feet are comparatively broad and flat. Finally, the voice is soft and pleasant, as I have noticed amongst several of the negro tribes, especially the Somal. Briefly, having once seen the little man it would be impossible to forget him, or to mistake the strongly marked and peculiar type to which he belongs.

Besides studying the pygmy there was little to do on board the *Flora*. A lumpy sea sent all the passengers to their berths, and a thick fog hid from us every beauty of the view. Despite the late hour, we landed at unfortunate Corfu; and found the Israelitic shopkeepers demanding such exaggerated prices for lace, arms, ornaments, and other *bibelots*, that purchase was out of the question. At last as the Bora, or north-easter, was threatening to set in, we landed at Trieste on Saturday, May 12th, two months and ten days after my departure; and, restored to marvellous good health and spirits, I was once more, so to speak, at home.

CONCLUSION.

THESE pages have made public property a secret jealously kept by me, because it was not wholly my own, during the last twenty-three years. My reconnaissance of the Midianite coast-lands in April 1877 has not only proved the existence of gold in the Arabian Peninsula, so long denied by the highest authorities: it has introduced another rich metalliferous region to the world. By discovering vasts deposits of iron in manifold shapes, it has shown the curious error of the ancient and classical geographers; and it has remarkably confirmed the list of metals, "the gold and the silver, the brass (copper), the iron, the tin, and the lead," taken from the Midianites (Num. xxxi. 22); adding to them zinc, antimony, and wolfram, or tungsten; with others of minor importance.

The Khedivial Expedition was, it is true, prevented, by the advanced season, from carrying out the discovery; from tracing the valleys to their water-sheds, and from laying down the superficies and the limits of the new Ophir. These measures, which may result in opening an unworked California, must be left to a "serious exploration," of which H.H. the Viceroy has courteously invited me to take the lead.

The once wealthy and commerical Land of Midian, now "destitute of that whereof it was once full," has become a desolation among the nations. The cities and goodly castles of the sea-board are ruinous heaps, almost level with the ground. "The Desert has resumed its rights; the intrusive hand of cultivation has been driven back; the race that dwelt here have perished; and their works now look abroad in loneliness and silence over the mighty waste." The interior, formerly so rich in oases if not in smiling field and pasture-land, has been disforested to a howling wilderness; and the area of some three thousand square miles, which, thirty-one centuries ago, could send into the field 135,000 swordsmen, is abandoned to a few hundreds of a mongrel Egypto-Bedawi race, half peasants, half nomads, whose only objects in life are to plunder, maim, and murder one another.

But Destruction is a mere phase of Reproduction; and man can do again what man has undone. The winter climate of Midian is admirable; and even a population of European miners could work in it from October to May. The summers, though hot, are not unhealthy, and the lofty and picturesque mountain ranges that line the coast are ready-made

Sanitaria. Every valley, with its perennial spring, which these rain-attractors draw from the clouds, is capable of cultivation ; of smiling once more with garden, orchard, and luxuriant field.

Upon a coast-line shown by the chart to be only eighteen (dir. geog.) miles in length, the Expedition found three large mining-establishments, the Wadies Taryam, Sharmá, and Aynúnah, where, I have reason to think, the precious metals were worked till the seventh century of our era, and perhaps much later. If the Ancients, with their imperfect technological appliances, could make these places pay, *à fortiori* we Moderns may hope to turn them into sources of wealth ; whilst the interior, should it be what I am convinced it is, will presently cause a total change in the condition of North-Western Arabia. Under the progessive and civilising rule of Egypt, which may now be said to have entered into the community of European nations, Midian will awake from her long and deadly lethargy ; her skeletons of departed glory will revive ; and she will enjoy a happier and more vigorous life than any she has yet known.

I finished my sixteen days in the old land, whose novelties are so striking, with the conviction that Voltaire was, for once, in error when he wrote—
" Nous ne vivons jamais, nous attendons la vie."

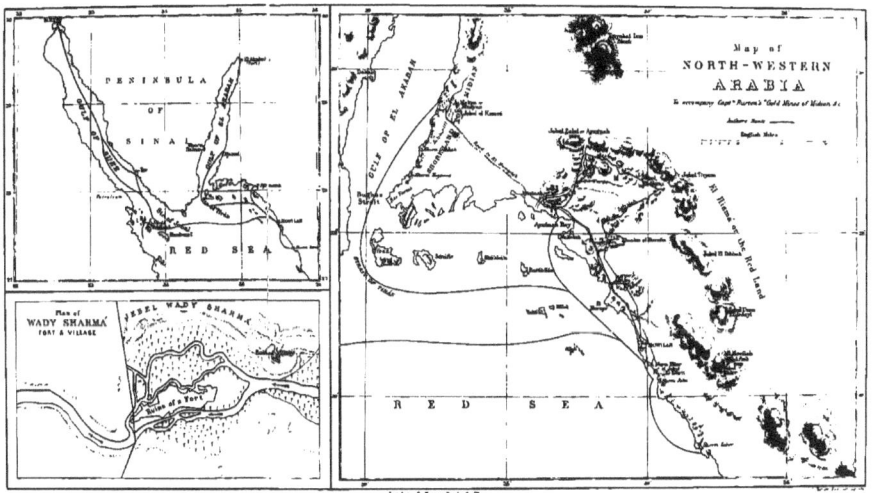

APPENDIX I.

A.

LIST OF SUPPLIES FOR A DESERT EXCURSION, of six to ten persons, lasting sixteen days, and a cruise of five (total twenty-one days), supplied by Madame Chiaramonti, of Suez.

MATÉRIEL.

Chairs (rickety), table, napkins: to be returned after the Expedition.

15 (20)* cases wine, *vin ordinaire* (tolerable).
1 case wine, assorted (Faval for Madeira, and not drinkable).
5 cases cognac (peculiarly bad).
5 (12) bottles absinthe.
15 kilogr. ground coffee.
2½ kilogr. tea.
5 (2) kilogr. chocolate.
100 tins preserved meats, of sorts.
2 bales rice.
5 sheep, with fodder for 10 (3) days.
30 fowls, with food for ditto (3).
400 eggs (should have been greased).
50 kilogr. sugar.
15 (20) boxes butter. 10 okes (each 3lbs. 3oz.) common butter.
10 tins concentrated milk.
15 kilogr. cheese.
10 kilogr. Italian pastes (vermicelli, etc.). Italian pastes, assorted, *pâtes assorties*.

* The numbers in parentheses are the number which ought to have been taken.

24 kilogr. bread.
2 quintals charcoal (coals carried to Newcastle !).
1 bag of potatoes.
20 (10) kilogr. beans and haricots (very useful).
45 (60) kilogr. onions.
50 kilogr. flour.
150 (172) kilogr. biscuits.
10 kilogr. chewing-tobacco (useful as presents, and smoked by the Arabs who never chew).
25 kilogr. salt.
2 kilogr. natron (intended as presents to the Arabs. Nonsense !).
20 packets candles.
3 dozen boxes matches.
5 (10) okes Turkish tobacco.
10 (20) boxes Zenobia cigars (smoked by friends).
1 box cigarette paper (all exhausted, much wasted).
48 (100) bottles soda.
24 bottles *lemônade gazeuse* (nauseous stuff).
6 (12) bottles syrup.
6 (12) bottles oil.
4 (6) bottles vinegar.
4 (12) cases beer.
20 bottles pickles.
10 okes common soap (much wasted).
1 case dried dessert-fruits (raisins very good against thirst).
200 (400) oranges and lemons.
10 pots mustard.
200 g. sulphate of quinine.
12 parasols (coarse make, and very useful).

Besides which, we carried some " Merceries," when a good housewife would have sufficed; Phénol (carbolic acid), good for bruises; *vinaigre de toilette*, utterly useless, and other notions, which were given away.

The total expenditure upon these stores was about 2,500 francs, (=£100). Madame Chiaramonti also claimed fifty francs for lost napkins and other damages. The two French servants received each 150 francs, with twenty-five of bakhshísh.

APPENDIX I. 395

B.

LIST OF EXPENDITURES made during the Expedition commanded by Captain R. F. Burton, from March 29th to April 22nd, 1877.

Piastres.	Parahs.	
186	0	Telegrams.
2,124	0	Hotel expenses.
10,648	0	Cost of provisions, six to ten persons for twenty-one days.
6,098	0	Total hire of camels.
2,680	0	Total cost of guides, Shaykhs, and ship-expenses.
520	0	For Sanbúks from El Muwayléh to Wady Aynúnah.
430	20	For boots, water-carriers, and messenger.
1,200	0	Advanced at Suez to Haji Wali.
440	0	Advanced by M. Marie to Expedition.
400	0	Cost of two microscopes.
1,400	0	Wages of two cooks during Expedition.
100	0	Wages of Ali, the servant.
203	20	Hire of a special camel to the Hismá, or *Terre-Rouge*.
10	20	Postages.
220	0	Cost of bags, etc.
50	0	Cost of porterage and carriages at Suez.
1,563	0	Advanced to Expedition, to Mr. Clarke.
28,263	20	(which have been duly paid from the moneys in charge of Ámir Effendi Ruschdi, of the État Major, acting under orders of the leader of the Expedition).

The total sum supplied to the Expedition, by the order of H.H. the Viceroy, and H.H. Prince Husayn Kamil Pasha, Minister of the Interior, was: dollars 1073 (1=18·20 piastres tariff), Turkish sovereigns 150 (=100 piastres tariff). This re-reduced to piastres at the current rates, the total would be 34,850·20; and the expenditure being 28,263·20, the surplus remaining in hand was, piastres 6,577, or $177·75. This sum was duly returned by me to H.H. Prince Husayn Kamil Pasha, Minister of Finance, etc.

APPENDIX II.

LIST OF CAPTAIN BURTON'S "LAND OF MIDIAN" PLANTS.

(*Supplied by the kindness of Professor Balfour, of the University, and Mr. Webb, Royal Botanic Garden, Edinburgh.*)

Cleome droserifolia.
Zilla myagroides.
Fagona cistoides.
  ,, arabica.
Zygophyllum simplex.
  ,, album.
Crassocephalum flavum.
Macrorhynchus nudicantis.
Centaurea procurrens.
Cucumis colocynthus.
Polypogon monopeliensis.
Glycine schimperi.
Leobordea lotoides.
Tephrosa apollinea.
Salsola vermiculata.
Scirpus holoschænus.
Stipa tortilis.
Solanum nigrum.
Lavendula coronopifolia.
Echium glomeratum.
Silene picta.
Erodium arabicum.
Plantago psyllium.
  ,, saxatilis.
Euphorbia chamæsyce.
  ,, cornuta.

Anagallis arvensis.
Aizoon canariense.
Veronica anagallis.
Asphodelus fistulosus.
Anchusa, with yellow flowers.
Veronica, near Beccabunga.
Salvia.
Suæda.
Santolina fragrantissima, not in flower.
Cotula.
Hagioscris, sp. cf.
Picris, near Sprengeriana.
Cf. Asterothix asperrimum.
Glysophylla libanotica?
Genista ferox, barren shoot only.
Rumex vesicarius, young male?
  ,, or bucephaloporus.
Parietaria.
Statice cf. græca.
Salvia, near molucella.
Salvia, cf. ægyptica.
Plantago, cf. cretica.
Reseda, same as Lowne's No. 2.
Malcolmia ægyptica.

APPENDIX III.

LIST OF INSECTS.

HYMENOPTERA.
Formicidæ.
Camponotus sericeus, Fabr.

LIPIDOPTERA.
Synchlœ daplidice, Linn.
Sphingomorpha chlorea, Guenei.

DIPTERA.
Tabanus rufipes, Walk.

ORTHOPTERA.
Fam. Mantidæ.
Eremiophila khamisin, Lefeb.

Fam. Gryllidæ.
Gryllus campestris, Linn.

Fam. Locustidæ.
Pœcilocera bufonia, Klug.
Œdipoda cærulans, Latr.
Forficula bimaculata, Pal. de Beam.

HEMIPTERA.
Nepa rufa, Linn.

APPENDIX IV.

SPECIMENS OF REPTILES PRESENTED BY CAPTAIN BURTON TO THE BRITISH MUSEUM.

1. Three lizards, viz., *Acanthodactylus cantoris, Uromastyx spinipes,* and *Ceramodactylus doriæ.* The first is a species ranging from Northern India through Sindh into Persia; the second is common in Northern Africa; the third has been discovered in Persia only some four years ago.

2. Two snakes, both belonging to *Zamenis ventrimaculatus,* a species common in the Indo-African region.

3. Three toads (*Bufo*). They are too young to be specifically determined, but probably *Bufo pantherinus.*

A. GÜNTHER.

British Museum, 21*st March,* 1878.

THE CRIMEA AND TRANSCAUCASIA.

Being the Narrative of a Journey in the Kouban, Gouria, Georgia, Armenia, Ossety, Imeritia, Swannety, and Mingrelia, and in the Tauric Range.

By J. BUCHAN TELFER, R.N., F.R.G.S.

With two Maps and numerous Illustrations. Two vols., medium 8vo. Cloth, price 36s.

"Volumes replete with valuable matter in great variety."—SATURDAY REVIEW.
"Important and substantially interesting contributions to works on Caucasia."—ACADEMY.

THE SUEZ CANAL.

Letters and Documents Descriptive of its Rise and Progress in 1854-56.

By FERDINAND DE LESSEPS.

Translated by N. D'ANVERS. Demy 8vo. Cloth, price 10s. 6d.

"The letters are pleasant, gossiping letters of an able, energetic man."—STANDARD.

A TRIP TO CASHMERE AND LADAK.

By COWLEY LAMBERT, F.R.G.S.

With Illustrations. Crown 8vo, price 7s. 6d.

"All who may have an idea of following Mr. Lambert's example, and going for a month's hunting in Cashmere, will thank him very heartily for having published the details of his journey. Mr. Lambert writes pleasantly and chattily; his accounts of sport are interesting, and he gives a spirited description of the life and doings of himself and the three friends who accompanied him. Cashmere is indeed a hunter's paradise."—STANDARD.

THE LARGE AND SMALL GAME OF BENGAL AND THE NORTH-WESTERN PROVINCES OF INDIA.

By CAPTAIN J. H. BALDWIN, F.Z.S., Bengal Staff Corps.

4to., with numerous Illustrations. Second Edition. Cloth, price 21s.

"Will be read with profit by naturalists, with pleasure by all who delight in sport and adventure, and with special interest and profit by residents or intending visitors to India."—ATHENÆUM.

"We find much that we can conscientiously praise and recommend; the author is a hardy, well-travelled, and genuine sportsman. . . . The narrative is sensible, manly, and perspicuous."—SATURDAY REVIEW.

THE NILE WITHOUT A DRAGOMAN.

By FREDERICK EDEN. Second Edition. Crown 8vo. Price 7s. 6d.

"Should any of our readers care to imitate Mr. Eden's example, and wish to see things with their own eyes and shift for themselves next winter in Upper Egypt, they will find this book a very agreeable guide."—TIMES.

"His book becomes one of real adventure, and interesting."—ATHENÆUM.

"All that could be seen or was worth seeing in nature or in art, is here graphically set down."—SPECTATOR.

C. KEGAN PAUL & CO., 1, PATERNOSTER SQUARE, LONDON.

A LIST OF

C. KEGAN PAUL & CO.'S
PUBLICATIONS.

THE

NINETEENTH CENTURY.

A Monthly Review.

EDITED BY JAMES KNOWLES.

Price 2s. 6d.

VOLUMES I. & II., PRICE 14s. EACH, CONTAIN CONTRIBUTIONS BY

ALFRED TENNYSON.
THE RIGHT HON. W. E. GLADSTONE, M.P.
CARDINAL MANNING.
VISCOUNT STRATFORD DE REDCLIFFE.
THE DUKE OF ARGYLL.
THE BISHOP OF GLOUCESTER AND BRISTOL.
THE DEAN OF ST. PAUL'S.
ARCHIBALD FORBES.
MATTHEW ARNOLD.
PROFESSOR HUXLEY.
PROFESSOR CLIFFORD.
JAMES ANTHONY FROUDE.
EDWARD DICEY.
SIR JOHN LUBBOCK.
DR. W. B. CARPENTER.
W. CROOKES, F.R.S.
REV. J. BALDWIN BROWN.
REV. DR. MARTINEAU.
REV. J. G. ROGERS.
DR. WARD.
REV. R. W. DALE.
PROFESSOR CROOM ROBERTSON.
FREDERIC W. H. MYERS.
ARTHUR ARNOLD.
JAMES SPEDDING.
RIGHT HON. JAMES STANSFELD, M.P.
FREDERIC HARRISON.
GEORGE J. HOLYOAKE.
REV. A. H. MACKONOCHIE.
CANON T. T. CARTER.
CANON BARRY.
LORD SELBORNE.

SIR JAMES FITZJAMES STEPHEN.
C. A. FYFFE.
M. E. GRANT DUFF, M.P.
T. BRASSEY, M.P.
SIR T. BAZLEY, M.P.
RIGHT HON. LYON PLAYFAIR, M.P.
LORD BLACHFORD.
SIR JULIUS VOGEL.
PROFESSOR HENRY MORLEY.
W. R. GREG.
W. R. S. RALSTON.
E. D. J. WILSON.
HENRY IRVING.
SIR THOMAS WATSON, M.D.
R. H. HUTTON.
EDGAR BOWRING.
LADY POLLOCK.
JOHN FOWLER.
GEORGE VON BUNSEN.
W. G. PEDDER.
W. H. MALLOCK.
GEORGE PERCY BADGER, D.C.L.
ROSWELL FISHER.
PROFESSOR COLVIN.
J. NORMAN LOCKYER.
PROFESSOR HUNTER.
COLONEL GEORGE CHESNEY.
SIR ERSKINE PERRY.
SIR HENRY SUMNER MAINE.
REV. N. K. CHERRILL, M.A.
REV. MALCOLM MACCOLL.
GODFREY TURNER.
CHARLES GRANT.

1 *Paternoster Square,*
London.

A LIST OF

C. KEGAN PAUL & CO.'S PUBLICATIONS.

ABDULLA (*Hakayit*)—AUTOBIOGRAPHY OF A MALAY MUNSHI. Translated by J. T. THOMSON, F.R.G.S. With Photo-lithograph Page of Abdulla's MS. Post 8vo. price 12s.

ADAMS (*A. L.*) *M.A., M.B., F.R.S., F.G.S.*—FIELD AND FOREST RAMBLES OF A NATURALIST IN NEW BRUNSWICK. With Notes and Observations on the Natural History of Eastern Canada. Illustrated. 8vo. price 14s.

ADAMS (*F. O.*) *F.R.G.S.*—THE HISTORY OF JAPAN. From the Earliest Period to the Present Time. New Edition, revised. 2 volumes. With Maps and Plans. Demy 8vo. price 21s. each.

A. K. H. B.—A SCOTCH COMMUNION SUNDAY, to which are added Certain Discourses from a University City. By the Author of 'The Recreations of a Country Parson.' Second Edition. Crown 8vo. price 5s.

ALLEN (*Rev. R.*) *M.A.*—ABRAHAM; HIS LIFE, TIMES, AND TRAVELS, 3,800 years ago. With Map. Second Edition. Post 8vo. price 6s.

ALLEN (*Grant*) *B.A.*—PHYSIOLOGICAL ÆSTHETICS. Crown 8vo. 9s.

ANDERSON (*Rev. C.*) *M.A.*—NEW READINGS OF OLD PARABLES. Demy 8vo. price 4s. 6d.

CHURCH THOUGHT AND CHURCH WORK. Edited by. Second Edition. Demy 8vo. price 7s. 6d.

WORDS AND WORKS IN A LONDON PARISH. Edited by. Second Edition. Demy 8vo. price 6s.

THE CURATE OF SHYRE. Second Edition. 8vo. price 7s. 6d.

ANDERSON (*R. C.*) *C.E.*—TABLES FOR FACILITATING THE CALCULATION OF EVERY DETAIL IN CONNECTION WITH EARTHEN AND MASONRY DAMS. Royal 8vo. price £2. 2s.

ARCHER (*Thomas*)—ABOUT MY FATHER'S BUSINESS. Work amidst the Sick, the Sad, and the Sorrowing. Crown 8vo. price 5s.

ASHTON (*J.*)—ROUGH NOTES OF A VISIT TO BELGIUM, SEDAN, AND PARIS, in September 1870-71. Crown 8vo. price 3s. 6d.

1,78.

BAGEHOT (Walter)—THE ENGLISH CONSTITUTION. A New Edition, Revised and Corrected, with an Introductory Dissertation on Recent Changes and Events. Crown 8vo. price 7s. 6d.

LOMBARD STREET. A Description of the Money Market. Seventh Edition. Crown 8vo. price 7s. 6d.

SOME ARTICLES ON THE DEPRECIATION OF SILVER, AND TOPICS CONNECTED WITH IT. Demy 8vo. price 5s.

BAGOT (Alan)—ACCIDENTS IN MINES. Crown 8vo. cloth. 6s.

BALDWIN (Capt. J. H.) F.Z.S. Bengal Staff Corps.—THE LARGE AND SMALL GAME OF BENGAL AND THE NORTH-WESTERN PROVINCES OF INDIA. 4to. With numerous Illustrations. Second Edition. Price 21s.

BARTLEY (G. C. T.)—DOMESTIC ECONOMY : Thrift in Every-Day Life. Crown 8vo. 2s.

BAUR (Ferdinand) Dr. Ph., Professor in Maulbronn.—A PHILOLOGICAL INTRODUCTION TO GREEK AND LATIN FOR STUDENTS. Translated and adapted from the German. By C. KEGAN PAUL, M.A. Oxon., and the Rev. E. D. STONE, M.A., late Fellow of King's College, Cambridge, and Assistant Master at Eton. Crown 8vo. price 6s.

BECKER (Bernard H.)—THE SCIENTIFIC SOCIETIES OF LONDON. Crown 8vo. price 5s.

BENNIE (Rev. J. N.) M.A.—THE ETERNAL LIFE. Sermons preached during the last twelve years. Crown 8vo. price 6s.

BERNARD (Bayle)—SAMUEL LOVER, HIS LIFE AND UNPUBLISHED WORKS. In 2 vols. With a Steel Portrait. Post 8vo. price 21s.

BISCOE (A. C.)—THE EARLS OF MIDDLETON, Lords of Clermont and of Fettercairn, and the Middleton Family. Crown 8vo. price 10s. 6d.

BISSET (A.)—HISTORY OF THE STRUGGLE FOR PARLIAMENTARY GOVERNMENT IN ENGLAND. 2 vols. Demy 8vo. price 24s.

BLANC (H.) M.D.—CHOLERA : HOW TO AVOID AND TREAT IT. Popular and Practical Notes. Crown 8vo. price 4s. 6d.

BONWICK (J.) F.R.G.S.—PYRAMID FACTS AND FANCIES. Crown 8vo. price 5s.

BOWEN (H. C.) M.A., Head Master of the Grocers' Company's Middle Class School at Hackney.

STUDIES IN ENGLISH, for the use of Modern Schools. Small crown 8vo. price 1s. 6d.

BOWRING (L.) C.S.I.—EASTERN EXPERIENCES. Illustrated with Maps and Diagrams. Demy 8vo. price 16s.

BOWRING (Sir John).—AUTOBIOGRAPHICAL RECOLLECTIONS OF SIR JOHN BOWRING. With Memoir by LEWIN B. BOWRING. Demy 8vo. price 14s.

BRADLEY (F. H.)—ETHICAL STUDIES. Critical Essays in Moral Philosophy. Large post 8vo. price 9s.

MR. SIDGWICK'S HEDONISM : an Examination of the Main Argument of 'The Methods of Ethics.' Demy 8vo. sewed, price 2s. 6d.

C. Kegan Paul & Co.'s Publications. 5

BROOKE (*Rev. S. A.*) *M.A., Chaplain in Ordinary to Her Majesty the Queen, and Minister of Bedford Chapel, Bloomsbury.*
LIFE AND LETTERS OF THE LATE REV. F. W. ROBERTSON, M.A., Edited by.
I. Uniform with the Sermons. 2 vols. With Steel Portrait. Price 7s. 6d.
II. Library Edition. 8vo. With Two Steel Portraits. Price 12s.
III. A Popular Edition. In 1 vol. 8vo. price 6s.

THE FIGHT OF FAITH. Sermons preached on various occasions. Third Edition. Crown 8vo. price 7s. 6d.

THEOLOGY IN THE ENGLISH POETS.—Cowper, Coleridge, Wordsworth, and Burns. Third Edition. Post 8vo. price 9s.

CHRIST IN MODERN LIFE. Eleventh Edition. Crown 8vo. price 7s. 6d.

SERMONS. First Series. Ninth Edition. Crown 8vo. price 6s.

SERMONS. Second Series. Third Edition. Crown 8vo. price 7s.

FREDERICK DENISON MAURICE: The Life and Work of. A Memorial Sermon. Crown 8vo. sewed, price 1s.

BROOKE (*W. G.*) *M.A.*—THE PUBLIC WORSHIP REGULATION ACT. With a Classified Statement of its Provisions, Notes, and Index. Third Edition, revised and corrected. Crown 8vo. price 3s. 6d.

SIX PRIVY COUNCIL JUDGMENTS—1850–72. Annotated by. Third Edition. Crown 8vo. price 9s.

BROUN (*J. A.*)—MAGNETIC OBSERVATIONS AT TREVANDRUM AND AUGUSTIA MALLEY. Vol. I. 4to. price 63s.
The Report from above, separately sewed, price 21s.

BROWN (*Rev. J. Baldwin*) *B.A.*—THE HIGHER LIFE. Its Reality, Experience, and Destiny. Fourth Edition. Crown 8vo. price 7s. 6d.

DOCTRINE OF ANNIHILATION IN THE LIGHT OF THE GOSPEL OF LOVE. Five Discourses. Second Edition. Crown 8vo. price 2s. 6d.

BROWN (*J. Croumbie*) *LL.D.*—REBOISEMENT IN FRANCE; or, Records of the Replanting of the Alps, the Cevennes, and the Pyrenees with Trees, Herbage, and Bush. Demy 8vo. price 12s. 6d.

THE HYDROLOGY OF SOUTHERN AFRICA. Demy 8vo. price 10s. 6d.

BROWNE (*Rev. M. E.*)—UNTIL THE DAY DAWN. Four Advent Lectures. Crown 8vo. price 2s. 6d.

BURTON (*Mrs. Richard*)—THE INNER LIFE OF SYRIA, PALESTINE, AND THE HOLY LAND. With Maps, Photographs, and Coloured Plates. 2 vols. Second Edition. Demy 8vo. price 24s.

CARLISLE (*A. D.*) *B.A.*—ROUND THE WORLD IN 1870. A Volume of Travels, with Maps. New and Cheaper Edition. Demy 8vo. price 6s.

CARNE (*Miss E. T.*)—THE REALM OF TRUTH. Crown 8vo. price 5s. 6d.

CARPENTER (*W. B.*) *LL.D., M.D., F.R.S., &c.*—THE PRINCIPLES OF MENTAL PHYSIOLOGY. With their Applications to the Training and Discipline of the Mind, and the Study of its Morbid Conditions. Illustrated. Fourth Edition. 8vo. price 12s.

CHILDREN'S TOYS, and some Elementary Lessons in General Knowledge which they Teach. With Illustrations. Crown 8vo. price 5s.

CHRISTOPHERSON (The Late Rev. Henry) M.A.—SERMONS. With an Introduction by John Rae, LL.D., F.S.A. First Series. Crown 8vo. price 7s. 6d.

SERMONS. With an Introduction by John Rae, LL.D., F.S.A. Second Series. Crown 8vo. price 6s.

CLODD (Edward) F.R.A.S.—THE CHILDHOOD OF THE WORLD : a Simple Account of Man in Early Times. Third Edition. Crown 8vo. price 3s.
 A Special Edition for Schools. Price 1s.

THE CHILDHOOD OF RELIGIONS. Including a Simple Account of the Birth and Growth of Myths and Legends. Third Thousand. Crown 8vo. price 5s.
 A Special Edition for Schools. Price 1s. 6d.

COLERIDGE (Sara)—PHANTASMION. A Fairy Tale. With an Introductory Preface by the Right Hon. Lord Coleridge, of Ottery St. Mary. A New Edition. Illustrated. Crown 8vo. Cloth, price 7s. 6d.

MEMOIR AND LETTERS OF SARA COLERIDGE. Edited by her Daughter. With Index. 2 vols. With Two Portraits. Third Edition, Revised and Corrected. Crown 8vo. price 24s.
Cheap Edition. With one Portrait. Price 7s. 6d.

COLLINS (Mortimer)—THE SECRET OF LONG LIFE. Dedicated by special permission to Lord St. Leonards. Fourth Edition. Large crown 8vo. price 5s.

COLLINS (Rev. R.) M.A.—MISSIONARY ENTERPRISE IN THE EAST. With special reference to the Syrian Christians of Malabar, and the Results of Modern Missions. With Four Illustrations. Crown 8vo. price 6s.

CONWAY (Moncure D.)—REPUBLICAN SUPERSTITIONS. Illustrated by the Political History of the United States. Including a Correspondence with M. Louis Blanc. Crown 8vo. price 5s.

COOKE (Prof. J. P.) of the Harvard University.—SCIENTIFIC CULTURE. Crown 8vo. price 1s.

COOPER (T. T.) F.R.G.S.—THE MISHMEE HILLS : an Account of a Journey made in an Attempt to Penetrate Thibet from Assam, to open New Routes for Commerce. Second Edition. With Four Illustrations and Map. Post 8vo. price 10s. 6d.

CORY (Lieut.-Col. Arthur)—THE EASTERN MENACE ; OR, SHADOWS OF COMING EVENTS. Crown 8vo. price 5s.

COX (Rev. Samuel)—SALVATOR MUNDI ; or, Is Christ the Saviour of all Men ? Second Edition. Crown 8vo. cloth, price 5s.

CROMPTON (Henry) — INDUSTRIAL CONCILIATION. Fcap. 8vo. price 2s. 6d.

CURWEN (Henry)—SORROW AND SONG ; Studies of Literary Struggle. Henry Mürger—Novalis—Alexander Petöfi—Honoré de Balzac—Edgar Allan Poe— André Chénier. 2 vols. crown 8vo. price 15s.

C. Kegan Paul & Co.'s Publications. 7

DANCE (Rev. C. D.)—RECOLLECTIONS OF FOUR YEARS IN VENEZUELA. With Three Illustrations and a Map. Crown 8vo. price 7s. 6d.

D'ANVERS (N. R.)—THE SUEZ CANAL : Letters and Documents descriptive of its Rise and Progress in 1854-56. Translated by FERDINAND DE LESSEPS. Demy 8vo. price 10s. 6d.

DAVIDSON (Rev. Samuel) D.D., LL.D.—THE NEW TESTAMENT, TRANSLATED FROM THE LATEST GREEK TEXT OF TISCHENDORF. A New and thoroughly revised Edition. Post 8vo. price 10s. 6d.

CANON OF THE BIBLE : Its Formation, History, and Fluctuations. Second Edition. Small crown 8vo. price 5s.

DAVIES (G. Christopher)—MOUNTAIN, MEADOW, AND MERE : a Series of Outdoor Sketches of Sport, Scenery, Adventures, and Natural History. With Sixteen Illustrations by Bosworth W. Harcourt. Crown 8vo. price 6s.

DAVIES (Rev. J. L.) M.A.—THEOLOGY AND MORALITY. Essays on Questions of Belief and Practice. Crown 8vo. price 7s. 6d.

DAWSON (Geo.), M.A.—PRAYERS, WITH A DISCOURSE ON PRAYER. Edited by his Wife. Fifth Edition. Crown 8vo. 6s.

SERMONS ON DISPUTED POINTS AND SPECIAL OCCASIONS. Edited by his Wife. Second Edition. Crown 8vo. price 6s.

DE KERKADEC (Vicomtesse Solange)—A CHEQUERED LIFE, being Memoirs of the Vicomtesse de Leoville Meilhan. Edited by. Crown 8vo. price 7s. 6d.

DE L'HOSTE (Col. E. P.)—THE DESERT PASTOR, JEAN JAROUSSEAU. Translated from the French of Eugène Pelletan. With a Frontispiece. New Edition. Fcp. 8vo. cloth, price 3s. 6d.

DE REDCLIFFE (Viscount Stratford) P.C., K.G., G.C.B.—WHY AM I A CHRISTIAN ? Fifth Edition. Crown 8vo. price 3s.

DE TOCQUEVILLE (A.)—CORRESPONDENCE AND CONVERSATIONS OF, WITH NASSAU WILLIAM SENIOR, from 1834 to 1859. Edited by M. C. M. SIMPSON. 2 vols. post 8vo. price 21s.

DOWDEN (Edward) LL.D.—SHAKSPERE : a Critical Study of his Mind and Art. Third Edition. Post 8vo. price 12s.

DREW (Rev. G. S.) M.A.—SCRIPTURE LANDS IN CONNECTION WITH THEIR HISTORY. Second Edition. 8vo. price 10s. 6d.

NAZARETH : ITS LIFE AND LESSONS. Third Edition. Crown 8vo. price 5s.

THE DIVINE KINGDOM ON EARTH AS IT IS IN HEAVEN. 8vo. price 10s. 6d.

THE SON OF MAN : His Life and Ministry. Crown 8vo. price 7s. 6d.

DREWRY (G. O.) M.D.—THE COMMON-SENSE MANAGEMENT OF THE STOMACH. Fourth Edition. Fcp. 8vo. price 2s. 6d.

DREWRY (G. O.) M.D., and BARTLETT (H. C.) Ph.D., F.C.S. CUP AND PLATTER : or, Notes on Food and its Effects. Small 8vo. price 2s. 6d.

EDEN (Frederick)—THE NILE WITHOUT A DRAGOMAN. Second Edition. Crown 8vo. price 7s. 6d.

ELSDALE (Henry)—STUDIES IN TENNYSON'S IDYLLS. Crown 8vo. cloth, price 5s.

ESSAYS ON THE ENDOWMENT OF RESEARCH. By Various Writers.
List of Contributors. —Mark Pattison, B.D.—James S. Cotton, B.A.—Charles E. Appleton, D.C.L.—Archibald H. Sayce, M.A.—Henry Clifton Sorby, F.R.S.—Thomas K. Cheyne, M.A.—W. T. Thiselton Dyer, M.A.—Henry Nettleship, M.A. Square crown 8vo. price 10s. 6d.

EVANS (Mark)—THE STORY OF OUR FATHER'S LOVE, told to Children. being a New and Enlarged Edition of Theology for Children. With Four Illustrations. Fcp. 8vo. price 3s. 6d.

A BOOK OF COMMON PRAYER AND WORSHIP FOR HOUSEHOLD USE, compiled exclusively from the Holy Scriptures. Fcp. 8vo. price 2s. 6d.

THE GOSPEL OF HOME LIFE. Crown 8vo. cloth, price 4s. 6d.

FAVRE (Mons. J.)—THE GOVERNMENT OF THE NATIONAL DEFENCE. From the 30th June to the 31st October, 1870. Translated by H. CLARK. Demy 8vo. price 10s. 6d.

FOLKESTONE RITUAL CASE : the Arguments, Proceedings, Judgment, and Report. Demy 8vo. cloth, price 25s.

FOOTMAN (Rev. H.) M.A.—FROM HOME AND BACK ; or, Some Aspects of Sin as seen in the Light of the Parable of the Prodigal. Crown 8vo. price 5s.

FOWLE (Rev. T. W.) M.A.—THE RECONCILIATION OF RELIGION AND SCIENCE. Being Essays on Immortality, Inspiration, Miracles, and the Being of Christ. Demy 8vo. price 10s. 6d.

FOX-BOURNE (H. R.)— THE LIFE OF JOHN LOCKE, 1632–1704. 2 vols. demy 8vo. price 28s.

FRASER (Donald)—EXCHANGE TABLES OF STERLING AND INDIAN RUPEE CURRENCY, upon a new and extended system, embracing Values from One Farthing to One Hundred Thousand Pounds, and at rates progressing, in Sixteenths of a Penny, from 1s. 9d. to 2s. 3d. per Rupee. Royal 8vo. price 10s. 6d.

FRERE (Sir H. Bartle E.) G.C.B., G.C.S.I.—THE THREATENED FAMINE IN BENGAL : How it may be Met, and the Recurrence of Famines in India Prevented. Being No. 1 of 'Occasional Notes on Indian Affairs.' With 3 Maps. Crown 8vo. price 5s.

FRISWELL (J. Hain.)—THE BETTER SELF. Essays for Home Life. Crown 8vo. price 6s.

GARDNER (J.) M.D.—LONGEVITY : THE MEANS OF PROLONGING LIFE AFTER MIDDLE AGE. Fourth Edition, revised and enlarged. Small crown 8vo. price 4s.

GILBERT (Mrs.)—AUTOBIOGRAPHY AND OTHER MEMORIALS. Edited by Josiah Gilbert. Third Edition. With Steel Portrait and several Wood Engravings. Crown 8vo. price 7s. 6d.

GILL (Rev. W. W.) B.A.—MYTHS AND SONGS FROM THE SOUTH PACIFIC. With a Preface by F. Max Müller, M.A., Professor of Comparative Philology at Oxford. Post 8vo. price 9s.

GODKIN (James)—THE RELIGIOUS HISTORY OF IRELAND : Primitive, Papal, and Protestant. Including the Evangelical Missions, Catholic Agitations, and Church Progress of the last half Century. 8vo. price 12s.

GODWIN (William)—WILLIAM GODWIN: HIS FRIENDS AND CONTEMPORARIES. With Portraits and Facsimiles of the Handwriting of Godwin and his Wife. By C. KEGAN PAUL. 2 vols. Large post 8vo. price 28s.

THE GENIUS OF CHRISTIANITY UNVEILED. Being Essays never before published. Edited, with a Preface, by C. Kegan Paul. Crown 8vo. price 7s. 6d.

GOODENOUGH (Commodore J. G.) R.N., C.B., C.M.G.—JOURNALS OF, during his Last Command as Senior Officer on the Australian Station, 1873-1875. Edited, with a Memoir, by his Widow. With Maps, Woodcuts, and Steel Engraved Portrait. Second Edition. Post 8vo. price 14s.

An Abridged Edition. With Portrait. Crown 8vo. price 5s.

GOODMAN (W.) CUBA, THE PEARL OF THE ANTILLES. Crown 8vo. price 7s. 6d.

GOSPEL (THE) OF HOME LIFE. Crown 8vo. cloth, price 4s. 6d.

GOULD (Rev. S. Baring) M.A.—THE VICAR OF MORWENSTOW: a Memoir of the Rev. R. S. Hawker. With Portrait. Third Edition, revised. Square post 8vo. 10s. 6d.

GRANVILLE (A. B.) M.D., F.R.S., &c.—AUTOBIOGRAPHY OF A. B. GRANVILLE, F.R.S., &c. Edited, with a Brief Account of the Concluding Years of his Life, by his youngest Daughter, Paulina B. Granville. 2 vols. With a Portrait. Second Edition. Demy 8vo. price 32s.

GREY (John) of Dilston. — MEMOIRS. By JOSEPHINE E. BUTLER. New and Revised Edition. Crown 8vo. price 3s. 6d.

GRIFFITH (Rev. T.) A.M.—STUDIES OF THE DIVINE MASTER. Demy 8vo. price 12s.

GRIFFITHS (Capt. Arthur)—MEMORIALS OF MILLBANK, AND CHAPTERS IN PRISON HISTORY. With Illustrations by R. Goff and the Author. 2 vols. post 8vo. price 21s.

GRIMLEY (Rev. H. N.) M.A., Professor of Mathematics in the University College of Wales, and Chaplain of Tremadoc Church.

TREMADOC SERMONS, CHIEFLY ON THE SPIRITUAL BODY, THE UNSEEN WORLD, AND THE DIVINE HUMANITY. Second Edition. Crown 8vo. price 6s.

GRUNER (M. L.)—STUDIES OF BLAST FURNACE PHENOMENA. Translated by L. D. B. GORDON, F.R.S.E., F.G.S. Demy 8vo. price 7s. 6d.

GURNEY (Rev. Archer)—WORDS OF FAITH AND CHEER. A Mission of Instruction and Suggestion. Crown 8vo. price 6s.

HAECKEL (Prof. Ernst)—THE HISTORY OF CREATION. Translation revised by Professor E. RAY LANKESTER, M.A., F.R.S. With Coloured Plates and Genealogical Trees of the various groups of both plants and animals. 2 vols. Second Edition. Post 8vo. cloth, price 32*s.*

THE HISTORY OF THE EVOLUTION OF MAN. With numerous Illustrations. 2 vols. Post 8vo.

HARCOURT (Capt. A. F. P.)—THE SHAKESPEARE ARGOSY. Containing much of the wealth of Shakespeare's Wisdom and Wit, alphabetically arranged and classified. Crown 8vo. price 6*s.*

HAWEIS (Rev. H. R.) M.A.—CURRENT COIN. Materialism—The Devil—Crime—Drunkenness—Pauperism—Emotion—Recreation—The Sabbath. Crown 8vo. price 6*s.*

SPEECH IN SEASON. Third Edition. Crown 8vo. price 9*s.*

THOUGHTS FOR THE TIMES. Eleventh Edition. Crown 8vo. price 7*s.* 6*d.*

UNSECTARIAN FAMILY PRAYERS for Morning and Evening for a Week, with short selected passages from the Bible. Square crown 8vo. price 3*s.* 6*d.*

HAYMAN (H.) D.D., late Head Master of Rugby School.—RUGBY SCHOOL SERMONS. With an Introductory Essay on the Indwelling of the Holy Spirit. Crown 8vo. price 7*s.* 6*d.*

HELLWALD (Baron F. Von)—THE RUSSIANS IN CENTRAL ASIA. A Critical Examination, down to the Present Time, of the Geography and History of Central Asia. Translated by Lieut.-Col. Theodore Wirgman, LL.B. With Map. Large post 8vo. price 12*s.*

HINTON (J.)—THE PLACE OF THE PHYSICIAN. To which is added ESSAYS ON THE LAW OF HUMAN LIFE, AND ON THE RELATIONS BETWEEN ORGANIC AND INORGANIC WORLDS. Second Edition. Crown 8vo. price 3*s.* 6*d.*

PHYSIOLOGY FOR PRACTICAL USE. By Various Writers. With 50 Illustrations. 2 vols. Second Edition. Crown 8vo. price 12*s.* 6*d.*

AN ATLAS OF DISEASES OF THE MEMBRANA TYMPANI. With Descriptive Text. Post 8vo. price £6. 6*s.*

THE QUESTIONS OF AURAL SURGERY. With Illustrations. 2 vols. Post 8vo. price £6. 6*s.*

LIFE AND LETTERS. Edited by ELLICE HOPKINS. Crown 8vo.

H. J. C.—THE ART OF FURNISHING. A Popular Treatise on the Principles of Furnishing, based on the Laws of Common Sense, Requirement, and Picturesque Effect. Small crown 8vo. price 3*s.* 6*d.*

HOLROYD (Major W. R. M.)—TAS-HIL UL KALAM; or, Hindustani made Easy. Crown 8vo. price 5*s.*

HOOPER (Mary)—LITTLE DINNERS: HOW TO SERVE THEM WITH ELEGANCE AND ECONOMY. Thirteenth Edition. Crown 8vo. price 5*s.*

COOKERY FOR INVALIDS, PERSONS OF DELICATE DIGESTION, AND CHILDREN. Crown 8vo. price 3*s.* 6*d.*

EVERY-DAY MEALS. Being Economical and Wholesome Recipes for Breakfast, Luncheon, and Supper. Second Edition. Crown 8vo. cloth, price 5*s.*

C. Kegan Paul & Co.'s Publications. 11

HOPKINS (M.)—THE PORT OF REFUGE ; or, Counsel and Aid to Ship-masters in Difficulty, Doubt, or Distress. Second and Revised Edition. Crown 8vo. price 6s.

HORNE (William) M.A.—REASON AND REVELATION : an Examination into the Nature and Contents of Scripture Revelation, as compared with other Forms of Truth. Demy 8vo. price 12s.

HORNER (The Misses)—WALKS IN FLORENCE. A New and thoroughly Revised Edition. 2 vols. Crown 8vo. Cloth limp. With Illustrations.
  VOL. I.—Churches, Streets, and Palaces. Price 10s. 6d.
  VOL. II.—Public Galleries and Museums. Price 5s.

HULL (Edmund C. P.)—THE EUROPEAN IN INDIA. With a Medical Guide for Anglo-Indians. By R. R. S. MAIR, M.D., F.R.C.S.E. Second Edition, Revised and Corrected. Post 8vo. price 6s.

HUTTON (James)—MISSIONARY LIFE IN THE SOUTHERN SEAS. With Illustrations. Crown 8vo. price 7s. 6d.

JACKSON (T. G.)—MODERN GOTHIC ARCHITECTURE. Crown 8vo. price 5s.

JACOB (Maj.-Gen. Sir G. Le Grand) K.C.S.I., C.B.—WESTERN INDIA BEFORE AND DURING THE MUTINIES. Pictures drawn from Life. Second Edition. Price 7s. 6d.

JENKINS (E.) and RAYMOND (J.) Esqs.—A LEGAL HANDBOOK FOR ARCHITECTS, BUILDERS, AND BUILDING OWNERS. Second Edition, Revised. Crown 8vo. price 6s.

JENKINS (Rev. R. C.) M.A.—THE PRIVILEGE OF PETER and the Claims of the Roman Church confronted with the Scriptures, the Councils, and the Testimony of the Popes themselves. Fcap. 8vo. price 3s. 6d.

JENNINGS (Mrs. Vaughan)—RAHEL: HER LIFE AND LETTERS. With a Portrait from the Painting by Daffinger. Square post 8vo. price 7s. 6d.

JONES (Lucy)—PUDDINGS AND SWEETS; being Three Hundred and Sixty-five Receipts approved by experience. Crown 8vo. price 2s. 6d.

KAUFMANN (Rev. M.) B.A.—SOCIALISM : Its Nature, its Dangers, and its Remedies considered. Crown 8vo. price 7s. 6d.

KING (Alice)—A CLUSTER OF LIVES. Crown 8vo. price 7s. 6d.

KINGSFORD (Rev. F. W.) M.A., Vicar of St. Thomas's, Stamford Hill; late Chaplain H. E. I. C. (Bengal Presidency).
  HARTHAM CONFERENCES ; or, Discussions upon some of the Religious Topics of the Day. 'Audi alteram partem.' Crown 8vo. price 3s. 6d.

KINGSLEY (Charles) M.A.—LETTERS AND MEMORIES OF HIS LIFE. Edited by his WIFE. With Two Steel Engraved Portraits, and Illustrations on Wood, and a Facsimile of his Handwriting. Eleventh Edition. 2 vols. Demy 8vo. price 36s.
  ALL SAINTS' DAY, and other Sermons. Edited by the Rev. W. HARRISON. Crown 8vo. price 7s. 6d.

LACORDAIRE (Rev. Père)—LIFE : Conferences delivered at Toulouse. A New and Cheaper Edition. Crown 8vo. price 3s. 6d.

LAMBERT (Cowley) F.R.G.S.—A TRIP TO CASHMERE AND LADAK. With Illustrations. Crown 8vo. price 7s. 6d.

LAURIE (J. S.)—EDUCATIONAL COURSE OF SECULAR SCHOOL BOOKS FOR INDIA :—

THE FIRST HINDUSTANI READER. Stiff linen wrapper, price 6d.
THE SECOND HINDUSTANI READER. Stiff linen wrapper, price 6d.
THE ORIENTAL (ENGLISH) READER. Book I., price 6d.; II., price 7½d.; III., price 9d.; IV., price 1s.
GEOGRAPHY OF INDIA; with Maps and Historical Appendix, tracing the Growth of the British Empire in Hindustan. Fcap. 8vo. price 1s. 6d.

L. D. S.—LETTERS FROM CHINA AND JAPAN. With Illustrated Title-page. Crown 8vo. price 7s. 6d.

LEATHES (Rev. S.) M.A.—THE GOSPEL ITS OWN WITNESS. Crown 8vo. price 5s.

LEE (Rev. F. G.) D.C.L.—THE OTHER WORLD; or, Glimpses of the Supernatural. 2 vols. A New Edition. Crown 8vo. cloth, price 15s.

LENOIR (J.)—FAYOUM; or, Artists in Egypt. A Tour with M. Gérome and others. With 13 Illustrations. A New and Cheaper Edition. Crown 8vo. price 3s. 6d.

LIFE IN THE MOFUSSIL; or, Civilian Life in Lower Bengal. By an Ex-Civilian. Large post 8vo.

LORIMER (Peter) D.D.—JOHN KNOX AND THE CHURCH OF ENGLAND. His Work in her Pulpit, and his Influence upon her Liturgy, Articles, and Parties. Demy 8vo. price 12s.

LOTHIAN (Roxburghe)—DANTE AND BEATRICE FROM 1282 TO 1290. A Romance. 2 vols. Post 8vo. cloth, price 24s.

LOVER (Samuel) R.H.A.—THE LIFE OF SAMUEL LOVER, R.H.A.; Artistic, Literary, and Musical. With Selections from his Unpublished Papers and Correspondence. By BAYLE BERNARD. 2 vols. With a Portrait. Post 8vo. price 21s.

LOWER (M. A.) M.A., F.S.A.—WAYSIDE NOTES IN SCANDINAVIA. Being Notes of Travel in the North of Europe. Crown 8vo. price 9s.

LYONS (R. T.) Surg.-Maj. Bengal Army.—A TREATISE ON RELAPSING FEVER. Post 8vo. price 7s. 6d.

MACAULAY (J.) M.A., M.D. Edin.—THE TRUTH ABOUT IRELAND : Tours of Observation in 1872 and 1875. With Remarks on Irish Public Questions. Being a Second Edition of 'Ireland in 1872,' with a New and Supplementary Preface. Crown 8vo. price 3s. 6d.

MACLACHLAN (A. N. C.) M.A.—WILLIAM AUGUSTUS, DUKE OF CUMBERLAND : being a Sketch of his Military Life and Character, chiefly as exhibited in the General Orders of His Royal Highness, 1745-1747. With Illustrations. Post 8vo. price 15s.

MAIR (R. S.) M.D., F.R.C.S.E.—THE MEDICAL GUIDE FOR ANGLO-INDIANS. Being a Compendium of Advice to Europeans in India, relating to the Preservation and Regulation of Health. With a Supplement on the Management of Children in India. Crown 8vo. limp cloth, price 3s. 6d.

MANNING (*His Eminence Cardinal*)— ESSAYS ON RELIGION AND LITERATURE. By various Writers. Third Series. Demy 8vo. price 10s. 6d.

THE INDEPENDENCE OF THE HOLY SEE. With an Appendix containing the Papal Allocution and a translation. Crown 8vo. cloth, price 5s.

THE TRUE STORY OF THE VATICAN COUNCIL. Crown 8vo. cloth, price 5s.

MARRIOTT (*Maj.-Gen. W. F.*) *C.S.I.*—A GRAMMAR OF POLITICAL ECONOMY. Crown 8vo. price 6s.

MAUGHAN (*W. C.*)—THE ALPS OF ARABIA; or, Travels through Egypt, Sinai, Arabia, and the Holy Land. With Map. Second Edition. Demy 8vo. price 5s.

MAURICE (*C. E.*)—LIVES OF ENGLISH POPULAR LEADERS. No. 1.— STEPHEN LANGTON. Crown 8vo. price 7s. 6d. No. 2.—TYLER, BALL, and OLDCASTLE. Crown 8vo. price 7s. 6d.

MAZZINI (*Joseph*) — A Memoir. By E. A. V. Two Photographic Portraits. Second Edition. Crown 8vo. price 5s.

MEDLEY (*Lieut.-Col. J. G.*) *R.E.*—AN AUTUMN TOUR IN THE UNITED STATES AND CANADA. Crown 8vo. price 5s.

MENZIES (*Sutherland*)—MEMOIRS OF DISTINGUISHED WOMEN. 2 vols. Post 8vo. price 10s. 6d.

MICKLETHWAITE (*J. T.*) *F.S.A.*—MODERN PARISH CHURCHES: Their Plan, Design, and Furniture. Crown 8vo. price 7s. 6d.

MILNE (*James*)—TABLES OF EXCHANGE for the Conversion of Sterling Money into Indian and Ceylon Currency, at Rates from 1s. 8d. to 2s. 3d. per Rupee. Second Edition. Demy 8vo. Cloth, price £2. 2s.

MIVART (*St. George*) *F.R.S.*—CONTEMPORARY EVOLUTION: An Essay on some recent Social Changes. Post 8vo. price 7s. 6d.

MOCKLER (*E.*)—A GRAMMAR OF THE BALOOCHEE LANGUAGE, as it is spoken in Makran (Ancient Gedrosia), in the Persia-Arabic and Roman characters. Fcap. 8vo. price 5s.

MOFFAT (*R. S.*)—ECONOMY OF CONSUMPTION: a Study in Political Economy. Demy 8vo.

MOORE (*Rev. D.*) *M.A.*—CHRIST AND HIS CHURCH. By the Author of 'The Age and the Gospel,' &c. Crown 8vo. price 3s. 6d.

MORE (*R. Jasper*)—UNDER THE BALKANS. Notes of a Visit to the District of Philippopolis in 1876. With a Map, and Illustrations from Photographs. Crown 8vo. cloth, price 6s.

MORELL (*J. R.*)—EUCLID SIMPLIFIED IN METHOD AND LANGUAGE. Being a Manual of Geometry. Compiled from the most important French Works, approved by the University of Paris and the Minister of Public Instruction. Fcap. 8vo. price 2s. 6d.

MORSE (*E. S.*) *Ph.D.*—FIRST BOOK OF ZOOLOGY. With numerous Illustrations. Crown 8vo. price 5s.

MUSGRAVE (*Anthony*)—STUDIES IN POLITICAL ECONOMY. Crown 8vo. price 6s.

NEWMAN (*J. H.*) *D.D.*—CHARACTERISTICS FROM THE WRITINGS OF. Being Selections from his various Works. Arranged with the Author's personal Approval. Third Edition. With Portrait. Crown 8vo. price 6s.

*** A Portrait of the Rev. Dr. J. H. Newman, mounted for framing, can be had price 2s. 6d.

NICHOLAS (*T.*)—THE PEDIGREE OF THE ENGLISH PEOPLE. Demy 8vo. cloth.

NOBLE (*J. A.*)—THE PELICAN PAPERS. Reminiscences and Remains of a Dweller in the Wilderness. Crown 8vo. price 6s.

NORMAN PEOPLE (THE), and their Existing Descendants in the British Dominions and the United States of America. Demy 8vo. price 21s.

NOTREGE (*John*) *A.M.*—THE SPIRITUAL FUNCTION OF A PRESBYTER IN THE CHURCH OF ENGLAND. Crown 8vo. cloth, red edges, price 3s. 6d.

ORIENTAL SPORTING MAGAZINE (THE). A Reprint of the first 5 Volumes, in 2 Volumes. Demy 8vo. price 28s.

PARKER (*Joseph*) *D.D.*—THE PARACLETE: An Essay on the Personality and Ministry of the Holy Ghost, with some reference to current discussions. Second Edition. Demy 8vo. price 12s.

PARR (*Harriet*)—ECHOES OF A FAMOUS YEAR. Crown 8vo. price 8s. 6d.

PAUL (*C. Kegan*)—WILLIAM GODWIN: HIS FRIENDS AND CONTEMPORARIES. With Portraits and Facsimiles of the Handwriting of Godwin and his Wife. 2 vols. Square post 8vo. price 28s.

THE GENIUS OF CHRISTIANITY UNVEILED. Being Essays by William Godwin never before published. Edited, with a Preface, by C. Kegan Paul. Crown 8vo. price 7s. 6d.

PAYNE (*Prof. J. F.*)—LECTURES ON EDUCATION. Price 6d. each.
I. Pestalozzi: the Influence of His Principles and Practice.
II. Fröbel and the Kindergarten System. Second Edition.
III. The Science and Art of Education.
IV. The True Foundation of Science Teaching.

A VISIT TO GERMAN SCHOOLS: ELEMENTARY SCHOOLS IN GERMANY. Notes of a Professional Tour to inspect some of the Kindergartens, Primary Schools, Public Girls' Schools, and Schools for Technical Instruction in Hamburgh, Berlin, Dresden, Weimar, Gotha, Eisenach, in the autumn of 1874. With Critical Discussions of the General Principles and Practice of Kindergartens and other Schemes of Elementary Education. Crown 8vo. price 4s. 6d.

PENRICE (*Maj. J.*) *B.A.*—A DICTIONARY AND GLOSSARY OF THE KO-RAN. With Copious Grammatical References and Explanations of the Text. 4to. price 21s.

PERCEVAL (*Rev. P.*) — TAMIL PROVERBS, WITH THEIR ENGLISH TRANSLATION. Containing upwards of Six Thousand Proverbs. Third Edition. Demy 8vo. sewed, price 9s.

PESCHEL (*Dr. Oscar*)—THE RACES OF MAN AND THEIR GEOGRAPHICAL DISTRIBUTION. Large crown 8vo. price 9s.

PIGGOT (J.) F.S.A., F.R.G.S.—PERSIA—ANCIENT AND MODERN. Post 8vo. price 10s. 6d.

PLAYFAIR (Lieut-Col.), Her Britannic Majesty's Consul-General in Algiers.
TRAVELS IN THE FOOTSTEPS OF BRUCE IN ALGERIA AND TUNIS. Illustrated by facsimiles of Bruce's original Drawings, Photographs, Maps, &c. Royal 4to. cloth, bevelled boards, gilt leaves, price £3. 3s.

POOR (H. V.)—MONEY AND ITS LAWS : embracing a History of Monetary Theories &c. Demy 8vo. price 21s.

POUSHKIN (A. S.)—RUSSIAN ROMANCE. Translated from the Tales of Belkin, &c. By Mrs. J. Buchan Telfer (*née* Mouravieff). Crown 8vo. price 7s. 6d.

POWER (H.)—OUR INVALIDS : HOW SHALL WE EMPLOY AND AMUSE THEM? Fcp. 8vo. price 2s. 6d.

PRESBYTER—UNFOLDINGS OF CHRISTIAN HOPE. An Essay shewing that the Doctrine contained in the Damnatory Clauses of the Creed commonly called Athanasian is Unscriptural. Small crown 8vo. price 4s. 6d.

PRICE (Prof. Bonamy) — CURRENCY AND BANKING. Crown 8vo. price 6s.

PROCTOR (Richard A.) B.A.—OUR PLACE AMONG INFINITIES. A Series of Essays contrasting our little abode in space and time with the Infinities around us. To which are added Essays on 'Astrology,' and 'The Jewish Sabbath.' Third Edition. Crown 8vo. price 6s.

THE EXPANSE OF HEAVEN. A Series of Essays on the Wonders of the Firmament. With a Frontispiece. Third Edition. Crown 8vo. price 6s.

RANKING (B. M.)—STREAMS FROM HIDDEN SOURCES. Crown 8vo. price 6s.

RIBOT (Prof. Th.)—ENGLISH PSYCHOLOGY. Second Edition. A Revised and Corrected Translation from the latest French Edition. Large post 8vo. price 9s.

HEREDITY : A Psychological Study on its Phenomena, its Laws, its Causes, and its Consequences. Large crown 8vo. price 9s.

RINK (Chevalier Dr. Henry)—GREENLAND : ITS PEOPLE AND ITS PRODUCTS. By the Chevalier Dr. HENRY RINK, President of the Greenland Board of Trade. With sixteen Illustrations, drawn by the Eskimo, and a Map. Edited by Dr. Robert Brown. Crown 8vo. price 10s. 6d.

RUSSELL (Major Frank S.)—RUSSIAN WARS WITH TURKEY, PAST AND PRESENT. With Maps. Second Edition. Crown 8vo. price 6s.

RUSSELL (W. C.)—MEMOIRS OF MRS. LÆTITIA BOOTHBY. Crown 8vo. price 7s. 6d.

ROBERTSON (*The late Rev. F. W.*) *M.A., of Brighton.*—LIFE AND LETTERS OF. Edited by the Rev. Stopford Brooke, M.A., Chaplain in Ordinary to the Queen.
    I. Two vols., uniform with the Sermons. With Steel Portrait. Crown 8vo. price 7s. 6d.
    II. Library Edition, in Demy 8vo. with Two Steel Portraits. Price 12s.
    III. A Popular Edition, in 1 vol. Crown 8vo. price 6s.

SERMONS. Four Series. Small crown 8vo. price 3s. 6d.

NOTES ON GENESIS. Crown 8vo. price 5s.

EXPOSITORY LECTURES ON ST. PAUL'S EPISTLES TO THE CORINTHIANS. A New Edition. Small crown 8vo. price 5s.

LECTURES AND ADDRESSES, with other Literary Remains. A New Edition. Crown 8vo. price 5s.

AN ANALYSIS OF MR. TENNYSON'S 'IN MEMORIAM.' (Dedicated by Permission to the Poet-Laureate.) Fcp. 8vo. price 2s.

THE EDUCATION OF THE HUMAN RACE. Translated from the German of Gotthold Ephraim Lessing. Fcp. 8vo. price 2s. 6d.

    The above Works can also be had, bound in half-morocco.

    ** A Portrait of the late Rev. F. W. Robertson, mounted for framing, can be had, price 2s. 6d.

RUTHERFORD (*John*)—THE SECRET HISTORY OF THE FENIAN CONSPIRACY: its Origin, Objects, and Ramifications. 2 vols. Post 8vo. cloth, price 18s.

SCOTT (*W. T.*)—ANTIQUITIES OF AN ESSEX PARISH; or, Pages from the History of Great Dunmow. Crown 8vo. price 5s.; sewed, 4s.

SCOTT (*Robert H.*)—WEATHER CHARTS AND STORM WARNINGS. Illustrated. Crown 8vo. price 3s. 6d.

SENIOR (*N. W.*)—ALEXIS DE TOCQUEVILLE. Correspondence and Conversations with Nassau W. Senior, from 1833 to 1859. Edited by M. C. M. Simpson. 2 vols. Large post 8vo. price 21s.

JOURNALS KEPT IN FRANCE AND ITALY. From 1848 to 1852. With a Sketch of the Revolution of 1848. Edited by his Daughter, M. C. M. Simpson. 2 vols. Post 8vo. price 24s.

SEYD (*Ernest*) *F.S.S.*—THE FALL IN THE PRICE OF SILVER. Its Causes, its Consequences, and their Possible Avoidance, with Special Reference to India. Demy 8vo. sewed, price 2s. 6d.

SHELLEY (*Lady*)—SHELLEY MEMORIALS FROM AUTHENTIC SOURCES. With (now first printed) an Essay on Christianity by Percy Bysshe Shelley. With Portrait. Third Edition. Crown 8vo. price 5s.

SHILLITO (*Rev. Joseph*)—WOMANHOOD: its Duties, Temptations, and Privileges. A Book for Young Women. Crown 8vo. price 3s. 6d.

SHIPLEY (*Rev. Orby*) *M.A.*—CHURCH TRACTS: OR, STUDIES IN MODERN PROBLEMS. By various Writers. 2 vols. Crown 8vo. price 5s. each.

SHUTE (*Richard*) *M.A.*—A DISCOURSE ON TRUTH. Post 8vo. price 9s.

SMEDLEY (M. B.)—BOARDING-OUT AND PAUPER SCHOOLS FOR GIRLS. Crown 8vo. price 3s. 6d.

SMITH (Edward) M.D., LL.B., F.R.S.—HEALTH AND DISEASE, as Influenced by the Daily, Seasonal, and other Cyclical Changes in the Human System. A New Edition. Post 8vo. price 7s. 6d.

PRACTICAL DIETARY FOR FAMILIES, SCHOOLS, AND THE LABOURING CLASSES. A New Edition. Post 8vo. price 3s. 6d.

TUBERCULAR CONSUMPTION IN ITS EARLY AND REMEDIABLE STAGES. Second Edition. Crown 8vo. price 6s.

SMITH (Hubert)—TENT LIFE WITH ENGLISH GIPSIES IN NORWAY. With Five full-page Engravings and Thirty-one smaller Illustrations by Whymper and others, and Map of the Country showing Routes. Third Edition. Revised and Corrected. Post 8vo. price 21s.

SOME TIME IN IRELAND. A Recollection. Crown 8vo. price 7s. 6d.

STEVENSON (Rev. W. F.)—HYMNS FOR THE CHURCH AND HOME. Selected and Edited by the Rev. W. Fleming Stevenson.
The most complete Hymn Book published.
The Hymn Book consists of Three Parts :—I. For Public Worship.—II. For Family and Private Worship.—III. For Children.
⁎⁎* Published in various forms and prices, the latter ranging from 8d. to 6s. Lists and full particulars will be furnished on application to the Publishers.

SULLY (James) M.A. — SENSATION AND INTUITION. Demy 8vo. price 10s. 6d.

PESSIMISM : a History and a Criticism. Demy 8vo. price 14s.

SYME (David)—OUTLINES OF AN INDUSTRIAL SCIENCE. Crown 8vo. price 6s.

TELFER (J. Buchan) F.R.G.S., Commander R.N.—THE CRIMEA AND TRANS-CAUCASIA. With numerous Illustrations and Maps. Second Edition. 2 vols. Royal 8vo. medium 8vo. price 36s.

THOMPSON (Rev. A. S.)—HOME WORDS FOR WANDERERS. A Volume of Sermons. Crown 8vo. price 6s.

TRAHERNE (Mrs. A.)—THE ROMANTIC ANNALS OF A NAVAL FAMILY. A New and Cheaper Edition. Crown 8vo. price 5s.

UMBRA OXONIENSIS—RESULTS OF THE EXPOSTULATION OF THE RIGHT HON. W. E. GLADSTONE, in their Relation to the Unity of Roman Catholicism. Large fcp. 8vo. price 5s.

UPTON (Capt. Richard D.)—NEWMARKET AND ARABIA. An Examination of the Descent of Racers and Coursers. With Pedigrees and Frontispiece. Post 8vo. price 9s.

VAMBERY (Prof. A.)—BOKHARA : Its History and Conquest. Second Edition. Demy 8vo. price 18s.

VYNER (Lady Mary)—EVERY DAY A PORTION. Adapted from the Bible and the Prayer Book, for the Private Devotions of those living in Widowhood. Collected and Edited by Lady Mary Vyner. Square crown 8vo. cloth extra, price 5s.

WELLS (Capt. John C.) R.N.—SPITZBERGEN—THE GATEWAY TO THE POLYNIA ; or, a Voyage to Spitzbergen. With numerous Illustrations by Whymper and others, and Map. New and Cheaper Edition. Demy 8vo. price 6s.

B

WETMORE (W. S.)—COMMERCIAL TELEGRAPHIC CODE. Second Edition. Post 4to. boards, price 42s.

WHITE (A. D.) LL.D.—WARFARE OF SCIENCE. With Prefatory Note by Professor Tyndall. Crown 8vo. price 3s. 6d.

WHITNEY (Prof. William Dwight)—ESSENTIALS OF ENGLISH GRAMMAR, for the Use of Schools. Crown 8vo. price 3s. 6d.

WHITTLE (J. L.) A.M.—CATHOLICISM AND THE VATICAN. With a Narrative of the Old Catholic Congress at Munich. Second Edition. Crown 8vo. price 4s. 6d.

WILBERFORCE (H. W.)—THE CHURCH AND THE EMPIRES. Historical Periods. Preceded by a Memoir of the Author by John Henry Newman, D.D. of the Oratory. With Portrait. Post 8vo. price 10s. 6d.

WILKINSON (T. L.)—SHORT LECTURES ON THE LAND LAWS. Delivered before the Working Men's College. Crown 8vo. limp cloth, price 2s.

WILLIAMS (A. Lukyn)—FAMINES IN INDIA; their Causes and Possible Prevention. The Essay for the Le Bas Prize, 1875. Demy 8vo. price 5s.

WILLIAMS (Chas.)—THE ARMENIAN CAMPAIGN. A Diary of the Campaign of 1877 in Armenia and Koordistan. Large post 8vo. cloth, price 10s. 6d.

WILLIAMS (Rowland) D.D.—LIFE AND LETTERS OF; with Extracts from his Note-Books. Edited by Mrs. Rowland Williams. With a Photographic Portrait. 2 vols. large post 8vo. price 24s.

PSALMS, LITANIES, COUNSELS, AND COLLECTS FOR DEVOUT PERSONS. Edited by his Widow. New and Popular Edition. Crown 8vo. price 3s. 6d.

WILLIS (R.) M.D.—SERVETUS AND CALVIN: a Study of an Important Epoch in the Early History of the Reformation. 8vo. cloth, price 16s.

WILSON (H. Schütz)—STUDIES AND ROMANCES. Crown 8vo. price 7s. 6d.

WILSON (Lieut.-Col. C. T.)—JAMES THE SECOND AND THE DUKE OF BERWICK. Demy 8vo. price 12s. 6d.

WINTERBOTHAM (Rev. R.) M.A., B.Sc.—SERMONS AND EXPOSITIONS. Crown 8vo. price 7s. 6d.

WOOD (C. F.)—A YACHTING CRUISE IN THE SOUTH SEAS. With six Photographic Illustrations. Demy 8vo. price 7s. 6d.

WRIGHT (Rev. David) M.A.—WAITING FOR THE LIGHT, AND OTHER SERMONS. Crown 8vo. price 6s.

WYLD (R. S.) F.R.S.E.—THE PHYSICS AND THE PHILOSOPHY OF THE SENSES; or, the Mental and the Physical in their Mutual Relation Illustrated by several Plates. Demy 8vo. price 16s.

YONGE (C. D.)—HISTORY OF THE ENGLISH REVOLUTION OF 1688. Crown 8vo. price 6s.

YOUMANS (Eliza A.)—AN ESSAY ON THE CULTURE OF THE OBSERVING POWERS OF CHILDREN, especially in connection with the Study of Botany. Edited, with Notes and a Supplement, by Joseph Payne, F.C.P., Author of 'Lectures on the Science and Art of Education,' &c. Crown 8vo. price 2s. 6d.

FIRST BOOK OF BOTANY. Designed to Cultivate the Observing Powers of Children. With 300 Engravings. New and Enlarged Edition. Crown 8vo. price 5s.

YOUMANS (Edward L.) M.D.—A CLASS BOOK OF CHEMISTRY, on the Basis of the New System. With 200 Illustrations. Crown 8vo. price 5s.

THE INTERNATIONAL SCIENTIFIC SERIES.

I. THE FORMS OF WATER IN CLOUDS AND RIVERS, ICE AND GLACIERS. By J. Tyndall, LL.D., F.R.S. With 25 Illustrations. Seventh Edition. Crown 8vo. price 5s.

II. PHYSICS AND POLITICS; or, Thoughts on the Application of the Principles of 'Natural Selection' and 'Inheritance' to Political Society. By Walter Bagehot. Third Edition. Crown 8vo. price 4s.

III. FOODS. By Edward Smith, M.D., LL.B., F.R.S. With numerous Illustrations. Fourth Edition. Crown 8vo. price 5s.

IV. MIND AND BODY: the Theories of their Relation. By Alexander Bain, LL.D. With Four Illustrations. Fifth Edition. Crown 8vo. price 4s.

V. THE STUDY OF SOCIOLOGY. By Herbert Spencer. Sixth Edition. Crown 8vo. price 5s.

VI. ON THE CONSERVATION OF ENERGY. By Balfour Stewart, M.A., LL.D., F.R.S. With 14 Illustrations. Third Edition. Crown 8vo. price 5s.

VII. ANIMAL LOCOMOTION; or, Walking, Swimming, and Flying. By J. B. Pettigrew, M.D., F.R.S., &c. With 130 Illustrations. Second Edition. Crown 8vo. price 5s.

VIII. RESPONSIBILITY IN MENTAL DISEASE. By Henry Maudsley, M.D. Second Edition. Crown 8vo. price 5s.

IX. THE NEW CHEMISTRY. By Professor J. P. Cooke, of the Harvard University. With 31 Illustrations. Third Edition. Crown 8vo. price 5s.

X. THE SCIENCE OF LAW. By Professor Sheldon Amos. Second Edition. Crown 8vo. price 5s.

XI. ANIMAL MECHANISM: a Treatise on Terrestrial and Aerial Locomotion. By Professor E. J. Marey. With 117 Illustrations. Second Edition. Crown 8vo. price 5s.

XII. THE DOCTRINE OF DESCENT AND DARWINISM. By Professor Oscar Schmidt (Strasburg University). With 26 Illustrations. Third Edition. Crown 8vo. price 5s.

XIII. THE HISTORY OF THE CONFLICT BETWEEN RELIGION AND SCIENCE. By J. W. Draper, M.D., LL.D. Tenth Edition. Crown 8vo. price 5s.

XIV. FUNGI: their Nature, Influences, Uses, &c. By M. C. Cooke, M.D., LL.D. Edited by the Rev. M. J. Berkeley, M.A., F.L.S. With numerous Illustrations. Second Edition. Crown 8vo. price 5s.

XV. THE CHEMICAL EFFECTS OF LIGHT AND PHOTOGRAPHY. By Dr. Hermann Vogel (Polytechnic Academy of Berlin). Translation thoroughly revised. With 100 Illustrations. Third Edition. Crown 8vo. price 5s.

XVI. THE LIFE AND GROWTH OF LANGUAGE. By William Dwight Whitney, Professor of Sanscrit and Comparative Philology in Yale College, Newhaven. Second Edition. Crown 8vo. price 5s.

XVII. MONEY AND THE MECHANISM OF EXCHANGE. By W. Stanley Jevons, M.A., F.R.S. Third Edition. Crown 8vo. price 5s.

XVIII. THE NATURE OF LIGHT. With a General Account of Physical Optics. By Dr. Eugene Lommel, Professor of Physics in the University of Erlangen. With 188 Illustrations and a Table of Spectra in Chromo-lithography. Second Edition. Crown 8vo. price 5s.

XIX. ANIMAL PARASITES AND MESSMATES. By Monsieur Van Beneden, Professor of the University of Louvain, Correspondent of the Institute of France. With 83 Illustrations. Second Edition. Crown 8vo. price 5s.

XX. FERMENTATION. By Professor Schützenberger, Director of the Chemical Laboratory at the Sorbonne. With 28 Illustrations. Second Edition. Crown 8vo. price 5s.

20 *A List of*

XXI. THE FIVE SENSES OF MAN. By Professor Bernstein, of the University of Halle. With 91 Illustrations. Second Edition. Crown 8vo. price 5*s*.

XXII. THE THEORY OF SOUND IN ITS RELATION TO MUSIC. By Professor Pietro Blaserna, of the Royal University of Rome. With numerous Illustrations. Second Edition. Crown 8vo. price 5*s*.

Forthcoming Volumes.

Prof. W. KINGDON CLIFFORD, M.A. The First Principles of the Exact Sciences Explained to the Non-Mathematical.

Prof. T. H. HUXLEY, LL.D., F.R.S. Bodily Motion and Consciousness.

W. B. CARPENTER, LL.D., F.R.S. The Physical Geography of the Sea.

Sir JOHN LUBBOCK, Bart., F.R.S. On Ants and Bees.

Prof. W. T. THISELTON DYER, B.A., B.Sc. Form and Habit in Flowering Plants.

Mr. J. NORMAN LOCKYER, F.R.S. Spectrum Analysis.

Prof. MICHAEL FOSTER, M.D. Protoplasm and the Cell Theory.

H. CHARLTON BASTIAN, M.D., F.R.S. The Brain as an Organ of Mind.

Prof. A. C. RAMSAY, LL.D., F.R.S., Earth Sculpture: Hills, Valleys, Mountains, Plains, Rivers, Lakes; how they were produced, and how they have been destroyed.

Prof. J. ROSENTHAL. General Physiology of Muscles and Nerves.

P. BERT (Professor of Physiology, Paris). Forms of Life and other Cosmical Conditions.

Prof. CORFIELD, M.A., M.D. (Oxon.) Air in its Relation to Health.

MILITARY WORKS.

ANDERSON (*Col. R. P.*)—VICTORIES AND DEFEATS: an Attempt to explain the Causes which have led to them. An Officer's Manual. Demy 8vo. price 14*s*.

ARMY OF THE NORTH GERMAN CONFEDERATION: a Brief Description of its Organisation, of the Different Branches of the Service and their *rôle* in War, of its Mode of Fighting, &c. Translated from the Corrected Edition, by permission of the Author, by Colonel Edward Newdigate. Demy 8vo. price 5*s*.

BRIALMONT (*Col. A.*)—HASTY INTRENCHMENTS. Translated by Lieut. Charles A. Empson, R.A. With Nine Plates. Demy 8vo. price 6*s*.

BLUME (*Maj. W.*)—THE OPERATIONS OF THE GERMAN ARMIES IN FRANCE, from Sedan to the end of the War of 1870-71. With Map. From the Journals of the Head-quarters Staff. Translated by the late E. M. Jones, Maj. 20th Foot, Prof. of Mil. Hist., Sandhurst. Demy 8vo. price 9*s*.

BOGUSLAWSKI (*Capt. A. von*)—TACTICAL DEDUCTIONS FROM THE WAR OF 1870-1. Translated by Colonel Sir Lumley Graham, Bart., late 18th (Royal Irish) Regiment. Third Edition, Revised and Corrected. Demy 8vo. price 7*s*.

CLERY (*C.*) *Capt.*—MINOR TACTICS. With 26 Maps and Plans. Third and revised Edition. Demy 8vo. cloth, price 16*s*.

DU VERNOIS (Col. von Verdy)—STUDIES IN LEADING TROOPS. An authorised and accurate Translation by Lieutenant H. J. T. Hildyard, 71st Foot. Parts I. and II. Demy 8vo. price 7s.

GOETZE (Capt. A. von)—OPERATIONS OF THE GERMAN ENGINEERS DURING THE WAR OF 1870-1. Published by Authority, and in accordance with Official Documents. Translated from the German by Colonel G. Graham, V.C., C.B., R.E. With 6 large Maps. Demy 8vo. price 21s.

HARRISON (Lieut.-Col. R.) — THE OFFICER'S MEMORANDUM BOOK FOR PEACE AND WAR. Oblong 32mo. roan, elastic band and pencil, price 2s. 6d. ; russia, 5s.

HELVIG (Capt. H.)—THE OPERATIONS OF THE BAVARIAN ARMY CORPS. Translated by Captain G. S. Schwabe. With Five large Maps. In 2 vols. Demy 8vo. price 24s.

TACTICAL EXAMPLES : the Battalion. Translated from the German by Col. Sir Lumley Graham. With nearly 300 Diagrams. Demy 8vo. cloth, price 15s.

HOFFBAUER (Capt.)—THE GERMAN ARTILLERY IN THE BATTLES NEAR METZ. Based on the Official Reports of the German Artillery. Translated by Captain E. O. Hollist. With Map and Plans. Demy 8vo. price 21s.

LAYMANN (Capt.) — THE FRONTAL ATTACK OF INFANTRY. Translated by Colonel Edward Newdigate. Crown 8vo. price 2s. 6d.

MIRUS (Maj.-Gen. von) — CAVALRY FIELD DUTY. Translated by Major Frank S. Russell 14th (King's) Hussars. Crown 8vo. cloth limp, price 7s. 6d.

PAGE (Capt. S. F.)—DISCIPLINE AND DRILL. Cheaper Edition. Crown 8vo. price 1s.

PUBLIC SCHOOLBOY : the Volunteer, the Militiaman, and the Regular Soldier. Crown 8vo. cloth, price 5s.

SCHELL (Maj. von)—THE OPERATIONS OF THE FIRST ARMY UNDER GEN. VON GOEBEN. Translated by Col. C. H. von Wright. Four Maps. demy 8vo. price 9s.

THE OPERATIONS OF THE FIRST ARMY UNDER GEN. VON STEINMETZ. Translated by Captain E. O. Hollist. Demy 8vo. price 10s. 6d.

SCHELLENDORF (Major-Gen. B. von) THE DUTIES OF THE GENERAL STAFF. Translated from the German by Lieutenant Hare. Vol. I. Demy 8vo. cloth, 10s. 6d.

SCHERFF (Maj. W. von)—STUDIES IN THE NEW INFANTRY TACTICS. Parts I. and II. Translated from the German by Colonel Lumley Graham. Demy 8vo. price 7s. 6d.

SHADWELL (Maj.-Gen.) C.B.—MOUNTAIN WARFARE. Illustrated by the Campaign of 1799 in Switzerland. Being a Translation of the Swiss Narrative compiled from the Works of the Archduke Charles, Jomini, and others. Also of Notes by General H. Dufour on the Campaign of the Valtelline in 1635. With Appendix, Maps, and Introductory Remarks. Demy 8vo. price 16s.

SHERMAN (Gen. W. T.)—MEMOIRS OF GENERAL W. T. SHERMAN, Commander of the Federal Forces in the American Civil War. By Himself. 2 vols. With Map. Demy 8vo. price 24s. Copyright English Edition.

STUBBS (Lieut.-Col. F. W.) — THE REGIMENT OF BENGAL ARTILLERY. The History of its Organisation, Equipment, and War Services. Compiled from Published Works, Official Records, and various Private Sources. With numerous Maps and Illustrations. 2 vols. demy 8vo. price 32s.

STUMM (Lieut. Hugo), German Military Attaché to the Khivan Expedition.—RUSSIA'S ADVANCE EASTWARD. Based on the Official Reports of. Translated by Capt. C.E.H.VINCENT, With Map. Crown 8vo. price 6s.

VINCENT (*Capt. C. E. H.*)—ELEMENTARY MILITARY GEOGRAPHY, RECONNOITRING, AND SKETCHING. Compiled for Non-commissioned Officers and Soldiers of all Arms. Square crown 8vo. price 2s. 6d.

WICKHAM (*Capt. E. H., R.A.*)—INFLUENCE OF FIREARMS UPON TACTICS : Historical and Critical Investigations. By an OFFICER OF SUPERIOR RANK (in the German Army). Translated by Captain E. H. Wickham, R.A. Demy 8vo. price 7s. 6d.

WOINOVITS (*Capt. I.*) — AUSTRIAN CAVALRY EXERCISE. Translated by Captain W. S. Cooke. Crown 8vo. price 7s.

WARTENSLEBEN (*Count H. von.*)—THE OPERATIONS OF THE SOUTH ARMY IN JANUARY AND FEBRUARY, 1871. Compiled from the Official War Documents of the Head-quarters of the Southern Army. Translated by Colonel C. H. von Wright. With Maps. Demy 8vo. price 6s.

THE OPERATIONS OF THE FIRST ARMY UNDER GEN. VON MANTEUFFEL. Translated by Colonel C. H. von Wright. Uniform with the above. Demy 8vo. price 9s.

WHITE (*Capt. F. B. P.*)—THE SUBSTANTIVE SENIORITY ARMY LIST—MAJORS AND CAPTAINS. 8vo. sewed, price 2s. 6d.

POETRY.

ABBEY (*Henry*)—BALLADS OF GOOD DEEDS, and other Verses. Fcp. 8vo. cloth gilt, price 5s.

ADAMS (*W. D.*—LYRICS OF LOVE, from Shakespeare to Tennyson. Selected and arranged by. Fcp. 8vo. cloth extra, gilt edges, price 3s. 6d.

Also, a Cheaper Edition. Fcp. 8vo. cloth, 2s. 6d.

ADAMS (*John*) *M.A.* — ST. MALO'S QUEST, and other Poems. Fcp. 8vo. price 5s.

ADON—THROUGH STORM AND SUNSHINE. Illustrated by M. E. Edwards, A. T. H. Paterson, and the Author. Crown 8vo. price 7s. 6d.

AURORA : a Volume of Verse. Fcp. 8vo. cloth, price 5s.

BARING (*T. C.*) *M.A., M.P.*—PINDAR IN ENGLISH RHYME. Being an Attempt to render the Epinikian Odes with the principal remaining Fragments of Pindar into English Rhymed Verse. Small 4to. price 7s.

BAYNES (*Rev. Canon R. H.*) *M.A.*)—HOME SONGS FOR QUIET HOURS. Third Edition. Fcp. 8vo. cloth extra, price 3s. 6d.

This may also be had handsomely bound in morocco with gilt edges.

Also, a Cheaper Edition. Fcp. 8vo. price 2s. 6d.

BENNETT (*Dr. W. C.*)—BABY MAY : Home Poems and Ballads. With Frontispiece. Crown 8vo. cloth elegant, price 6s.

BABY MAY AND HOME POEMS. Fcp. 8vo. sewed, in Coloured Wrapper, price 1s.

NARRATIVE POEMS AND BALLADS. Fcp. 8vo. sewed, in Coloured Wrapper, price 1s.

SONGS FOR SAILORS. Dedicated by Special Request to H.R.H. the Duke of Edinburgh. With Steel Portrait and Illustrations. Crown 8vo. price 3s. 6d.

An Edition in Illustrated Paper Covers, price 1s.

SONGS OF A SONG WRITER. Crown 8vo. price 6s.

BOSWELL (*R. B.*) *M.A., Oxon.* — METRICAL TRANSLATIONS FROM THE GREEK AND LATIN POETS, and other Poems. Crown 8vo. price 5s.

BRYANT (*W. C.*)—POEMS. Red-line Edition. With 24 Illustrations and Portrait of the Author. Crown 8vo. cloth extra, price 7s. 6d.

A Cheap Edition, with Frontispiece. Small crown 8vo. price 3s. 6d.

BUCHANAN (*Robt.*)—POETICAL WORKS. Collected Edition, in 3 vols. with Portrait. Crown 8vo. price 6s. each.

MASTER-SPIRITS. Post 8vo. price 10s. 6d.

BULKELEY (*Rev. H. J.*)—WALLED IN, and other Poems. Crown 8vo. price 5*s*.

COSMOS : a Poem. Fcp. 8vo. price 3*s*. 6*d*.

CALDERON'S DRAMAS: the Wonder-Working Magician—Life in a Dream—the Purgatory of St. Patrick. Translated by Denis Florence MacCarthy. Post 8vo. price 10*s*.

CARPENTER (*E.*)—NARCISSUS, and other Poems. Fcp. 8vo. price 5*s*.

COLLINS (*Mortimer*)—INN OF STRANGE MEETINGS, and other Poems. Crown 8vo. cloth, price 5*s*.

CORY (*Lieut.-Col. Arthur*) — IONE : a Poem in Four Parts. Fcp. 8vo. cloth, price 5*s*.

CRESSWELL (*Mrs. G.*)—THE KING'S BANNER : Drama in Four Acts. Five Illustrations. 4to. price 10*s*. 6*d*.

DENNIS (*J.*)—ENGLISH SONNETS. Collected and Arranged. Elegantly bound. Fcp. 8vo. price 3*s*. 6*d*.

DE VERE (*Aubrey*)—ALEXANDER THE GREAT : a Dramatic Poem. Small crown 8vo. price 5*s*.

THE INFANT BRIDAL, and other Poems. A New and Enlarged Edition. Fcp. 8vo. price 7*s*. 6*d*.

THE LEGENDS OF ST. PATRICK, and other Poems. Small crown 8vo. price 5*s*.

ST. THOMAS OF CANTERBURY : a Dramatic Poem. Large fcp. 8vo. price 5*s*.

ANTAR AND ZARA: an Eastern Romance. INISFAIL, and other Poems, Meditative and Lyrical. Fcp. 8vo. price 6*s*.

THE FALL OF RORA, THE SEARCH AFTER PROSERPINE, and other Poems, Meditative and Lyrical. Fcp. 8vo. 6*s*.

DOBSON (*Austin*) — VIGNETTES IN RHYME, and Vers de Société. Third Edition. Fcp. 8vo. price 5*s*.

PROVERBS IN PORCELAIN. By the Author of 'Vignettes in Rhyme.' Third Edition. Crown 8vo. price 6*s*.

DOWDEN (*Edward*) *LL.D.*—POEMS. Second Edition. Fcp. 8vo. price 5*s*.

DOWNTON (*Rev. H.*) *M.A.*—HYMNS AND VERSES. Original and Translated. Small crown 8vo. cloth, price 3*s*. 6*d*.

DURAND (*Lady*)—IMITATIONS FROM THE GERMAN OF SPITTA AND TERSTEGEN. Fcp. 8vo. price 4*s*.

EDWARDS (*Rev. Basil*) — MINOR CHORDS ; or, Songs for the Suffering : a Volume of Verse. Fcp. 8vo. cloth, price 3*s*. 6*d*.; paper, price, 2*s*. 6*d*.

ELLIOTT (*Ebenezer*), *The Corn Law Rhymer.*—POEMS. Edited by his son, the Rev. Edwin Elliott, of St. John's, Antigua. 2 vols. crown 8vo. price 18*s*.

EROS AGONISTES : Poems. By E. B. D. Fcp. 8vo. price 3*s*. 6*d*.

EYRE (*Maj.-Gen. Sir V.*) *C.B., K.C.S.I., &c.*—LAYS OF A KNIGHT-ERRANT IN MANY LANDS. Square crown 8vo. with Six Illustrations, price 7*s*. 6*d*.

FERRIS (*Henry Weybridge*) — POEMS. Fcp. 8vo. price.5*s*.

GARDNER (*H.*)—SUNFLOWERS : a Book of Verses. Fcp. 8vo. price 5*s*.

GOLDIE (*Lieut. M. H. G.*)—HEBE : a Tale. Fcp. 8vo. price 5*s*.

HARCOURT (*Capt. A. F. P.*)—THE SHAKESPEARE ARGOSY. Containing much of the wealth of Shakespeare's Wisdom and Wit, alphabetically arranged and classified. Crown 8vo. price 6*s*.

HEWLETT (*Henry G.*)—A SHEAF OF VERSE. Fcp. 8vo. price 3*s*. 6*d*.

HOLMES (*E. G. A.*)—POEMS. Fcp. 8vo. price 5*s*.

HOWARD (*Rev. G. B.*) — AN OLD LEGEND OF ST. PAUL'S. Fcp. 8vo. price 4*s*. 6*d*.

HOWELL (*James*)—A TALE OF THE SEA, Sonnets, and other Poems. Fcp. 8vo. price 5*s*.

HUGHES (*Allison*) — PENELOPE, and other Poems. Fcp. 8vo. price 4*s*. 6*d*.

INCHBOLD (*J. W.*)—ANNUS AMORIS Sonnets. Fcp. 8vo. price 4*s*. 6*d*.

KING (*Mrs. Hamilton*)—THE DISCIPLES: a New Poem. Third Edition, with some Notes. Crown 8vo. price 7s. 6d. ASPROMONTE, and other Poems. Second Edition. Fcp. 8vo. price 4s. 6d.

KNIGHT (*A. F. C.*)—POEMS. Fcp. 8vo. price 5s.

LADY OF LIPARI (THE): a Poem in Three Cantos. Fcp. 8vo. price 5s.

LOCKER (*F.*)—LONDON LYRICS. A New and Revised Edition, with Additions and a Portrait of the Author. Crown 8vo. cloth elegant, price 6s.
Also, a Cheaper Edition. Fcp. 8vo. price 2s. 6d.

LUCAS (*Alice*)—TRANSLATIONS FROM THE WORKS OF GERMAN POETS OF THE 18TH AND 19TH CENTURIES. Fcp. 8vo. price 5s.

MORICE (*Rev. F. D.*) *M.A.*—THE OLYMPIAN AND PYTHIAN ODES OF PINDAR. A New Translation in English Verse. Crown 8vo. price 7s. 6d.

MORSHEAD (*E. D. A.*)—THE AGAMEMNON OF ÆSCHYLUS. Translated into English Verse. With an Introductory Essay. Crown 8vo. cloth, price 5s.

NEW WRITER (*A*)—SONGS OF TWO WORLDS. By a New Writer. Third Series. Second Edition. Fcp. 8vo. price 5s.

THE EPIC OF HADES. By the Author of 'Songs of Two Worlds.' Third Edition. Fcp. 8vo. price 7s. 6d.

NICHOLSON (*Edward B.*) *Librarian of the London Institution*—THE CHRIST CHILD, and other Poems. Crown 8vo. cloth, price 4s. 6d.

NOAKE (*Major R. Compton*) — THE BIVOUAC; or, Martial Lyrist. With an Appendix: Advice to the Soldier. Fcp. 8vo. price 5s. 6d.

NORRIS (*Rev. Alfred*) — THE INNER AND OUTER LIFE POEMS. Fcp. 8vo. cloth, price 6s.

PAYNE (*John*)—SONGS OF LIFE AND DEATH. Crown 8vo. cloth, price 5s.

PAUL (*C. Kegan*)—GOETHE'S FAUST. A New Translation in Rhyme. Crown 8vo. price 6s.

PEACOCKE (*Georgiana*)—RAYS FROM THE SOUTHERN CROSS: Poems. Crown 8vo. with Sixteen Full-page Illustrations by the Rev. P. Walsh, cloth elegant, price 10s. 6d.

PENNELL (*H. Cholmondeley*)—PEGASUS RESADDLED. By the Author of 'Puck on Pegasus,' &c. &c. With Ten Full-page Illustrations by George Du Maurier. Fcp. 4to. cloth elegant, 12s. 6d.

PFEIFFER (*Emily*)—GLAN ALARCH: His Silence and Song: a Poem. Crown 8vo. price 6s.

GERARD'S MONUMENT and other Poems. Second Edition. Crown 8vo. cloth, price 6s.

POWLETT (*Lieut. N.*) *R.A.*—EASTERN LEGENDS AND STORIES IN ENGLISH VERSE. Crown 8vo. price 5s.

RHOADES (*James*)—TIMOLEON: a Dramatic Poem. Fcp. 8vo. price 5s.

SCOTT (*Patrick*) — THE DREAM AND THE DEED, and other Poems. Fcp. 8vo. price 5s.

SONGS FOR MUSIC. By Four Friends. Square crown 8vo. price 5s. Containing Songs by Reginald A. Gatty, Stephen H. Gatty, Greville J. Chester, and Juliana Ewing.

SPICER (*H.*)—OTHO'S DEATH WAGER: a Dark Page of History Illustrated. In Five Acts. Fcp. 8vo. cloth, price 5s.

STONEHEWER (*Agnes*)—MONACELLA: a Legend of North Wales. A Poem. Fcp. 8vo. cloth, price 3s. 6d.

SWEET SILVERY SAYINGS OF SHAKESPEARE. Crown 8vo. cloth gilt, price 7s. 6d.

TAYLOR (*Rev. J. W. A.*) *M.A.*—POEMS. Fcp. 8vo. price 5s.

TAYLOR (*Sir H.*)—Works Complete in Five Volumes. Crown 8vo. cloth, price 30s.

TENNYSON (*Alfred*) — HAROLD: a Drama. Crown 8vo. price 6s.

QUEEN MARY: a Drama. New Edition. Crown 8vo. price 6s.

TENNYSON (A.)—Works Complete :—
THE IMPERIAL LIBRARY EDITION. Complete in 7 vols. demy 8vo. price 10s. 6d. each; in Roxburgh binding, 12s. 6d. (*See p.* 31.)

AUTHOR'S EDITION. In Six Volumes. Post 8vo. cloth gilt ; or half-morocco. Roxburgh style. (*See p.* 31.)

CABINET EDITION. 12 Volumes. Each with Frontispiece. Fcp. 8vo. price 2s. 6d. each. (*See p.* 31.)

CABINET EDITION. 12 vols. Complete in handsome Ornamental Case. (*See p.* 31).

Original Editions :—
POEMS. Small 8vo. price 6s.

MAUD, and other Poems. Small 8vo. price 3s. 6d.

THE PRINCESS. Small 8vo. price 3s. 6d.

IDYLLS OF THE KING. Small 8vo. price 5s.

IDYLLS OF THE KING. Complete. Small 8vo. price 6s.

THE HOLY GRAIL, and other Poems. Small 8vo. price 4s. 6d.

GARETH AND LYNETTE. Small 8vo. price 3s.

ENOCH ARDEN, &c. Small 8vo. price 3s. 6d.

IN MEMORIAM. Small 8vo. price 4s.

SELECTIONS FROM THE ABOVE WORKS. Super royal 16mo. price 3s. 6d. ; cloth gilt extra, price 4s.

SONGS FROM THE ABOVE WORKS. 16mo. cloth, price 2s. 6d.

POCKET VOLUME EDITION. 13 vols. in neat case, price 36s. Ditto, ditto. Extra cloth gilt, in case, price 42s.

SHILLING EDITION OF THE POETICAL WORKS. In 10 vols. pocket size, 1s. each, sewed.

TENNYSON'S IDYLLS OF THE KING, and other Poems. Illustrated by Julia Margaret Cameron. 2 vols. folio. half-bound morocco, cloth sides, price £6. 6s. each.

TENNYSON FOR THE YOUNG AND FOR RECITATION. Specially arranged. Fcp. 8vo. 1s. 6d.

TENNYSON BIRTHDAY BOOK. Edited by Emily Shakespear. 32mo. cloth limp, 2s. ; cloth extra, 3s.

THOMPSON (Alice C.)—PRELUDES : a Volume of Poems. Illustrated by Elizabeth Thompson (Painter of 'The Roll Call'). 8vo. price 7s. 6d.

THOUGHTS IN VERSE. Small crown 8vo. price 1s. 6d.

THRING (Rev. Godfrey), B.A.—HYMNS AND SACRED LYRICS. Fcp. 8vo. price 5s.

TODD (Herbert) M.A.—ARVAN ; or, the Story of the Sword. A Poem. Crown 8vo. price 7s. 6d.

TODHUNTER (Dr. J.) — LAURELLA, and other Poems. Crown 8vo. price 6s. 6d.

TURNER (Rev. C. Tennyson)—SONNETS, LYRICS, AND TRANSLATIONS. Crown 8vo. cloth, price 4s. 6d.

WATERFIELD (W.) — HYMNS FOR HOLY DAYS AND SEASONS. 32mo. cloth, price 1s. 6d.

WAY (A.) M.A.—THE ODES OF HORACE LITERALLY TRANSLATED IN METRE. Fcp. 8vo. price 2s.

WILLOUGHBY (The Hon. Mrs.)—ON THE NORTH WIND—THISTLEDOWN : a Volume of Poems. Elegantly bound, small crown 8vo. price 7s. 6d.

LIBRARY NOVELS.

AYRTON (J. C.)—A SCOTCH WOOING. 2 vols. crown 8vo.

BLUE ROSES ; or, Helen Malinofska's Marriage. By the Author of 'Véra.' Fifth Edition. 2 vols. cloth, gilt tops, 12s.

BUNNETT (F. E.)—LINKED AT LAST. Crown 8vo.

CADELL (Mrs. H. M.)—IDA CRAVEN : a Novel. 2 vols. crown 8vo.

CARR (Lisle)—JUDITH GWYNNE. 3 vols. Second Edition. Crown 8vo.

CHAPMAN (*Hon. Mrs. E. W.*) — A CONSTANT HEART : a Story. 2 vols. cloth, gilt tops, 12*s*.

CLAYTON (*Cecil*) — EFFIE'S GAME ; How She Lost and how She Won : a Novel. 2 vols.

COLLINS (*Mortimer*) — THE PRINCESS CLARICE : a Story of 1871. 2 vols.

SQUIRE SILCHESTER'S WHIM. 3 vols.

MIRANDA : a Midsummer Madness. 3 vols.

CONYERS (*Ansley*) — CHESTERLEIGH. 3 vols. crown 8vo.

COTTON (*R. T.*) — MR. CARINGTON : a Tale of Love and Conspiracy. 3 vols. crown 8vo.

DE WILLE (*E.*) — UNDER A CLOUD ; or, Johannes Olaf: a Novel. Translated by F. E. Bunnètt. 3 vols. Crown 8vo.

EILOART (*Mrs.*) — LADY MORETOUN'S DAUGHTER. 3 vols. crown 8vo.

FAITHFULL (*Mrs. Francis G.*) — LOVE ME, OR LOVE ME NOT. 3 vols. crown 8vo.

FENN (*G. M.*) — A LITTLE WORLD : a Novel. In 3 vols.

FISHER (*Alice*) — HIS QUEEN. 3 vols. crown 8vo.

FOTHERGILL (*Jessie*) — ALDYTH : a Novel. 2 vols. crown 8vo. 21*s*.

HEALEY : a Romance. 3 vols. cr. 8vo.

GRAY (*Mrs. Russell*) — LISETTE'S VENTURE : a Novel. 2 vols. crown 8vo.

GRIFFITHS (*Capt. Arthur*) — THE QUEEN'S SHILLING : a Novel. 2 vols.

HAWTHORNE (*Julian*) — BRESSANT : a Romance. 2 vols. crown 8vo.

IDOLATRY : a Romance. 2 vols. cr. 8vo.

HAWTHORNE (*Nathaniel*) — SEPTIMIUS : a Romance. Second Edition. Crown 8vo. cloth, price 9*s*.

HEATHERGATE : a Story of Scottish Life and Character. By a New Author. 2 vols. crown 8vo.

HOGAN, M.P. : a Novel. 3 vols. cr. 8vo.

HOCKLEY (*W. B.*) — TALES OF THE ZENANA ; or, a Nuwab's Leisure Hours. By the Author of 'Pandurang Hari.' With a Preface by Lord Stanley of Alderley. 2 vols. crown 8vo. cloth, price 21*s*.

INGELOW (*Jean*) — OFF THE SKELLIGS. (Her First Romance.) 4 vols. cr. 8vo.

KEATINGE (*Mrs.*) — HONOR BLAKE : the Story of a Plain Woman. 2 vols. crown 8vo.

LISTADO (*J. T.*) — CIVIL SERVICE : a Novel. 2 vols. crown 8vo.

LOVEL (*Edward*) — THE OWL'S NEST IN THE CITY : a Story. Crown 8vo. price 10*s*. 6*d*.

MACDONALD (*G.*) — MALCOLM : a Novel. 3 vols. Second Edition. Crown 8vo.

ST. GEORGE AND ST. MICHAEL. 3 vols. crown 8vo.

MARKEWITCH (*B.*) — THE NEGLECTED QUESTION. Translated from the Russian by the Princess Ourousoff. 2 vols. crown 8vo. 14*s*.

MARSHALL (*H.*) — THE STORY OF SIR EDWARD'S WIFE : a Novel. Crown 8vo. price 10*s*. 6*d*.

MORLEY (*Susan*) — AILEEN FERRERS : a Novel. 2 vols. crown 8vo.

THROSTLETHWAITE : a Novel. 3 vols. Crown 8vo.

MARGARET CHETWYND : a Novel. 3 vols. crown 8vo.

MOSTYN (*Sydney*) — PERPLEXITY : a Novel. 3 vols. crown 8vo.

MY SISTER ROSALIND : a Novel. By the Author of 'Christiana North,' and 'Under the Limes.' 2 vols.

SAUNDERS (*John*) — ISRAEL MORT, OVERMAN : a Story of the Mine. 3 vols. crown 8vo.

SAUNDERS (*Katherine*) — THE HIGH MILLS : a Novel. 3 vols. crown 8vo.

C. Kegan Paul & Co.'s Publications.

FARQUHARSON (M.)
I. ELSIE DINSMORE. Crown 8vo. price 3s. 6d.
II. ELSIE'S GIRLHOOD. Crown 8vo. price 3s. 6d.
III. ELSIE'S HOLIDAYS AT ROSELANDS. Crown 8vo. price 3s. 6d.

HERFORD (*Brooke*)—THE STORY OF RELIGION IN ENGLAND: a Book for Young Folk. Crown 8vo. cloth, price 5s.

INGELOW (*Jean*) — THE LITTLE WONDER-HORN. With Fifteen Illustrations. Small 8vo. price 2s. 6d.

KER (*David*) — THE BOY SLAVE IN BOKHARA: a Tale of Central Asia. With Illustrations. Crown 8vo. price 5s.

THE WILD HORSEMAN OF THE PAMPAS. Illustrated. Crown 8vo. price 5s.

LEANDER (*Richard*) — FANTASTIC STORIES. Translated from the German by Paulina B. Granville. With Eight Full-page Illustrations by M. E. Fraser-Tytler. Crown 8vo. price 5s.

LEE (*Holme*)—HER TITLE OF HONOUR. A Book for Girls. New Edition. With a Frontispiece. Crown 8vo. price 5s.

LEWIS (*Mary A.*) —A RAT WITH THREE TALES. With Four Illustrations by Catherine F. Frere. Price 5s.

LITTLE MINNIE'S TROUBLES: an Everyday Chronicle. With Four Illustrations by W. H. Hughes. Fcap. price 3s. 6d.

MC CLINTOCK (*L.*)—SIR SPANGLE AND THE DINGY HEN. Illustrated. Square crown 8vo. price 2s. 6d.

MAC KENNA (*S. J.*)—PLUCKY FELLOWS. A Book for Boys. With Six Illustrations. Fourth Edition. Crown 8vo. price 3s. 6d.

AT SCHOOL WITH AN OLD DRAGOON. With Six Illustrations. Third Edition. Crown 8vo. price 5s.

MALDEN (*H. E.*)—PRINCES AND PRINCESSES: Two Fairy Tales. Crown 8vo. cloth.

NAAKE (*J. T.*) — SLAVONIC FAIRY TALES. From Russian, Servian, Polish, and Bohemian Sources. With Four Illustrations. Crown 8vo. price 5s.

PELLETAN (*E.*)—THE DESERT PASTOR. JEAN JAROUSSEAU. Translated from the French. By Colonel E. P. De L'Hoste. With a Frontispiece. New Edition. Fcap. 8vo. price 3s. 6d.

REANEY (*Mrs. G. S.*)—WAKING AND WORKING; or, From Girlhood to Womanhood. With a Frontispiece. Crown 8vo. price 5s.

SUNBEAM WILLIE, and other Stories. Three Illustrations. Royal 16mo. price 1s. 6d.

BLESSING AND BLESSED: a Story of Girl Life. Crown 8vo. cloth, price 5s.

SUNSHINE JENNY and other Stories. 3 Illustrations. Royal 16mo. cloth, price 1s. 6d.

ROSS (*Mrs. E.*), ('Nelsie Brook')— DADDY'S PET. A Sketch from Humble Life. With Six Illustrations. Royal 16mo. price 1s.

SADLER (*S. W.*) *R.N.*—THE AFRICAN CRUISER: a Midshipman's Adventures on the West Coast. With Three Illustrations. Second Edition. Crown 8vo. price 3s. 6d.

SEEKING HIS FORTUNE, and other Stories. With Four Illustrations. Crown 8vo. price 3s. 6d.

SEVEN AUTUMN LEAVES FROM FAIRY LAND. Illustrated with Nine Etchings. Square crown 8vo. price 3s. 6d.

STRETTON (*Hesba*), Author of 'Jessica's First Prayer.'

MICHEL LORIO'S CROSS and other Stories. With Two Illustrations. Royal 16mo. price 1s. 6d.

THE STORM OF LIFE. With Ten Illustrations. Sixteenth Thousand. Royal 16mo. price 1s. 6d.

THE CREW OF THE DOLPHIN. Illustrated. Thirteenth Thousand. Royal 16mo. price 1s. 6d.

STRETTON (*Hesba*), Author of 'Jessica's First Prayer.'

CASSY. Thirty-fourth Thousand. With Six Illustrations. Royal 16mo. price 1s. 6d.

THE KING'S SERVANTS. Thirty-eighth Thousand. With Eight Illustrations. Royal 16mo. price 1s. 6d.

LOST GIP. Fifty-fourth Thousand. With Six Illustrations. Royal 16mo. price 1s. 6d.

⁎ *Also a handsomely bound Edition, with Twelve Illustrations, price 2s. 6d.*

DAVID LLOYD'S LAST WILL. With Four Illustrations. Royal 16mo. price 2s. 6d.

THE WONDERFUL LIFE. Twelfth Thousand. Fcap. 8vo. price 2s. 6d.

A NIGHT AND A DAY. With Frontispiece. Eighth Thousand. Royal 16mo. limp cloth, price 6d.

FRIENDS TILL DEATH. With Illustrations and Frontispiece. Twentieth Thousand. Royal 16mo. price 1s. 6d.; limp cloth, price 6d.

STRETTON (*Hesba*), Author of 'Jessica's First Prayer.'

TWO CHRISTMAS STORIES. With Frontispiece. Fifteenth Thousand. Royal 16mo. limp cloth, price 6d.

MICHEL LORIO'S CROSS, AND LEFT ALONE. With Frontispiece. Twelfth Thousand. Royal 16mo. limp cloth, price 6d.

OLD TRANSOME. With Frontispiece. Twelfth Thousand. Royal 16mo. limp cloth, price 6d.

⁎ *Taken from 'The King's Servants.'*

THE WORTH OF A BABY, and How Apple-Tree Court was Won. With Frontispiece. Fifteenth Thousand. Royal 16mo. limp cloth, price 6d.

SUNNYLAND STORIES. By the Author of 'Aunt Mary's Bran Pie.' Illustrated. Small 8vo. price 3s. 6d.

WHITAKER (*Florence*)—CHRISTY'S INHERITANCE. A London Story. Illustrated. Royal 16mo. price 1s. 6d.

ZIMMERN (*H.*)—STORIES IN PRECIOUS STONES. With Six Illustrations. Third Edition. Crown 8vo. price 5s.

A LIST
OF THE COLLECTED EDITIONS OF
MR. TENNYSON'S WORKS.

THE IMPERIAL LIBRARY EDITION,
COMPLETE IN SEVEN OCTAVO VOLUMES.
Cloth, price 10s. 6d. per vol.; 12s. 6d. Roxburgh binding.

CONTENTS.

Vol. I.—MISCELLANEOUS POEMS.
II.—MISCELLANEOUS POEMS.
III.—PRINCESS, AND OTHER POEMS.
Vol. IV.—IN MEMORIAM and MAUD.
V.—IDYLLS OF THE KING.
VI.—IDYLLS OF THE KING.
VII.—DRAMAS.

Printed in large, clear, old-faced type, with a Steel Engraved Portrait of the Author, the set complete, price £3. 13s. 6d. *⁎* *The handsomest Edition published.*

THE AUTHOR'S EDITION,
IN SIX VOLUMES. Bound in cloth, 38s. 6d.

CONTENTS.

Vol. I.—EARLY POEMS and ENGLISH IDYLLS. 6s.
II.—LOCKSLEY HALL, LUCRETIUS, and other Poems. 6s.
III.—THE IDYLLS OF THE KING, complete. 7s. 6d.
Vol. IV.—THE PRINCESS and MAUD. 6s.
V.—ENOCH ARDEN and IN MEMORIAM. 6s.
VI.—QUEEN MARY and HAROLD. 7s.

This Edition can also be had bound in half-morocco, Roxburgh, price 1s. 6d. per vol. extra.

THE CABINET EDITION,
COMPLETE IN TWELVE VOLUMES. Price 2s. 6d. each.

CONTENTS.

Vol. I.—EARLY POEMS. Illustrated with a Photographic Portrait of Mr. Tennyson.

II.—ENGLISH IDYLLS, and other POEMS. Containing an Engraving of Mr. Tennyson's Residence at Aldworth.

III.—LOCKSLEY HALL, and other POEMS. With an Engraved Picture of Farringford.

IV.—LUCRETIUS, and other POEMS. Containing an Engraving of a Scene in the Garden at Swainston.

V.—IDYLLS OF THE KING. With an Autotype of the Bust of Mr. Tennyson by T. Woolner, R.A.

Vol. VI.—IDYLLS OF THE KING. Illustrated with an Engraved Portrait of 'Elaine,' from a Photographic Study by Julia M. Cameron.

VII.—IDYLLS OF THE KING. Containing an Engraving of 'Arthur,' from a Photographic Study by Julia M. Cameron.

VIII.—THE PRINCESS. With an Engraved Frontispiece.

IX.—MAUD and ENOCH ARDEN. With a Picture of 'Maud,' taken from a Photographic Study by Julia M. Cameron.

X.—IN MEMORIAM. With a Steel Engraving of Arthur H. Hallam, engraved from a picture in possession of the Author, by J. C. Armytage.

XI.—QUEEN MARY: a Drama. With Frontispiece by Walter Crane.

XII.—HAROLD: a Drama. With Frontispiece by Walter Crane.

⁎ *These Volumes may be had separately, or the Edition complete, in a handsome ornamental case, price 32s.*

THE MINIATURE EDITION,
IN THIRTEEN VOLUMES.

CONTENTS.

Vol. I.—POEMS.
II.—POEMS.
III.—POEMS.
IV.—IDYLLS OF THE KING.
V.—IDYLLS OF THE KING.
VI.—IDYLLS OF THE KING.
Vol. VII.—IDYLLS OF THE KING.
VIII.—IN MEMORIAM.
IX.—PRINCESS.
X.—MAUD.
XI.—ENOCH ARDEN.
XII.—QUEEN MARY.

VOL. XIII.—HAROLD.

Bound in imitation vellum, ornamented in gilt and gilt edges, in case, price 42s. This Edition can also be had in plain binding and case, price 36s.

LONDON: PRINTED BY
SPOTTISWOODE AND CO., NEW-STREET SQUARE
AND PARLIAMENT STREET